m on the

versity, Chicago, IL, USA)

The Loyola University Symposiu
Human Rights of Children

Series editor: James Garbarino (Loyola Uni

For other titles published in this series, go to
www.springer.com/series/7885

James Garbarino · Garry Sigman
Editors

A Child's Right to a Healthy Environment

Springer

Editors
James Garbarino
Center for the Human Rights of Children
Department of Psychology
Loyola University
1032 W Sheridan Rd
119 Coffey Hall
Chicago, IL 60660
USA
jgarbar@luc.edu

Garry Sigman
Stritch School of Medicine
Maywood, IL
USA
gsigman@lumc.edu

ISBN 978-1-4419-6789-3 e-ISBN 978-1-4419-6791-6
DOI 10.1007/978-1-4419-6791-6
Springer New York Dordrecht Heidelberg London

Library of Congress Control Number: 2010936454

Printed on acid-free paper

Springer is part of Springer Science+Business Media (www.springer.com)

Preface

This volume resulted from the inaugural Symposium of the Loyola University Center for the Human Rights of Children, held in April 2008, in Chicago. The theme of the Symposium was "The Right to a Healthy Environment." Each of the chapters contained within this volume was presented at the Symposium and each is offered here to contribute to an interdisciplinary understanding of the meaning, significance, challenges to, and implementation of the human rights approach to important issues in the health and well-being of children and youth.

Children's rights are human rights. As a Jesuit University, Loyola has a special obligation in matters of human rights, particularly as a reflection of the U.S. Catholic Bishops' principle that "...human dignity can be protected and a healthy community can be achieved only if human rights are protected and responsibilities met." The Loyola University Center for the Rights of Children exists to represent, coordinate, and stimulate efforts of the University community to understand, protect, and apply the human rights of children in the face of injustice and poverty of body, mind, and spirit. It seeks guidance and inspiration from the tradition of Catholic teachings on social justice ("the passion which animates Roman Catholic social thought is a feeling of affective solidarity with aggrieved people") as well as the UN Convention on the Rights of the Child and the global movement for children's rights that the Convention represents. It does so with respect for the rights and responsibilities of parents, teachers, and other caregivers entrusted with raising children.

As articulated by Loyola President Fr. Michael Garanzini, the framework for the Center's work flows from the University's mission: "Our commitment to address the challenges of social inequality and social injustice around the belief that faith and the desire for human progress come from the same root within our human natures ... It demands that we engage and challenge one another to examine and change the conditions that promote injustice and victimize ourselves and others." And it asks us to "remember the delicate way that faith can be used to assist us in opening our minds, not closing them, as so often appears to be the case when religious thinking comes into play." Loyola's efforts to work within this framework are manifest in three principal ways: "through the curriculum, through our research and attempts to influence leaders and policy makers, and through our direct encounter with victims of injustice and the systems that promote, even in unwittingly, dehumanization and injustice."

Beyond these general imperatives, the Jesuit commitment to higher education has more specific mandates (as articulated by Fr. Peter-Hans Kolvenbach, SJ, The Superior General of the Order of the Society of Jesus, commenting upon "Commitment to Justice in Jesuit Higher Education").

* "Personal involvement with innocent suffering, with the injustice others suffer, is the catalyst for solidarity which then gives rise to intellectual inquiry and moral reflection.... Students in the course of their formation, must let the gritty reality of this world into their lives, so they can learn to feel it, think about it critically, respond to its suffering, and engage it constructively.... They should learn to perceive, think, judge, choose and act for the rights of others, especially the disadvantaged and the oppressed."

* "Every discipline, beyond its necessary specialization, must engage with human society, human life, and the environment in appropriate ways, cultivating moral concern about how people ought to live together...Adopting the point of view of those who suffer injustice, our professors seek the truth and share their search and its results with our students....To make sure that the real concerns of the poor find their place in research, faculty members need an organic collaboration with those in the Church and in society who work among and for the poor and actively seek justice....when faculty do take up inter-disciplinary dialogue and socially-engaged research in partnership with social ministries, they are exemplifying and modeling knowledge which is service, and students learn by imitating them as 'masters of life and moral commitment'..."

By launching the Loyola University Symposium on the Human Rights of Children, the Center has sought to bring this Jesuit commitment to fruition in the academic community. Designed as a biennial program, it brings together scholars, advocates, practitioners, and students from Loyola University and around the world to present and discuss their work in understanding and advancing the human rights of children. We hope this volume contributes to this process.

About the Editors

James Garbarino is the founding Director of the Center for the Human Rights of Children at Loyola University Chicago; the current Maude C. Clarke Chair in Humanistic Psychology. Before arriving at Loyola, he was Cornell University's Elizabeth Lee Vincent Professor of Human Development and codirector of the Family Life Development Center. He received his bachelor's degree from St. Lawrence University and a doctorate in human development and family studies from Cornell University. From 1985 to 1994, he was President of the Erikson Institute for Advanced Study in Child Development. Dr. Garbarino has served as a consultant to a wide range of organizations, including the National Committee to Prevent Child Abuse, the National Institute for Mental Health, the American Medical Association, the U.S. Advisory Board on Child Abuse and Neglect, and the Federal Bureau of Investigation. He also serves as an expert witness in criminal and civil cases involving issues of violence and children. Books he has authored or edited include: *Children and the Dark Side of Human Experience: A Spiritual Memoir*, *See Jane Hit: Why Girls Are Growing More Violent and What We Can Do About It*, and *Words Can Hurt Forever: How to Protect Adolescents from Bullying, Harassment, and Emotional Violence*. His work has also been featured in television, magazines, and newspapers, including appearances on "The Today Show," "Dateline," and "Larry King Live." Dr. Garbarino has received numerous awards, including the first C. Henry Kempe Award from the National Conference on Child Abuse and Neglect, Fellow of the American Psychological Association, Spencer Fellow by the National Academy of Education, National Fellow by the Kellogg Foundation, and the President's Celebrating Success Award from the National Association of School Psychologists. He is a former president of the American Psychological Association's Division on Child, Youth, and Family Services.

Garry Sigman, M.D., is an Associate Professor at the Loyola Stritch School of Medicine. He is the Director of Adolescent Medicine at the Loyola University Medical Center and serves as Vice-Chairman for Administration, in the Department of Pediatrics. He trained in General Academic Pediatrics at the University of Rochester, and was a Scholar-in-Residence at the Lutheran General Hospital's Center for Clinical Ethics. He is a member of the American Academy of Pediatrics Task Force on Mental Health. He has served as Chairman of the Illinois Chapter of the AAP's Committee on Adolescence. He is a founding member of the Academy for Eating Disorders. He served as member and chairman of the American Academy of Pediatric's Institutional Review Board. He has served on many committees locally and nationally related to the prevention and treatment of adolescent health problems. He lectures widely in behavioral medicine, clinical ethics, and adolescent medicine and has a series of publications that relate to those disciplines.

Contents

Contributors

Alastair Ager
Professor of Clinical Population and Family Health, Program on Forced Migration and Health, Columbia University, Mailman School of Public Health
aa2468@columbia.edu

Neil Boothby
Mailman School of Public Health, Program on Forced Migration and Health, Colombia University, 60 Haven Avenue, New York, NY 10032, USA
nb2101@columbia.edu

Edmund B. Bruyere
Department of Psychology, Loyola University,
6525 N Sheridan Road, 669 Damen Hall, Chicago, IL 60626, USA
ebruyere@luc.edu

Jaap E. Doek
UN Committee on the Rights of the Child, Amsterdam, The Netherlands
JaapEDoek@cs.com

John Donoghue
Department of History, Loyola University, 6525 N Sheridan Rd,
Chicago, IL 60626, USA
jdonoghue@luc.edu

William French
Department of Theology, Center for Christian Ethics, Loyola University,
6525 N Sheridan Rd, 443 Crown Center, Chicago, IL 60626, USA
wfrench@luc.edu

James Garbarino
Center for the Human Rights of Children, Department of Psychology,
Loyola University, 1032 W Sheridan Rd, 119 Coffey Hall,
Chicago, IL 60660, USA
jgarbar@luc.edu

James Gilligan
Clinical Professor of Psychiatry, School of Medicine, Adjunct Professor, School of Law, and Collegiate Professor, School of Arts and Sciences, New York University, Silver Center for Arts and Science, Room 908, 100 Washington Square East, 10003 New York, NY, USA
jamesgilliganmd@att.net

Robin Kimbrough-Melton
Institute on Family and Neighborhood Life, Clemson University, 225 South Pleasantburg Drive, Suite B 11, 29607 Greenville, SC, USA
rkimbro@clemson.edu

Gary B. Melton
Institute on Family and Neighborhood Life, Clemson University, University Center, 225 South Pleasantburg Drive, Suite B-11, Greenville, SC 29607, USA
gmelton@clemson.edu

Garry Sigman
Loyola University Medical Center, 2160 S First Ave, Maywood, IL 60153, USA
gsigman@lumc.edu

Shweta Singh
Department of Social Work, School of Social Work, Loyola University Chicago, 820 N Michigan Avenue, Lewis Tower 1237, Chicago, IL 60611, USA
ssingh9@luc.edu

Anita Weinberg
ChildLaw Policy Institute, Loyola University Chicago School of Law, Chicago, IL, USA
aweinbe@luc.edu

Kim C. Williamson
Department of Biology, Loyola University, 6525 N Sheridan Rd, Chicago, IL 60626, USA
kwilli4@luc.edu

Part I
Perspectives on Healthy Environments for Children

Chapter 1
"To Such as These, the Kingdom of Heaven Belongs"[1]: Religious Faith as a Foundation for Children's Rights[2]

Gary B. Melton

When the topic of religion enters discourse on children's rights, all too often it is to lament the influence of certain religions on the status and well-being of children. At worst, there is concern that participation in religious life may directly place children at risk of harm. As is well known to the general public, some religious denominations have accrued huge liabilities as a result of sexual abuse of children by clergy and others in religious occupations (Associated Press, 2005). At the time of the symposium from which this book developed, cable news cameras were focused nearly around the clock on the compound of a polygamist sect in Texas from which hundreds of children were placed in emergency custody of the state. The Texas case was a variation on long-standing concerns about religious communities with unconventional sexual mores and child-rearing practices (Lilliston, 1997) or even satanic rituals (Goodman et al., 1997).

Is Religion Related to Risk for Children?

Advocates sometimes also express concern about the relation of fundamentalist religious beliefs (apart from bizarre or criminal practices) to sexual exploitation or, more commonly, psychological and physical abuse. As a purely statistical matter,

[1]Matthew 19:14; see also Luke 18:15–17, Mark 10:13–16, and Matthew 18:1–5.

[2]Reflecting the Jesuit underpinnings of the center that sponsored the symposium on which this book is based and the largely Protestant communities in which Strong Communities for Children (discussed at some length in this chapter) is located, the examples in this chapter predominantly reflect Christian traditions. However, most of the arguments and conclusions apply with equal force to other great religions, which in varying degrees share values of compassion, justice, and neighborly love, particularly in relation to children. (For primary source materials and commentary on beliefs about childhood in Buddhism, Christianity, Confucianism, Hinduism, Islam, and Judaism, see Browning & Bunge, 2009.)

G.B. Melton (✉)
Institute on Family and Neighborhood Life, Clemson University, University Center,
225 South Pleasantburg Drive, Suite B-11, Greenville, SC 29607, USA
e-mail: gmelton@clemson.edu

J. Garbarino and G. Sigman (eds.), *A Child's Right to a Healthy Environment*,
The Loyola University Symposium on the Human Rights of Children 1,
DOI 10.1007/978-1-4419-6791-6_1,

religious fundamentalism is an indicator of risk for sexual abuse (Stout-Miller, Miller, & Langenbrunner, 1997) and frequent use of corporal punishment (Straus, 1994).

It is important, of course, not to ascribe causality on the bases of simple correlations or even to posit profiles of abusive adults that include religion as an element. It is likely that such statistical relationships at least partially reflect other factors (e.g., social class) that happen to be associated with both family dysfunction and fundamentalism.

Nonetheless, parental punitiveness (for that matter, punitiveness of church employees, such as child care workers) sometimes may reflect distortions of the doctrine of original sin – asserting, in effect, that children are intrinsically evil creatures who must be tamed for their own good. Such ideas are well ingrained in America's puritanical heritage (famously, in Jonathan Edwards' deliberately frightening sermons about or toward purportedly hell-bound children; see Brekus, 2001), but they also appear today in the popular tracts for parents by James Dobson (2004) and some other key figures in the Religious Right (see Bunge, 2001, and Mercer, 2005, for critical discussion of such commentary).

Probably more often, however, religion is regarded less as threatening than simply as irrelevant to children's safety and well-being – benign but insignificant. Notwithstanding a burgeoning literature associating religiosity with young people's health and adjustment (Roehlkepartain & Benson, in press), social scientists and child advocates alike have largely overlooked the protective roles that religious organizations can play. This point was dramatically illustrated in a data base search that I conducted in September 2007. A PsycInfo search in which "*child abuse*" or "*child maltreatment*" was paired with *religion* or *church* failed to reveal a single published discussion of religious institutions' involvement in initiatives or programs to prevent child abuse and neglect.[3] Similarly, the topic does not appear in the 500+ pages of the handbook of the American Professional Society on Abuse of Children (Myers et al., 2002) or the 29 chapters of the handbook compiled by the National Center for Injury Prevention and Control, a unit of the Centers for Disease Control and Prevention (Doll, Bonzo, Mercy, & Sleet, 2007).

In the broad view, perhaps the most serious lapse is in religious leaders' common failure to recognize the important roles that they and their congregations can play in the coalescence of community resources to protect children and promote their interests. Ironically and tragically, their attention often has been deflected by concern with risk management within churches themselves. To prevent further violations of trust and the resulting extensive adverse publicity and costly legal judgments against churches, many congregations (even entire denominations) have diligently attempted to create *safe sanctuaries* (Barnett, 2005; J. T. Melton, 1998, 2003; Paulson, 2006). It is likely that the publicity surrounding social condemnation and

[3] Subsequently, one study (Kim, 2008) documented possible protective effects of religiosity on the mental health of maltreated children in low-income families (specifically, lower frequency of internalizing symptoms among girls, and lower frequency of externalizing symptoms among boys). However, this study (see also Holmes, 2008) also did not address organizational activities of churches and other faith-based organizations to mitigate the harm of child abuse and neglect or to prevent it altogether.

legal penalties against individual offenders and the religious organizations that employed them had both deterrent and educative effects that reduced the prevalence of church-based abuse (U. S. Conference of Catholic Bishops, 2005; Finkelhor & Jones, 2006; G. B. Melton, 1985). Such precautions have probably reduced opportunities for church-based misconduct by any remaining would-be offenders against children. Unfortunately, however, most congregations have failed to go a step further – to appreciate the more extensive and more constructive roles that churches and other faith-based organizations may have in building a system of family support that might guarantee children's personal security (cf. Melton & Barry, 1994; Thompson, 1995; U.S. Advisory Board on Child Abuse and Neglect, 1993).

Of course, in some instances, as already noted, churches' lack of engagement in the protection of children's rights is the result of doctrine or ideology, not merely negligence or misplaced emphasis. Some fundamentalist congregations perceive their mission not to extend from personal to social evangelism (see Chaves, Konieczny, Beyerlein, & Barman, 1999). Others may confuse their conservative political orientation with Biblical mandates. This neglect of important potential contributions by religious communities to the creation of safety nets for families with children has been amplified by the vociferous rejection of children's rights by some groups in the Religious Right, such as the Eagle Forum[4] and Focus on the Family[5] (see also Fagan, 2001, writing on behalf of The Heritage Foundation).

In short, churches often have left tasks undone when they could have contributed affirmatively to children's status and well-being. Whether because of inadequate attention, misplaced priorities, or theological conservatism, many (maybe even most) churches have neglected to weave safety nets for children and families throughout the community, even when those same institutions have vigorously sought to prevent church-based child abuse.

Moreover, some congregations and religious movements have occasionally – even frequently – taken actions that were arguably contrary to children's interests. Those organizations have actively and even specifically striven to create and sustain a climate that has impeded recognition and implementation of children's rights. Although there is clearly some foundation for concern, therefore, about an expanded engagement by communities of faith in matters pertaining to children's rights, the bigger message – the idea that drives most of the remainder

---

[4] Using the term *"children's rights"*, a Google search of the Eagle Forum's Web site (http://www.eagleforum.org) on September 1, 2009, yielded 112 documents. The general tone is illustrated by the first document appearing in the search: *The New World Order Wants Your Children.*

[5] Consider, e.g., the following juxtaposition of *rights* on the Web site of Focus on the Family:

> Danger seems to be everywhere, even generating new buzzwords. *Terrorism* is a buzzword that has come into common use only in the past few years. Other common buzzwords [of the contemporary era] include ***rights***, *access, gay, lesbian, bisexual, transgender, binge, purge, chat rooms, morning-after pill, body art, piercing, cutting, X, Meth, date-rape drugs, crack-baby, huffing, parental consent* and many additional slang words used for various sexual behaviors.
>
> (Klepacki, n.d., ¶ 8, emphasis added)

of this chapter – people of faith and the religious organizations of which they are a part can and should be leading forces in achieving realization of children's rights.

Churches' Support for Children's Rights and Families' Well-Being

Eliminating Risk to Children in the Church

Nonetheless, there is little factual foundation for the fear that children today are often at risk of harm because of exploitive or bizarre behavior of certain church officials.[6] Indeed, *contemporary* evidence of church-based abuse of children is virtually nonexistent (Finkelhor, 2003; Paulson, 2006; U.S. Conference of Catholic Bishops, 2005). Although new revelations continue to appear, the "new" cases generally refer to behavior that occurred at least a generation ago and usually involve individuals who have already been removed from parish ministry or who have died. Moreover, anonymous surveys of pupils and staff in parochial schools have generally not uncovered any instances of abuse. Although sexual abuse may once have been a crime of opportunity for unscrupulous adults in some religious settings, the heightened vigilance and special opprobrium for offenders in church vocations and volunteer positions have made religious institutions especially safe today.

Promoting Children's Rights in Public Life

Religious Proponents of US Ratification of International Instruments

In the same vein, although some religious groups have led the opposition to legal recognition of children's rights, many more denominations have been strong proponents of the U.S. ratification of the Convention on the Rights of the Child (1989). For example, the partners of the Campaign for the U.S. Ratification (2009) have included groups affiliated with African Methodist Episcopal, American Baptist, Catholic, Episcopal, Evangelical Lutheran, Jewish, Mennonite, Unitarian Universalist, United Church of Christ, and United Methodist denominations – only

[6] The mismatch in this instance between factual accuracy on the one hand and media messages and public beliefs on the other is directly analogous to the "stranger danger" or the "culture of fear" in relation to child abduction (Glassner, 2000).

a portion of the denominations that have endorsed ratification of the Convention.[7] ChildFund International (formerly the Christian Children's Fund), Church Women United, Church World Service, and World Vision are among the other faith-based partners of the Campaign.

World Vision

More importantly, at least in practical terms, many churches and other institutions of faith have taken important and thoughtful steps toward recognition of children's rights in the organizations' own work and advocacy of children's rights in the broader context. Some of the most far-reaching efforts in that regard have come from World Vision International (WVI), a source that some might regard as improbable. An evangelical international humanitarian organization, WVI is compatible with the new movement of theologically conservative, socially engaged Christians (cf. Wallis, 2000).

Framing its arguments in terms of scriptural themes of justice, compassion, and grace, WVI (Miller, 2007; World Vision, 2002) has been a staunch supporter of children's rights. In so doing, WVI has made clear that its position is based on theological grounds, not secular ethics or law:

> World Vision believes that the respect for the rights of others is a religious duty corollary to the obligations to honor those who are equal before God and, in particular, to "creat[e] room for people to be what God intends them to be" (World Vision, 2002, p. 11). Permitting or committing a wrong against children – violation of the dignity of the people of God – is also a wrong against God. World Vision argues that such wrongs are sufficiently egregious that they demand action by the *community* (ultimately including a system of rights guaranteed by secular law) to ensure that the children of God – all children – are protected.
>
> (G. B. Melton & Anderson, 2008, p. 175)

This core idea – enabling children to be (and presumably become) all that God intends them to be – is a restatement of World Vision's historic poignant statement of purpose:

> Our Vision for Every Child, Life in All Its Fullness
>
> Our prayer for every heart, the will to make it so.
>
> (World Vision New Zealand, n.d., p. 1)

This notion might be further restated as the right of every child to expression of a God-given personality (status as a unique person; cf. G. B. Melton, 2005) and the corollary obligation of every adult to enable fulfillment of this right. This idea is clearly explained in WVI's current statement of Core Values. Noting Jesus's "special concern for children" and "his challenge to unjust attitudes and systems," WVI (2007)

---

[7] The list also includes at least the following: Adventist; Bahai; Baptist World Alliance Council; Buddhist; Greek Orthodox; Salvation Army; United Church of Christ; National Council of Churches; Young Men's and Young Women's Christian Associations (U.S. Committee for UNICEF, n.d.).

emphasized its central concern for human rights and the religious underpinnings of this principle:

> We regard all people as created and loved by God. We give priority to people before money, structure, systems, and other institutional machinery. We act in ways that respect dignity, uniqueness, and intrinsic worth of every person…. We celebrate the richness of diversity in human personality, culture and contribution. (¶ 8)[8]

Presbyterian Church (USA)

Of course, WVI puts its values into action in many instances of advocacy and humanitarian relief for children and for the adults who care for them. In at least some instances, ordinary Christian denominations (not just action-oriented faith-based humanitarian organizations) as national or international institutions have gone beyond doctrinal explication of the meaning and significance of children's rights. In effect, they not only have stated the case for children's rights and taught members about the centrality of this idea within denominational tenets, but they also have created structures for congregants to give life to these abstract ideas.

One of the most ambitious has been the Presbyterian Church (USA), which established a Decade of the Child in 2001–2011. The Decade of the Child (n.d.) is framed as a systematic collective and individual time to renew congregational vows made at the time of infant baptism and the Eucharist. Specifically, Presbyterian leaders called on congregations in the denomination to welcome children into the community (a renewal of the baptismal commitment) band to consider that pledge as they join at the Lord's Table as a community of God. Presbyterian leaders have reminded congregants that "[c]aring for all children, both those within and those beyond our church walls, is a just way to respond to God's grace and live out our promises" (*Decade of the Child*, n.d., ¶ 5).

This denominational emphasis builds on the articulation of *A Vision for Children and the Church* (General Assembly, 1993) that in concept established goals much like those followed by World Vision. Affirming children not only as gifts from God "to the whole of the human community," but also as participants in ministry within and beyond their congregations, the Presbyterians poetically established an expectation of respect for children as people of God:

---

[8]See also Garbarino (2009): "Children have human rights because each of us is one of God's Children, and thus beyond the authority of human beings and institutions that may wish to use or degrade us" (p. 4).

For a similar perspective, see Vailaau (2009), who provides a Christian theology of childhood, amplified by an exposition of Samoan cultural norms and values. Vailaau is particularly pointed in his analysis of the prohibition of corporal punishment, currently a hot issue in New Zealand, among scores of other countries. Noting that many believe erroneously that the Old Testament commands physically assaultive punishment of children, Vailaau (2009, p. 10) makes the powerful argument that "it is hard to conceive of Jesus ever hitting a child for any reason. The very suggestion is contradictory both to what He taught and the way He lived."

> We hope for a world where children can find a safe place;
>
> where all ages, races, genders, creeds, and abilities are recognized, valued, and celebrated;
>
> where all adults hear the voices of children and speak with as well as for them;
>
> where all children have "first call" on the world's resources and first place in the mind and hearts of the world's adults.
>
> (General Assembly, 1993)

Building on these sentiments, many Presbyterian (USA) congregations have joined in a new network, Presbyterians in Covenant with Children (*A New Network*, n.d.), which "unites…congregations and groups in intentional ministries of justice and compassion with and for children in our congregations, communities, nation and world through worship, education, service and advocacy" (*A New Network*, n.d., ¶ 1). Moreover, the denomination itself has established an Office of Child Advocacy (2009a, 2009b; see also "Red Hand Day," 2009), which has put much of its resources into advocacy for the U.S. ratification and implementation of the Convention on the Rights of the Child (1989), care for the most vulnerable children (e.g., child soldiers; children subject to trafficking), facilitation of children's own understanding of social issues, support for children's own ministries to less advantaged children (see, e.g., http://www.presbykids4kids.org), and education of congregations about children's issues. Typically, the Office of Child Advocacy works in collaboration with other denominational entities (e.g., Presbyterian Peacemaking Program; Presbyterian Women) and thus serves as a catalyst for continued consideration of *A Vision for Children and the Church* and realization of the Decade of the Child.

The Episcopal Church

The tenets expressed in the Presbyterian vision statement were echoed in the Episcopal Church's (General Convention, 2000) *Children's Charter for the Church*. Analogizing to children as "treasure" (cf. Psalm 127:4, in re children as gifts; for explication, see the slide presentation in General Convention, 2000), the Episcopal national governing body "ask[ed] each committee, commission, and program of the Episcopal Church, as it plans for the future, to consider how its ministry will positively impact the lives of children in the church and in the world, how it will be impacted by children, and how it will encourage children's full participation in the worship and mission of the church" (see *Implementing a Children's Charter*, n.d., Appendix 6, ¶ 1).

The Episcopal General Convention's broad directive interestingly went farther than many statements on children's ministries in two ways. First, the endorsement of the Charter was unusual and maybe even unique in its depth and breadth. The General Convention stated an expectation that *all* church bodies would consider the Children's Charter "as a continuing vision of The Episcopal Church's ministry in nurturing children, ministering to and advocating on behalf of children, and supporting children in their ministries" (*Implementing a Children's Charter*, n.d., Appendix 6, ¶ 2).

Thus, the General Convention (2000) continued and expanded a process that had already begun, diocese by diocese and even congregation by congregation (*Implementing a Children's Charter*, n.d.), to contribute to a transformation in the denomination's relationship with the children who are part of its communities.

Second, the General Convention adopted a policy that heightened the priority given to ministries to children and that, less typically, recognized children themselves as participants in the priesthood of believers (see *Implementing a Children's Charter*, n.d.). Hence, the Children's Charter called its congregations and members not only "to love, shelter and protect children within [their] own community and in the world" (General Convention, 2000, ¶ 5) but also "to advocate for the integrity of childhood and the dignity of all children at every level of our religious, civic and political structures" (General Convention, 2000, ¶ 8).

Recalling Isaiah's (11:6) prophecy that "a child shall lead them," the Episcopal leaders pledged "to appreciate children's abilities and readiness to represent Christ and his church, to bear witness to him wherever they may be, and according to gifts given them, to carry on Christ's work of reconciliation in the world, and to take their place in the life, worship and governance of the church" (General Convention, 2000, ¶ 11). In a sense, the Episcopal Children's Charter thus gave form and specificity to the Presbyterian (General Assembly, 1993) vision of a church "where all adults hear the voices of children and speak with as well as for them."

United Methodist Church

Building on the Wesleyan tradition of social evangelism, the leaders of the United Methodist Church (UMC; General Conference, 2000/2004) have gone to another level by placing the situation for children and the church's obligations in that regard into a sociopolitical context. In eight pages of small type, the UMC advocated specific political steps, with particular attention to children's rights, as antidotes to the excesses of globalization, corollary increases in inequality, and sometimes perverse incentive systems.

Like WVI and other religious entities with a broad social agenda, the UMC has grounded its challenge to the prevailing political, economic, and social norms in terms of human rights. Its commitment to human rights is further grounded in its respect for human beings, which in turn is derived from its theological understanding, not an ethical–philosophical analysis per se.

Accordingly, after repeatedly quoting Psalm 8:4–5,[9] the UMC (2000/2004) proclaimed:

---

[9] "What are human beings that you are mindful of them, mortals that you care for them? Yet you have made them a little lower than God [or divine beings, or angels] and crowned them with glory and honor."

On the same point, the UMC statement also cited Genesis 1:27 (adapted): "God created human beings, in the image of God they were created...."

> Human dignity is the foundation of all human rights. It is inherent and inborn. Human dignity is the image of God in each human being. Human dignity is the sum total of all human rights. We protect human dignity with human rights. Human rights are the building blocks of human dignity. They are...God's gift of love for everyone. Human rights, being the expression of the wholeness and fullness of human dignity, are indivisible and interdependent. (¶ 6)

The UMC (2000/2004) further emphasized that human rights law is a tool in the protection of human dignity:

> As peoples and governments increase the catalogue of rights that are recognized and protected, protections not only increase, but so do our approximation of and striving for human dignity. To be engaged in the human rights struggle is to accept God's gift of love in Jesus Christ who has come to affirm all God's people as they are – as individuals and people in community together. (¶ 7)

Recognizing Jesus's affirmation of the place of children in the kingdom of heaven (Matthew 19:14), the UMC (General Conference, 2000/2004) unequivocally held that "children's rights are human rights" (¶ 16). Building on its general recognition of the importance of international human rights law in protecting divinely ordained dignity of human beings, the UMC reiterated its strong and unequivocal support for the U.S. ratification of the Convention on the Rights of the Child (1989) and full implementation of the Convention elsewhere. In a section entitled "Receiving the reign of God as a little child," the UMC (General Conference, 2000/2004) gave special attention to a long list of basic entitlements that the denomination recognizes for children: "food, shelter, clothing, health care, and emotional well-being" and especially protection from exploitation and abuse (¶ 14).

In a relatively lengthy passage (¶¶ 17–20), the UMC leaders emphasized that they had been "called to join the international campaign" to prevent the proliferation of small arms and land mines, the use of children as soldiers, the accessibility of guns to children and even the production of war toys for children's play – societal policies and practices that constitute "a culture of violence which denies human rights, snuffs out precious human life, and debases human dignity" (¶ 18):

> There is something wrong in our sense of the moral when children are put in harm's way. No boy or girl must be sent to the front lines of war, battles, and conflict. The field of play must not be replaced with the field of combat. War games are not child games. Playgrounds are for children; battlegrounds are not. (¶ 20)

The calling to join international action illustrates the UMC's recognition that "civil society" provides a context for leadership from local to global levels to establish "just, participatory, and sustainable communities" (¶ 13). At its best, the communion of people of faith offers the opportunity to add passion – a sense of righteousness grounded in a collective calling – to debates about human rights and to action to fulfill them by framing such events in the context of prophetic justice (cf. Franklin, 1997, 2007; Resner, 2008).

Catholic Church

Historically, the Catholic Church has been the denomination best positioned to exercise such a role, at least at national and global levels.[10] Besides its sheer size and its corresponding influence in both North (Eastern and Western Europe; North America) and South (Africa; Latin America), the Catholic Church, uniquely, is an embodiment of spiritual, economic, and political power through the statehood of the Holy See.

This general significance has been heightened in recent years in regard to children's issues by the common (although questionably accurate) identification of Catholic priests as the major culprits in church-based abuse of children – so much so that AmericanCatholic.org features an ongoing news section on "The Church and Sexual Abuse" (see *The Catholic Church*, 1996–2009; see also *Boston Globe*, 2004). In positive terms, however, for centuries the Catholic Church has been, worldwide, a major provider of advocacy, care, education, and humanitarian relief for children and families (see, e.g., Bice, 2009a; Caritas Internationalis, 2009; Catholic Relief Services, 2009).[11] Today, that work extends to more than 300,000 church-administered settings for education, child care, and social services (Tomasi, 2007).

In its multiple roles – e.g., a communion of believers; a political authority; an advocacy organization; a service provider – the Catholic Church has been especially influential in the development of a global consensus for children's rights.[12] During the decade-long drafting of the Convention on the Rights of the Child (1989), religion was the direct focus (in relation, e.g., to children's freedom of religion) or the underlying basis for most of the particularly contentious issues (in relation, e.g., to the legitimacy of foster care and adoption and to the definition of childhood and, therefore, the scope of children's right to life). In that context, the Holy See's continuing endorsement of the Convention provided an important indicator that the Convention is not anti-religion in tone or scope (Johnson, 1992). At this writing, as a reflection of its continuing commitment to the ideals embodied in the Convention on the occasion of the 20th anniversary of its adoption by the United Nations, the International Catholic Child Bureau (Bice, 2009b) is leading a world appeal for mobilization on behalf of children.

---

[10]Of course, the Jesuit order has been especially engaged in the promotion of social justice (Society of Jesus in the United States, 2009), a tradition that is reflected in the center (and the university of which it is a part) that sponsored the symposium on which this book is based.

[11]A particularly noteworthy example is Istituto degli Innocenti (2007), usually regarded as the first residential care facility for children and appropriately located on Piazza della Santissima Annunziata, the setting in Florence, Italy, for veneration of the Virgin Mary. Today (more than 600 years after its establishment) Istituto degli Innocenti is the home of UNICEF's primary research center, a related Italian governmental research center, and various services for children.

[12]Catholic theology about justice for children has been heavily influenced by the work of Karl Rahner (see Hinsdale, 2001, for an analysis, with accompanying commentary by Bunge, 2001).

Pope John Paul II's (1990) rationale for Catholic support for the Convention rested on a theological framework similar to that proclaimed by Protestant leaders:

> The Holy See's prompt accession to the Convention on the Rights of the Child...accords with the Catholic Church's bi-millenary tradition of service to those in material or spiritual need, especially the weaker members of the human family, among whom children have always received special attention. In the Child of Bethlehem, Christians contemplate the uniqueness, the dignity and the need for love of every child. In the example and teaching of her Founder, the Church perceives a mandate to devote special care to the needs of children (cfr. Mark 10:14); indeed, in the Christian view, our treatment of children becomes a measure of our fidelity to the Lord himself (cfr. Matthew 18:5). (¶ 3)

Reflecting the sense of prophetic justice to which I have referred, the pope continued:

> The Church has a vivid perception of the immense burden of suffering and injustice borne by the children of the world. In my own ministry and pastoral journeys, I am a witness of the heartbreaking plight of millions of children in every continent. They are most vulnerable because they are less able to make their voice heard. My contribution to this Summit [for the World's Children], Mr. Secretary General, is meant to reinforce before this powerful Assembly the often wordless but no less significant and insistent appeal which the children of the world address to those who have the means and the responsibility to make better provision for them.
>
> *The children of the world cry out for love.* In this case, love stands for the real concern of one human being for another, for the good that each owes to the other in the bond of our common humanity. A child cannot survive physically, psychologically, and spiritually without the solidarity which makes us all responsible for all, a responsibility which assumes particular intensity in the self-giving love of parents for their offspring. (¶¶ 4–5, emphasis in the original)

Child-Inclusive Communities of Faith

The Doctrinal Foundation

Although there are segments of the religious community that remain suspicious of – or even hostile to – children's rights, this review of illustrative denominational actions on children's issues reasonably leads to the conclusion that people of faith are natural child advocates. Even though the potential for religious leadership in such matters has seldom been fully achieved, it is unlikely that any other sector of society is as poised ideologically (doctrinally) to be advocates of children's rights.[13]

At root, the actions that are needed to provide support for children and their families can be found in the Golden Rule (Luke 6:31; Matthew 7:12) – usually recognized as a religiously (Biblically) grounded guide to human relations even by the individuals who are wary not only of government-supported social programs, but also of the faith-based or faith-related initiatives that go beyond the "programs"

[13] For an analysis of Jesus's teachings about children, see Gundry-Volf (2001).

expressly mentioned in the Bible (e.g., care for widows and orphans [e.g., James 1:27]; visitation of prisoners [e.g., Matthew 25:36]; food and clothing for people in poverty [e.g., Matthew 25:35–36]). Found in some form in all religions, the Golden Rule is not without logical challenges, notably in relation to individual and group differences in preferences (Duxbury, 2008).[14] However, the embedded idea of reciprocal obligations for neighborliness is virtually beyond debate. A society in which people are as attentive to others as themselves is a place where almost everyone would want to live and, in particular, to rear their children.

The fundamental theological premise on which religiously motivated advocacy for children's rights can be found in the following syllogism:

1. People are created in the image of God and, by that status, owed great respect.
2. Although "the least of these," children are people in the kingdom of God.
3. Therefore, children, by such a status, are owed great respect.

This point can be amplified – and moved toward a program of action – by these additional premises:

4. By their nature, the requisites for assurance of respectful treatment of children of God (in effect, all of us) are so fundamental that they rise to the level of rights – shared obligations to assure the fulfillment of such rights in secular society and the religious community itself.
5. Therefore, children, as people of God, have rights, the protection of which is a matter of community responsibility.
6. Communities of believers must organize to fulfill such duties.

Application to Children

This set of successive logical corollaries from central tenets of faith applies in substantial measure in relation to *human* rights and the relationships required to sustain them. However, such concepts have special significance in regard to children. Perhaps the most obvious point in that regard is that, whether because of immaturity or social status, children are usually not in a position to vindicate their rights. Indeed, young children are obviously not able even to secure the material and emotional support needed for their survival. At the same time, older children often have been systematically excluded from meaningful participation in community life, even though they have the capacity in many ways to be *neighbors* and themselves to serve others in the community. In that context, assurance of the respect that children are owed requires watchfulness and responsive action.

Moreover, in the contemporary era, reliance on parents alone is clearly not a reasonable strategy for the protection of children's integrity as persons (if indeed

[14] The power of the Christian version of the Golden Rule would have been greater if it were framed as a duty to act toward others as *they* would want.

such an approach was ever reasonable). In an era in which (across a period of roughly four decades) young people – including young parents – have become increasingly isolated, distrustful, and disengaged (see, e.g., Bennett, 1998; Fukuyama, 1995/1996, 1999/2000; Putnam, 1995, 2000; Rahn & Transue, 1998; Uslaner, 2002), the safety and well-being of children are increasingly difficult to secure (see, e.g., G. B. Melton & Lyons, in prep.; Twenge, 2000). Moreover, as young parents are increasingly isolated and therefore lacking in social support, the number of adults per household continues to drop so that all too often parents are caring for children alone (Popenoe, 1990, 1993). They are doing so in a world that they often regard as scary and overwhelming and in which there are generational decreases in real income combined with increases in debt load (Ackerman & Alstott, 1999; Kamenetz, 2006; Perrucci & Wysong, 1999) so that even buying help as a commodity (or a professional service) is more difficult (cf. G. B. Melton, 1992). The combination of economic and social poverty or near-poverty is all too common and all too dangerous for children (see, e.g., Coulter, Crampton, Irwin, Spilsbury, & Korbin, 2007; Garbarino, 1995; Garbarino & Kostelny, 1994). We also know that parents' own social networks provide useful points of entry for children into community life and that such experiences with unrelated adults are important resources in social development (see, e.g., Cochran & Brassard, 1979).

Accordingly, if children's rights are to be protected, then parents and other caregivers must also be respected and supported. In the Clemson University Institute on Family and Neighborhood Life, we strive in our own version of the Golden Rule to create settings in which *every child and every parent will know that if they have a reason to celebrate, worry, or grieve, someone will notice, and someone will care.* Such settings do not just happen, however. Their presence in community life requires conscious planning to make such connections easy to fulfill – so that indeed they become a seamless part of everyday life. Another mantra of our Institute – *People shouldn't have to ask!* – provides the principle by which such transformation occurs. Opportunities to notice and care for one's neighbors (including children and parents) must be built in. Religious life offers not only the structures, but also the motivation for creation of such a shalom community[15] – norms of service expressed in the context of a set of ongoing relationships among people who believe that they can make a difference in the broader community on behalf of their own and their neighbors' families.

At its best, therefore, community life is the product of both a theology that supports recognition of human rights and an organizational context that facilitates expression of such convictions:

> By fully acknowledging children's humanity, the great religions accept the duty to respect children's dignity and, therefore, to protect them against threats to their personal security. By undertaking an ethic of service, communities of faith provide the ethos in which to

[15] For an example, see Jeremiah 29:4–8. Jeremiah preached that the Hebrews in exile in Babylon should not only form a community for themselves – building houses, planting gardens, establishing families – but, radically, that they should also pray for and in general promote the welfare of Babylon itself.

> make such a duty meaningful. By recognizing that such a duty applies even when its fulfillment is inconvenient or its benefits apply to those who are powerless and unattractive, religious communities provide the dedication and the outreach needed to establish places of acceptance for ostracized or withdrawn families. In so doing, communities of faith can become cornerstones of support for parents and other caregivers.
>
> (Melton & Anderson, 2008, p. 176)

Communities That Are Welcoming to Children and Families

In Christian teaching, as the discussion thus far makes clear, the recognition of children's humanity and the relation of human beings to God combine to create duty of respect for children (and their parents) as people – in effect, for recognition of children's rights. This duty is enhanced by the fact of children's dependency and the corresponding reality that children's well-being is affected by their being (or not being) a part of a functioning community. Religious obligations to children both build from and support broader community life.

But there is more. The Christian Gospel makes clear that adults have an affirmative duty to *welcome* children to the community (Luke 9:48; Matthew 18:3–5),[16] not just to protect them from harm. In this regard, one of the characteristics of churches that makes them ripe for mobilization on behalf of children's rights is that they are intergenerational. Indeed, although the specific practices vary, religious institutions typically have a "career ladder" by which children assume increasingly complex tasks in the particular community of faith. Thus, for example, churches and other religious organizations often include opportunities for even very young children to participate in worship services (through children's choirs or storytime), somewhat older children to join in community service and in more central roles in worship (e.g., service as acolytes), and adolescents to create or implement their own church-based youth organizations or even to serve in congregational governance bodies.

Religious institutions also generally have ritualized procedures for welcoming children into the congregation at various levels of engagement. Hence, an initial congregational commitment to a child typically occurs soon after birth in infant baptism, infant dedication, or naming ceremonies. Rites of passage for full participation in the religious community often happen in early adolescence in the form of rituals that are accompanied by family and community celebrations (e.g., baptism,

---

[16] See also Matthew 25:34–35, 40:

> Come, you that are blessed by my Father, inherit the kingdom prepared for you from the foundation of the world; for I was hungry and you gave me food, I was thirsty and you gave me something to drink. I was a stranger and you welcomed me.... Truly I tell you, just as you did it to one of the least of these who are members of my family, you did it to me.

Given the other passages in which Jesus referred to "the least of these" (see footnote 1 *supra*), this quote about Jesus's prophecy in the Final Judgment can be read, as in other passages, to assert that failure to welcome a child – or someone in another vulnerable group – would be tantamount to excluding Jesus himself.

confirmation, first communion, or bar/bat mitzvah). In the same manner, children often encounter graduation ceremonies as they progress across levels of religious education, installation ceremonies as they assume offices in a youth group, scouting, or the congregation as a whole, and so forth. In addition, young people's achievements not only in the church per se but also in other contexts (for example, school) are often celebrated in religious ceremonies. Hence, congregations that have given little systematic attention to welcome the youngest among them still routinely introduce young people to the community and provide significant roles for them in the life of the church or other institution itself.

Compatibility with Religious Values and Goals

Hence, there is a logical flow from religious beliefs to the recognition of human rights. It is important to note, however, that the converse is also true. By their nature, as discussed, for example, in the United Methodist statement presented *supra*, human rights documents are consonant with religious values. Indeed, secular action in support of human rights can be meaningfully understood as a tool in the expression of theological values and the pursuit of religious goals.

Most fundamentally, human rights instruments begin with respect for the value of every person. They are especially respectful of those experiences that define who we are. Hence, human rights instruments protect the relationships, especially those within the family, that are entwined in one's personality. Such instruments also commonly require governments to be respectful of expressions of spirituality.

Although human rights instruments are designed to affirm the norms of the global community, they also intended (like institutions of faith) to be transformative – in effect, to make the Golden Rule preeminent in everyday life and thus to reinforce the sense of oneness across the broader community. Accomplishment of these noble goals requires engagement by and within the primary institutions of the community.[17]

In this context, the position taken by some groups in the Religious Right that the Convention on the Rights of the Child (1989) is anti-family and anti-religion is either misinformed, unreasonable, or disingenuous. The Convention is fundamentally community-oriented. It requires national governments to assist communities in

---

[17] In a speech at the United Nations in 1958 (quoted by Lash, 1972), Eleanor Roosevelt, the mother of international human rights law, eloquently expressed the importance of conceptualizing the fulfillment of human rights (whether for children or other people) as a matter of everyday life:

> Where, after all, do universal human rights begin? In small places, close to home – so close and so small they cannot be seen on any maps of the world. Yet they are the world of the individual person; the neighborhood he lives in, the school or college he attends; the factory, farm, or office where he works. Such are the places where every man, woman, and child seeks equal justice, equal opportunity, equal dignity without discrimination. Unless these rights have meaning there, they have little meaning anywhere. Without concerted citizen action to uphold them close to home, we shall look in vain for progress in the larger world. (p. 79).

fulfilling their responsibility to protect and promote family (including extended-family) relationships that are crucial to the development of the child's unique personality (cf. G. B. Melton, 2005).

In that regard, one of the ways in which the Convention was groundbreaking was its recognition of children's right to a *family environment*, a right (unlike a hypothetical right to a family) that governments can in fact enforce (see G. B. Melton, 1996). Accordingly, the drafters of the Convention recognized "that the child, for the full and harmonious development of his or her personality should grow up in a family environment, in an atmosphere of happiness, love and understanding," and "that the child should be fully prepared to live an individual life in society,... brought up in..the spirit of peace, dignity, tolerance, freedom, equality, and solidarity" (Convention, 1989, preamble).

Practical Reasons for Engaging Religious Institutions in Child Advocacy

The emphasis in this chapter has been on doctrinal reasons for church involvement in promotion of children's rights. As the example of intergenerational membership, activities, and leadership illustrate, however, some institutional characteristics of churches make them especially good candidates for promotion of children's well-being, recognition of their rights, and protection of children from harm.

Perhaps the simplest reason is *ubiquity*. No matter where one lives in the United States, there are churches. Often there are also ashrams, mosques, synagogues, and temples. Even in long-declining communities where schools and businesses have closed, small churches with part-time pastors can be found in many of the store-fronts that have been vacated. Hence, the religious sector is especially well suited to the application of a universal approach (as embedded in rights discourse) because religious institutions can be found even in communities where other institutions are absent. Analogously, religious institutions have important societal roles (e.g., refugee resettlement; moral education; rites of passage) that are widely accepted even in the most secular societies – so much so that the church may be entangled in civil government in such societies.

Religious communities also offer *structures* for expression of human rights and for improvement of the status and well-being of children in the community. Propelled in that regard by the exceptional *motivation* that people of faith often bring to community service, the organizational capacity of religious organizations (when viewed with ordinary metrics of financial and human capital) is often surprising:

> Whatever one's theology may be (indeed, regardless of whether one is a religious adherent at all), one must recognize the special motivation associated with religious faith and, perhaps even more so, active engagement in a community of faith. The norm of altruism is energized by the special confidence that comes with faith. As a result, even small congregations with few tangible resources often have substantial human and social capital.
>
> (G. B. Melton & Anderson, 2008, p. 176)

Ironically, religious faith offers the foundation for a "can-do" orientation (in psychological terms, a strong sense of efficacy), even if it is accompanied by belief in an omniscient and omnipotent deity (see, e.g., Bryd, Hageman, & Isle, 2007; Pargament, 1992). Although people of faith sometimes feel called to be ascetics immersed in prayer and meditation, the stronger pull – usually much stronger pull – is outward. Religious faith promotes an optimistic viewpoint grounded in the belief that, through faith, all things are possible, and it thus facilitates civic engagement. This sense of confidence is modulated by the humility that emanates from an appreciation of the place of any individual in relation to all of God's creation. An attitude of service is the logical result of this combination of religious devotion, sense of efficacy, and concern for "the least" among us.

Accordingly, religious communities offer structures for moral leadership and public service on behalf or marginal and excluded children and families (cf. U.S. Advisory Board on Child Abuse and Neglect, 1993). Churches commonly have their own outlets for community service (for example, denominational campaigns and congregational councils for social justice; inter-faith ministries to people in times of crisis; faith-based social service agencies [e.g., Catholic Charities; Jewish Family Services; Lutheran Immigration Services]; women's missionary societies). Moreover, as parishioners carry their faith into other settings (e.g., civic clubs; workplaces), the boundaries of religious institutions – and, therefore, of their emphases on service – can become quite diffuse. Congregations can in fact become beacons of light in care for children across the community.

In that regard, the wall of separation between church and state in the USA often combines with religious institutions' institutional culture (including parishioners' sense of moral responsibility) to enable a special *responsiveness* to family needs. Even in denominations with an episcopal structure (hence, in principle, a top-down orientation to the definition and implementation of church emphases), the external constraints on congregational action are usually quite limited, in relation to governmental and corporate organizations. Therefore, religious institutions can typically respond to family needs – and implement children's rights – quickly, flexibly, and informally. Although a gatekeeper may control access to congregational resources, emergency relief can often be rapidly obtained (e.g., small financial resources in a pastor's discretionary fund; staff and/or lay resources in "compassion ministries").

Perhaps most importantly, religious institutions have widely recognized *societal roles – missions*, if you will – that potentially place them at the center of the community in guarding children's interests and supporting their families. The U.S. Advisory Board on Child Abuse and Neglect (1993) identified three such roles. Perhaps the most obvious attribute of this sort is one that has been implicit in much of this discussion. Religious congregations are called to be *communities of service*, expressing the value of loving care that is embedded in the Golden Rule, showing humility and generosity in the stewardship of God-given resources, and respecting the dignity of all human beings, no matter how powerless or needy.

A more challenging role is to be *places of acceptance*. Religious institutions' mission of reconciliation of those who have been estranged from the community may be critical in ensuring that children are not subjected to de facto punishment for the real or perceived sins of their parents (see Convention on the Rights of the Child, 1989, art. 1, § 2). In the same vein, the outreach of people of faith may be important in ensuring that parents (whether withdrawn, ostracized, or simply impoverished) and, therefore, their children are not deprived of the social and material support necessary for their healthy development and personal security (see, e.g., Convention, 1989, arts. 5 & 27, § 3).

In such circumstances, faith-based institutions may be important partners with other private-sector organizations (e.g., secular social service agencies) and with government in fulfilling children's social, economic, and cultural rights in a "friendly," respectful, and personally responsive manner. At one level, such assistance is potentially significant because of its direct instrumental effects. At another, such assistance is apt to have indirect effects on children's well-being by its influence on parents' perceived personal and collective efficacy (beliefs that they and their neighbors have the means of positively influencing their children's well-being) and, therefore, their motivation to supervise their children closely and to ensure the availability of safe environments for their schooling and play (see, e.g., Hurley, 2004; Sampson, Raudenbush, & Earls, 1997).

As the U.S. Advisory Board further recognized, religious organizations can have other indirect influence on the fulfillment of children's rights by acting as *moral beacons* shedding light on the moral imperative of treating children like people and providing guidance about means by which such obligations might be fulfilled. Although churches and other religious institutions are not the only potential sources of such guidance, they are especially well positioned by historic mission and social expectation to provide prophetic leadership in the pursuit of social justice, whether through "witness" by example, exhortations from the pulpit (cf. Resner, 2008), special observances (e.g., Blue Ribbon Sabbath), or campaigns throughout the congregation, the denomination, or the broader community of faith.

Strong Communities for Children[18]

Scope and Effects

Each of these functions was an important element of Strong Communities for Children, a unique population-wide initiative that my colleagues and I undertook

[18]The conceptual foundation, practical strategies, and community effects of Strong Communities have been described in detail in a series of publications: e.g., a special issue of *Family and Community Health* (G. B. Melton & Holaday, 2008), a special section of *Child Abuse and Neglect* (G. B. Melton, in prep.-b), much of an edited book (G. B. Melton, in prep.-a), and a book chapter (G. B. Melton, 2009).

The initiative was supported in substantial part by a generous long-term grant from The Duke Endowment to the Clemson University Research Foundation. The opinions expressed in this chapter are not necessarily those of The Endowment or its trustees, staff, or advisors.

for the prevention of child abuse and neglect in parts of two counties in the Upstate region of South Carolina (population of approximately 125,000). The first large-scale effort to implement the neighborhood-based strategy for child protection that the U.S. Advisory Board on Child Abuse and Neglect (1993) recommended, Strong Communities engaged all sectors of the community in supporting parents and ensuring children's personal security. The formal launch of the initiative occurred in March 2002, and phase-out of external support began in June 2008.

Strong Communities resulted in an impressive and continuously increasing level of community engagement in achieving the goals of the initiative. More than 5,000 individuals were known to have contributed more than 60,000 h in the initiative – probably substantial underestimates of the actual level of engagement because an objective was to institutionalize new norms across the community (hence, eventually to make activities seem to be natural behavior in the relevant setting, not special events in Strong Communities). Moreover, the volunteers were a cross-section of the community in relation to age, gender, and ethnicity.

Apart from the community engagement in enhancing support for children and families (no mean feat in itself), there was strong evidence that the safety of children in the Strong Communities area improved as a result of the initiative. Surveys of randomly selected parents of young children elicited increased social support, more frequent help from others, greater sense of community and personal efficacy, more frequent positive parental behavior, more frequent use of household safety devices, less frequent disengaged (inattentive) parenting, and less frequent neglect – in each instance, across time and in relation to randomly selected parents in comparison communities elsewhere in South Carolina. There was also a nearly significant trend toward less frequent assaultive behavior (physical discipline) by parents ($p<0.06$).

Moreover, surveys of parents, teachers, and fifth graders (particularly the children themselves) showed, across time and relative to their peers in comparison with elementary schools, greater perceived safety at and en route to and from school. The surveys also indicated that the service-area schools became more welcoming to parents. Although the initiative was aimed primarily at parents of preschool, kindergarten, and primary-grade children, there is good reason to believe that these changes were spillover effects of the Strong Communities initiative. Of course, families with young children often have older children. Moreover, changes in school climate (in this case, attitudes and behavior related to parental participation in the school) are not likely to be limited to a single grade level. Also, comparisons across communities in relation to other typical social indicators (e.g., unemployment; adolescent pregnancy) and major events did not support the alternative hypothesis that changes in both parental self-reports and school surveys were the product of a coincident phenomenon unrelated to the initiative.

Church Involvement

In achieving change across the area, Strong Communities involved widely diverse community institutions (e.g., businesses; civic clubs; fire departments; schools). However, it was obvious that churches and their active members were at the forefront of the movement. Numerous indicators contributed to this conclusion:

1. About three-fourths of the volunteers in Strong Communities, and virtually all of the volunteer leaders reported being active in a church. Many described their service as an outgrowth of their faith, even if they were recruited from an institution other than a church.
2. Like most volunteers in other projects, most of the volunteers in Strong Communities reported an altruistic motive – giving back to the community – for their service. Unlike other projects, however, volunteers reported few self-centered motives (e.g., networking for business purposes).
3. More than one-fourth of the volunteers were recruited through a church – about 40% more than any other institution.
4. The length of retention of the church-based volunteers was second only to those who were recruited through fire departments.
5. Journalists regularly conducted interviews of outreach workers about their logs. More than one-fourth of the statements about particular organizations involved churches – obviously a minority but still 50% more than any other sector.
6. Nearly 200 churches participated in the initiative (nearly twice as many as were engaged in 2004).
7. The number of types of activities in which the churches participated as part of their work in Strong Communities grew dramatically across the service area. Churches expressed their engagement in the initiative through a stunning array of activities (see G. B. Melton & Anderson, 2008, p. 180, Table 1).
8. The average depth of involvement – in effect, the centrality of Strong Communities themes and activities in congregational life – also grew dramatically. For example, the number of congregations observing Blue Ribbon Sabbath grew from about 75 in 2004 to more than 120 in 2007. Even more impressively, the number of congregations who extended their observance from distribution of blue ribbons and bulletin inserts to special worship services or volunteer activities increase from 0 in 2004 to 60 in each instance.
9. Churches in the Strong Communities service area were much more likely than churches in other eligible communities to embrace related projects (e.g., provision by church-based volunteers of mentoring and other support for prisoners' families [Building Dreams] and of individualized support and care, sometimes including extended 24-h care, to children and families in high need [Safe Families]).

Strong Communities was unusual not only in the centrality of church involvement in a community-wide initiative (in effect, a social movement toward fulfillment of children's right to personal security) but also in the breadth and depth of participation from the religious sector. To appreciate the meaning of this summative observation, it is useful to know a bit about the sociology of the communities in which Strong Communities was undertaken. Upstate South Carolina has an unusually high level of religious participation (Newport, 2006), but an even more unusual proportion of people of faith in that area are evangelical Christians.[19] In the South Carolina (Southern) Baptist Convention alone, there are almost 2,000 churches (see http://images.acswebnetworks.com/2013/1271/churchlisting082509cityabcformat.pdf). This number does not include non-denominational (unaffiliated) and historically Black (Missionary) Baptist churches. Partly as a reflection of the theological conservatism that is modal in the area, ministerial alliances and interfaith councils are largely absent in the participating communities, so that cooperation across denominational lines (including related ethnic and racial lines) had been a rare event.

However, Strong Communities apparently transcended theological boundaries, just as it bridged common divisions in regard to politics, gender, age, and population density (e.g., congregation size). Reflecting the broader community, approximately 70% of the congregations specifically mentioned in the journalists' accounts about participation in Strong Communities were Baptist, pentecostal, or independent evangelical. A slightly higher proportion (about 80%) of the workers' statements mentioning religious organizations referred to such fundamentalist and pentecostal congregations.

In such a context, the remarkable engagement of faith-based institutions in Strong Communities indicated the breadth of potential church involvement in community transformation on behalf of children. Experience in the initiative ran counter to the common observation that socially active congregations tend to be associated with relatively liberal "mainstream" or African American denominations (Billingsley, 2002; Chaves, Konieczny, Beyerlein, & Barman, 1999). This broad engagement of religious congregations in the Strong Communities initiative *has* occurred – and, therefore, obviously *can* occur – when people of widely diverse theology are presented with mission-relevant justifications for their participation. The appeal of such an initiative rests at least in part in the nearly universal acceptance of the Golden Rule (cf. Duxbury, 2008, on the broad applicability of the concept in law).

---

[19] Nonetheless, the participants in Strong Communities included numerous congregations in mainstream Christian denominations and minority (non-Christian) religious traditions. The diversity of the religious beliefs represented in the initiative is illustrated by the project's faculty and staff. The author himself is a member of a Unitarian Universalist fellowship. Most Unitarian Universalists today do not regard themselves as Christian, although the historic roots of the denomination are in Christianity. Drawing from multiple sources (including but by no means limited to Judeo-Christian texts), the UU faith is an excellent illustration of the broad spiritual foundation of respect for human rights. In fact, UUs' first principle is "the inherent worth and dignity of every person" (Unitarian Universalist Association, 2009).

Among the other religious traditions represented by faculty and staff in Strong Communities were agnostic, independent evangelical, Baptist (both Missionary Baptist and Southern Baptist), Catholic, Jewish, Presbyterian, Russian Orthodox, and United Methodist. Other traditions represented among the participating congregations included African Methodist Episcopal, Bahai, Church of Christ, Episcopal, Full Gospel, Lutheran, Pentecostal, and Wesleyan.

Of course, the message of Strong Communities was fully compatible with the Christian social gospel. For example, Eastminster Presbyterian Church (USA), a suburban congregation that includes an unusually large number of families with children, institutionalized Strong Families among its members by establishing Network 6:2 (see Taylor & McLeigh, in press). The name for the Network was modeled after Galatians 6:2, in which Paul urged the early Christians to "bear one another's burdens" and assured them that "in this way [they] will fulfill the law of Christ."

Responding to bulletin inserts (including a pledge card to be placed in the offering basket) and a related sermon on Blue Ribbon Sabbath, initial participants in Network 6:2 promised to be available to each other and to the community at large as part of an email-based system of initiating the gift and the receipt of family assistance, such as child care, transportation, home repairs, Spanish–English interpretation, and intercessory prayer. In addition to pledging to provide such occasional help, participants indicated a willingness to "pray about being 'hooked'" in long-term service through Building Dreams, Safe Families, volunteer coordination, or an ongoing support group. Subsequently, the Network agreed to ensure that every member of the group was given a family meal by the Network at least once a month, with an expectation that the time that would have been spent in meal preparation would ordinarily be used as unencumbered time for family activities. The Network's tasks were conceptualized as being grounded in Biblically mandated hospitality (see Pohl, 1999, for book-length conceptual discussion, related materials for adult religious education, and relevant scriptural citations in both the Jewish and Christian traditions).

A prominent part of the congregation's substantial and diverse commitments to Strong Communities, the Network was conceived as a strategy for fulfillment of Strong Communities' assurance of "noticing" and "caring," particularly in regard to the related goal of "leaving no family outside." Church leaders hoped that Network 6:2 would be a means to help members to "see" seemingly hidden needs in the congregation and the community at large.

A moderate-sized congregation, Eastminster has about 400 members, with an average weekly attendance of approximately 200. On the Sunday in April 2008 when the Network was announced, 80 individuals joined. That number soon grew to 120 people in 100 households. By the end of 2008, the Network had received 112 requests for assistance, divided more or less equally from the congregation itself and from the broader community. Within about 8 months, these requests had elicited at least 834 h of volunteer service, enhanced by donations of money and materials (altogether, more than $32,500 in contributions of time and tangible resources).

Conclusions: Mr. Rogers' Neighborhood

Going beyond the scriptures, the practices undertaken in Strong Communities by churches as well as other community institutions fit well with secular visions of humane societies. In that regard, the late children's television personality Fred

Rogers ("Mr. Rogers") made some especially insightful observations about the relationships that support children's healthy development. Although he used other terminology, he understood the *helping paradox* (Riessman & Carroll, 1995) – the reality that helpers often experience more benefit than do those whom they assist.

Building from this insight, Mr. Rogers recognized that parents' motivation to give of themselves – in effect, the "glue" that cements parent–child attachments – comes from the existential rewards that accompany such special relationships:

> In the giving of help, a parent experiences one of the best feelings that any of us can have: that life has meaning because we are needed by someone else. Watching a baby grow with our help tells us other things we like to feel about ourselves: that we are competent and loving.
>
> (Rogers, 2003, p. 82)

Children surely saw Mr. Rogers as a gentle adult friend, and most of their parents probably perceived him as a helpful but perhaps somewhat naïve expert on early childhood development. Nonetheless, Mr. Rogers' use of a secular mass medium was an efficient and effective expression of his desire as a person of faith to serve others. Mr. Rogers' most fundamental professional identity – an ordained pastor in the Presbyterian Church (USA) – was unknown, I am sure, to virtually all of his viewers and the great majority of their parents. Theological education and, perhaps more importantly, the faith that guided it were the sources of Mr. Rogers' concern for all of the children who watched his show *and* their parents.

In one of his last interviews, Mr. Rogers was asked what his message would be "if [he] had *one final broadcast, one final opportunity* to address [his] television neighbors, and [he] could tell them the single most important lesson of [his] life." In his typical slow cadence, Mr. Rogers responded,

> Well, I would want [those] who were listening somehow to know that they had unique value, that there isn't anybody in the whole world exactly like them and that there never has been and there never will be.
>
> And that they are loved by the Person who created them, in a unique way.
>
> If they could know that really know it and have that behind their eyes, they could look with those eyes on their neighbor and realize, "My neighbor has unique value too; there's never been anybody in the whole world like my neighbor, and there never will be." If they could value that person – if they could love that person – in ways that we know that the Eternal loves us, then I would be very grateful.
>
> (Hollingsworth, 2005, pp. 160–161)

It is such a value of respect for human dignity that is at the root of advocacy of children's rights, just as Mr. Rogers sought not only to protect children, but also to promote their participation in a community – both "real-life" relationships and a mythical supportive and educational neighborhood – and to support their parents in ensuring children's personal security but also enabling their self-expression. That nearly final interview showed an exquisite awareness that such experiences are fundamentally spiritual – not matters of sectarian religion per se but instead of human connections that provide a glimpse of the divine through living expression of love for one another (especially "the least of these") and for the Creator.

Whatever the distinctive attributes of particular theological traditions may be, religious institutions and the people of faith who comprise them are surely called to lead the fulfillment of the vision that Mr. Rogers described. Although such organizations have too often approached children's issues timidly or defensively, it is time to recognize that churches and other religious institutions are well suited by doctrine, mission, structure, and resources to be at the forefront of the quest for recognition and fulfillment of children's rights. Although the record is by no means spotless, ample evidence is already present to demonstrate that churches do have the potential to "see" the "Vision" in World Vision – "life in all its fullness" for every child – and to make that vision real in all of the communities of which children are or could be a part. Be it so.

References

(1996–2009). *The Catholic Church and sexual abuse by priests archive*. Retrieved from http://www.americancatholic.org/News/ClergySexAbuse/.

A new network: Presbyterians in Covenant with Children. (n.d.). Retrieved September 14, 2009, from http://www.pcusa.org/children/covenant.htm.

Ackerman, B., & Alstott, A. (1999). *The stakeholder society*. New Haven, CT: Yale University Press.

Associated Press. (2005). *Sex abuse scandals cost church $1 billion*. Retrieved June 10, 2005, from http://www.TheState.com.

Barnett, R. (2005). *Churches take steps to prevent sex abuse of kids*. Retrieved March 13, 2005, from http://www.greenvilleonline.com.

Bennett, S. E. (1998, September). Young Americans' indifference to media coverage of public affairs. *PSOnline*, pp. 535–541. (Available at http://www.apsanet.org).

Bice. (2009a). *Bice: International Catholic Child Bureau* [Web site]. Retrieved September 17, 2009, from http://www.biceinternational.org/index.php.

Bice. (2009b). *World appeal to a new mobilization for childhood*. Retrieved September 17, 2009, from http://www.biceinternational.org/ewb_pages/w/world-appeal-to-a-new-mobilization-for-childhood-geneva-june-2009.php.

Billingsley, A. (2002). *Mighty like a river: The black church and social reform*. New York: Oxford University Press.

Boston Globe. (2004). *Spotlight investigation: Abuse in the Catholic Church*. Retrieved September 17, 2009, from http://www.boston.com/globe/spotlight/abuse/.

Brekus, C. A. (2001). Children of wrath, children of grace: Jonathan Edwards and the Puritan culture of child rearing. In M. J. Bunge (Ed.), *The child in Christian thought* (pp. 300–328). Grand Rapids, MI: Eerdmans.

Browning, D. S., & Bunge, M. J. (2009). *Children and childhood in world religions: Primary sources and texts*. New Brunswick, NJ: Rutgers University Press.

Bryd, K. R., Hageman, A., & Isle, D. B. (2007). Intrinsic motivation and subjective well-being: The unique contribution of intrinsic religious motivation. *International Journal for the Psychology of Religion, 17*, 141–156.

Bunge, M. J. (2001). Introduction. In M. J. Bunge (Ed.), *The child in Christian thought* (pp. 1–28). Grand Rapids, MI: Eerdmans.

Campaign for U.S. Ratification of the Convention on the Rights of the Child. (2009). *Partners*. Retrieved from http://childrightscampaign.org/crcindex.php?sNav=about_snav.php&sDat=partners_dat.php.

Caritas Internationalis. (2009). *Caritas.org*. Retrieved from http://www.caritas.org.

Catholic Relief Services. (2009). *Catholic relief services: Giving hope to a world of need.* Retrieved from http://www.crs.org.

Chaves, M., Konieczny, M. E., Beyerlein, K., & Barman, E. (1999). The national congregations study: Background, methods, and selected results. *Journal for the Scientific Study of Religion, 38*, 458–476.

Cochran, M. M., & Brassard, J. A. (1979). Child development and personal social networks. *Child Development, 50*, 601–616.

Convention on the Rights of the Child. (1989). U.N. Doc. A/Res/44/25.

Coulter, C. J., Crampton, D. S., Irwin, M., Spilsbury, J. C., & Korbin, J. E. (2007). How neighborhoods influence child maltreatment: A review of the literature and alternate pathways. *Child Abuse & Neglect, 31*, 1117–1142.

Decade of the Child. (n.d.). Retrieved from http://www.pcusa.org/children/about.htm.

Dobson, J. C. (2004). *The new strong-willed child: Birth through adolescence.* Carol Stream, IL: Tyndale House.

Doll, L. S., Bonzo, S. E., Mercy, J. A., & Sleet, D. A. (Eds.). (2007). *Handbook of injury and violence prevention.* New York: Springer.

Duxbury, N. (2008). *Golden Rule reasoning, moral judgement and law.* (John M. Olin Program in Law and Economics Working Paper Series, No. 47). Charlottesville: University of Virginia, School of Law.

Fagan, P. F. (2001, February 5). How U.N. conventions on women's and children's rights undermine family, religion, and sovereignty. *Heritage Foundation Backgrounder* (Report No. 1407).

Finkelhor, D. (2003). The legacy of the clergy abuse scandal. *Child Abuse & Neglect, 27*, 1225–1229.

Finkelhor, D., & Jones, L. (2006). Why have child maltreatment and child victimization declined? *Journal of Social Issues, 62*, 685–716.

Franklin, R. M. (1997). *Another day's journey: Black churches confronting the American crisis.* Minneapolis: Augsburg Fortress.

Franklin, R. M. (2007). *Crisis in the village: Restoring hope in African American communities.* Minneapolis: Augsburg Fortress.

Fukuyama, F. (1996). *Trust: The social virtues and the creation of prosperity.* New York: Free Press. (Originally published 1995).

Fukuyama, F. (2000). *The great disruption: Human nature and the reconstitution of the social order.* New York: Touchstone. (Originally published 1999).

Garbarino, J. (1995). Growing up in a socially toxic environment: Life for children and families in the 1990s. In G. B. Melton (Ed.), *Nebraska Symposium on Motivation* (*The individual, the family, and social good: Personal fulfillment in times of change* (pp, Vol. 42, pp. 1–20). Lincoln: University of Nebraska Press.

Garbarino, J., & Kostelny, K. (1994). Neighborhood-based programs. In G. B. Melton & F. D. Barry (Eds.), *Protecting children from abuse and neglect* (pp. 304–352). New York: Guilford.

General Convention, Episcopal Church. (2000). *Children's charter for the church.* Adopted by Resolution 2000-D045 as "a continuing vision of The Episcopal Church's ministry in nurturing children, ministering to and advocating on behalf of children, and supporting children in their ministries." Retrieved from http://www.episcopalchurch.org/documents/Child_Charter_8.5x11.pdf.

General Assembly, Presbyterian Church (USA). (1993). *A vision for children and the church.* Retrieved from http://www.pcusa.org/phewa/childabusevision.htm.

General Conference, United Methodist Church. (2004). *Globalization and its impact on human dignity and human rights.* Resolution adopted in 2000 and amended and re-adopted in 2004. Retrieved from http://archives.umc.org/interior.asp?ptid+4&mid=1016.

Glassner, B. (2000). *The culture of fear: Why Americans are afraid of the wrong things.* New York: Basic Books.

Goodman, G. S., Quas, J. A., Bottoms, B. L., Qin, J., Shaver, P. R., Orcult, H., et al. (1997). Children's religious knowledge: Implications for understanding satanic ritual allegations. *Child Abuse & Neglect, 21*, 1111–1130.

Gundry-Volf, J. M. (2001). The least and the greatest: Children in the New Testament. In M. J. Bunge (Ed.), *The child in Christian thought* (pp. 29–60). Grand Rapids, MI: Eerdmans.
Hinsdale, M. A. (2001). "Infinite openness to the infinite": Karl Rahner's contribution to modern Catholic thought on the child. In M. J. Bunge (Ed.), *The child in Christian thought* (pp. 406–445). Grand Rapids, MI: Eerdmans.
Hollingsworth, A. (2005). *The simple faith of Mister Rogers: Spiritual insights from the world's most beloved neighbor*. Nashville: Integrity.
Holmes, K. (2008). The roles of religion and spirituality in child maltreatment. *[American Psychological Association] Section on Child Maltreatment Newsletter, 13*(1), 6–7.
Hurley, D. (2004, January 6). *On crime as science (a neighbor at a time).* Retrieved November 27, 2009, from http://crab.rutgers.edu/~goertzel/CollectiveEfficacyEarls.html.
Implementing a Children's Charter for the Church: A study guide for congregations. (n.d.). Retrieved from http://www.episcopalchurch.org/documents/implementingcc.pdf.
Istituto degli Innocenti. (2007, April 2). *The children's Renaissance* [News release]. Retrieved from http://www.istitutodeglinnocenti.it/notizia.jsf?idNot=568.
John Paul II. (1990, September 22). [*Letter to Secretary General Javier Pérez de Cuellar on the occasion of the World Summit for Children.*] Retrieved from http://www.vatican.va/holy_father/john_paul_ii/letters/1990/documents/hf_jp-ii_let_19900922_de-cuellar_en.html.
Johnson, D. (1992). Cultural and regional pluralism in the drafting of the U. N. Convention on the Rights of the Child. In M. D. A. Freeman & P. E. Veerman (Eds.), *The ideologies of children's rights* (pp. 95–114). Dordrecht, The Netherlands: Martinus Nijhoff.
Kamenetz, A. (2006). *Generation debt: How our future was sold out for student loans, bad jobs, no benefits, and tax cuts for rich geezers – and how to fight back.* New York: Riverhead.
Kim, J. (2008). The protective effects of religiosity on maladjustment among maltreated and non-maltreated children. *Child Abuse & Neglect, 32*, 711–720.
Klepacki, L. (n.d.). *Dear Mom & Dad: Teach, instruct, discuss.* Retrieved from http://www.citizenlink.org/FOSI/abstinence/parents/A000001024.cfm.
Lash, J. P. (1972). *Eleanor: The years alone*. New York: Norton.
Lilliston, L. (1997). Children of communal new religious members: Psychosocial functioning. *American Journal of Forensic Psychology, 15*, 57–85.
Melton, G. B. (Ed.). (1985). *Nebraska Symposium on Motivation: Vol. 33. The law as a behavioral instrument.* Lincoln: University of Nebraska Press.
Melton, G. B. (1992). It's time for neighborhood research and action. *Child Abuse & Neglect, 16*, 909–913.
Melton, G. B. (1996). The child's right to a family environment: Why children's rights and family values are compatible. *The American Psychologist, 51*, 1234–1238.
Melton, J. T. (1998). *Safe sanctuaries: Reducing the risk of child abuse in the church.* Nashville: Discipleship Resources.
Melton, J. T. (2003). *Safe sanctuaries for youth: Reducing the risk of abuse in youth ministries.* Nashville: Discipleship Resources.
Melton, G. B. (2005). Building humane communities respectful of children: The significance of the Convention on the Rights of the Child. *The American Psychologist, 60*, 918–926.
Melton, G. B. (2009). How Strong Communities restored my faith in humanity: Children *can* live in safety. In K. A. Dodge & D. L. Coleman (Eds.), *Preventing child maltreatment: Community approaches* (pp. 82–101). New York: Guilford.
Melton, G. B. (Ed.). (in prep.-a). *Good neighbors: Safe and humane communities for children and families*. Dordrecht, Netherlands: Springer.
Melton, G. B. (Ed.). (in prep.-b). Strong communities: Community wide prevention of child abuse and neglect [Special section]. *Child Abuse and Neglect.*
Melton, G. B., & Anderson, D. (2008). From safe sanctuaries to strong communities: The role of communities of faith in child protection. *Family & Community Health, 31*, 173–185.
Melton, G. B., & Barry, F. D. (Eds.). (1994). *Protecting children from abuse and neglect: Foundations for a new national strategy*. New York: Guilford.
Melton, G. B. & Holaday, B. J. (Eds.). (2008). Strong communities as safe havens for children [Special issue]. *Family and Community Health, 31*(2), 83–185.

Mercer, J. A. (2005). *Welcoming children: A practical theology of childhood*. Saint Louis: Chalice Press.
Miller, J. (2007). *Churches as change agents: Guidelines for child participation in periodic reporting of the Convention on the Rights of the Child*. Mississauga, Ontario: World Vision Canada.
Myers, J. E. B., Berliner, L., Briere, J., Hendrix, C. T., Jenny, C., & Reid, T. A. (Eds.) (2002). *The APSAC handbook on child maltreatment* (2nd ed.). Thousand Oaks, CA: Sage.
Newport, F. (2006, April 27). *Church attendance lowest in New England, highest in South*. Retrieved from http://www.gallup.com/poll/22579/church-attendance-lowest-new-england-highest-south.aspx?version=print.
Office of Child Advocacy, Presbyterian Church (USA). (2009a, March 25–27). *Update from Office of child advocacy*. Report to the General Assembly Mission Council, Presbyterian Church (USA). Retrieved from http://www.pcusa.org/gamc/business/march09/information/200.pdf.
Office of Child Advocacy, Presbyterian Church (USA). (2009b, September 23–24). *Update from Office of child advocacy*. Report to the General Assembly Mission Council, Presbyterian Church (USA). Retrieved from http://www.pcusa.org/gamc/business/sept09/information/239.pdf.
Pargament, K. I. (1992). Of means and ends: Religion and the search for significance. *International Journal for the Psychology of Religion, 2*, 201–229.
Paulson, M. (2006, April 8). Diocese progresses on child protection: Abuse board revision urged. *Boston Globe*, B1, B4.
Perrucci, R., & Wysong, E. (1999). *The new class society*. Lanham, MD: Rowman & Littlefield.
Pohl, C. (1999). *Making room: Recovering hospitality as a Christian tradition*. Grand Rapids, MI: Eerdman.
Popenoe, D. (1990). Family decline in America. In D. Blankenhorn, S. Bayme, & J. B. Elshtain (Eds.), *Rebuilding the nest: A new commitment to the American family* (pp. 39–51). Milwaukee: Family Service America.
Popenoe, D. (1993). American family decline, 1960–1990: A review and appraisal. *Journal of Marriage and the Family, 55*, 527–555.
Putnam, R. D. (1995). Bowling alone. *Journal of Democracy, 6*, 65–78.
Putnam, R. D. (2000). *Bowling alone: The collapse and revival of American community*. New York: Simon & Schuster.
Rahn, W. M., & Transue, J. E. (1998). Social trust and value change: The decline of social capital in American youth, 1976–1995. *Political Psychology, 19*, 545–565.
Red Hand Day: the effort continues. (2009, February 12). *Swords into plowshares: Reflections from the Presbyterian Peacemaking Program*. Retrieved from http://presbyterian.typepad.com/peacemaking/2009/02/red-hand-day-the-effort-continues.html.
Resner, A., Jr. (2008). *Just preaching: Prophetic voices for economic justice*. Saint Louis: Chalice Press.
Riessman, F., & Carroll, D. (1995). *Redefining self-help in the human services: Policy and practice*. New York: Wiley.
Roehlkepartain, E. C. & Benson, P. L. (in press). Children, religion, and spiritual development: Reframing a research agenda. In A. Ben-Arieh, J. Cashmore, G. S. Goodman, & G. B. Melton (Eds.), *Children in childhood: A research handbook*. London: Sage.
Rogers, E. M. (2003). *Diffusion of innovations* (5th ed.). New York: Free Press.
Sampson, R., Raudenbush, S. W., & Earls, F. (1997). Neighbors and violent crime: A multilevel study of collective efficacy. *Science, 277*, 918–924.
Society of Jesus in the United States. (2009). *A faith that does justice*. Retrieved September 17, 2009, from http://www.jesuit.org/SocialJustice/default.aspx.
Stout-Miller, R., Miller, L. S., & Langenbrunner, M. R. (1997). Religiosity and child sexual abuse: A risk factor assessment. *Journal of Child Sexual Abuse, 6*(4), 15–34.
Straus, M. (1994). *Beating the devil out of them: Corporal punishment in American families*. New York: Lexington Books.
Taylor, D. & McLeigh, J. (in press). "Bear one another's burdens": A church and a community in transformation. In G. B. Melton (Ed.), *Good neighbors: Safe and humane communities for children and families*. Dordrecht, Netherlands: Springer.

Thompson, R. A. (1995). *Preventing child maltreatment through social support: A critical analysis*. Thousand Oaks, CA: Sage.
Tomasi, S.M. (2007, March 23). *Intervention of the Holy See at the ordinary session of the United Nations Convention on the Rights of the Child*. Address by the Holy See's permanent observer to the United Nations to the meeting of the Human Rights Council, Geneva. Retrieved from http://www.vatican.va/roman_curia/secretariat_state/2007/documents/rc_seg-st_20070323_children_en.html.
Twenge, J. M. (2000). The age of anxiety? Birth cohort change in anxiety and neuroticism, 1952–1993. *Journal of Personality and Social Psychology, 79*, 1007–1021.
U. S. Conference of Catholic Bishops, Office of Media Relations. (2005, February 18). *CARA report on 2004 allegations released*. Retrieved from http://www.usccb.org/comm/archives/2005/05-040.shtml.
U.S. Advisory Board on Child Abuse and Neglect. (1993). *Neighbors helping neighbors: A new national strategy for the protection of children*. Washington, DC: U.S. Government Printing Office.
U.S. Committee for UNICEF. (n.d.). *U.S. organizations which endorse the U.N. Convention on the Rights of the Child*. Retrieved from http://www.abanet.org/intlaw/committees/public_II/human_rights/entitiessuppcrc.pdf.
Unitarian Universalist Association. (2009, November 9). *Our principles*. Retrieved from http://www.uua.org/visitors/6798.shtml.
Uslaner, E. M. (2002). *The moral foundations of trust*. Cambridge, England: Cambridge University Press.
Vailaau, N. (2009). *A theology of children*. Wellington: Barnardos New Zealand & Royal New Zealand Plunket Society.
Wallis, J. (2000). *Faith works*. New York: Random House.
World Vision. (2002). Protecting children: a Biblical Perspective on child rights. Monrovia, CA: Author.
World Vision International. (2007, October 15). *Core values*. Retrieved from http://www.wvi.org/wvi/wviweb.nsf/maindocs/7A0A54FD44BC11C38825737500737C8A?opendocument.
World Vision New Zealand. (n.d.). *About world vision*. Retrieved from https://worldvision.org.nz/PDF/resources/About_World_Vision.pdf.

Chapter 2
Preventing Childhood Malaria: Strategies That Work Today and Directions for the Future

Kim C. Williamson

Introduction

Malaria, an ancient plague named "Mal Air" by the Italians for its association with swampy areas, remains the most lethal single agent for children under the age of 5: it is responsible for 8% of all deaths in this population. One million children die each year, which is equivalent to one death every 30 s approximately the same number of people that die from HIV each year. Public awareness and funding for treatment and control has trailed significantly. One of the reasons for this is that 90% of the deaths are confined to children (Johansson, Newby, Renshaw, & Wardlaw, 2007). In addition, they live in sub-Saharan African, and so they are largely invisible to the industrialized world. However, malaria can be transmitted throughout the tropics and in temperate zones, including the USA and Europe, and it is as lethal to nonimmune adults as it is to young children. As with all infectious diseases drug-resistant strains have developed posing increased risk to travelers and residents. A number of economists also suggest that endemic diseases such as malaria are one of the primary obstacles to economic development (Teklehaimanot, McCord, & Sachs, 2007). In the case of malaria, 40% of the world's population is affected.

The parasite is introduced by the bite of an infectious mosquito, invades liver cells and then replicates in red blood cells. Every 2 days a single parasite multiplies into ~16 new parasites. This ruptures the RBC, releasing the parasites which are then free to invade new RBC and start the cycle over. The material released also causes fever, the only early symptom. The problem is that children often get fevers and most will resolve in a few days. However, if the infant has malaria, the fever does not go away but it gets progressively worse. As the parasite replicates, it adheres to the cells lining the capillaries, and as the number of infected red blood cells increases, the adherent cells can occlude the vessel blocking blood flow. This can lead to organ damage, coma, and death. In pregnant women, parasites sequester in the placenta affecting fetal development.

K.C. Williamson (✉)
Department of Biology, Loyola University, 6525 N Sheridan Rd, Chicago, IL 60626, USA
e-mail: kwilli4@luc.edu

J. Garbarino and G. Sigman (eds.), *A Child's Right to a Healthy Environment*, The Loyola University Symposium on the Human Rights of Children 1,
DOI 10.1007/978-1-4419-6791-6_2,

As mentioned, the primary symptom of malaria is a fever and the only way to distinguish between malaria, which could be lethal if not treated, and a self-resolving common cold is to analyze a blood sample for the presence of parasites. In other words, a visit to a health clinic is necessary, which is not a trivial task for rural families whose livelihood is subsistence farming. Even if care is free, there are significant costs associated with taking the time and using limited resources to travel to and from the clinic with a sick child. Once at the clinic the malaria test is straightforward, only if you have a microscope or other commercially available tests. The next question is whether the clinic has the appropriate antimalarial drugs available. Supply, cost, and the drug sensitivity of the parasite are all issues. Imagine investing time, energy, and resources into carrying your child to the clinic, often by foot, only to find that there are no drugs or the drugs you get do not work. This outcome also makes it much less likely that the family will take the effort to visit the clinic the next time someone has a fever.

Unfortunately, this is not a hypothetical scenario. Over the past 30 years, parasites that are resistant to chloroquine, the mainstay of antimalarial treatment since the 1950s, have spread throughout the world (Hoffman & Miller, 1996). Chloroquine was in many respects a "wonder drug." A 3-day oral dose was effective against all four human malaria parasites, *Plasmodium malariae*, *ovale*, *vivax*, and *falciparum,* the last of which causes the most mortality. Chloroquine was inexpensive to produce, relatively nontoxic to humans and safe for use by children and pregnant women. There were no other antimalarials that even came close, and so public health officials were hesitant to change their drug recommendation until 60–70% of the malaria cases were insensitive to chloroquine, and it became apparent that the death rate was rising (Bryce, Boschi-Pinto, Shibuya, & Black, 2005). The second choice, Fansidar, a combination of pyrimethamine and sulfadoxine, was more expensive and drug-resistant parasites were also known to exist.

Through the 1990s, there was an overall decline in child mortality from all causes as the United Nations started to implement the Convention on the Rights of the Child that was adopted in 1989. Article 6 of the convention states that every child has the inherent right to life and that parties shall ensure to the maximum extent possible the survival and development of the child. Article 24 expands this by recognizing the right of the child to enjoy the highest attainable standard of health; in particular, the parties shall take appropriate measures:

24.2.a. To diminish infant and child mortality
24.2.b. To ensure provision of necessary medical assistance and healthcare
24.2.d. To ensure appropriate pre-natal and post-natal healthcare for mothers
24.4. To promote and encourage international cooperation

All of these matters have been lacking for children in the case of malaria risk and disease. In spite of the overall decline in child mortality, the death rate due to malaria increased during the 1990s. This caused real concern and in 1998 the Roll Back Malaria (RBM) Partnership was begun as a collaborative effort between the World Health Organization (WHO), the United Nations Children's Fund (UNICEF), the United Nations Development Programme (UNDP) and the World Bank. Since then additional governmental and private foundations, such as the Global fund for AIDS, TB and Malaria, the Bill and Melinda Gates Foundation, and the US Presidents Initiative against Malaria, have become involved in increasing the funds available from <$ 100 million in 1998 to $1 billion in 2008. The costs are high. With the tools currently available, it is estimated that three billion dollars a year would be required to control the disease and eliminate malaria mortality (Teklehaimanot, McCord, & Sachs, 2007). The only way to eliminate the need for control strategies is to develop new reagents that can effectively eradicate malaria. Some of these exciting recent advances are discussed at the end of talk. First, the basic targets of the RBM campaign, prompt effective chemotherapy, and protective measures which include insecticide treated-bed nets are discussed.

Chemotherapy

During the 1990s, as chloroquine-resistant parasites were spreading through Africa, a compound found in Wormwood or *Artemisia annua* that had been used as a fever treatment in China for centuries was actively being developed as an oral drug (Jiang et al. 1982; Cai, 1981; Gu, Liu, & Lu, 1981). This has been successful, and several artemisinin formulations, including combinations with other drugs, are commercially available from companies based in China as well as from Novartis. The use of two distinct antimalarial drugs in Artemisinin Combination Therapy or ACT is intended to decrease the development of drug resistance, as has been done with HIV medications. In 2002, WHO officially changed its recommendation to treat malaria to ACT. Novartis has agreed to provide the drug at cost, but it still costs greater than $1 per treatment, which is ten times more expensive than chloroquine. When you take into account the 300–400 million malaria cases annually, this increase has serious economic consequences. Initially, the production could not keep up with demand, but capacity has increased, as has the availability of *Artemisia annua* (Walther & Walther, 2007). Deliveries of ACT increased from 4 to 50 million treatments between 2004 and 2006 and the cost decreased to $1 per treatment. Formulations that are easy for young children to take by masking the bitter taste are still being evaluated. Major research efforts are also being directed toward the production of synthetic analogs and bacterial production methods that could reduce costs significantly (Linares & Rodriguez, 2007; Nosten & White, 2007). These and other projects are discussed in the Future Directions Section.

Intermittent antimalarial treatment of individuals at high risk for malaria, such as pregnant women, is also being used as a prevention strategy. It has been shown to protect women from severe malarial anemia and to improve the birth weights of their babies (Shulman et al., 1999). The current recommendation endorsed by the WHO and the United States Center for Disease Control (CDC) is that, during at least two of her routine antenatal clinic visits each pregnant woman should receive a treatment dose of an effective antimalarial drug. Due to concerns about the safety of ACT during pregnancy, the drug most commonly used for Intermittent Preventive

Treatment in pregnancy (IPTp) is sulfadoxine-pyrimethamine, even though some malaria parasites are resistant. This IPT strategy is also being tested for use in children as part of the Expanded Programme on Immunization (EPI). However, concerns about increasing the development of resistant parasites coupled with the paucity of good alternative antimalarial drugs has slowed its implementation (Walther & Walther, 2007).

Prevention

Insecticide Treated Bed Nets

Evidence for the efficacy of insecticide-treated bed nets (ITNs) has been growing since the first encouraging reports from small-scale trials in Gambia in 1987 (Snow, Rowan, & Greenwood, 1987; Snow, Rowan, Lindsay, & Greenwood, 1988; D'Alessandro et al., 1995). A large-scale trial in Western Kenya demonstrated that the use of ITN reduced the incidence of child mortality (16–20%), particularly among infants <12 months old (23–26%), and clinical malaria (44%) (Phillips-Howard et al., 2003; ter Kuile et al., 2003). A review of community randomized ITN trials indicated that ITN usage reduced the incidence of uncomplicated malaria episodes by 50 and 62% in areas of stable and unstable malaria transmission, respectively (Lengeler 2000). Increasing bed net usage to 80% of all children <5 years old and pregnant women in malaria endemic areas is one of the primary RBM targets (Johansson et al., 2007). Recently, a technique has been developed to incorporate insecticide directly into the fibers that will be used to make the net. This process has increased the effective life of the nets from 6 months to 5 years. These long-lasting insecticidal nets (LLIN) can be washed and reused. However, the nets remain expensive ranging from $5 to 7 dollars each, and so subsidized distribution programs and marketing approaches are needed to achieve high coverage (Teklehaimanot et al., 2007). ITN usage increased by three- to fivefold in 17 sub-Saharan countries between 2000 and 2005 and progress continues to be made (Johansson et al., 2007).

Mosquito Control

Indoor residual spraying (IRS) is also an effective approach to reduce malaria transmission in sub-Saharan Africa. Dichloro-diphenol-trichloroethane (DDT) remains the most economical and long last-lasting effective insecticide (Sadasivaiah, Tozan, & Breman, 2007). However, it persists in the environment for a long time, and it has been reported to have adverse effects on birds, although there is no clear evidence of toxicity to humans. The use of DDT was banned in the USA in 1972, and in 2001, the Stockholm convention included it on its list of persistent organic pollutants that were targeted for elimination. A provision allowed for DDT to be used for disease vector control when locally safe, effective, and affordable alternatives are not available. Pyrethoids, which are used in ITN, are more environmentally friendly and can be used as an alternative to DDT. However, they are more expensive and evidence of resistance has been seen which could affect the efficacy of ITN as well. The development of alternative economical insecticides remains a major need.

Public Health

Educating parents and community healthcare workers about the importance of prompt diagnosis and appropriate treatment for fevers, as well as completing the full treatment course are other key components to reduce mortality and the spread of resistant parasites (Walther & Walther, 2007). Both education and access to prompt treatment requires a good local public health system, including the coverage of rural areas where malaria is most prevalent. In coastal Kenya, only 32% of the population lives within 2 km of a government dispensary or private clinic, therefore it is a long walk to obtain treatment (Goodman et al., 2007). The WHO is increasingly encouraging home-based management; however, this also has associated risks. In Togo and again in coastal Kenya, 69–70% of young children (<5 years old) with fevers were treated with medicine obtained from a medicine-seller rather than a village health worker, even though the medicine from the health worker is cheaper. The medicine sellers are usually closer, open longer hours, less likely to be out of medicine, and perceived as friendlier, and more approachable; however, they are also less likely to distribute the correct medicine and dose. Preliminary studies indicate that training improves the distribution of the appropriate dose and medication and demonstrates the efficacy of including the medicine sellers, local faith-based organizations, and schools in the public health campaigns. Developing and maintaining these education and healthcare programs is expensive and accounts for over 50% of the cost of malaria control (Teklehaimanot et al., 2007). Large-scale sustained implementation of these techniques could eliminate deaths from malaria, but new strategies are needed to actually eradicate the disease.

Ongoing monitoring of malaria cases and the environmental conditions known to be associated with increased transmission is also needed to provide time for public heath officials to respond to outbreaks (Breman & Holloway, 2007). Such surveillance is also critical for the early identification of the development of resistant parasites or mosquitoes. Early warning of changes in the pattern of disease allows time to identify the cause and develop an effective response.

The Future

The complete genomes of the three organisms involved, humans, *Plasmodium falciparum* parasites, and *Anopheles* mosquito, have been released and are fully accessible on the web (Gardner et al., 2002; Holt et al., 2002; Venter et al., 2001; www.genome.gov, www.plasmDB.org, agambiae.vectorbase.org). This provides key resources for investigators to identify unique genes that can be targeted for drug and/or vaccine development. High throughput techniques also allow genetic comparisons of isolates from all over the world that have a variety of characteristics. The information obtained can be used to link specific genes with specific characteristics that contribute to virulence. For example, the parasite gene that confers resistance to chloroquine was identified using this strategy (Fidock et al., 2000).

Chemotherapy Development

Several approaches have been taken to identify new drug candidates. The comparative genomic analysis described above revealed a set of genes that are more closely related to bacteria than to other higher organisms such as humans. Some of these genes are similar to those that are already known to be the target of antibiotics that have been approved for human use, including doxycycline, clindamycin, and rifampicin (Goodman, Su, & McFadden, 2007). These compounds are now being tested for efficacy against malaria. Once an effective compound is identified a series of related structures are produced to attempt to improve specificity against malaria. This type of ongoing optimization has also been used to develop new derivatives of chloroquine and artemisinin that are also effective against the parasite (Medicines for Malaria Venture, www.mmv.org). The development of high throughput assays for in vitro antimalarial activity has facilitated screening large libraries of compounds (Weisman et al., 2006).

In addition to targeting the parasite directly, therapies can be developed against the pathology caused by malaria. Many of the symptoms of severe malaria are thought to be due to red blood cell rupture during the release of the parasite and the ability of *Plasmodium falciparum* to adhere to the endothelial cells that line capillaries. It has recently been shown that intravenous administration of the amino acid, arginine, reversed the endothelial dysfunction associated with severe malaria (Yeo et al., 2007). The clinical effectiveness of this treatment is now being evaluated. Similar approaches could be taken to enhance or reverse other physiologic and immunologic responses to the parasite. Advances in understanding the genes that are involved in malaria susceptibility, as well as the development of a protective immune response could also contribute to the identification of high risk individuals and allow customized treatment (Knight, 2005; Taylor, Ferdig, Su, & Wellems, 2000)

Vaccines

Ideally, a malaria vaccine would be safe and affordable. It would be administered as part of the ongoing EPI and confer lifelong immunity against the disease.

Currently, none of the available malaria vaccine candidates meet these criteria, but they could provide partial protection against severe disease and contribute an integrated malaria control strategy. In light of this, the WHO determined that a malaria vaccine with an effectiveness of 30–50% would be justified to be licensed in light of the magnitude of malaria's morbidity and mortality (Moorthy, Reed, & Smith, 2007).

Malaria vaccines have been traditionally divided into preerythrocytic or sporozoite vaccines, blood stage or merozoite vaccines, and mosquito stage or transmission blocking vaccines depending on the stage of the parasite life cycle that is targeted. To date, over 40 malaria proteins have been identified as possible vaccine candidates (Hoffman & Miller, 1996; Girard, Reed, Friede, & Kieny, 2007). The most advanced candidate to date is a preerythrocytic vaccine that will be the primary focus of this discussion. A preerythrocytic vaccine targets the sporozoite released during the bite of an infected mosquito and blocks the development of the disease. If partially effective, it could decrease parasite burden and consequently lower the incidence of clinical disease. The other types of vaccines do not prevent the initial infection, but could protect against the expansion of the parasite population in the blood or block transmission to the mosquito and spread to another human.

The importance of sporozoites as vaccine candidates was highlighted by the finding that radiation-attenuated *Plasmodium* sporozoites induced protective immunity in immune-naïve vertebrate hosts (Mulligan, Russell, & Mohan, 1941; Nussenzweig, Vanderberg, Most, & Orton, 1967). These encouraging results were then confirmed in humans using irradiated *Plasmodium falciparum* sporozoites (Clyde, 1975; Clyde, McCarthy, Miller, & Hornick, 1973; Clyde, Most, McCarthy, & Vanderberg, 1973; Rieckmann, 1990; Rieckmann et al., 1974; Hoffman et al., 2002). Volunteers exposed to irradiated sporozoites administered via mosquito bites developed protection against subsequent challenges with infectious parasites. Protection was directly related to the number of immunizing bites (Hoffman et al., 2002). However, this vaccine approach was thought to be impractical because it requires a large number of infectious sporozoites that can only be produced in mosquitoes. The use of subunit vaccines produced using recombinant DNA techniques developed in the 1980s seemed like a much more reasonable approach to an economical malaria vaccine and were the focus of further research efforts.

The first step in developing a subunit vaccine is to identify a parasite protein that is the target of a protective immune response. Many years of research resulted in the identification of a protein on the sporozoite surface, the Circumsporozoite Protein (CSP), that is an important vaccine target (Hoffman, Franke, Holligdale, & Druilhe, 1996). This work led to the addition of a portion of the CSP protein to the hepatitis B subunit vaccine, and the combination called RTS,S, is currently the most advanced malaria vaccine. Plans are in place for a large clinical trial in the near future (Aponte et al., 2007). The encouraging RTS,S vaccine results are a major milestone in malaria vaccine development. Although the current RTS,S formulation still does not confer sterilizing immunity, the studies to date all consistently demonstrate a 20–60% decrease in severe malaria in children under 1 year of age (Aponte et al., 2007; Alonso et al. 2004; 2005; Bojang et al., 2001; Macete et al., 2007). In conjunction with the other available malaria control measures, such as ITN and prompt ACTs treatment, this vaccine could be an important component of an integrated strategy to eliminate malaria mortality. Further investigation into the mode of action of RTS,S may also facilitate the development of other malaria vaccines.

More research is required to identify parasite components that trigger a fully protective immune response. It is clear that an immune response can be stimulated by the vaccine candidates that are currently available, but the response is not strong enough to completely block parasite development. People living in endemic areas have a similar response to natural exposure to the parasites. Multiple exposures are needed to gradually develop protection against clinical symptoms, but even after many years they are still not completely protected (Schofield & Mueller, 2006).

Clearly, there is strong selective pressure on both the parasite and the human to coexist. It could be argued that a moderate host immune response maintained by continual re-exposure to the parasite evolved to balance damage caused by the parasite and the host immune response. One of the strategies used by the parasite to evade our immune response is varying the type of proteins on its surface (Smith & Craig, 2005). To become immune, a person has to generate a response to a number of these different types of proteins. This also means that a vaccine might need to include a variety of protein types to be effective. Advances in basic immunology leading to methods to increase the immune response to parasite proteins and to promote long-lasting immunity should contribute to the efficacy of future malaria vaccines.

After 25 years of focusing primarily on subunit vaccines, there is now renewed interest in developing whole parasite vaccine strategies, such as irradiated attenuated sporozoites (Hoffman et al., 2002; Labaied et al., 2007; Mueller, Labaied, Kappe, & Matuschewski, 2005). The recent demonstration that genetically attenuated sporozoites also effectively induce sterilizing immunity in mice provides an alternative to irradiation. However, it still remains unlikely that an attenuated sporozoite vaccine will be widely distributed until an efficient in vitro system is developed to produce infectious attenuated sporozoites. Other methods that have been shown to effectively provide protection against clinical malaria, such as the use of low dose parasite inoculation, passive transfer of antibodies from immune adults to malaria patients, or vaccination with parasite-produced antigens, all raise similar cost, safety, and production concerns (Pombo et al., 2002; Cohen, Mc, & Carrington, 1961; Bouharoun-Tayoun, Attanath, Sabchareon, Chongsuphajaisiddhi, & Druilhe, 1990). Further evaluation of the protective immune responses induced by these methods and coupled with the recent identification of the set of genes expressed at each stage of the life cycle (Tarun et al., 2008; Young et al., 2005; Le Roch, Johnson, & Florens, 2004; Bozdech et al. 2003) with innovative techniques to economically produce attenuated-parasites and/or reproduce a protective immune response should lead to advances that could be applied in the field.

Mosquito Control

Historically, insect vectors have been important targets for disease control programs (Catteruccia, 2007). The success of ITN and IRS programs in decreasing malaria mortality and morbidity are recent examples. However, as with malaria chemotherapy, the development of resistance to the limited number of cost effective insecticides available is a concern and additional economical, ecologically safe alternatives are needed. Other strategies include the development of biological control measures, such as using species of bacteria, fungus or fish that specifically affect mosquitoes instead of other animals (Breman & Holloway, 2007; Schote et al., 2005; Blanford et al., 2005; Knols, Bossin, Mukabana, & Robinson, 2007; Lacey, 2007). Advances in genetic engineering have also led to the production of *Anopheles* mosquitoes that have a very limited ability to transmit parasites that cause malaria in rodents. (Ito, Ghosh, Moreira, Wimmer, & Jacobs-Lorena, 2002). Unfortunately, there was no reduction in the ability of these mosquitoes to transmit the human malaria parasite, *P. falciparum*, but similar techniques are being used to identify modifications that will block *P. falciparum* transmission (Knols et al., 2007).

Summary

The tools are currently available to effectively treat malaria, but as with many resources the problem is distribution. Individuals with malaria symptoms need access to prompt diagnosis and treatment with the appropriate drugs. Currently, both infrastructure and cost are major obstacles. The UN's efforts to promote the Rights of Children have increased global awareness of the problem and catalyzed steps to improve the situation. Public health programs through the RBM campaign and its many public and private partners are having an immediate effect, but these initial efforts have also served to reveal the magnitude of the problem. Active engagement and empowerment of the people directly affected to creatively address the problem utilizing established community networks will also be critical to sustainability. Further advances in the development of new drugs, vaccines, and mosquito control methods are needed to augment our ability to efficiently and economically eliminate malaria mortality and hopefully one day eradicate the disease completely.

Acknowledgments Kim C. Williamson received financial support from Public Health Service grants AI40592 and AI48826 from the National Institute of Allergy and Infectious Disease.

References

Alonso, P. L., Sacarlal, J., Aponte, J. J., et al. (2004). Efficacy of the rts, s/as02a vaccine against Plasmodium falciparum infection and disease in young African children: Randomised controlled trial. *Lancet, 364*, 1411–1420.

Alonso, P. L., Sacarlal, J., Aponte, J. J., et al. (2005). Duration of protection with rts, s/as02a malaria vaccine in prevention of Plasmodium falciparum disease in Mozambican children: Single-blind extended follow-up of a randomised controlled trial. *Lancet, 366*, 2012–2018.

Aponte, J. J., Aide, P., Renom, M., et al. (2007). Safety of the rts, s/as02d candidate malaria vaccine in infants living in a highly endemic area of Mozambique: A double blind randomised controlled phase I/IIb trial. *Lancet, 370*, 1543–1551.

Bojang, K. A., Milligan, P. J., Pinder, M., et al. (2001). Efficacy of RTS, S/AS02 malaria vaccine against Plasmodium falciparum infection in semi-immune adult men in the Gambia: A randomised trial. *Lancet, 358*, 1927–1934.

Bouharoun-Tayoun, H., Attanath, P., Sabchareon, A., Chongsuphajaisiddhi, T., & Druilhe, P. (1990). Antibodies that protect humans against Plasmodium falciparum blood stages do not on their own inhibit parasite growth and invasion in vitro, but act in cooperation with monocytes. *The Journal of Experimental Medicine, 172*, 1633–1641.

Bozdech, Z., Llinas, M., Pulliam, B. L., Wong, E. D., Zhu, J., & DeRisi, J. L. (2003). The transcriptome of the intraerythrocytic developmental cycle of Plasmodium falciparum. *PLoS Biology, 1*, E5.

Blanford, S., Chan, B. H., Jenkins, N., et al. (2005). Fungal pathogen reduces potential for malaria transmission. *Science, 308*, 1638–1641.

Breman, J. G., & Holloway, C. N. (2007). Malaria surveillance counts. *The American Journal of Tropical Medicine and Hygiene, 77*, 36–47.

Bryce, J., Boschi-Pinto, C., Shibuya, K., & Black, R. E. (2005). Group WHOCHER. Who estimates of the causes of death in children. *Lancet, 1*, 885–888.

Cai, X. Z. (1981). Observation of therapeutic effect of single-dose combined administration of qinghaosu, sulphomethoxine, pyrimethamine and primaquine in the treatment of chloroquine-resistant malignant malaria (author's transl). *Chung Hua Nei Ko Tsa Chih, 20*, 724–727.

Catteruccia, F. (2007). Malaria vector control in the third millennium: Progress and perspectives of molecular approaches. *Pest Management Science, 63*, 634–640.

Clyde, D. F. (1975). Immunization of man against falciparum and vivax malaria by use of attenuated sporozoites. *The American Journal of Tropical Medicine and Hygiene, 24*, 397–401.

Clyde, D. F., McCarthy, V. C., Miller, R. M., & Hornick, R. B. (1973). Specificity of protection of man immunized against sporozoite-induced falciparum malaria. *The American Journal of the Medical Sciences, 266*, 398–403.

Clyde, D. F., Most, H., McCarthy, V. C., & Vanderberg, J. P. (1973). Immunization of man against sporozoite-induced falciparum malaria. *The American Journal of the Medical Sciences, 266*, 398–403.

Cohen, S., Mc, G. I., & Carrington, S. (1961). Gamma-globulin and acquired immunity to human malaria. *Nature, 192*, 733–737.

D'Alessandro, U., Olaleye, B. O., McGuire, W., et al. (1995). Mortality and morbidity from malaria in Gambian children after introduction of an impregnated bednet programme. *Lancet, 345*, 479–483.

Fidock, D. A., Nomura, T., Talley, A. K., et al. (2000). Mutations in the P. falciparum digestive vacuole transmembrane protein pfcrt and evidence for their role in chloroquine resistance. *Molecular Cell, 6*, 861–871.

Gardner, M. J., Hall, N., Fung, E., et al. (2002). Genome sequence of the human malaria parasite Plasmodium falciparum. *Nature, 419*, 498–511.

Girard, M. P., Reed, Z. H., Friede, M., & Kieny, M. P. (2007). A review of human vaccine research and development: Malaria. *Vaccine, 13*, 1263–1276.

Goodman, C., Brieger, W., Unwin, A., Mills, A., Meek, S., & Greer, G. (2007). Medicine sellers and malaria treatment in sub-Saharan Africa: What do they do and how can their practice be improved? *The American Journal of Tropical Medicine and Hygiene, 77*, 203–218.

Goodman, C. D., Su, V., & McFadden, G. I. (2007). The effects of anti-bacterials on the malaria parasite Plasmodium falciparum. *Molecular and Biochemical Parasitology, 152*, 181–191.

Gu, H. M., Liu, M. Z., Lu, B. F., et al. (1981). Antimalarial effect and toxicity of methyl-dihydro-artemisinine in animals (author's transl). *Chung Kuo Yao Li Hsueh Pao, 2*, 138–144.

Hoffman, S. L., Franke, E. D., Hollingdale, M. R., & Druilhe, P. (1996). Attacking the infected hepatocyte. In S. L. Hoffman (Ed.), *Malaria vaccine development: A multi-immune response approach* (pp. 35–75). Washington, D.C.: American Society for Microbiology.

Hoffman, S. L., Goh, L. M., Luke, T. C., et al. (2002). Protection of humans against malaria by immunization with radiation-attenuated Plasmodium falciparum sporozoites. *The Journal of Infectious Diseases, 185*, 1155–1164.

Hoffman, S. L., & Miller, L. H. (1996). *Perspectives on malaria vaccine development.* ASM Press. Washington, D.C.

Holt, R. A., Subramanian, G. M., Halpern, A., et al. (2002). The genome sequence of the malaria mosquito anopheles Gambia. *Science, 298*, 129–149.

Ito, J., Ghosh, A., Moreira, L. A., Wimmer, E. A., & Jacobs-Lorena, M. (2002). Transgenic anopheline mosquitoes impaired in transmission of a malaria parasite. *Nature, 417*, 452–455.

Jiang, J. B., Li, G. Q., Guo, X. B., Kong, Y. C., & Arnold, K. (1982). Antimalarial activity of mefloquine and qinghaosu. *Lancet, 1*, 885–888.

Johansson, E.W., Newby, H., Renshaw, M., & Wardlaw, T. (2007). Malaria & children. United Nations Children's Fund.

Knight, J. C. (2005). Regulatory polymorphisms underlying complex disease traits. *Journal of Molecular Medicine, 83*, 97–109.

Knols, B. G., Bossin, H. C., Mukabana, W. R., & Robinson, A. S. (2007). Transgenic mosquitoes and the fight against malaria: Managing technology push in a turbulent GMO world. *The American Journal of Tropical Medicine and Hygiene, 77*, 232–242.

Labaied, M., Harupa, A., Dumpit, R. F., Coppens, I., Mikolajczak, S. A., & Kappe, S. H. (2007). Plasmodium yoelii sporozoites with simultaneous deletion of p52 and p36 are completely attenuated and confer sterile immunity against infection. *Infection and Immunity, 75*, 3758–3768.

Lacey, L. A. (2007). Bacillus thuringiensis serovariety israelensis and Bacillus sphaericus for mosquito control. *Journal of the American Mosquito Control Association, 23*(2 Suppl), 133–163.

Lengeler, C. (2004). Insecticide-treated bed nets and curtains for preventing malaria. *Cochrane Database System Review* (2):CD000363.

Le Roch, K. G., Johnson, J. R., Florens, L., et al. (2004). Global analysis of transcript and protein levels across the Plasmodium falciparum life cycle. *Genome Research, 14*, 2308–2318.

Linares, G. E., & Rodriguez, J. B. (2007). Current status and progresses made in malaria chemotherapy. *Current Medicinal Chemistry, 14*, 289–314.

Macete, E., Aponte, J. J., Guinovart, C., et al. (2007). Safety and immunogenicity of the RTS, S/AS02 candidate malaria vaccine in children aged 1–4 in Mozambique. *Tropical Medicine and International Health, 12*, 37–46.

Moorthy, V., Reed, Z., & Smith, P. G. (2007). Efficacy WHOSGoMoMV. Measurement of malaria vaccine efficacy in phase III trials: Report of a WHO consultation. *Vaccine, 13*, 1263–1276.

Mueller, A. K., Labaied, M., Kappe, S. H., & Matuschewski, K. (2005). Genetically modified Plasmodium parasites as a protective experimental malaria vaccine. *Nature, 433*, 164–167.

Mulligan, H. W., Russell, P. F., & Mohan, B. N. (1941). Active immunization of fowls against Plasmodium gallinaceum by infections of killed homologous sporozoites. *Journal of Malaria Institute of India, 4*, 24–34.

Nosten, F., & White, N. J. (2007). Artemisinin-based combination treatment of falciparum malaria. *The American Journal of Tropical Medicine and Hygiene, 77*, 181–192.

Nussenzweig, R. S., Vanderberg, J., Most, H., & Orton, C. (1967). Protective immunity produced by the injection of x-irradiated sporozoites of Plasmodium berghei. *Nature, 216*, 160–162.

Phillips-Howard, P. A., Nahlen, B. L., Kolczak, M. S., et al. (2003). Efficacy of permethrin-treated bed nets in the prevention of mortality in young children in an area of high perennial malaria transmission in western Kenya. *The American Journal of Tropical Medicine and Hygiene, 68*, 23–29.

Pombo, D. J., Lawrence, G., Hirunpetcharat, C., et al. (2002). Immunity to malaria after administration of ultra-low doses of red cells infected with Plasmodium falciparum. *Lancet, 360*, 610–617.

Rieckmann, K. H. (1990). Human immunization with attenuated sporozoites. *Bulletin of the World Health Organization, 55*, 363–365.
Rieckmann, K. H., Carson, P. E., Beaudoin, R. L., Cassells, J. S., & Sell, K. W. (1974). Letter: Sporozoite induced immunity in man against an Ethiopian strain of Plasmodium falciparum. *Transactions of the Royal Society of Tropical Medicine and Hygiene, 76*, 812–818.
Sadasivaiah, S., Tozan, Y., & Breman, J. G. (2007). Dichlorodiphenyltrichloroethane (DDT) for indoor residual spraying in Africa: How can it be used for malaria control? *The American Journal of Tropical Medicine and Hygiene, 77*, 249–263.
Schofield, L., & Mueller, I. (2006). Clinical immunity to malaria. *Current Molecular Medicine, 6*, 205–221.
Scholte, E. J., Ng'habi, K., Kihonda, J., et al. (2005). An entomopathogenic fungus for control of adult African malaria mosquitoes. *Science, 308*, 1641–1642.
Shulman, C. E., Dorman, E. K., Cutts, F., et al. (1999). Intermittent sulphadoxine-pyrimethamine to prevent severe anaemia secondary to malaria in pregnancy: A randomised placebo-controlled trial. *Lancet, 353*, 632–636.
Smith, J. D., & Craig, A. G. (2005). The surface of the Plasmodium falciparum-infected erythrocyte. *Current Issues in Molecular Biology, 7*, 81–93.
Snow, R. W., Rowan, K. M., & Greenwood, B. M. (1987). A trial of permethrin-treated bed nets in the prevention of malaria in Gambian children. *Transactions of the Royal Society of Tropical Medicine and Hygiene, 76*, 812–818.
Snow, R. W., Rowan, K. M., Lindsay, S. W., & Greenwood, B. M. (1988). A trial of bed nets (mosquito nets) as a malaria control strategy in a rural area of the Gambia, West Africa. *Transactions of the Royal Society of Tropical Medicine and Hygiene, 76*, 812–818.
Tarun, A. S., Peng, X., Dumpit, R. F., et al. (2008). A combined transcriptome and proteome survey of malaria parasite liver stages. *Proceedings of the National Academy of Sciences of the United States of America, 105*, 305–310.
Taylor, J. G., Ferdig, M. T., Su, X. Z., & Wellems, T. E. (2000). Toward quantitative genetic analysis of host and parasite traits in the manifestations of Plasmodium falciparum malaria. *Current Opinion in Genetics & Development, 10*, 314–319.
Teklehaimanot, A., McCord, G. C., & Sachs, J. D. (2007). Scaling up malaria control in Africa: An economic and epidemiological assessment. *American Journal of Tropic Medicine and Hygiene, 77*, 138–144.
ter Kuile, F. O., Terlouw, D. J., Kariuki, S. K., et al. (2003). Impact of permethrin-treated bed nets on malaria, anemia, and growth in infants in an area of intense perennial malaria transmission in western Kenya. *The American Journal of Tropical Medicine and Hygiene, 68*, 68–77.
Venter, J. C., Adams, M. D., Myers, E. W., et al. (2001). The sequence of the human genome. *Science, 291*, 1304–1351.
Walther, B., & Walther, M. (2007). What does it take to control malaria? *Annals of Tropic Medicine Parasitology, 86*, 207–215.
Weisman, J. L., Liou, A. P., Shelat, A. A., Cohen, F. E., Guy, R. K., & DeRisi, J. L. (2006). Searching for new antimalarial therapeutics amongst known drugs. *Chemical Biology & Drug Design, 67*, 409–416.
Yeo, T. W., Lampah, D. A., Gitawati, R., et al. (2007). Impaired nitric oxide bioavailability and l-arginine reversible endothelial dysfunction in adults with falciparum malaria. *The Journal of Experimental Medicine, 204*, 2693–2704.
Young, J. A., Fivelman, Q. L., Blair, P. L., et al. (2005). The Plasmodium falciparum sexual development transcriptome: A microarray analysis using ontology-based pattern identification. *Molecular and Biochemical Parasitology, 143*, 67–79.

Chapter 3
A Case Study of a Partnership in Chicago to Prevent Childhood Lead Poisoning

Anita Weinberg[*]

"When I think how much time has gone by and how much we know about it [lead poisoning], how dangerous it is, and how it should have been eliminated completely long ago...."

Former Chicago Alderman and civil rights attorney Leon M. Despres in a video made March 2008 when Despres was 100 years old (Lead Poisoning in Chicago, 2008).[1]

The Centers for Disease Control and Prevention (CDC) describe lead poisoning as a potentially devastating, but entirely preventable, disease caused primarily by exposure to dust from deteriorated paint on old housing (CDC, 2009). An estimated 434,000 children nationwide are lead poisoned[2] (Meyer et al., 2003). While lead

---

[*]Anita Weinberg is Clinical Professor and Director of the ChildLaw Policy Institute at Loyola University Chicago School of Law's Civitas ChildLaw Center. In this capacity, she also directs the Lead Safe Housing Initiative and is the Chair of the Illinois Lead Safe Housing Task Force which oversaw the work described in this chapter. The author wishes to acknowledge and thank the students and staff who have worked on the Lead Safe Housing Initiative over the last 10 years and recognize the passion, energy, and persistence of the members of the Illinois Lead Safe Housing Task Force, our community partners, and ad hoc coalitions without whom we would not be on our way to eliminate the scourge of childhood lead poisoning within Chicago and other parts of Illinois. Special appreciation goes to The Chicago Community Trust, the US Environmental Protection Agency, the Centers for Disease Control and Prevention, and the Chicago Department of Public Health for their support of this work. In addition, our efforts would not have been possible without the in-kind support of Loyola University Chicago's School of Law.

[1]Lead Poisoning in Chicago: A Historical Perspective (found at leadsafeillinois.org). Despres, a Chicago alderman from 1955 to 1975, introduced Chicago's first lead paint ordinance. Despres, who was Of Counsel, Despres Schwartz & Geoghegan, died in May 2009.

A. Weinberg (✉)
ChildLaw Policy Institute, Loyola University Chicago School of Law, Chicago, IL, USA
e-mail:aweinbe@luc.edu

J. Garbarino and G. Sigman (eds.), *A Child's Right to a Healthy Environment*,
The Loyola University Symposium on the Human Rights of Children 1,
DOI 10.1007/978-1-4419-6791-6_3,

poisoning crosses all barriers of race, income, and geography, some populations and geographic areas face disproportionately high risk for lead exposure. Once poisoned, the damage to a child's developing brain is done and the focus must shift to addressing the problems caused by the poisoning and to avoiding further accumulation of lead in a child's body.

This chapter begins with a brief overview of lead poisoning and the importance of prevention. It then describes the evolution of efforts of a public–private–community–University partnership, overseen by Loyola University Chicago School of Law's ChildLaw Center, to tackle the problem of childhood lead poisoning in Chicago and to refocus state and city efforts toward prevention. In conclusion, challenges and lessons learned are discussed.

The public's focus on a particular issue can be fickle. This is true for legislators as well as lay people. According to Professor Aaron Wildavsky, "A problem is a problem only if something can be done about it" (Anderson, 2003). Problems become public problems when they – actually or potentially – affect a substantial number of people or a higher proportion of some communities than others, have broad impact including consequences for more people than those directly affected, and involve the use of substantial common resources, or alter the way the community functions or allocates its resources (Anderson, 2003; Christoffel, 2000). It is under these conditions that advocacy efforts may be successful. But their success depends not only on having an identified and possible response or solution, but also on how that problem is articulated, and brought to the attention of decision makers, as well as on timing. And even when these criteria are met, it is unlikely that decision makers will assume responsibility for addressing them. Separate streams of problems, solutions, and politics must come together for an issue to become part of a public policy agenda, resulting in potential governmental action and toward potential change (For more discussion on how an issue becomes part of the public policy agenda, see Kingdon, 2003).

Public policy advocacy is a never-ending cycle, or a feedback loop that includes several stages which can be described as conceptually sequential, but in practice, more often than not, are simultaneous and repetitive. The workings of the policy process have been described as "organized anarchy" (Kingdon, 2003). Reform is organic. It can be messy; more often than not, it is nonlinear. A range of strategies for influencing policy are available, including public education, community organizing, coalition building, legislative and policy advocacy, and litigation. Strategy selection depends in part on whether one is advocating from within – or without – the institutions being impacted, trying to influence state and/or local policy, whether this is a community-based initiative or comes from the top-down, the

[2]Lead also has been described as "an environmental and public health hazard of global proportions" (UNEP & UNCEF, 1997). Lead clearly comes under the protections and agenda of the United Nations Convention on the Rights of the Child, and Agenda 21, a comprehensive plan of action adopted at the Earth Summit in 1992, in that these documents call for the protection of children and the environment from the negative effects of "human impacts on the environment."

extent to which partnerships can be developed, and perception of the problem's urgency. Strategies are determined and change, based on the personalities of those seeking change and those whose opinions need to be influenced for the change to occur. Other key factors include the populations most affected by the problem, available research and data, whether one is responding to a specific crisis or seeking general progress, accountability for the problem, and media attention. In addition, strategies are tied to whether resources are available or can be found to address the problem or whether one is dependent on goodwill and/or mandates and enforcement.

The partnership described in this article used an integrative advocacy model to address the public health and housing problem of childhood lead poisoning. This approach integrated a unique set of strategies and tactics, including public education, organizing, coalition building, legislative and policy advocacy, and policy implementation. It is hoped that this discussion will be helpful to other organizing efforts regardless of their specific focus.

History of Lead

Lead is a heavy metal used in many materials and products; it does not break down in the environment. Once lead is dispersed and redeposited in the environment, it will remain to poison generations of children unless it is contained or removed. Lead has no positive value to the human body and has not been shown to be safe at any level (Stapleton, 1994). While lead is toxic to many different organs in the body, the most severe damage is to a child's developing brain and nervous system. Undue lead exposure is defined by blood lead level, the amount of lead concentration in the blood. This number is established by the CDC and the World Health Organization. In the 1960s, children were considered "lead poisoned" only if the blood lead level was 60 μg/dL (micrograms per deciliter) or higher. Since 1991, the official definition for lead poisoning has been 10 μg/dL. We know now that children are being harmed at even lower levels (Lanphear, Dietrich, Auinger, & Cox, 2000; Lanphear et al., 2005; Canfield et al., 2003; Nigg et al., 2008).

At extremely high levels, lead poisoning can cause severe neurologic problems and seizure, coma, and death (Meyer et al., 2003). Today, most children are lead poisoned at low and moderate levels causing subtle brain damage resulting in reduced intelligence, learning disabilities, speech disorders, hyperactivity, shortened attention span, and behavioral disorders (Lanphear et al., 2005; Nigg et al., 2008). Research also links low levels of lead exposure to lower IQ scores and to juvenile delinquency (Needleman et al., 1996; Dietrich et al., 2001; Needleman et al., 2002; Lynch & Stretesky, 2004; Reyes, 2007). More recent studies are beginning to show that early lead exposure is also a risk factor for criminal behavior, including violent crime, in adulthood (Wright et al., 2008).

The dangers posed by lead were known centuries ago. A Greek physician in 2000 BC noted that "Lead makes the mind give way" (UNEP & UNICEF, 1997). More recently, concluding a letter to a journalist in 1786, Benjamin Franklin wrote: "This, my dear friend, is all I can at present recollect on the Subject. You will see by it, that the Opinion of this mischievous Effect from Lead is at least about Sixty Years old; and you will observe with Concern how long a useful Truth may be known, and exist, before it is generally receiv'd and practis'd on" (Franklin, 1786).

Moreover, in 1910, during a Committee Hearing in the US House of Representatives, a witness testifying about a proposed bill that would restrict the use of lead paint in housing and thus might prevent thousands of children from becoming lead poisoned over the course of the century proclaimed: "The most eminent scientists and doctors of Great Britain reached the conclusion that white lead is a poison. I say it is a poison, it matters not in what form you approach it…" (Warren, 2000).

France and Austria banned or restricted the use of white lead for interior paint in 1909.[3] By 1934, at least ten other countries had banned its use, including Tunisia, Greece, Czechoslovakia, Great Britain, Sweden, Belgium, Poland, Spain, Yugoslavia, and Cuba. In 1922, the Third International Labor Conference of the League of Nations recommended the banning of white lead for interior use (Markowitz & Rosner, 2002).

But it was not until the mid-twentieth century that USA began to focus seriously on the problem of lead poisoning. Chicago was the first city, in 1972, to enact an ordinance to limit the lead content in paint to <0.6%, recognizing the dangers of lead poisoning to children and its impact on communities. The city also established a lead unit within the city's Department of Buildings, and an increased vigilance in screening for lead poisoning in children. Parallel efforts around the country were creating broader awareness of the range of lead hazards that were harming children. By the 1970s, the federal government was responding to the problem as well: lead in residential paint was phased out and completely banned by the Consumer Product Safety Commission in 1978 (16 CFR Part 1303 – US Code of Federal Regulation). The US Environmental Protection Agency (EPA) phased out leaded gasoline between 1973 and 1996 (US Environmental Protection Agency, 2009). The EPA also placed strict limits on the amount of lead in drinking water and on the amount of lead emitted from industrial facilities. It also phased out lead in pesticides. With the assistance of the US Food and Drug Administration (FDA), the use of lead solder in domestically canned food and beverages has been virtually eliminated. In addition, the FDA has established strict standards concerning the amount of lead that can leach from US manufactured ceramic ware into beverages and food (President's Task Force, 2000a, 2000b). Federal laws also have been passed requiring the use of lead safe work practices in federally subsidized work, and

[3]White lead is the paint pigment composed of lead carbonate or lead sulfate.

disclosure of known lead hazards in homes built before 1978 (Residential Lead-Based Paint Hazard Reduction Act of 1992).[4]

As a result of these federal laws, the blood lead levels of US children aged 1–6 years declined dramatically from the late 1970s to the early 1990s. Since lead is not biodegradable, it continues to be a source of lead poisoning in children unless it is properly removed or contained. While children can be exposed to lead through a number of sources, most children are lead poisoned in their own homes through exposure to lead dust or paint chips from deteriorated lead paint surfaces, or when lead-painted surfaces are disturbed during home renovation or repainting (Nevin & Jacobs, 2006). The greatest risk is lead-contaminated dust generated from the friction of opening and closing windows and doors.

As older homes are more likely to have lead paint on their windows, doors, and walls, and fall into disrepair, the age of housing stock affects the risk of children's exposure to lead hazards. For example, although lead paint has been banned in USA since 1978, approximately 24 million housing units have deteriorated lead paint and dangerous levels of lead-contaminated house dust. One or more young children live in more than four million of these units (CDC, 2009).

Impact of Lead on Our Children, Communities, and Future

Lead is most hazardous to the nation's 24 million children aged 6 years and younger because their brains and nervous systems are still developing. Children aged 1–3 years are at the greatest risk of lead poisoning because of normal hand-to-mouth activity: they crawl and put their hands in their mouths, ingesting the lead dust that has settled on the floor or their toys. Young children's increased mobility makes lead hazards more accessible. Children absorb up to 50% of the lead they ingest, compared to adults who retain only 10% (Oliveira, Aro, Sparrow, and Hu, 2002).

Lead can also be transmitted to a fetus if the mother ingests lead while pregnant or has been exposed to high levels of lead in the past, usually due to occupational

---

[4]While the primary focus of concern for children in USA is deteriorating lead paint in housing built prior to 1978, children in other parts of the world are being harmed in large numbers not only by lead sold in residential paint still being manufactured and sold in parts of the world, but also from a number of other sources including lead from battery recycling plants, smelters, medicinal products, and gasoline (UNEP & UNICEF, 1997). See also, for example, Associated Press (January 4, 2009), *Lead for car batteries poisons an African town*, last retrieved October 21, 2009 from http://www.msnbc.com/id/28484477/print/1/displaymode/1098; The Times of India (September 27, 2009), *Lead poisons 121 children in eastern China*, last retrieved October 21, 2009 from http://timesofindia.com/articleshow/msid-5061493,prtpage-1.cms; For an update on efforts to phase out leaded gasoline around the globe, see Clearing-House for the Partnership for Clean Fuels and Vehicles (2008) Global strategies for phase-out of leaded gasoline of the partnership for clean fuels and vehicles. Last retrieved November 3, 2009 from http://www.unep.org/pcfv/PDF/PCFVLeadStrategy-Mar08.pdf.

exposure, pica, or having grown up outside USA (Binns, 2008). During pregnancy, the lead stored in bones is released into the blood stream, and lead crosses the placental barrier throughout the gestation period, including the period during which the central nervous system is formed.

While children living in wealthy communities also are at risk, lead poisoning disproportionately affects children of color and implicates environmental justice issues. Bernard Lafayette, Jr., Director, Center for Nonviolence and Race Studies, noted, "Tell you why we're still battling this problem of lead poisoning – it's because of the people who are affected by it, are not people who are in power. One problem is that the bodies of people who are victimized are African American" (Lead Poisoning in Chicago, 2008). For cases where race or ethnicity was known, data for the period 1997–2001 showed that approximately 17% of children who were identified as lead poisoned were non-Hispanic whites, 60% were non-Hispanic blacks, 16% were Hispanic, and 7% were other races or ethnicities (Meyer et al., 2003). Children living at or below the poverty level who live in older housing are at greatest risk and disproportionately affected by lead (CDC, 2009). In total, 41% of low-income housing has lead paint hazards compared to 18% of middle- and upper-income housing (Jacobs et al., 2002).

The economic costs of lead poisoning also impact communities, and local and state governments. Society pays a huge price not only in human terms but also in billions of dollars to treat the problems caused by lead poisoning, including learning disabilities, increased need for special education services and high crime rates, and chronic health problems (President's Task Force, 2000a, 2000b; Landrigan, Schechter, Lipton, Fahs, & Schwartz, 2002; Korfmacher, 2003; Gould, 2009). Research suggests that early lead exposure may also be linked to problems that develop later in life, including vascular and kidney disease, hypertension, Alzheimer's disease, stroke, diabetes, cancer, and osteoporosis. These estimates do not include the costs of addressing these problems.

The Chicago Lead Project

> *Despite that lead paint was banned in housing more than 25 years ago, children, primarily in poor and minority communities continue to be poisoned in their own homes because their homes have not been renovated or were poorly renovated, because each time an old window is opened, peeling lead paint turns to lead dust, and because people track lead paint from Chicago's old rear porches throughout the house (Woltjen 2002).*

When we began our work, Illinois represented over 20% of all children in the country with elevated lead levels, and 11% or over 26,000 Illinois children were lead poisoned (Illinois Department of Public Health, 1999). Cook County had one of the most severe childhood lead poisoning problems of any metropolitan area in the country, more than six times the national rate (Goldman, 1998). The actual numbers probably were higher, because fewer than 25% of children in Cook County were tested for lead, despite an Illinois law requiring testing children 6 years of age and younger living in communities identified as high risk based on age of housing stock and poverty. African–American children were more than three times as likely to be affected by lead poisoning as Caucasian children. Hispanic children faced nearly twice the risk. Most of this increased risk is attributed to the fact that minorities are more likely to live in older housing stock – built before leaded paint in residential buildings was banned in 1978 – which is more likely to have lead-based paint (IDPH, 2001).

More than one out of every four children, aged 6 years and younger, tested for lead in Cook County between July 1995 and June 1997, showed lead levels that placed them at danger for harmful effects. Chicago had the majority of these cases, approximately 16,000. The Illinois Department of Public Health (IDPH) had identified all of Chicago and much of suburban Cook County as high-risk areas for lead poisoning. The State of Illinois ranked 10th out of the 50 states in the age of its housing stock (CDC, 1997). In Chicago, more than 70% of the housing units were built prior to 1960, and an estimated 88,000 Chicago units were at high risk for lead hazards (U.S. Census Bureau, 2003).

Chicago and Illinois still have some of the highest numbers of lead-poisoned children, but the numbers have decreased significantly. In 2007, Illinois identified 7,260 children as lead poisoned; Chicago had less than 4,000 children identified with lead levels of 10 μg/dL or above. Still, fewer than 35% of children are tested for lead poisoning even in communities where testing is required (IDPH, 2007). While these numbers have gone down significantly, given recent research indicating that children are being harmed at much lower levels than previously thought, Chicago and Illinois children are still at great risk: the IDPH estimates that more than 81,000 children had lead levels between 5 and 9 μg/dL in 2001 (IDPH, 2001) and the Chicago Department of Public Health (CDPH) reports that over 20,000 children had lead levels $\geq$5 μg/dL in 2007 (CDPH, 2007).

When the Chicago project began, the greatest obstacles to preventing childhood lead poisoning were lack of awareness of lead as a problem and a lack of funds to remediate the lead hazards. Lead had already been eliminated from many sources, so this misconception that lead was no longer a problem existed among parents, property owners, media, policy makers, and legislators. In addition, removing deteriorated lead paint from a home correctly can cost up to $10,000. Only a few federally funded clean-up programs existed in Illinois and these were small pilot projects. No public resources were available to most property owners faced with the problem of cleaning up lead paint contamination. In addition, many families with lead-poisoned children were renting apartments with lead hazards. All too often, this led to a tug of war between landlords and tenants, as families continued to live in, and pay rent for, apartments that were poisoning their children, while negotiating with the landlords to get the lead contamination cleaned up. Some owners of low-income properties chose to abandon their properties when the city required remediation of a hazardous unit, since abatement costs were prohibitive and loans difficult to obtain (Goldman, 1998).

The following sections describe the evolution of a public–private–University–community partnership to tackle the problem of childhood lead poisoning in Chicago, and identify and discuss the challenges to carry out the effort and lessons learned.

Background

In 1999, representatives from Children and Youth 2000, a not-for-profit organization established to create and maintain public/private partnerships on child and adolescent health issues in the Chicago metropolitan area, asked Loyola University Chicago's Civitas ChildLaw Center to assume responsibility for staffing and chairing a statewide Task Force focused on Lead Safe Housing. Children and Youth 2000, which was shutting down, had organized the Task Force at the behest of the National Center for Lead Safe Housing and on the recommendation of the CDPH in an effort to develop and implement lead safe housing standards while preserving affordable housing. The Task Force, the only statewide advocacy organization in Illinois focused on childhood lead poisoning, was comprised of representatives of property management and insurance agencies, the statewide realtor association, and child health and lead advocacy groups; officials from the city, county, and State public health, housing, and economic development-related agencies; physicians; and parents of lead-poisoned children.

Loyola's ChildLaw Center, founded in 1993, is part of Loyola University Chicago School of Law and is committed to promoting justice for children through interdisciplinary service, teaching, and scholarship. Its advocacy efforts had been focused on juvenile justice and child protection. When the Center was approached by Children and Youth 2000, the Center's leadership was just adding a policy component and was intrigued by the possibility of focusing on a health issue that impacted so many underrepresented children and families being served by the Center. Set within a University setting, the Center was perceived by the Task Force members as a neutral player with no bias other than concern for children.

The charge to the ChildLaw Center was twofold: (1) to reach a consensus among a diverse group of individuals and organizations (the Task Force members) on the substance of a document that delineated the practices and standards needed to achieve lead safe housing on the part of property owners and tenants, and (2) to reach a consensus among the same group on the manner in which the document (hereafter referred to as "the standards") would be used.

The Task Force's diversity was not only its greatest strength but also posed its greatest challenge. The first few meetings showed that the group was not going to reach an agreement on the document's content. Lead advocates on the Task Force demanded that the standards be legislated. Representatives of the insurance and realtors industries refused to compromise and argued that their memberships would voluntarily comply with the standards but that they would not agree to a legislative mandate. Moreover, they added that their industries had sufficient power in the state legislature to win any legislative battles – a claim that was correct. The Task Force had not spent time building a strong coalition; instead, it had focused on drafting a document that could educate stakeholders on making housing lead safe.

To their credit, the Task Force members recognized that while the group's diversity posed challenges, it also made for a powerful force when agreements could be reached. Members unanimously agreed that the Task Force was in a unique position to work toward housing that is lead safe. While the diversity and potential conflicting interests of its members might sometimes slow the process, it also provided for a unique opportunity to discuss issues and reach consensus on the best ways to address housing problems. With Loyola's involvement, the Task Force gained staff including student researchers, an "impartial" Chair (who is also the author of this article and directed the policy initiative at the Center), and expertise from a number of University departments.[5] A professor in the Environmental Studies/Chemistry Department had been involved in training elementary grade students to test for lead paint in their homes, while using graduate students to decipher the results; the University's Stritch School of Medicine operated a lead clinic and its faculty members worked closely with the Cook County Department of Public Health to address the problem of lead poisoning. Other departments interested in the issue because of the populations with whom they worked, included education, social work, nursing, and Loyola's Center for Urban Research and Learning.

Building Trust

While all members of the Task Force agreed on the general goal, frustration and distrust existed within the Task Force due to the lack of agreement on how the standards the Task Force had worked to develop over time were to be used. One of the Center's greatest challenges in keeping the Task Force together was to build trust. The group agreed to at least temporarily set aside the issue of legislation mandating the standards. Instead, one of the Task Force members, a pediatrician, agreed to post the standards on a website hosted by the children's hospital and university with which she was affiliated, and members agreed to disseminate the document among their own constituency groups. Members unanimously agreed that the Task Force was in a unique and positive position to undertake successfully efforts to work toward housing that is lead safe. The Center made a concerted effort to involve the range of stakeholders on the Task Force in non-threatening activities

[5]Over the years the Center has received grants from the Searle Funds at The Chicago Community Trust, the US EPA, and through a subcontract with the Chicago Department of Public Health and the CDC. In addition, a key source of support to the Task Force was its affiliation with Loyola University's ChildLaw Center and the in-kind resources and indirect services provided by the University through the involvement of faculty, staff, and students.

that supported mutual goals. The strategy was twofold: to recognize and utilize members' expertise so that they felt valued, and to provide on-going education about the problem and possible solutions at quarterly Task Force meetings so that their participation was beneficial to them.

The Center served in a research and educational capacity to the Task Force members. This was important in order for the Task Force members, with diverse interests and backgrounds, to become familiar with a range of issues concerning lead poisoning and housing, and in order for the diverse membership to discuss issues among the group and to bring back the information learned and discussed to their broader constituencies. Information was gathered on an array of efforts being undertaken in other parts of the country, including (1) programs and standards addressing the reduction or elimination of lead paint in housing, (2) recent studies on the effects of lead exposure, (3) lead awareness campaigns in several states, (4) current trends in state legislation supporting lead safe housing, (5) litigation efforts around the country, and (6) distribution of tobacco settlement monies in several states.

Based on this information and a 7-hour strategic planning session in 2001, the Task Force identified the following challenges to addressing lead poisoning of children:

- Cost of doing lead abatement work – on average, it could cost $10,000 per unit to remove lead hazards;
- Lack of understanding among property owners of the dangers to children along with the lack of financial resources for many property owners to address the problem;
- Incorrect and often dangerous information being provided to contractors and rehab workers by retailers about lead safe work practices;
- Lack of knowledge and skill among contractors and remodelers on working safely with lead paint;
- Lack of enforcement of existing codes requiring that properties be maintained, and of mitigation orders once inspections identified lead hazards in a residential building;
- Parents' reluctance to publicize their story because they felt guilty that they had not protected their child; they were embarrassed; and they did not want their child labeled. Parents who would have liked to tell their story often were fearful of reprisal and eviction from a landlord, or deportation if they were illegally living in the country and the apartment building. In addition, families had little choice in their housing given the limitation of affordable housing;
- Limited resources to offer affected families. The quandary faced was that while families needed to be educated about the hazards of lead paint and the risks to their children, there were limited, if any, resources with which to help the families address the problem. Thus, we were raising families' fears but offering little in return. At the same time, it was important to involve families and tell their story in order to gain the attention of the public, the media, policy makers, and legislators to advocate successfully for resources.

The Task Force members also agreed on the need to shift from a responsive to preventative approach. Federal and state law required a response only after a child was lead poisoned. Advocates frequently compared the situation to the canary in a mine shaft – one only became aware of the dangers after the canary died, or after a child was poisoned.

The stakeholders agreed on three areas on which to focus the Task Force's continuing attention:

- Promote public awareness;
- Advocate for policy reform to shift focus from responding to preventing lead poisoning;
- Foster collaborations to achieve the shared goal of eliminating childhood lead poisoning.

In addition, while not specifically stated, within the ChildLaw Center it was agreed that the Center would not engage in litigation specifically related to landlord–tenant issues and lead poisoning. Others could do litigation, but the Center could not effectively lead the diverse coalition if members could not trust one another and feel comfortable sharing information within the Task Force.

The Task Force made a concerted effort to involve the range of stakeholders in activities and to address their concerns. The first two projects focused on involving the Task Force members in working together to raise awareness: convening a community forum to focus attention on the problem of childhood lead poisoning in three communities; and preparing a Public Service Announcement and hosting an 11-week series on Public Access Television. Two other projects included Task Force collaboration focused on moving forward the advocates' policy agenda to enforce existing Codes and creative means of developing financial resources for making homes lead safe. These projects were drafting a Judicial Bench Book – a manual for judges in Chicago's Housing Court – that addressed the problem of lead poisoning and provided and summarized local, state, and federal laws and rules and regulations concerning lead paint; and beginning research on drafting a bill that would provide financial resources for property owners while focusing on code enforcement. Together, these projects also assisted in the goals of fostering collaborations and later policy reform and legislative efforts.

Community Summit

One of the ChildLaw Center's first efforts to integrate the University into its lead poisoning prevention work was to build on the University's biennial Forum on the Child and refocus the traditional conference model for exploring issues affecting urban children and the role of public policy in responding to children's needs, to an action-oriented response to a targeted issue. With assistance from several University departments, a representative from the CDPH, and three community agencies, the Center established an interactive partnership involving the University, governmental agencies, and three targeted communities in the Chicago metropolitan area. The communities were identified based on the extent of the problem of lead poisoning, University resources available in the communities, existing infrastructure within the communities to tackle the problem, and/or expressed interest by community-based organizations in the areas.

The partnership aimed to develop and implement workable strategies to reduce the problem of childhood lead poisoning in those communities and to create a model that could be used by other communities where children were at high risk for lead poisoning. The Forum functioned as a collaborative learning and planning vehicle for those who would be most directly involved in developing and implementing such a response. The ChildLaw Center's role was primarily to staff the preparation for the Forum and to facilitate follow-up community organizing around the developing strategic plans. The Center's work included convening the planning sessions prior to the Forum which were used to select the three targeted communities, identifying conference invitees, including representatives of the targeted communities, and developing the format for the Forum and strategic planning initiative, with a focus on creating a format that would best allow for carrying forward the strategic plans. The Center sought to avoid duplication of effort, and to learn from past experiences and to build on current initiatives. To that end, under the supervision of faculty, law students surveyed relevant agencies, organizations, and individuals to identify existing or past lead-related activities within the relevant communities; and national and state representatives and advocacy organizations to identify innovative lead prevention efforts that would be compiled as part of the materials for the working conference. Faculty recruited the targeted communities, and with student assistance planned the conference and convened and staffed the Forum and follow-up efforts. A working paper was drafted for use during the Forum. *Children in a Toxic World: A Working Paper on Community Efforts to End Childhood Lead Poisoning*, outlined the lead poisoning problem and its impact on the specific communities, and acknowledged and described current efforts underway in the communities to work on the problem, and creative ideas from elsewhere.

The Forum, held in October 2001, included a morning session during which participants learned about the problem of childhood lead poisoning; in the afternoon, the participants divided into breakout groups by community and, with a facilitator and student recorder, began developing action plans. Participants at the Forum included representatives from community-based groups; property owners; health and housing state and local government officials; university faculty and students from Nursing, Medicine, Social Work, Urban Studies, and Law; and other interested community members.

With the groundwork for an action-oriented partnership in place between Loyola, governmental agencies, and the communities, following the Forum, representatives began developing specific implementation strategies aimed at lead poisoning prevention tailored to each community's unique needs and circumstances. It was at one of these meetings that the State Representative from one of the communities attended and heard from a parent of a lead-poisoned child. Moved by what he had heard,

Representative Harry Osterman became our best ally and leader in tackling this problem in the Illinois General Assembly.

A key to success in this phase of work was the focus on the characteristics of the individual communities, the prior lead-related activities in the communities, and the strengths the community groups and members brought to the initiative. The effort was community driven, with the community deciding what it wanted to accomplish. The emphasis was on bringing together the churches, health and social service organizations, community organizing groups, and relevant businesses to work together to determine the approach that would work best in the community. The University's role was to facilitate this process, not to direct it. We have come back to this model for building community partnerships to address a problem several times over the course of the project.[6]

Chicago Public Access Cable TV

The ChildLaw Center, in cooperation with the Lead Safe Housing Task Force members, produced and hosted an 11-week series of public access cable television programs in the fall of 2002 on Channel 21 Hotline. Each 25-min program included a call-in segment. Members of the Task Force, ChildLaw Center staff, and other interested members of a growing coalition of community members, government representatives, and advocates participated as hosts and guest interviewees. For example, the Task Force members who were interviewed included the representative from the Chicago Realtor's Association, who was interviewed about funding for abatement and mitigation; a tenant organizer was interviewed about tenants' rights and lead disclosure laws; the attorney with the City's Corporation Counsel's Office who sat on the Task Force was interviewed about the Chicago Housing Court process; and a pediatrician was interviewed about preventive health care and screening for lead poisoning. A parent of a child with lead poisoning – also a Task Force member – was interviewed about the challenges of raising a child with lead poisoning. Members of the Task Force served as host and interviewer during the call-in show.

In addition, the ChildLaw Center worked with the Chicago Cable Access television to produce a public service announcement (PSA) about lead paint hazards on FYI TV 27. The PSA was aired over the next several years to correspond with Lead Poisoning Prevention week in October, and Lead Poisoning Prevention month in April.

---

[6] A similar format was successfully used at a Summit convened by the Center and its partners in September 2009 which brought together five communities in the greater Chicagoland area at high risk for lead hazards to tackle the problem of lead poisoning on a local and state policy level and to consider broader healthy housing issues.

Judicial Bench Book

Statewide, enforcement of the existing ordinances and state law regarding housing and lead paint violations was poor. With the assistance of Loyola law students, the ChildLaw Center drafted a Bench Book for judges in Chicago's Housing Court outlining local and state laws and regulations concerning lead paint violations. In 2002, the Supervising Judge of the Housing Court in the Circuit Court of Cook County disseminated the Bench Books to the judges in his division. Over the next 2 years, the Center began to adapt its Chicago Bench Book on Lead Poisoning Laws to several other jurisdictions within the state with high numbers of children who had been lead poisoned. In subsequent years, the IDPH planned to develop bench books for several jurisdictions as well, and the Center shared its research and materials in hopes that the state agency, charged with enforcing the laws, would be in a stronger position to distribute the Bench Books and assure that they were used. The CDC and a national advocacy organization focused on lead poisoning prevention used the Bench Book as a model for other jurisdictions.

Representatives for realtors and property owners did not oppose the development of the Bench Book, reasoning that the City primarily prosecuted repeat offenders and that this was an appropriate priority of the Task Force. In order to provide a neutral text, the initial Bench Brook cited only government sources in presenting the problem to avoid any charges that our research was biased against property owners.

State Legislative Initiative

By the summer and fall of 2002, the ChildLaw Center and Task Force envisioned a legislative effort that would include coalition building, education of legislators, and introduction of legislation by January of 2003. The Center, on behalf of the Illinois Lead Safe Housing Task Force, worked with Representative Osterman to introduce legislation to address childhood lead poisoning. Initially, it was hoped that the legislation would focus on a window replacement initiative in several communities at the greatest risk for lead poisoning throughout the state. Research had shown that replacing windows in old housing significantly reduced risk to children by reducing the amount of lead dust found on floors, windowsills, and window troughs generated by the friction of opening and closing windows. Young children are especially vulnerable because they play by the windows or handle toys on which lead dust has settled, and then put their hands or toys in their mouths (These findings have been further established in more recent research. See Nevin & Jacobs, 2006; Jacobs, 2007.). The initiative provided an opportunity to build on the expertise of the Task Force members and to bring together an expanded group of community, business, and government leaders to focus specifically on the initiative. It was intended that the group would include window manufacturers, building supplies companies, carpenters, property owners, tenants, government representatives, legislators, and others to address the problem of children being poisoned by lead paint.

The proposed legislation called for loans and grants to low-income property owners for window replacement, and community economic development through training and employment opportunities. The cost of implementing the bill, however, would have been approximately $25–$30 million, and the sponsoring representative and others were concerned that the state legislature was unlikely to make sufficient funds available to implement the legislation. It was therefore agreed to pursue an important, but less costly provision of the bill that would create an advisory council charged with developing and making recommendations to the Governor and General Assembly regarding development of a prevention-focused lead poisoning program. Although the Advisory Council's makeup closely mirrored that of the Task Force, the new Council would be established and charged with its responsibility by the legislature with the mandate of reporting back to the General Assembly and Governor. The Task Force members hoped that it would be more difficult for the state leadership to ignore a report that it had commissioned. Equally important, it was important to be responsive to the representative's desire to begin moving forward on a legislative agenda.

In February 2003, HB 3229, the Lead Safe Housing Advisory Council bill, was introduced. There is always a risk, in creating an advisory group, of making it seem like something is being done to address a problem when in fact it is not. And the bill did not approach the depth of the initial draft legislation establishing a grants and loans program. However, in a successful attempt to make the legislative effort worthwhile, a provision was included in the legislation requiring the Advisory Council be co-chaired by a representative from the IDPH and the author, who chaired the Illinois Lead Safe Housing Task Force and was a faculty member in Loyola's ChildLaw Center. This shared role assured that researchers and writers – through the assistance of law students and faculty – would be available to staff the Council and move the reform agenda forward. It also provided the authority of the IDPH to convene the meetings and print the final report. Both IDPH and the Center would have the ability to disseminate the report.

The ChildLaw Center and Lead Safe Housing Task Force used the introduction and passage of the bill as an opportunity to educate legislators, the Governor, and the public about the problem of childhood lead poisoning and the need for prevention.

The bill's signing in July 2003 also provided an opportunity for media attention, with a press conference held to discuss the problem of lead poisoning and the goals of the new law.

The final report, drafted by the Center staff and published in 2006, put forth more than 50 recommendations regarding lead screening, data sharing, targeting properties at risk, lead safe work practices, funding mechanisms, and education of the public (Illinois Lead Safe Housing Advisory Council, 2007). Voting on recommendations can be quite controversial. Even when individuals actively participate during meeting discussions, it is possible at the point of voting for members of a group to easily feel that their position has been misunderstood or not heard. It was important that Advisory Council members participated in the voting discussion and felt that their opinions were weighed because the goal for the recommendations was eventually to move them into legislation. In a very deliberate effort to ensure the integrity of the recommendations and report, the chairs facilitated a consensus decision-making process (Dressler, 2004).

About this time, the Center also began to have a limited, but more consistent presence in Springfield through the volunteer work of a lobbyist committed to children's issues and interested in lending his expertise to a compelling issue.

As the Center built its expertise in the field and put together coalitions, collaborating with a broad range of groups – community and governmental – the CDPH asked the Center to expand its public–private–University partnership and work with the City in developing a strategic plan for the City of Chicago to eliminate childhood lead poisoning by the year 2010.[7] The initial step was to plan and staff a Citywide Summit, modeled on the 2001 Community Summit, to define the major objectives and components of a strategic plan.

Emergence of the Chicago Plan

The strategic plan to eliminate childhood lead poisoning in Chicago (hereafter referred to as the Lead Safe Chicago Plan) was made possible by the coming together of existing groups concerned about lead poisoning of children due to lead paint, and their efforts to identify additional stakeholders needed to develop a blueprint for the city to eliminate lead poisoning.

The City of Chicago's Lead Committee (Lead Committee), which began meeting in 2000, consisted of the departments of health, environment, housing, budget, law, human services, and buildings. In early 2002, the Lead Committee, inspired by the federal strategy to eliminate childhood lead poisoning, identified the need to develop a citywide strategy to address childhood lead poisoning (President's Task Force, 2000a, 2000b). It was evident to this Committee that lead poisoning was a serious problem facing Chicago's children and that a partnership of housing, health, and environmental advocates was required to address this issue adequately. Simultaneously, the Illinois Lead Safe Housing Task Force was tackling the problem of lead poisoning. Development of the Lead Safe Chicago Plan began in the spring of 2002 when a small group of stakeholders from the Task Force and others met with CDPH (Steering Committee) to plan a Summit for March 2003 to serve as a kick-off strategy meeting. The Steering Committee included representatives

[7] A federal agenda also sought to eliminate childhood lead poisoning in the United States by the year 2010. (President's Task Force on Environmental Health Risks and Safety Risks to Children, 2000a, 2000b).

from the City of Chicago, the US EPA, the US Department of Housing and Urban Development (HUD), CDC, non-profit housing, and health groups.

During the planning meetings, members of the Steering Committee worked together to create a set of principles to guide the strategic planning process. The goals for the summit developed by the Steering Committee were threefold: (1) lay the groundwork to educate about the problem and existing efforts to address it; (2) engage participants and focus them on the impact of lead poisoning on Chicago's children and thus the future of the City; and (3) begin writing a blueprint for the City to tackle the problem. The Steering Committee sought to include individuals who might not have been familiar with the problem of childhood lead poisoning but had specific knowledge and/or resources that could lend additional perspectives on how to address the problem and garner broader audiences to whom to spread the message about lead poisoning, and individuals with related or specific expertise that is important to moving forward on specific steps, including those needed for buy-in and those needed to make implementation of any proposals possible. Invitees included local, state, and federal government and legislators; non-profit community-based organizations; and non-profit other groups, such as healthcare providers, environmental law clinics, legal aid, housing advocates, and others, including University, national organization, financial institution and foundation representatives, and the Task Force members. In addition, representatives participated from the Illinois Department of Children and Family Services, the Chicago Public Library, Chicago Public Schools, child welfare community, healthcare providers, childcare community, early childhood leaders, financial services, bank representatives, and foundations. The Summit also provided an opportunity to educate legislators about the problem within their districts, even if they did not attend the all-day program. Fact sheets specific to legislators' districts were sent with the invitations to legislators describing how the problem of lead poisoning impacted their communities.

Although the Steering Committee planned for 80–100 participants, the response greatly surpassed expectations. The conveners heard from innumerable individuals who had heard about the Summit and requested to be included. In March 2003, Lead Safe Chicago: A Citywide Summit to End Childhood Lead Poisoning brought together 150 invited guests, representing a broad spectrum of public, private, and non-profit organizations and agencies.

The morning session of the Summit provided participants with background information on lead poisoning so that the participants would have a shared basis from which to begin formulating ideas for the strategic plan. The director of the Lead Poisoning Prevention Unit of the CDPH gave a presentation on childhood lead poisoning in the City. Representatives from the EPA, HUD, and CDC provided overviews on their agency's role in addressing childhood lead poisoning. Representatives of these agencies were included as partners not only to provide the audience with information but also to ensure the representatives' presence to demonstrate to them the extent of interest, concern, and energy in Chicago to address this problem. The keynote speaker, a renowned researcher and professor, spoke on

The Legacy of Lead: Childhood Lead Poisoning in the 21st Century. Toward the end of the morning, the participants divided into concurrent working sessions and began the process, which continued through the afternoon, of drafting a strategic plan for the elimination of lead poisoning in the City of Chicago.

A consensus emerged from the Summit that a plan should focus on four key objectives: (1) leveraging dollars for making housing lead safe, (2) fostering compliance with lead safe housing practices, (3) increasing identification of children with lead poisoning, and (4) putting childhood lead poisoning on decision makers' radar screens. Working groups were developed to review, refine, and address each objective, and the working groups continued to meet following the Summit to work on implementing the action plans, during which priorities sometimes changed and evolved.[8]

Leveraging dollars working group: Directors and staff of lead poisoning prevention programs are painfully aware that housing cannot be made lead safe without more money. Conversations about money invariably dwell on the expenditure side of the ledger. The creation of a Chicago plan to end lead poisoning presented an opportunity to recast lead safety interventions as investments rather than expenditures that at the same time could upgrade affordable housing, stabilize distressed neighborhoods, lower healthcare costs, improve school performance, and reduce delinquent behavior. The objective of the "leveraging dollars working group" was to develop and implement creative mechanisms, including public–private partnerships, to leverage dollars to make housing lead safe.

Fostering compliance working group: While landlords, homeowners, contractors, and insurers all have a stake in making housing lead safe, the goal of achieving lead safe housing ultimately depends on the actions of property owners. The objective of the "fostering compliance working group" was to identify and develop a spectrum of rewards, sanctions, and incentives for increasing owners' motivation to prevent and control lead hazards and to create educational campaigns geared to property owners regarding lead poisoning. Much consideration went into determining the appropriate title for this working group. Because "enforcement," which is what many members were seeking, had a pejorative connotation, "fostering compliance" was used to imply an effort to collaborate and work together not only to enforce codes but also to provide supports.

Increasing identification working group: Because most children with lead poisoning do not have visible symptoms of lead poisoning, the only way to identify those with elevated blood lead levels is through a blood test. It is critical that such tests be performed as early as possible in order to limit children's exposure to the source of the poisoning, ensure that younger siblings are not poisoned, and access

[8]This strategic plan focused initial efforts on lead-based paint in housing because it was, and still is, considered the primary source of exposure for children. There are other sources of lead in the environment, however, which will need to be addressed before the problem can be completely eliminated.

remedial services that can mitigate the effects of the poisoning. The objective of this working committee was to increase the identification of children aged 0–3 years who were at the greatest risk for lead poisoning.

Putting childhood lead poisoning on decision makers' radar screen working group: Many people, including legislators and other decision makers, assumed that lead poisoning was eliminated decades ago. Lead paint is banned, leaded gasoline is no longer an option, and leaded pipes are not used. What they do not realize is that children continue to be poisoned, with devastating results for their communities. The objective of this working group was to develop creative mechanisms for raising awareness about childhood lead poisoning among decision makers and those with the power to make housing lead safe.

The Center and CDPH drafted the final strategic plan (Lead Safe Chicago, 2004) based upon the work of the committees. CDPH retains overall responsibility for work-plan implementation. The Task Force, under the leadership of the Center, provides monitoring and evaluation. The Task Force makes recommendations for corrective action and re-allocation of resources to assure that the outcome of eliminating childhood lead poisoning is achieved. The Task Force agreed to assume responsibility for on-going monitoring of the implementation of the plan when it became clear that no other organization appeared to be in a position to hold the City accountable in its work. While Chicago's City Council should have been the obvious monitor, there was concern that it would not undertake the effort responsibly.

Passage of the Illinois Lead Poisoning Prevention Act of 2006

While these efforts were underway, and waiting for publication of the Statewide Advisory Council's report, the Task Force members and Representative Osterman still wanted to move legislation, which would have a broader impact. On behalf of the Task Force, the Center drafted the Lead Poisoning Prevention Act of 2006. But this time there was even greater concern about what could be passed. Because any controversial legislation would receive the response that we should wait for the publication of the Advisory Council report, we sought to draft a bill that would be relatively non-controversial within the legislature. Advisory Council recommendations ranged from relatively innocuous provisions such as amending Illinois law to provide a state income tax form check-off to generate dollars for lead poisoning prevention, to passing a consumer tax on paint or imposing a fee on utilities to go toward a Lead Poisoning Prevention Fund. Equally important was that the provisions included in the bill be based on recommendations that had been supported by all members of the Advisory Council; they had the backing of tenant organizers, property owners, government agencies, and advocates. Moreover, an ongoing state budget crisis meant that the bills' provisions could not be vulnerable to a fiscal note indicating that the implementation of the bill would be costly.

Moving legislation at this time, even if not everything that was envisioned, was seen as a further opportunity to raise awareness, to have an impact on the problem, and to set the stage for movement toward passage of more costly programs and to keep the legislature engaged. The primary goal of the drafted legislation was lead poisoning prevention. As drafted, the bill placed responsibility on government, professionals, property owners, and organizations to help prevent lead poisoning; raised public awareness about the dangers of lead by requiring more information be made available for parents and consumers; required that products children eat, use, or wear be lead safe; prohibited property owners who fail to comply with the law from doing business with the State or State agencies; and imposed monetary fines for violations of some provisions of the law.

In advocating for the legislation, three messages were conveyed:

> Message 1:
> Our current focus has been responsive, responding only after a child is poisoned. This bill sets the stage to prevent childhood lead poisoning. The costs to society of childhood lead poisoning are prohibitive in human and financial terms, and the cost benefit of addressing this problem is fairly straightforward.
>
> Message 2:
> Lead poisoning is one of the few causes of social and learning problems we know how to fix and thus prevent. Unlike so many social ills, this problem can be eliminated in our lifetime. To tackle the problem, we need to replace pre-1978 windows, maintain lead safe homes and buildings, utilize lead safe work practices, raise awareness, and test children for lead.
>
> Message 3:
> While the number of lead-poisoned children in Illinois is falling, the problem is still significant, as shown by recent research finding that even lower levels of lead can harm children. To emphasize the significance of the problem to the legislators, fact sheets were drafted about childhood lead poisoning and the risk of lead hazards in the housing stock specific to their individual districts. Statewide maps also were disseminated to illustrate the point that childhood lead poisoning was neither a partisan nor a Chicago-only issue.

Key to the law, which was passed by the end of the session, was to begin to move toward a prevention-driven program (Illinois Lead Poisoning Prevention Act, 2006). The law establishes creative ways to raise awareness about the problem and places reasonable requirements on landlords, child care providers, hardware and retail stores selling paint supplies, and the state and local departments of public health to address the problem. Landlords, in addition to repairing lead hazards once a child is lead poisoned, as required under the old law, must now also post signs in common areas of buildings when a child has been poisoned in one of the units, putting residents on notice that there may be lead hazards in their unit as well. Child care centers are required to distribute lead poisoning information to parents of enrolled children, since that is the age group at the greatest risk. Hardware and retail stores selling paint removal products must display posters or distribute brochures about lead safe work practices. This hardware store effort was first undertaken as a pilot project in Chicago as part of the Lead Safe Chicago Plan under the joint efforts of CDPH, the University of Illinois at Chicago School of Public Health

Great Lakes Centers for Occupational and Environmental Safety and Health, and Loyola's ChildLaw Center. It evolved after a survey by law and public health students, modeled after a study in Indiana by Improving Kids' Environment, identified that stores were giving out insufficient or incorrect information about working with lead paint. We were able to point to its success on a local level in advocating for a similar statewide program.

The 2006 law also requires the IDPH and its local agencies to inspect buildings when a child younger than 3 years is poisoned at a blood lead level lower than what was required before, and upon the request of a parent of a child aged 6 years or younger, or a pregnant woman if more than two units in the building have had children identified as lead poisoned in the last 5 years. These are the populations at the greatest risk. If an inspection finds lead hazards, the property owner must repair the unit(s). Realtors supported these provisions recognizing that they targeted the populations at the greatest risk and that they were focused on repeat offenders who already should have known that they had lead hazards, since other children in the building already would have been identified as lead poisoned to trigger the inspection. The law also prohibits retailers from selling products used by children that are not lead safe.

While Center staff and the active support of Task Force members were crucial, it is unlikely that the legislation would have been passed without the consistent presence of a lobbyist at the Capital on a daily basis to ensure that the bill did not get dropped due to competing matters and time. The Task Force benefited by the volunteer efforts of the lobbyist committed to working on behalf of children's issues and later by a grant that allowed us to hire the lobbyist.

On-Going Efforts

Throughout this period, the Center through its students and staff undertook a range of other activities that strengthened its efforts to raise awareness, educate stakeholders, and move forward policy reform efforts. These activities included launching local and statewide Lead Safe Chicago (2004) and Illinois (2006) campaigns, which included developing a logo to establish a recognized "identity," starting up a website, reaching out to media outlets around the state, and publishing a quarterly newsletter circulated by email and distributed at conferences, trainings, meetings, and legislative events. Students interviewed and profiled families who could then be featured in discussions with legislators or the media, and planned and created exhibits and games to be used at a children's museum and at health fairs to describe the problem of lead poisoning. Students and faculty also made presentations to stakeholder groups targeting the message to the specific group. For example, meetings were held with property owner associations not only to encourage them to address lead hazards in their buildings, but also to remind them of the existing laws: a representative of the Center provided an overview of the problems of lead poisoning; a property owner or member of the realtor's association described efforts they had undertaken and/or why preventing lead hazards should be a priority; and a prosecuting attorney discussed the laws and enforcement issues. Students, staff, and the Task Force members also spoke at Chicago aldermanic community meetings where the audience was not only an alderman's constituents but the alderman who was in a position to work at changing policy.

Challenges Moving Forward

Loyola's ChildLaw Center has now been working on the problem of childhood lead poisoning for 10 years. During this time, the Center has successfully maintained and expanded partnerships in order to build coalitions; develop public, private, university, and community collaborations; and build trust among a group of stakeholders with diverse backgrounds, training, and special interests. All the groups, however, share the goal of eliminating childhood lead poisoning. The Center has kept the participants engaged and working together to create and negotiate solutions to achieve the shared goal, including through community organizing, coalition building, and policy and legislative advocacy. The Task Force remains the only advocacy organization in the state focused on lead poisoning prevention. It continues to have more than 90% attendance at its quarterly meetings and serves as an educational resource and place for brainstorming and initiating new ideas for/among stakeholders, the local and state government officials, advocates, community-based representatives, realtors, property owners, and parents who attend. The momentum and determined commitment to eliminate lead poisoning continue to exist among stakeholders. More recently, partnerships have grown due to increased attention to healthy housing, federal stimulus dollars, and new leadership at government levels.

Nevertheless, the Center and Task Force will face challenges in the coming months and years. It is always difficult to maintain coalitions and partnerships as new concerns or conflicts arise. The trust developed and history in working together should help to continue to maintain the working relationships. With growing local and national budget crises, there will be fewer financial resources to address the specific problem of lead poisoning and it will compete with many other public health issues and social problems. HUD, EPA, and CDC have shifted the focus from lead poisoning alone to include a broader focus on healthy homes. This can be positive, but it also requires conveying to families and the public a broader message in which lead may be lost. Over the years, we have informed decision makers that in fact the efforts and financial resources are paying off with lower numbers of lead-poisoned children. As research demonstrates that children are being harmed at even lower levels, however, and the numbers go up, not down, the message becomes more confusing and the sources of poisoning become even more difficult to address.

In the past, limited resources also have resulted in the state's public health department responding *after* a child has been lead poisoned rather than preventing it. In fact, through September 2008, its annual surveillance report specifically stated that the Department is "committed to monitoring the identification and treatment of lead poisoned children, in addition to identifying the source of the lead poisoning" – not a public health preventative approach. As resources continue to be limited, there is the danger that the focus on prevention will be lost.

Confounding this challenge is the difficulty of attracting media attention to the issue of lead paint in homes. Ironically, media has paid much attention to a different lead poisoning problem – the presence of lead paint in children's products – chiefly toys. While it is inexcusable that any parent should have to worry about their child being harmed by lead in a toy, lead paint in homes is a far more significant source of poisoning for children in USA.

Lastly, public health agencies are becoming more aware of refugee, internationally adopted, and recent immigrant children coming to USA lead poisoned due to lead sources in their native countries. Their blood lead levels rise after resettlement because of lead contamination in their new environments and continued use of imported products containing lead. Existing health burdens and cultural, language, and economic barriers compound the risk for lead poisoning after resettlement. For example, iron deficiency, prevalent among refugee children, increases lead absorption through the gastrointestinal tract. Exposure to small amounts of lead can result in very high blood lead levels in iron-deficient children. Outreach, education, and solutions differ somewhat from current efforts aimed at reducing the use of lead paint.

As the Task Force and Center move forward, the primary focus is fivefold:

1. maintain the public–private–community–University partnership and coalitions working toward the elimination of lead poisoning;
2. continue efforts to ensure implementation and enforcement of the 2006 Act and a Chicago ordinance that also was passed in 2006 reflecting changes in state law and that lowered the level of concern from ≥10 to ≥5 μg/dL for a child harmed by lead living in Chicago;
3. pursue current legislative and advocacy efforts to obtain state and federal dollars to eliminate lead hazards;[9]
4. help individual communities assume a greater role and take the initiative to address problems within their communities independent of, as well as in coordination with, city efforts;
5. involve leadership organizations working on issues or on behalf of constituencies that may be impacted by the resulting problems of childhood lead poisoning. These include child, health, and education advocacy organizations; affordable

[9]Most recently, on behalf of the Task Force, the Center successfully advocated for legislation that appropriates $5 million for a pilot program in two communities to remove lead hazards primarily through window replacement (Build Illinois Bond Fund, 2009). The program includes a community economic development aspect, providing incentives to contractors who train and hire community members to do the work, and supporting the purchase of windows manufactured and assembled in Illinois (Illinois Lead Poisoning Prevention Act, 2008).

housing groups; and environmental advocacy organizations. The goal is to involve these groups in strategic discussions on how to integrate education about the dangers of childhood lead poisoning and prevention initiatives into their work and public voice. As an example, in 2004, based largely on a Task Force member's efforts, a statewide child advocacy organization added information and data on childhood lead poisoning to its Kids Count report, and featured the efforts of one of the community's with which we worked as an example of "What's Working for Kids."

Lessons Learned

As the Center and Task Force moves forward with its agenda, the following Lessons Learned will inform its work.

Partnerships are key. This effort would not have been successful without the right people in the right place at the right time. Without the visionary leadership in the Lead Poisoning Prevention Unit at the CDPH during this period, it is likely that our efforts would have been far less expansive. There is no question, however, but that the city government also needed the strong advocacy arm and vision the Center brought to the effort. The importance of ongoing independent leadership to move slow-moving, recalcitrant bureaucracies cannot be overstated. Moreover, many of the projects undertaken are due to the creative thinking that results from a partnership of a broad range of individuals coming from different perspectives and experience, including the Task Force members and the greater coalition we built.

Use a strengths-based approach when working with community partners. Every community, through its residents and community-based groups and partners, has strengths, often untapped or unrecognized, that can and should be called upon when working together. The Center and Task Force members may have brought the issue of lead poisoning to the forefront within some of the communities with which we worked, and we sought to empower the communities by helping to facilitate the planning and implementation process. But the community members were the active participants and the work was built upon the talents, skills, knowledge, interests, energy, dreams, and connections of the community members.

Find the compelling message, make it simple, and convey it in different ways. The problem of lead poisoning can seem overwhelming – lead hazards are in millions of our homes; tens of thousands of young children are being poisoned. But it is hard to argue with the message that unlike the cause of so many other social problems, lead poisoning can be prevented and almost entirely eradicated, and we know exactly how to prevent it. Figure 3.1 was developed to simply and effectively convey our message. It was also effective to discuss how long we have known that lead is a problem to our children. A video made in 2008 tells the story of the fight against lead poisoning in Chicago through interviews with three early advocates who

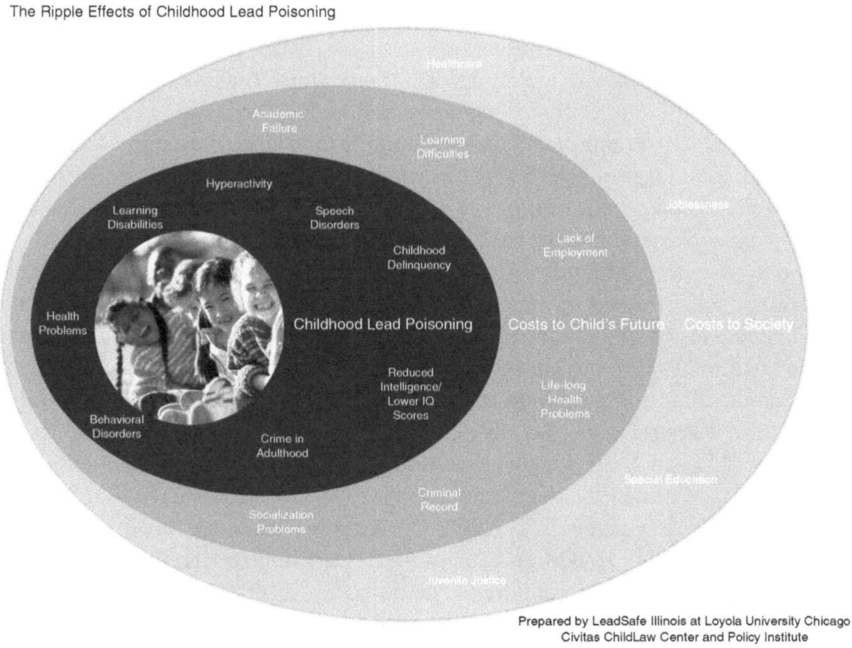

Fig. 3.1 The ripple effects of childhood lead poisoning

describe their efforts in the 1960s and the challenges they faced (Lead Poisoning in Chicago: A Historical Perspective, 2008).

Build Trust. The working relationships built over years as we sat around a table together sharing ideas, frustrations, and goals helped advocates and industry folks to trust one another. Seeking one another's support and expertise for trainings and drafting materials, and participating in meetings strengthened the trust. Credibility was built as we worked initially on less controversial solutions. Those wins led to greater trust and desire to keep working to tackle the problem. While not every activity or decision was discussed first with the full Task Force, every effort was made to be transparent and straightforward, sharing information and challenges. Sometimes those discussions occurred in smaller groups or an individual phone conversation, but any stakeholders affected by an action were consulted and/or informed about what was happening.

Trust and credibility also are keys to building relationships with legislators. It was because of the credibility earned during previous legislative initiatives that when child product and jewelry manufacturers' sought to weaken amendments to Illinois' 2006 lead poisoning prevention law, legislators contacted the Task Force and Center staff before taking a position on the amendments.

Compromise, but cautiously. Litigation against landlords would have been an obvious approach for the ChildLaw Center to pursue its role as a teaching institution for law students. But the cohesiveness of the coalition certainly was due in part to our decision not to litigate against property owners. Law students had many opportunities to develop their litigation techniques. Work on the lead project provided unique experience in policy reform, community organizing, and coalition building – all important skills for any lawyer.

The challenge to compromise on legislation is to balance the desire to see a law passed with the danger of negotiating away the importance of the bill. In an example of the need for compromise on the legislative front, the National Rife Association (NRA) was working behind the scenes to kill the Lead Poisoning Prevention Act of 2006, due to concerns that the bill would require a lead poisoning warning statement on the sale of boxes of ammunition in the state. As ironic as this sounds, the NRA's focus was on youth hunting. Furthermore, as tempting as it might have been for the coalition to become embroiled in a gun-rights fight, we also knew that the NRA had the clout in Springfield to kill our bill if it chose to do so. As a result, a compromise was struck. The law includes a specific exception which states that the definition of "Lead bearing substance" does not include firearm ammunition or components as defined by the Firearm Owners Identification Card Act (Illinois Lead Poisoning Prevention Act, 2006). On the other hand, the coalition held its ground when retailers sought an exemption for labeling on certain products that might come in contact with children. The purpose was not to prohibit the sale of ammunition, but to protect children from the sale of items used – or intended to be chewable – by children.

And finally, know your goal but be flexible on the road to achieving it. Our goal of eliminating childhood lead poisoning has not changed over the 10 years we have been working on the challenge. But as the above case study illustrates, as partnerships grew, and as obstacles and opportunities arose, the successes came about from a willingness to embrace – or at least be open to – shifted priorities and directions. As a result, Chicago and Illinois children are better protected from becoming lead poisoned than when this partnership began.

References

Anderson, J. E. (2003). *Public policymaking*. Boston: Houghton Mifflin Company.

Binns, H. (2008). Reducing fetal exposure to lead: a view towards the future. (PowerPoint presentation at the Illinois Lead Safe Housing Task Force, October 5, 2009)

Build Illinois Bond Fund (2009), P.A. 96-0039.

Canfield, R. L., et al. (2003). Intellectual impairment in children with blood lead concentrations below 10 μg per deciliter. *New England Journal of Medicine, 348*, 1517–1526.

CDPH (2007). Elevated Blood Lead Levels 2007 by Community Area. Data from Chicago Department of Public Health shared with author via email (February 11, 2009).

Cecil, K. M., et al. (2008). Decreased brain volume in adults with childhood lead exposure. *PLoS Medicine, 5*, e112.

Centers for Disease Control and Prevention. (1997). Chapter 1: Childhood lead poisoning in the United States. In *Screening young children for lead poisoning: Guidance for state and local public health officials* (pp. 13–20). Washington, DC: Author. Retrieved from http://www.cdc.gov/nceh/lead/publications/screening.htm

Centers for Disease Control and Prevention. (2009). Lead: Prevention Tips. Retrieved from http://www.cdc.gov/nceh/lead/tips.htm

Christoffel, K. K. (2000). Public health advocacy: process and product. *American Journal of Public Health, 90*, 722–726.

Dietrich, K. N., et al. (2001). Early exposure to lead and juvenile delinquency. *Neurotoxicology and Teratology, 23*, 511–518.

Dressler, L. (2004). *The consensus pocket guide: How to achieve high-commitment decisions.* Boulder: Blue Wing Consulting, LLC.

Franklin, B. (1786). *The famous Benjamin Franklin letter of lead poisoning.* Retrieved from http://www.ledizolv.com/LearnAbout/LeadHazards/benfranklin.asp

Goldman, J. (1998). *Silent Epidemic: Childhood lead poisoning in Cook County.* Chicago: Lead Elimination Action Drive.

Gould, E. (2009). Childhood lead poisoning: conservative estimates of the social and economic benefits of lead hazard control. *Environmental Health Perspectives, 117*, 1162–1167.

Gulson, B. L., et al. (1997). Pregnancy increases mobilization of lead from maternal skeleton. *Journal of Laboratory and Clinical Medicine, 130*, 51–62.

Hornung, R. W., Lanphear, B. P., & Dietrich, K. N. (2009). Age of greatest susceptibility to childhood lead exposure: a new statistical approach. *Environmental Health Perspectives, 117*, 1309–1312.

Illinois Department of Public Health. (2005). *Childhood lead poisoning surveillance report.* Springfield, IL: Author. Retrieved from http://www.idph.state.il.us/health/clpsr/clps0506.htm

Illinois Department of Public Health. (2001). *Get the lead out – childhood lead poisoning surveillance report.* Springfield, IL: Author. Retrieved from http://www.eric.ed.gov/ERICDocs/data/ericdocs2sql/content_storage_01/0000019b/80/1a /b8/bc.pdf

Illinois Department of Public Health. (1999). *Get the lead out – childhood lead poisoning surveillance report.* Springfield, IL: Author. Retrieved from http://www.idph.state.il.us/health/clpsr/clps9900.htm

Illinois Department of Public Health. (2002). *Get the lead out: Renovation. How to safely remove paint.* Springfield, IL: Author. Retrieved from http://www.idph.state.il.us/envhealth/pdf/Lead_Renovation.pdf

Illinois Lead Poisoning Prevention Act, 410 ILCS 43/15 (2008). Retrieved from http://ilga.gov/legislation/publicacts/fulltext.asp?Name=095-0492&GA=095

Illinois Lead Poisoning Prevention Act, 410 ILCS §45 (2006). Retrieved from http://www.ilga.gov/legislation/ilcs/ilcs3.asp?ActID=1523&ChapAct=410%A0ILCS%A045/&ChapterID=35&ChapterName=PUBLIC+HEALTH&ActName=Lead+Poisoning+Prevention+Act%2E

Illinois Lead Safe Housing Advisory Council. (2007). *Illinois Lead Safe Housing Advisory Council recommendations: a report to the Illinois General Assembly pursuant to Public Act 93-0789.* Springfield, IL: Illinois Department of Public Health.

Jacobs, D. E., et al. (2002). The prevalence of lead-based paint hazards in U.S. housing. *Environmental Health Perspectives, 110*, A599–A606.

Jacobs, D. E. (2007). Written statement of Dave E. Jacobs, Before the U.S. Senate Environment and Public Works Committee.

Jusko, T. A., et al. (2008). Blood lead concentrations less than 10 micrograms per deciliter and child intelligence at 6 years of age. *Environmental Health Perspectives, 116*, 243–248.

Kemper, A. R., Bordley, W. C., & Downs, S. M. (1998). Cost-effectiveness analysis of lead poisoning screening strategies following the 1997 guidelines of the Centers for Disease Control and Prevention. *Archives of Pediatrics and Adolescent Medicine, 152*, 1202–1208.

Kingdon, J. W. (2003). *Agendas, alternatives, and public policies.* New York: Longman Classics.

Korfmacher, K. S. (2003). *Long-term costs of lead poisoning: how much can New York save by stopping lead?* Retrieved from http://www.sehn.org/tccpdf/lead%20costs%20NY.pdf

Landrigan, P. J., Schechter, C. B., Lipton, J. M., Fahs, M. C., & Schwartz, J. (2002). Environmental pollutants and disease in American children: Estimates of morbidity, mortality, and costs for lead poisoning, asthma, cancer, and development disabilities. *Environmental Health Perspectives, 110*, 721–728.

Lanphear, B. P., Dietrich, K. N., Auinger, P., & Cox, C. (2000). Cognitive deficits associated with blood lead concentrations ≤10 μg/dl in U.S. children and adolescents. *Public Health Reports, 115*, 521–529.

Lanphear, B. P., et al. (2005). Low-level environmental lead exposure and children's intellectual function: an international pooled analysis. *Environmental Health Perspectives, 113*, 894–899.

Lead-Bearing Substances ordinance, Municipal Code of the City of Chicago, §7-4. (2006). Retrieved from http://www.amlegal.com/nxt/gateway.dll/Illinois/chicago_il/municipalcodeofchicago?f=templates$fn=default.htm$3.0$vid=amlegal:chicago_il

Lead poisoning in Chicago: a historical perspective. (2008). Retrieved from www.leadsafeillinois.org

Lead Poisoning Prevention Code, 77 Ill. Adm. Code 845 (2008). Retrieved from http://www.ilga.gov/commission/jcar/admincode/077/07700845sections.html

Lead Renovation, Repair, and Painting, 40 C.F.R. § 745 (2001).

Lead Safe Chicago. (2004). *Lead Safe Chicago: a plan to eliminate childhood lead poisoning in Chicago by 2010*. Chicago, IL: Retrieved from http://www.luc.edu/law/academics/special/pdfs/lead_safe_chicago_plan.pdf

Lynch, M. L., & Stretesky, P. B. (2004). The relationship between lead and crime. *Journal of Health and Social Behavior, 45*, 214–229.

Markowitz, G., & Rosner, D. (2002). *Deceit and denial: The deadly politics of industrial pollution*. Berkeley: University of California Press.

Meyer et al. (2003). Surveillance for elevated blood lead levels among children – United States, 1997 – 2001. *Morbidity and Mortality Weekly Report* (Sept 12, 2003/52(SS10);1–21.

National Research Council. (1993). *Measuring lead exposure in infants, children, and other sensitive populations*. Washington, DC: National Academy Press. Retrieved from http://www.eric.ed.gov/ERICWebPortal/custom/portlets/recordDetails/detailmini.jsp?_nfpb=true&_&ERICExtSearch_SearchValue_0=ED367476&ERICExtSearch_SearchType_0=no&accno=ED367476

Needleman, H. L., et al. (1996). Bone lead levels and delinquent behavior. *Journal of the American Medical Association, 275*, 363–369.

Needleman, H. L., et al. (2002). Bone lead levels in adjudicated delinquents: A case control study. *Neurotoxicology and Teratology, 24*, 711–717.

Nevin, R., Jacobs, D. E., Berg, M., & Cohen, J. (2008). Monetary benefits of preventing childhood lead poisoning with lead safe window replacement. *Environmental Research, 106*, 410–419.

Nevin, R. (2009). Trends in preschool lead exposure, mental retardation, and scholastic achievement: Association or causation? *Environmental Research, 109*, 301–310.

Nevin, R. (2007). Understanding international crime trends: the legacy of preschool lead exposure. *Environmental Research, 101*, 315–336.

Nevin, R., & Jacobs, D. E. (2006). Windows of opportunity: lead poisoning prevention, housing affordability, and energy conservation. *Housing Policy Debate, 17*, 185–207.

Nigg, J. T., et al. (2008). Low blood lead level associated with clinically diagnosed attention-deficit/hyperactivity disorder and medicated by weak cognitive control. *Biological Psychiatry, 63*, 325–331.

Oliveira, S., Aro, A., Sparrow, D., & Hu, H. (2002). Season modifies the relationship between bone and blood lead levels: The Normative Aging study. *Archives of Environmental Health, 57*, 466–472.

President's Task Force on Environmental Health Risks and Safety Risks to Children. (2000a). Appendix: methodology used to project numbers of lead poisoned children and trends in the American housing stock, 2000–2010. In *Eliminating childhood lead poisoning: a federal strategy targeting lead paint hazards, Appendix*. Retrieved from http://www.cdc.gov/nceh/lead/about/fedstrategy2000.pdf

President's Task Force on Environmental Health Risks and Safety Risks to Children. (2000b). *Eliminating childhood lead poisoning: a federal strategy targeting lead paint hazards*. Retrieved from http://www.cdc.gov/nceh/lead/about/fedstrategy2000.pdf

Residential Lead-Based Paint Hazard Reduction Act of 1992, Pub. L. No. 102-550, §§1001-1061, 106 Stat. 3897 (2005).

Reyes, J. W. (2007). Environmental policy as social policy? The impact of childhood lead exposure on crime. *The B.E. Journal of Economic Analysis and Policy, 1*, Article 51.

Rules and Regulations, Municipal Code of the City of Chicago. (1997). Retrieved from http://egov.cityofchicago.org/webportal/COCWebPortal/COC_ATTACH/LeadReg_1may08.html

Schwartz, J. (1993). Societal benefits of reducing lead exposure. *Environmental Research, 66*, 105–124.

Stapleton, R. M. (1994). *Lead is a silent hazard*. New York: Walker & Company.

United Nations Environment Programme (UNEP) & United Nations Children's Fund (UNICEF). (1997). *Childhood lead poisoning information for advocacy and action*. Retrieved from http://www.chem.unep.ch/irptc/Publications/leadpoison/lead_eng.pdf

U.S. Census Bureau. (2003). *Census 2000 summary file 3, matrices H36, H37, H38, and H39*. Retrieved from http://factfinder.census.gov.

U.S. Department of Housing and Urban Development. (1997). Chapter 7: Lead-based paint inspection. In *Guidelines for the evaluation and control of lead-based paint hazards in housing* (pp. 7-1–7-40). Washington, DC: Retrieved from http://www.hud.gov/offices/lead/lbp/hudguidelines/Ch07.pdf

U.S. Environmental Protection Agency (2009). EPA takes final step in phase out of leaded gasoline. EPA press release January 29, 1996. Retrieved from http://www.epa.gov/history/topics/lead/02.htm

U.S. Office of Housing and Urban Development. (2001). National Survey of Lead and Allergens in Housing.

Warren, C. (2000). *Brush with death: A social history of lead poisoning*. Baltimore: The Johns Hopkins University Press.

Weinberg, A. (2002). Lead Poisoning Threatens Children's Health, Legal System Responds. *Public Interest Law Reporter, 14*, 14–20.

Wright, J. P., et al. (2008). Association of prenatal and childhood blood lead concentrations with criminal arrest in early adulthood. *PLoS Med, 5*, e101.

Part II
Why Is Protecting the Human Rights of Children so Difficult?

Chapter 4
Spare the Rod: Why Are More American Children Victims and Perpetrators of Violence Than Those of Any Other Developed Country?

James Gilligan

Children are perhaps the last of the great demographic groups that our society has finally begun to recognize as being systematically discriminated against, and in some ways even persecuted – though I should add that the battle for recognition of that fact is still an ongoing struggle that is far from won. We have already dealt with many other demographic groups of whom one could have said the same thing – for example, many minority groups, the poor, the disabled, women, and gays – the only difference being that with them, the recognition of their plight and the taking of concrete steps to amend it was begun decades ago, whereas the recognition of the degree to which we have been simultaneously and disproportionately punitive toward and neglectful of our own children is still only minimally recognized and mostly denied, whether at the level of public opinion in general, or of meaningful national policy changes in particular. That the face-saving defense mechanism of denial is the cause of our blindness toward the facts is the only explanation I can think of to explain the continuation of our indefensible treatment of our own children, given that the facts of their situation and the means of solving it have been laid out so clearly by the pioneering and dedicated advocates for children in our nation who have been tirelessly trying to bring this problem to our attention – among them scholars (James Garbarino), legislators (Congressman George Miller), and philanthropists (Irving Harris). This chapter can be read as one extended argument for the proposition that while we have already identified race, class and gender as categories that need to be addressed in order to bring to an end the discrimination that occurs against blacks and other minority groups, the poor, women and gays, we now need to add age – specifically, young age: childhood, adolescence and young adulthood – to the list as the next category we need to include in our roster of socially important areas where fundamental progress is urgently needed.

J. Gilligan (✉)
Clinical Professor of Psychiatry, School of Medicine, Adjunct Professor, School of Law, and Collegiate Professor, School of Arts and Sciences, New York University, Silver Center for Arts and Science, Room 908, 100 Washington Square East, 10003 New York, NY, USA
e-mail: jamesgilliganmd@att.net

J. Garbarino and G. Sigman (eds.), *A Child's Right to a Healthy Environment*, The Loyola University Symposium on the Human Rights of Children 1,
DOI 10.1007/978-1-4419-6791-6_4,

I make no claims as to which of the above areas of reform is most important or pivotal. Clearly, they are not only all important, they are all equally indispensable in the effort to transform our society into one that is consistently life-affirming rather than, as it now is, too often life-destroying. Indeed, this whole chapter will illustrate my belief that one cannot understand or undo any one of the four patterns of discrimination I have mentioned without understanding the interaction between them, and the ways in which they reinforce each other. Thus, my theoretical model here is interactionist, not reductionist. Rather than attempting to reduce all discrimination to the one form that will explain all the others, I attempt to show how they all interact with and reinforce each other. In doing so, I hope to make it clear why it is so unfortunate that we have not yet, as a nation, recognized that our treatment of children and youth is just as urgently in need of fundamental reform as is our treatment of the other demographic groups just mentioned – minorities, the poor, and those defined by their sexual identity or orientation. This chapter is devoted to data and arguments in support of that proposition.

From 1954 on, after the Supreme Court decision of that year, Brown v. Board of Education, and the refusal in 1955 by Rosa Parks to move to the back of the bus in Montgomery, Alabama, we have, as a nation, at least been discussing, and have taken many concrete steps to remedy, many of the more outrageous forms of discrimination by whites against blacks, and then by extension many other racial and ethnic minority groups. And while we are far from having eliminated racial discrimination, the fact that it exists is almost universally recognized to a degree that was never true before the 1950s, when it was simply taken for granted that blacks were sharecroppers, not landowners, and in movies were always servants or laborers, never protagonists or heroes (without anyone's noticing that these trivial truisms were part of the same social system that created much more tragic realities – that in city after city, black babies and their mothers both died at two to four times the rate of white ones, or that year after year, the death rates among blacks in general was 30–40% higher than it was for whites).

Since that time, real social, legal, political, and economic progress has been made in some limited areas, and it is no longer publicly acceptable to be as openly racist as it was 50 or 60 years ago; yet, the life-and-death discrepancies just mentioned have not been eliminated. Racism continues or is revived, albeit in more disguised and underground ways than it used to be. But the fact that it exists has been recognized so widely since the mid-1950s that the debate over how to deal with it is still a prominent part of our national political discussion.

Then, in 1962, Michael Harrington published an article and book, The Other America, which President Kennedy happened to read about poverty in the USA, and the fact that even though the Depression had ended, the New Deal had eliminated or neutralized many of the causes of economic hardship, and we had experienced an unprecedented degree of prosperity ever since the end of World War II, America still had a major problem with poverty – both absolute poverty and relative poverty – more than many European countries whose history of even greater class stratification had been radically ameliorated by the postwar creation of social-democratic welfare states. So we began a war on poverty under Democratic presidents, alternating with a war on the poor under Republican ones. Again, these are wars that are from over, but the issues being fought over are at least part of recognized public discourse. Some on the right, to be sure, deny that poverty in this country still exists, but it is harder than before to take them seriously. (Which is probably a mistake politically, even if it is not one intellectually, since as the current deep recession shows, the power of those on the right to prevent the elimination of poverty and the achievement of social and economic equality in the USA has never been greater or more successful.)

In 1963, Betty Friedan published *The Feminine Mystique,* a watershed event that was the opening salvo of a huge new social program, the modem women's movement, or feminism. Her book stimulated and was followed by an outpouring of research, writing, and social policy advocacy by a large number of brilliant and articulate authors and activists such as Gloria Steinem, Kate Millett, Susan Brownmiller, Marilyn French, and (I am proud to say) Carol Gilligan, along with many others too numerous to mention, as a result of which the issue of the many forms of discrimination against women and girls has never been off the public agenda.

At the very end of that same decade, in 1969, the "Stonewall riots" in Greenwich Village put the issue of discrimination against gays on the public agenda, which it has never left (Carter, 2005). Prior to that event, even completely private, consensual sex between two adults of the same sex was a criminal act in 49 of the 50 states, homosexuals were considered "security risks" by the State Department, the FBI and the USA Post Office conducted surveillance operations to identify who was or was not gay, and from 1952 until 1973 my own profession, as (mis)represented by the American Psychiatric Association, declared homosexuality to be a form of sociopathic personality disorder, among the proposed "cures" for which, as demonstrated at APA meetings, was a course of electrical shocks.

Homophobia, the morbid fear and hatred of nonheterosexual individuals, is of course still rampant – in most states they cannot marry, even now it is legal in 22 of the United States, to fire people from their jobs (in all 50 states if they are in the military) because they are not heterosexual; and "hate crimes" against all of the demographic groups mentioned above continue to occur. But those facts are now well known, and the degree of discrimination suffered by all of these groups has been reduced enough that young people today are often amazed to discover just how bizarre and extensive it was even during the lifetimes of their parents. My point is not that these wars against discrimination have been won (they have not), merely that these wars are being fought, and that the issues over which they are being fought have been publicly and widely identified and recognized as such.

So we are dealing, sometimes effectually and sometimes ineffectually but at least openly and consciously, with the issues of racial and ethnic discrimination, poverty, and discrimination based on gender and sexual orientation. But we have never, to anywhere near the same degree, recognized, identified, or struggled against the many forms of discrimination that we still practice against one particular minority group, namely, children and adolescents. For example, children have never been the reason for major demonstrations in the streets, as all these other movements have. No national organizations with much influence, large membership, or significant financial resources have been formed to represent and advocate for the rights of children, on the scale of the many civil rights and feminist organizations and labor unions – not to mention the Democratic Party – that have been formed to perform that task for their members. Advocates for children and adolescents have never been numerous or powerful enough to be seen as capable of influencing political elections, as have those representing all the other groups I have mentioned.

We have certainly become increasingly aware of overt *child abuse* as a problem, ever since Kempe, Silverman, Steele, Droegemueller, and Silver (1962) published their historic article on the "battered child syndrome" in the *Journal of the American Medical Association*, and that was followed by new recognition of the various forms of sexual abuse as well, from incest to pedophilia. But we have not succeeded very well in going beyond these forms of physical and sexual violence against children which important as they are, are nevertheless limited to a minority of children: a minority that no matter how small is always too large, of course, but is still a minority – to discuss what Johann Galtung and other sociologists (and the "liberation theologians" of Latin America) have called the "structural violence" (Gilligan, 1999) to which a much, much larger proportion of children and youth – indeed, potentially all children simply by being identified as children – are not only vulnerable but are actually subjected. In what follows, I attempt to clarify what is meant by that concept, and to illustrate and document the disproportionate toll it takes on children and youth in this country.

But let me bring to your attention the degree to which children and youth in America are both victims and perpetrators of severe (lethal) violence, far beyond that which is seen among the young people of any other economically developed country on earth. As you can see in Fig. 4.1, (Richter, 1993) the homicide victimization rate among adolescents and young adults in the USA (ages 15–24) is a whole order of magnitude higher than it is in the 22 developed countries with which we are compared. The death rate from homicide ranges from less than one to a little more than two (per 100,000) in two thirds of the other countries and even in the country the youth homicide rates are closest to ours, Scotland, it is still only five. The average among all of them is about two. In the USA, by contrast, it is more than ten times as high as that: 22 for the entire youth population, 12 for white youth alone, and 85 for African–Americans in this age range. (I emphasize the latter two rates because I have frequently been asked whether our excess homicide rate, as compared with the other industrialized countries, is merely a function of the disproportionately high rates among African–Americans in the USA. The answer, as these figures show, is no; even for "white" American youth, the homicide rates are more than six times higher than they are among the almost entirely "white" populations of Western Europe and the other English-speaking democracies.)

I have just given you a cross-sectional study, comparing the rates of youth violence in the USA with the other industrialized nations of the world, during one point in time, namely, 1986–1987. Now, I am going to present you with longitudinal data, showing changes in the rates of youth violence in our own country alone, over an extensive time period, from 1955 to the 1990s. What we find when we examine the figures shown in Table 4.1 is something that was so shocking and unprecedented during the time it was happening that it unfortunately provoked many of our political

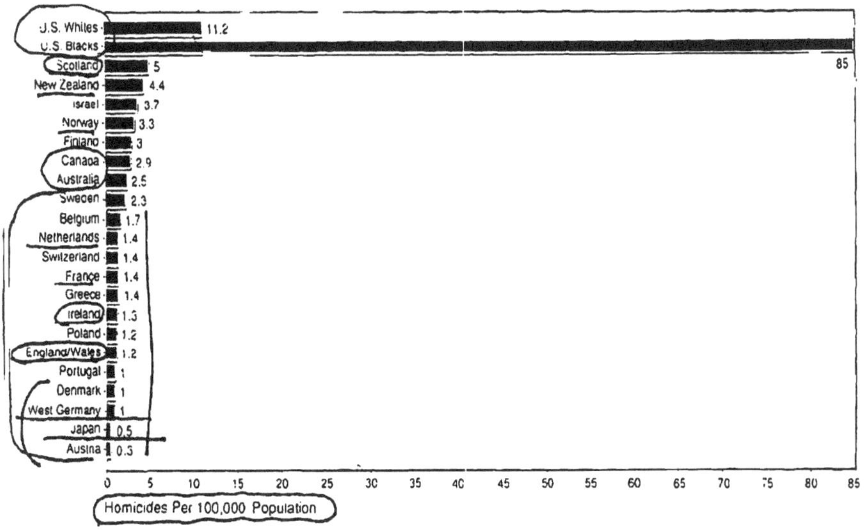

Fig. 4.1 Homicide Rates for Males 15–24 years of age. *Source*: From Richter, John E., "Community Violence and Children's Development: Toward a Research Agenda for the 1990s," pp. 3–6 in *Children and Violence,* edited by David Riess, John E. Richter, Marian Radke-Yarrow and David Scharff: New York: Guilford Press, 1993, Fig. 4.1, p. 4. Published simultaneously as *Psychiatry: Interpersonal and Biological Processes,* Vol. 56, No.1, Feb. 1993. Figure adapted from Fingerhut and Kleinman (1990). Data on total homicide death rate for all males 15–24 years of age are taken from *Vital Statistics of the USA,* 1987, p. 51, Table 1-10, compiled by the National Center for Health Statistics, Center for Disease Control, USA Public Health Service

Table 4.1 Increases in Youth Violence Rates 1955–1990/94

Year	Homicide offending rate (14–17-year olds)
1955	3.2
1984	6.2
1994	19.1
Net: sixfold increase in 40 years	
	Homicide victimization rate (15–19-year olds)
1955	3.2
1990	17.0
Net: fivefold increase in 35 years	
	Suicide rate (15–19-year olds)
1955	2.6
1956	2.3
1990	11.1
Net: fivefold increase in 35 years	

leaders and public commentators into a kind of "moral panic," a scapegoating condemnation of the young, based on a misunderstanding and distortion of the facts involved, rather than on a reasoned set of reflections on the facts and a patient attempt to learn what they had to teach us.

To speak of what happened in this country as an "epidemic" of violence is hardly an exaggeration. But more importantly, to frame it in those terms leads to a whole different way of thinking – e.g., to think of it as a problem in public health, in which our task is to learn what the causes of the epidemic are and what the cures and preventive interventions might consist of, rather than as a "crime wave," a sign of moral, legal, and criminal turpitude on the part of the young, to which the solution can only be to increase the severity of the punishments that we inflict on them.

As Table 4.1 shows, *the rates of both homicide and suicide among youth in this country increased five- and sixfold from the mid-1950s to the 1990s.* The suicide rate among 15–19-year olds increased from 2.3 (per 100,000) in 1956 to 11.1 in 1990, a fivefold increase in 35 years. The homicide offending rate (the rate at which these teenagers committed murders) likewise increased among 14–17-year olds from 3.2 in 1955 to 19.1 in 1994, a sixfold increase over 40 years. Finally, the homicide victimization rate (the rate at which they were murdered) among 15–19-year olds increased from 3.2 in 1955 to 17 in 1990, a more than fivefold increase in 35 years.

There are several aspects of these figures that are important to notice. The first is that these increases occurred not only for homicides, but also for suicides. I emphasize that point because during the 1990s, 44 states responded to the increase in juvenile homicides (while paying little or no attention to the suicides) by adopting new laws enabling them to try and sentence more children as adults and send them to adult prisons. Throughout the 1990s, from five to six thousand children were sent to adult prisons each and every year. In nearly half the states in this country, no age is specified as too young for such transfers; in the others, the minimum age ranges from 10 to 15 years. Legislatures throughout the country have authorized these transfers into the adult penal system despite repeated research evidence that children who are treated in that way are not only more likely to reoffend, especially in violent ways, after they are released, but they are also more likely to be raped, beaten,robbed, murdered, or to commit suicide, while they are in the adult prisons.

To add to the insanity of this, *most of the young people who are sent to the adult system are sent there for nonviolent crimes!* From 1987 to 1996, the percentage of children who were sent to adult courts for violent crimes (defined as murder, sexual assault, aggravated assault, and robbery) ranged from 28 to 43%; at no time did it reach even half of those sentenced. The remainder – the majority in each year – had committed nothing more serious than property crimes, violations of the drug laws, or offense against so-called public order (illegal gambling, prostitution, etc.) but not crimes of violence or crimes against the person Stahl (1999). And as I have long observed, from four decades of experience in the penal system, *the most effective way to turn a nonviolent person into a violent one is to send him to prison.*

So these policies of increasing punitiveness toward the young are not only counter-productive and self-defeating from the standpoint of the rational self-interest of the rest of us, but they are also indefensibly hypocritical and self-righteous. Once we had noticed that the young were not only committing six times more murders, but they also were committing five times more suicides, than they ever had before, we might have begun to ask not only what is wrong with them, but also what is wrong with us, or with our society as a whole, that we, the parents, have raised a whole generation of children who feel so desperately miserable and hopeless that they no longer care whether they themselves live or die – which is how you would have to feel before you could be capable of taking your own or someone else's life.

One empirical finding that is consistent with that latter generalization is the fact that throughout the developed world, at least, and in many developing countries as well, more murderers kill themselves than were ever killed by the state, even when execution was the standard punishment for murder (Wolfgang, 1958; West, 1967). As a result, the suicide rate among murderers in every country in which this has been studied is several hundred times higher than it is among nonhomicidal people in the same demographic groups. Once someone commits a murder, you know that he is also at very high risk for suicide (compared to the rest of us). I first learned this when I started providing psychiatric therapeutic programs to the Massachusetts prison system and discovered that the most intractably violent prisoners, the ones about whom we all are most justifiably concerned, had one life-and-death plan in common: they wanted to end their lives in a "blaze of glory," killing as many other people as possible until they themselves were shot to death by the police. Nor were these mere fantasies or idle boasts. Many of them had made, or eventually did make, attempts to do exactly that. And in our country as a whole, several hundred individuals every year in fact act out this scenario. This phenomenon is so common and well-known that the police have a nickname for it: "suicide by cop." Today, of course, you cannot read any daily newspaper without reading about the latest "suicide-bombing" in other parts of the world as well. Clearly, throughout the world, the link between suicidal and homicidal behavior is very strong. And the cause is the same: overwhelming humiliation and terminal despair as to the possibility of undoing it by any less destructive (and self-destructive) means (Gilligan, 2003).

Nevertheless, after the epidemic of mass murder school shootings that occurred in the 1990s (culminating most notoriously in the Columbine shootings), many journalists, politicians, and other commentators began speaking of America's teenagers as if they were immoral, selfish, spoiled monsters who were behaving so badly because we had been too kind, permissive, tolerant, and generous toward them, and that it was now time that we learned to get tougher and more punitive toward them; that the problem was with them (the dangerous and evil children) not with us (the well-meaning but naive and overly indulgent parents). One Texas legislator, for example, proposed a law reducing the age at which people could be subjected to capital punishment to the age of twelve.

Now, anyone who knew the first thing about the epidemiology of violence would know that many of the social and economic conditions that produce increases in homicide also produce corresponding increases in suicide. There is much evidence for that conclusion, including the fact that since these rates first began being recorded in this country on an annual basis, in 1900, suicide and homicide rates have tracked each other to a statistically significant degree; that is, when one of them increases or decreases, so does the other (as can be seen clearly in Figs. 4.8 and 4.9), which is at least consistent with the hypothesis that some of the conditions in this country that are causing a change in one of these forms of violence may well be causing the corresponding change in the other (Holinger, 1987).

Among the socioeconomic and psychological conditions that have been correlated with increases in the rates of both forms of violence are elevated rates of unemployment, impoverishment (especially relative poverty, and sudden downward social mobility), child abuse or neglect, and homelessness (Holinger, 1987) all of which tend to provoke the feelings of shame and humiliation, inferiority, failure, inadequacy, and worthlessness, which in turn can provoke the feelings of overwhelming rage alternating with utter despair and hopelessness. In other words, despair, hopelessness, humiliation, and feelings of failure and inadequacy have consistently been found, on psychological examination, to be among the most potent causes of both suicide and homicide – not insufficient punishment and too few threats.

The notion that you could deter murders in a group that is as suicidal as it is homicidal by threatening them with death is as insane as are the youth who are committing this violence. One has to wonder if those who advocate the death penalty as a means of deterring murder even noticed that virtually every one of the mass murdering school shooters either killed themselves as well (such as the two Columbine killers) or else expected to be killed, or asked to be killed, and were surprised when they were not. *From their standpoint, the death penalty is a reward and an encouragement to kill, not a punishment or a deterrent.*

Other important aspects of the trends in juvenile violence over the past half-century include the following facts:

1. First, it is no surprise that the rates of perpetration of homicides so closely paralleled the rates for victimization. As James Alan Fox (2000) has noticed, "age patterns are similar for victims and offenders, since most killings are intra-generational" (p 7).
2. As Figs. 4.2–4.9 (Holinger et al., 1994) show, the marked increase in both homicides and suicides that I am referring to here as an epidemic of lethal violence occurred among both white and black males, including both teenagers and those aged 20–24. However, it only occurred among males (of both races). White and black females both showed either relatively negligible increases, or actual decreases, during the periods in which males were undergoing these epidemics. Also, rates of both homicide and suicide were in every year (going back to 1933) from four to twelve times as high among the males in each age group as among the females in the same age group. Lethal violence of both sorts, homicide and suicide, is primarily male behavior, not female, both in epidemic years and in "normal" years.
3. As Figs. 4.2–4.7 also show, suicide rates every year were 50–100% higher among whites than among blacks, whereas homicide rates were seven to ten times higher among blacks than among whites. That is, even though the rates of change in both suicide and homicide were remarkably similar for blacks and whites (that is, when the data are graphed over time, the upward curves for each form of violence are almost exactly the same for whites and blacks), the baselines from which these changes start are very different. Thus, both the epidemic and the nonepidemic rates of suicide and homicide were to some extent distributed differently between the two social castes, with the highest rates of suicides occurring among the white males, and of homicides, among the black males, in both the epidemic and the "normal" years. How to explain this? Henry and Short (1954)

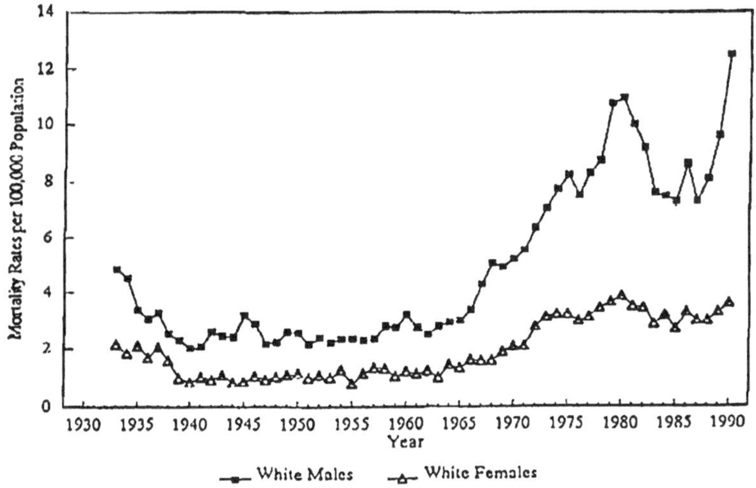

Fig. 4.2 USA Homicide Rates, white 15- to 19-year olds, 1993–1990. *Source*: Holinger, Paul C. et al., 1994, p. 54

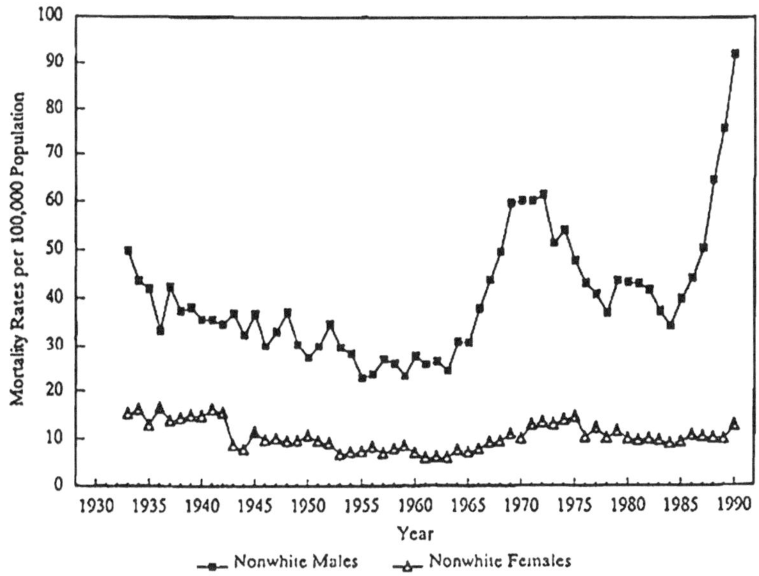

Fig. 4.3 USA Homicide Rates, nonwhite 15- to 19-year olds, 1993–1990. *Source*: Holinger, Paul C. et al., 1994, p. 55

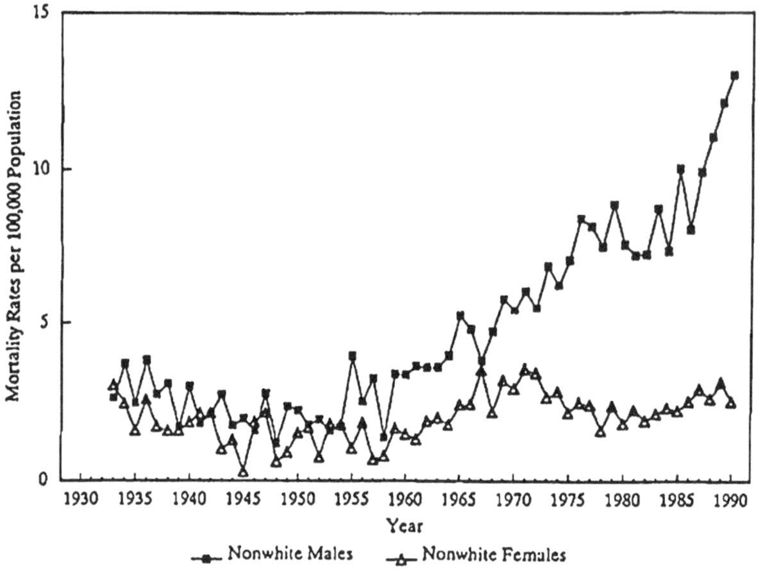

Fig. 4.4 USA Suicide Rates, white 15- to 19-year olds, 1993–1990. *Source*: Holinger, Paul C. et al., 1994, p. 47

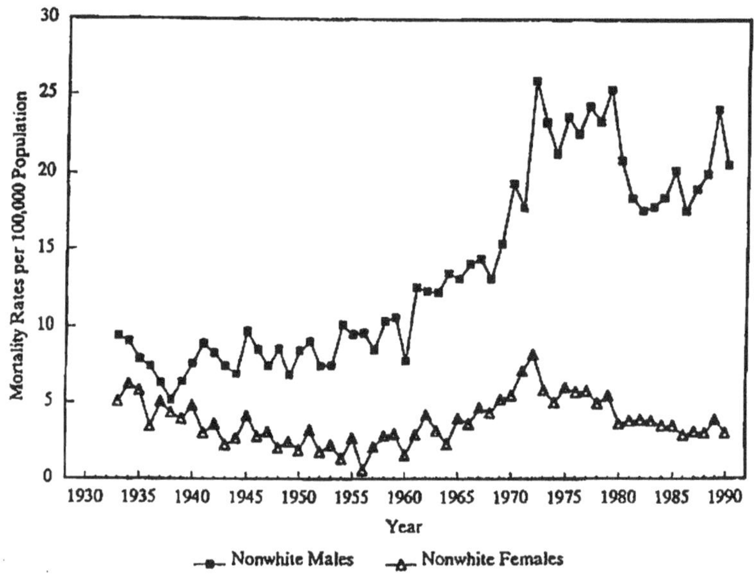

Fig. 4.5 USA Suicide Rates, nonwhite 20- to 24-year olds, 1993–1990. *Source*: Holinger, Paul C. et al., 1994, p. 49

who were among the first to call special attention to this by now well-known difference in patterns of violence between these two social castes, proposed an explanation that, while hardly comprehensive, appears to me to be persuasive as far as it goes. They suggested that whenever individuals or groups experience

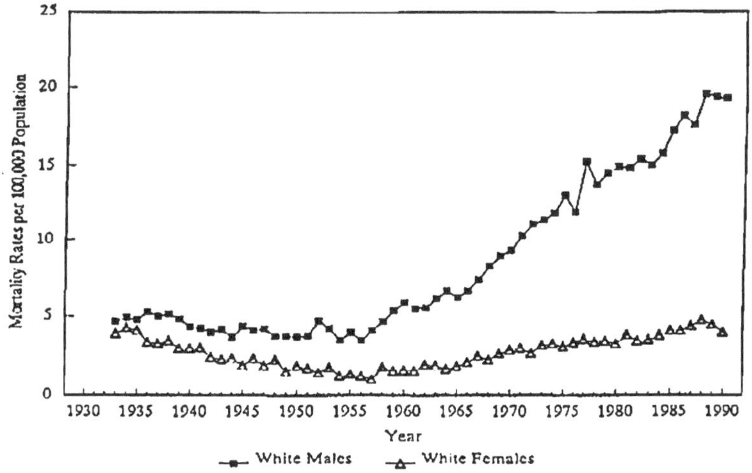

Fig. 4.6 USA Suicide Rates, white 15- to 19-year olds, 1993–1990. *Source*: Holinger, Paul C. et al., 1994, p. 46

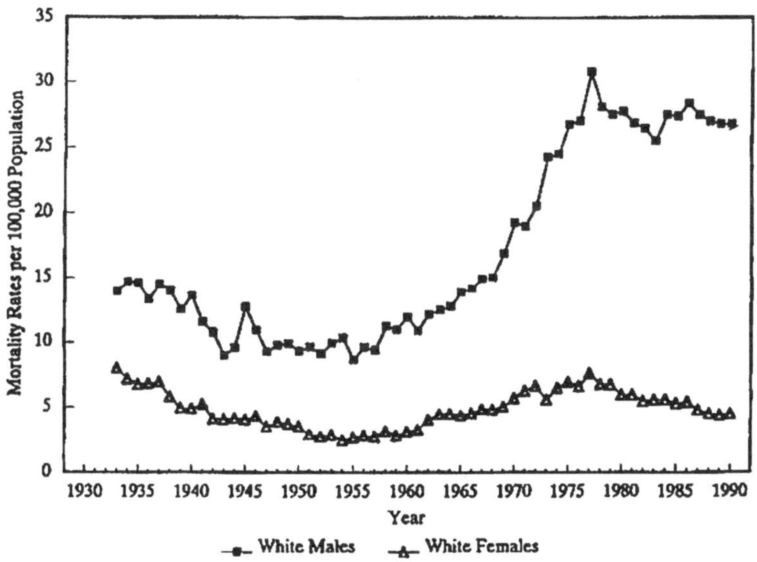

Fig. 4.7 USA Suicide Rates, white 20-24-year olds, 1993–1990. *Source*: Holinger, Paul C. et al., 1994, p. 48

and perceive themselves as relatively disadvantaged, powerless, and controlled by others (as African–Americans are more likely to than whites are, since that is more often exactly the reality of their social situation in our still hierarchical and racist society, in which they are far more likely to have to take orders from others than they are to be in a position to give orders to others), then they are more likely to interpret whatever misfortunes occur to them as not being their fault, but

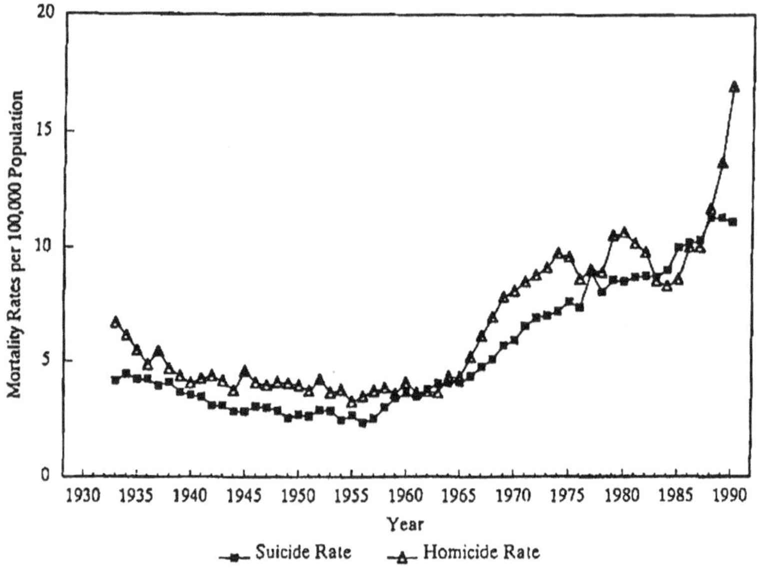

Fig. 4.8 USA Suicide and Homicide Rates, 15- to 19-year olds, 1993–1990. *Source*: Holinger, Paul C. et al., 1994, p. 60

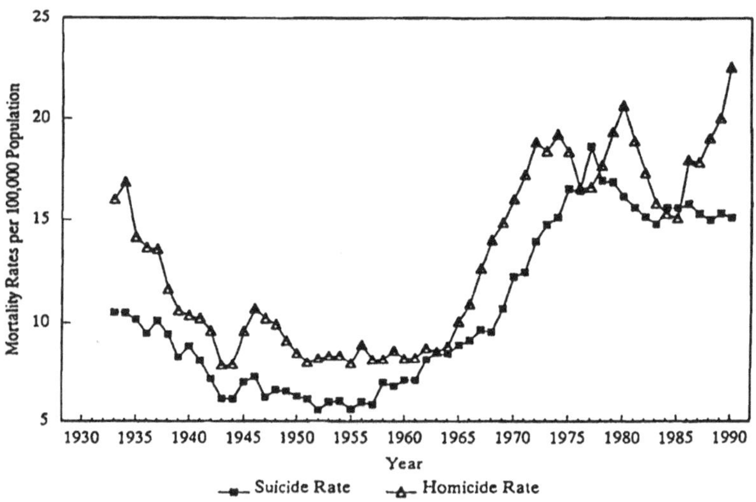

Fig. 4.9 USA Suicide and Homicide Rates, 15- to 19-year olds, 1993–1990. *Source*: Holinger, Paul C. et al., 1994, p. 61

rather the fault of others, against whom they then turn their rage (in the form of homicide). However, when individuals or groups perceive themselves as having relatively more advantages and power and control over their own fates (as whites in this country in fact do, compared with blacks), then they are more likely to interpret whatever misfortunes occur to them as being their own fault and thus to direct their anger at themselves (in the form of suicide).

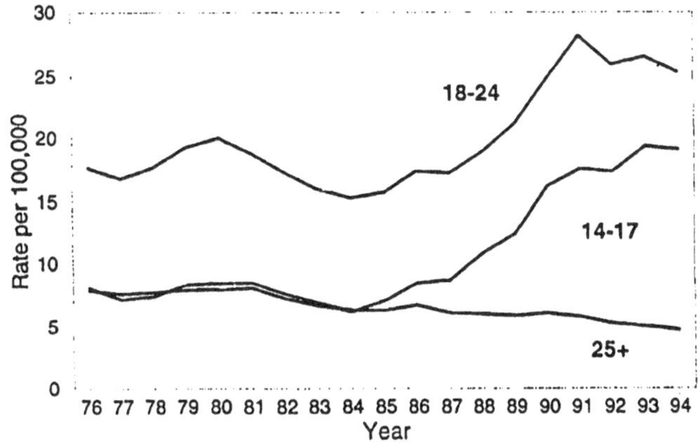

Fig. 4.10 *Source*: Holinger, Paul C. et al. *Suicide and Homicide among Adolescents,* NY: Guilford Press, 1994, Figs. 2–3 (their Figs. 4.5–4.6), pp. 54–55; Figs. 4–5 (4.1–4.2), pp. 46–47; Figs. 6–7 (4.7–4.8), pp. 56–57; Figs. 8–9 (4.3–4.4), pp. 48–49; Figs. 10–11 (4.9–4.10), p. 6061

Thus, in response to what outwardly might appear to be the same socioeconomic and psychological stress – say, being fired from one's job, or being unable to find a job in the first place, and experiencing the feelings of humiliation, rejection, impotence, rage, and despair that such an experience can engender – a black youth might respond with significantly different interpretations and hence different behavioral responses than a white one would: an "anger-out" response against others rather than an "anger-in" one against himself.

4. The increase in juvenile and youth homicides was not paralleled by an increase among adults over the age of 25. On the contrary, as Fig. 4.10 shows, rates among these older age groups actually declined during the years when they were increasing among the younger age groups (14–17- and 18–24-year olds). What Figures 4.2–4.3 and 4.11 also show is that a disproportionate amount of the increase in youth homicides that has occurred since the mid-1950s actually was concentrated in one 10-year period, 1984–1993 (which, not coincidentally, were years of Republican hegemony under Reagan and Bush Sr.). During those 10 years alone, the homicide offending rate among 14–17-year olds literally tripled. Such an extraordinary explosion of homicidal rage in such a brief period of time is, to the best of my knowledge, unprecedented in our history.

Where did this epidemic come from? The nation does not always experience an epidemic of homicides. Indeed, the only reason we can label this one, an epidemic, is by contrast with what might be called the more "normal" rates of lethal violence in the USA (if such a thing can ever be called "normal," other than in a statistical sense). During an entire quarter of a century, from 1942 to 1967, the age-adjusted US homicide rate (for all ages) ranged from 4.5 to 6, with an average of 5, per 100,000 per year. During that same time period, the homicide death rate among 15–19-year olds ranged from 3.2 to 6.1, with an average of about 4 (National Center for Health Statistics). Thus, not only were the overall homicide rates the

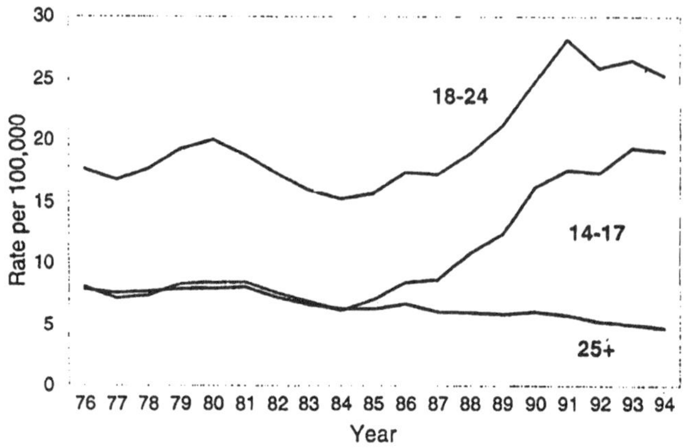

Fig. 4.11 From: Trends in Juvenile Violence, A report to the USA Attorney General on Current and Future Rates of Juvenile Offending, Fox, 1996, p. 8

lowest in the 20th century, the juvenile homicide rates were even lower than the rates for all ages. This was, not coincidentally, as I will show later, the age in which the country was ruled according to what has been called the "New Deal consensus," by the Roosevelt, Truman, Eisenhower, Kennedy and Johnson administrations, during which rates of economic inequality, insecurity, and unemployment decreased dramatically from the levels they had reached under Roosevelt's Republican predecessors, and then remained low; and rates of economic growth attained the highest levels of the century.

During the following quarter of a century, however, from 1968 on, the New Deal consensus was defeated by the success of the Republican party's "southern strategy," which enabled it to come to power on the back of the white backlash against civil rights for blacks and the conservative backlash against economic redistribution from the rich to the poor promised by the "war on poverty." Thus began the age of Nixon, Ford, Reagan, and the first Bush (with a short interlude occupied by Carter). Nixon took office in 1969, and from 1970 on, until Clinton had finally had time to undo the worst of what his Republican predecessors had wrought by the beginning of his second term, the nation went through the worst epidemic of suicides and homicides that it had seen since the last period of Republican hegemony, 1921–1933. One major cause of these epidemics of lethal violence during both periods of Republican domination of our social and economic life was the fact that in both periods their policies led to dramatic increases in the rates of both unemployment and economic inequality, and equally dramatic decreases in economic prosperity. While these socioeconomic changes were most obvious during the period leading up to and then culminating in the Great Depression of the 1930s, they also occurred during the period of Republican reaction that was ushered in by the Republican sweep of Congress in 1966 and its capture of the White House in 1968. By 1970, and continuing until 1997, by which time Clinton had been in office for 4 years, the homicide rates for the country as a whole (all ages) ranged from 8 to 11 (they never dropped below the epidemic "floor" of 8) and averaged roughly 10 per 100,000 – almost twice as high as they had been during the previous quarter of a century of Democratic/liberal hegemony.

But this epidemic of homicide became in reality an epidemic of youth homicides (involving teenagers and young adults below the age of 25), not of homicides among the population as a whole. This transformation into a youth violence epidemic did not happen over night, but it did happen; and it did not happen by accident, it happened for reasons that can be identified, understood and, if we wish to do so enough, remedied (as can the overall epidemics of violence, regardless of the age groups involved).

To understand the contribution that youth violence made to our national epidemic of violence, we might begin by noticing that although, as I stated above, youth homicide rates began increasing from 1955 on, they started from a low base rate (3.2/100,000) and actually did not reach epidemic levels (which I am defining as greater than 8) until 1970, the second year of Nixon's administration. Even then, however, they were still overshadowed by the much larger rates suffered (and inflicted) by older age groups. For example, as late as 1984, the homicide offending rate among adults older than 24 (25–34-year olds) was still twice as high as it was for 14–17-year olds, which had been the "normal" ratio between the two age groups for decades. (Specifically, the 1984 rate was 16.9 for 25–34-year olds, and 8.5 for 14–17-year olds).

However, the long-term trend to which I referred earlier was already operating: From 1980 on, the murder rate among all age groups over the age of 24 began declining, steadily and consistently, year after year, with almost no exceptions. Beginning in 1984 and 1985 on, however, the murder rate among those under the age of 25 (14–17-year olds and 18–24-year olds) increased equally consistently, year after year, until they finally reached levels never before recorded since these rates first began being measured. As a result, by 1993 (the first year of Clinton's administration) the murder rate among 14–17-year olds had changed from half as high as that among 25–34-year olds to twice as high! (The actual 1993 figures are: 30.2 for those 14–17, and 15.9 among 25–34-year olds.) This represented an unprecedented reversal in the age distribution of lethal violence in this country, and illustrates what I mean by saying that the epidemic of violence from 1970 to 1997 was transformed during the Reagan–Bush administration into an epidemic of youth violence. Between 1984 and 1993 alone the homicide offending rate among teenagers 14–17 years old increased by three and a half times, from 8.5 to 30.2, and that among young adults 18–24 years old almost doubled, from 21.4 to 41.3. By contrast, the corresponding rates among 25–34 years old declined during those same years from 22.2 to 15.9; and among 35–49 years old, from 13.3 to 7.4. So what we saw was a dramatic explosion of murder rates among the young, especially from 1984 on, combined with an almost as dramatic decrease in such rates among those in all age groups older than 25.

These trends apply as much to homicide victims as to homicide offenders. From 1955 to 1965, in fact from 1940 to 1965, the rate at which 15–19-year olds were murdered varied little, from 3.2 to 4.4, and was at all times below the national rate for all ages. But then, a cataclysmic change occurred in America's political, economic, and social life. Up to that point, our national ethos had been based on the "New Deal" consensus that followed Roosevelt's election in 1933, which removed the Republican leadership that had brought both economic and social disaster to the country: the Great Depression, which led to the worst epidemic of suicides and homicides in our recorded history up to that point. Roosevelt inherited from his Republican predecessors an unprecedented epidemic of violence, whose effect on our adolescent population (15–19-year olds) can be summarized in the fact that the homicide death rate for this group had risen to 6.7 by 1933, and the suicide rate to 10.5. Following Roosevelt's coming to power in March of that year, the teenage homicide rate fell by more than half in a year by year series of declines, to 4 by 1940, to 3.7 by 1944, and to 3.2 by 1955. The suicide rate, likewise, fell in half in similar fashion, reaching 5.6 by 1952.

The spirit of Roosevelt, and of the country that elected him (which is what I mean when I refer to our national value system at that time as the New Deal consensus), can be summarized in his statement that "The test of our progress is not whether we add more to the abundance of those who have much; it is whether we provide enough for those who have too little" (Bartlett, 1992; Roosevelt, 1937). This ethos – which, incidentally, was deliberately and enthusiastically embraced and even furthered by Eisenhower, despite his being nominally a Republican – did not come to an end until the late 1960s, when the conservative wing of the Republican party (which by that time included people like Strom Thurmond) rejected its moderate voices and ers of the white backlash against the civil rights revolution, and the closely linked backlash against the "war on poverty," the two Democratic programs that had done most to "provide enough for those who have too little." This reactionary turn came about in the Republican landslide in the Congressional elections of 1966, which commentators at the time recognized as the end of the Johnson era (even though 2 years remained in his now crippled administration), and then, definitively, in the presidential election 2 years later, which brought Nixon to power in 1968. Predictably, those events were followed by a reversal of the trend toward growing socioeconomic equality that had been the norm since 1933, and, as a direct result, a shocking increase in the adolescent murder rate, which went from 4.3 in 1965 to 8.1 by 1970 – a doubling of that violent death rate within a mere 5 years.

For the next quarter of a century, our national murder rates, both for adolescents and for all ages put together, fluctuated within but never fell below the floor of an epidemic range, but with particularly devastating effects on the teenage segment of the population. In fact, the teenage murder rate, which had already doubled once, *as* we just saw, under Nixon and the Republican Congress, doubled again, after Nixon was replaced, a few years later, by an even more openly and extremely antidemocratic Republican, Reagan, whose philosophy (and that of the country that elected him) can be summarized in his statement (the opposite of Roosevelt's, above) that "We're the party that wants to see an America in which people can still get rich" (Bartlett, 1992; Reagan, 1982).

Among the many ironies in this sorry saga is the fact that while a tiny minority of people who were already wealthy did indeed get much, much richer, the country as a whole experienced the most severe recessions, the highest unemployment rates, and the greatest gap in incomes and wealth between the rich and the poor, since similar Republicans had been in power from 1921 to 1933. Predictably, the teenage (15–19-year olds) murder rate doubled again, within one 5-year period – from 8.6 in 1985 to 17 in 1990. But it did not stop there. By 1993, Clinton's first year in office, it had reached the highest level ever recorded for this age group, 20.5. It then began falling consistently and steeply year after year, finally reaching a low of 9.6 by Clinton's last year in office, less than half of the rate he had inherited from his Republican predecessors.

The teenage suicide rate likewise exploded during the period of Republican hegemony that lasted from 1966–1968 to 1993. That rate had ranged from 2.3 to 4 from 1939 to 1965. During the Nixon–Ford administration, it doubled to 7.6, by 1975, and by Reagan's last year in office, 1988, it had more than tripled to 11.3. Following Clinton's assumption of power in 1993, these rates reversed course and began falling year by year, reaching a low of 8.0 by his last year in office, a decline of nearly 30%.

Bush Jr. arrived in the White House in 2001, following which these steep declines abruptly stopped, and the rates of both forms of lethal violence began drifting upward again. By 2004, the suicide rate for youths and young adults (aged 10–24) had registered the largest single-year increase in 15 years (going back to 1990), increasing by 8% in 1 year (CDC, 2007). A follow-up study 1 year later, studying the trend from 1996 to 2005, found that both the 2004 and 2005 rates were still significantly greater than the expected rates based on the 1996–2003 trend.... This same pattern of significance was also found ... in the 10- to 17-year and 18- to 19-year age groups.... In absolute numbers, in 2004 there were an estimated 326 excess suicide deaths among youth aged 10 to 19 years...compared with the number of deaths predicted by the regression model [that measured the slope of the trend since 1996]. In 2005, the overall number of "excessive deaths was 292" (Bridge et al., 2008).

By 2006, the last year for which we have comparable data, the teenage death rate from murder had reached 11; and although we will not know the results of Bush Jr.'s last years in office until 2011, we do know that the results so far appear to be consistent with what all previous Republican presidents except Eisenhower have produced.

The studies just quoted, which compared youth suicide rates in 2004 and 2005 with the trends in those rates from 1990 to 1996, respectively, failed to notice the correlation between these rates and the political party in power during the different time periods studied. Therefore, I have compared those rates as they varied under the different political parties in power at the times under investigation. What we find when we do that is consistent with what we have observed during the earlier time periods already discussed. Let me summarize the murder rates first.

From 1993 to 2000, Clinton's years in office, the murder rate among 15–19-year olds decreased from 20.5 to 9.6, an average decrease of 1.56 per year. During Bush Jr.'s years in office from 2001 to 2006, homicide rates in the same age group did not decrease; they increased – from 9.5 to 10.9, an average increase of 0.28 per year. If the homicide trend line observed during the Clinton years (a decrease of 1.56 per year) had continued throughout Bush's years in office, the murder rate in 2006 would have been not 10.9 but 0.24 (That is, 9.6 was the rate reached by 2000 after seven decreases of 1.56 per year. If we had experienced 6 further decreases of 1.56 per year, a total of 9.36, from the rate at which we started, 9.6, we would wind up with a net murder rate of 0.24 per 100,000 per year.) Now, the difference between 10.9 and 0.24 is 10.66, meaning that there was an excess of 10.66 youth homicides per year by the end of Bush's sixth year in office, compared with what we would have experienced if the trend line achieved during the Clinton years had continued. Since the Census Bureau's estimate of the population of 15–19-year olds in 2006 is 21,274,583, that means there were approximately 2,268 more murders in that age group alone during 2006 under the Bush administration than would have been expected if, say, the Republican members of the Supreme Court had not elected a Republican as president in 2000, and the Democratic candidate, Gore, had been allowed to continue the kinds of policies that had been in effect during the Democratic years of 1993–2000 (i.e. 10.66/100,000 × 21.2746 million = 2,268).

A similar analysis would show that there was also an excess of 277 adolescent suicides during Bush's first 6 years in office, compared with the number that would have occurred if the corresponding trend during the Clinton years had continued. All in all, then, there appear to have been more than 2,000 extra teenage deaths from violence (2,545 to be exact) during 2006 alone, than would have occurred if Democrats had remained in power and had achieved the same results that they attained during the years in which they were in power.

That is of course not an empirical prediction of what would necessarily have happened if Democrats had remained in power – trees do not grow to the sky, and homicide and suicide rates seldom decline to zero. But these vital statistics do show how dramatically different the trends in both violent death rates were under the last Democratic president compared with what they were under his Republican successor. Since these same partisan differences in murder rates have been occurring since at least the 1920s, as we have already seen, together with equally consistent partisan differences in rates of unemployment, recession, inequality, and other causes of severe socioeconomic stress and distress (Bartels, 2008) which have independently been found in dozens of studies to predict rates of homicide and suicide (Harris, 1996; Holinger, 1987; Hsieh & Pugh, 1999; James, 1995; Wilkinson, 1994, 2004) the changes in youth homicide rates that occurred between the Clinton years and the Bush years begins to appear to be more than an accident or a coincidence based on some unique, random, unrepeatable, inexplicable, and unpredictable combination of events that might have occurred between 1993–2000 and 2001–2006.

In other words, the reasons for these declines under Clinton and their arrest and reversal under Bush Jr. are not difficult to identify. The homicide and suicide rates in the USA under Clinton reached their lowest levels in 30 years, by 1997, the beginning of his second term in office, after – and only after – the unemployment rate reached the lowest level in 30 years, the median and the minimum wage both increased in real terms for the first time in 30 years, and the poverty rate among blacks and Latino families reached the lowest level since those figures first began being recorded. For all of those socioeconomic stressors (unemployment, poverty and inequality) have been independently identified in dozens of studies throughout the world as among the most powerful predictors of lethal violence rates. And while all decreased under Clinton, they all increased under Bush Jr. – as they have done so regularly under Republican administrations since at least 1900 that, despite the occasional exceptions, there is a statistically significant correlation between Republican occupation of the White House and all of those forms of economic stress and distress, as well as of increases in rates of both homicide and suicide.

For example, the homicide rate among those over the age of 24 (25–85+) also showed an excess during the Bush years over what they would have been if the trend line they showed under Clinton had continued. However, the size of the excess was only about 3.1 per 100,000, roughly one-third as high *as* it was among the 15–19-year olds. To put it another way, both the increases and the decreases in the homicide rate have been greater among adolescents than they have been among adults. One consequence of that difference between the two age groups is that the difference between the two political parties appears to be three times as powerful among teenagers as it is among adults. In that sense, the teenagers might be seen as the canaries in the mine-shaft, the highly sensitive barometer of the presence of the socioeconomic factors, and their psychological consequences, which lead to either increases or decreases in rates of homicide and suicide.

Or, conversely, it may be that the difference between the two political parties is much more a difference in their effect on youth than it is in their effect on adults. Clearly, we have been singling out the young people in our country more than the adults for exposure to whatever set of stresses or other conditions has been increasing their level of despair to truly suicidal and homicidal proportions, and we appear to have been doing that especially since we began electing leaders whose goal was to undo the social and economic reforms that occurred between roughly 1933 and 1966. And we have been simultaneously providing relatively greater protection from those same stresses and conditions to the adult and elderly populations. One might say that the Republican value system is gerontocratic rather than child-oriented.

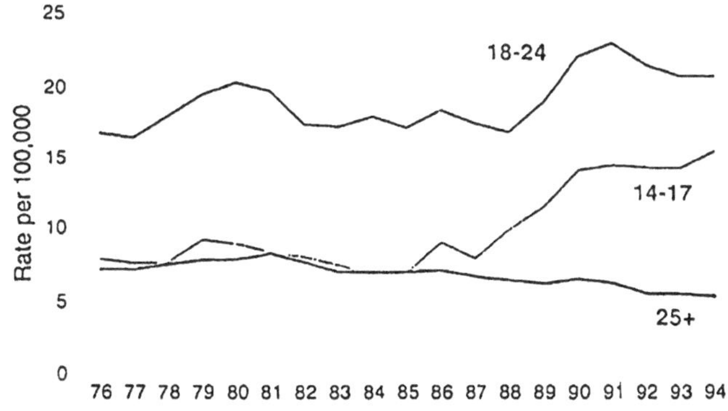

Fig. 4.12 USA Homicide Offending Rate by Age, White Males, 1976–94. *Source*: Fox, 1996, p. 8

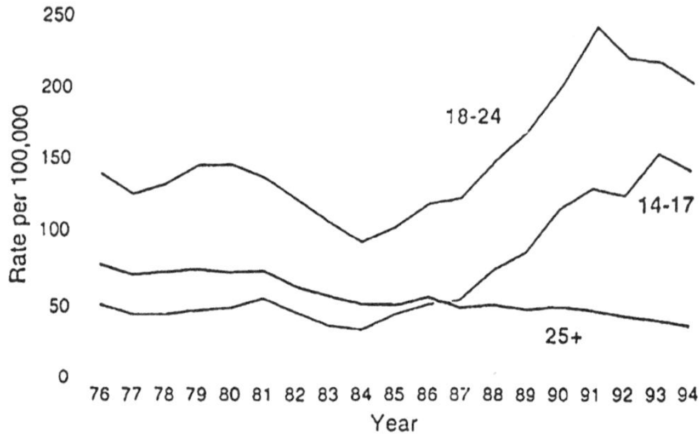

Fig. 4.13 USA Homicide Offending Rate by Age, Black Males, 1976–94. *Source*: Fox, 1996, p. 8

What might some of those stressors be, to which we are exposing our children more than the adult and elderly segments of our population? Clearly, there are many, since violence, like all behavior, is multidetermined, and results from the interaction between psychological, social, and economic, and even some biological variables. In no way can the etiology of violence be reduced to just one determinant. But a preliminary and partial first approximation toward answering the question I just raised might begin by reviewing the data in Fig. 4.14 (Black, 1991).

What we see there is a graphic illustration of at least one of the ways in which we have been discriminating against children in this country, and in favor of those who are older. This chart shows the degree to which we as a country, through our federal government, give economic support to people in different age groups. The top line shows the amount of money allocated to support the elderly from 1960 to 1990. As you can see, it was a huge increase, from roughly $3,000 in the early 1960s to nearly $11,000 in constant 1989 dollars, which was a perfectly wonderful thing to do. It meant the elderly changed from being the most impoverished age group in our society to being the one with the lowest poverty rate. The middle line shows that adults received an increase in their allotment, but nothing comparable to the increase given to the elderly – presumably because being young enough to work full-time and not yet burdened with the ailments that become more frequent with advancing age, they did not need so much extra help. In the very bottom row, you see children. At the very bottom, in more senses than one. You remember the old saying, "Women and children first?" Well, we tend to do the opposite in this country. Our motto seems to be "Women and children last."

By 1989, the federal government was contributing $10,923 to each elderly person, as compared with $744 for each child. One result of these policy differences has been that the poverty rate for those over 65 dropped from about 25% in 1970 to 11% in 1989, the lowest of any age group. During that same period, the poverty rate for children under 18 increased from 15% in 1970 to 20% in 1989 and even higher and 25% for children under the age of 6. "In real numbers," as Black summarized it, "that means 12.5 million children are living in poverty compared with 3.3 million senior

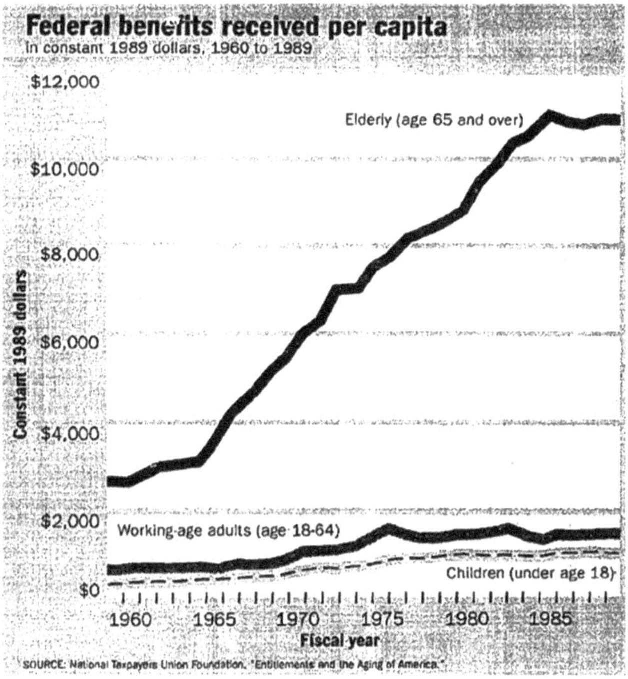

Fig. 4.14 From "Entitlements and the Aging of America," National Taxpayers Union Foundation. Reprinted in Black, Chris, "Robbing baby Peter to pay aging Paul," *Boston Globe,* Feb. 10, 1991, p. A32

citizens." That suggests that the Republican party, under whose rule these changes occurred between 1970 and the early 1990s, has been engaged in a generation of intergenerational warfare, with the age-group that votes (the elderly) winning a war against their own children, who do not. In reality, as James Will, the general counsel for the Children's Defense Fund, put it, "The problem isn't that we are helping the elderly too much, it is that we are helping children too little." In other words, this intergenerational warfare is completely unnecessary from every standpoint except that of an amoral struggle for political power – at the expense of our children, which ultimately means at the expense of the physical safety of everyone.

To summarize the results of these policies, then, the age group in our nation with the highest poverty rate is children. For all children (everyone under the age of 18), the poverty rate in 3 recent years, 1989, 1995, and 1996, was almost twice as high as that among persons 65 and older. Even more shocking, the poverty rate for the very youngest children, those under 6, was worst of all, more than twice as high as the poverty rate among the elderly. It has also been reported that the age group with the highest rate of homelessness is also – you guessed it – children. An article in the *New York Times* reports the shocking increase in the number of homeless children throughout the country over the past 2 years, as a result of the success the Republican ethos has had for the second time in less than a century in wrecking our economy (Eckholm, 2009).

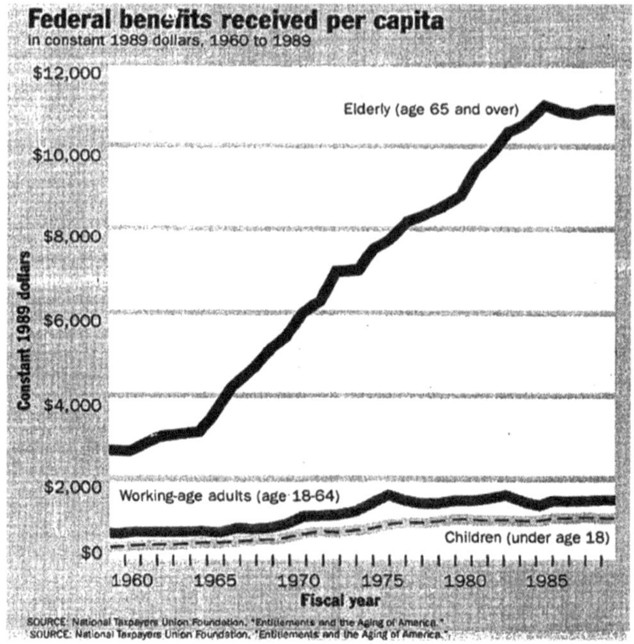

Fig. 4.15 *Source*: From "Entitlements and the Aging of America," National Taxpayers Union Foundation. Reprinted in Black, Chris, "Robbing baby Peter to pay aging Paul," *Boston Globe*, Feb. 10, 1991, p. A32

This situation did not develop overnight. It is a situation that has worsened over time, or at least over some times. For example, by one measure, the poverty rate among children under 18 in the USA increased from 15% in 1970 (the Nixon years) to 18% in 1990 (Bush Sr.), and increased again to 22% by 1993 (the rate Clinton inherited from the Republicans). Why that was so can be inferred from an examination of the average monthly payments families received from AFDC in constant 1991 dollars. In 1970, the average payment was $622; in 1980, $477; and by 1992 (the last of the Reagan–Bush years) it had dropped to $374 – 40% less than it had been a mere quarter of a century earlier.

Another important factor contributing to poverty among young people is their relatively high unemployment rate. In 1994, for example, the unemployment rate for workers aged 25–54 was 5. For those 20–24 it was twice as high: 10%. And for those aged 16–19, the rate was almost four times as high: 18% (Albelda & Folbre, 1996). But that is what makes the current recession, which the Obama administration inherited from its Republican predecessor, so alarming. As I write these words, the Sept. 4, 2009 *New York Times* (Rampell, 2009) posts the following news story:

> Pity the unemployed, but pity especially the young and unemployed. This August, the teenage unemployment rate – that is, the percentage of teenagers who wanted a job who could not find one – was 25.5%, its highest level since the government began keeping track of such statistics in 1948. Likewise, the percentage of teenagers over all who were working was at its lowest level in recorded history.

> ...Recessions disproportionately hurt America's youngest and most inexperienced workers, who are often the first to be laid off and the last to be rehired. Jobs for youth also never recovered after the last recession, in 2001. But this August found more than a quarter of the teenagers in the job market unable to find work, an unemployment rate nearly three times that of the non-teenage population (9%), and nearly four times that of workers over 55 (6.8%, also a record high for that age group).

The article goes on to comment that "Economists say there are multiple explanations for why young workers have suffered so much in this downturn, but *they mostly boil down to being at the bottom of the totem pole.*" Recent college graduates who are unable to find higher-paying jobs would be able to compete successfully against teenagers for jobs at Starbucks or Gap; and older workers, who cannot afford to retire since their homes and pension and investment funds have lost value, are not making way for younger replacements. Adding to the frustration, teenage employment is increasingly either a necessity (their family needs the money) or a prudent investment that our whole society can ill afford to forego: as the *Times* article observes, "Many college students need to work to pay for college. Half of traditional-age college students work 20 hours a week" (Rampell, 2009).

Proponents of the "free enterprise, unregulated market" economic philosophy have been so successful in misleading the voters into thinking that economics is a natural science that merely discovers inevitable and immutable laws of nature rather than being a description of the consequences of inventing and then imposing a certain arbitrary set of rules for playing games with the marketplace, that people sometimes look at unemployment figures such as those just reviewed as being merely an unfortunate consequence of the "business cycle," about which it is as impossible to do anything as it is to change the weather. But in fact, when we were faced with an even more severe unemployment crisis in the 1930s, Roosevelt immediately reduced the unemployment rate by the simple expedient of having the federal government hire millions of workers, which had the additional benefit of providing us with thousands of new hospitals, schools, libraries, roads, bridges, and other forms of infrastructure that have enriched both our spirits and our economy ever since. And with respect to the need, the young have to earn money to pay for college, there is no reason why a nation as rich as ours should not emulate every western European government and make college and graduate school educations free, as we already do for (but only for) primary and secondary education. Finally, we could learn another lesson from the social-democratic welfare states of western Europe, which have been much more successful than we have in providing generous unemployment benefits which, along with other aspects of their taxation and welfare policies, have turned inequitable pretax income patterns into much more equal posttax incomes, one side-benefit of which has been much lower rates of homicide, imprisonment, and other symptoms of social stress and conflict and of political and economic failure.

This is not to imply that they are utopias. The suicide rates in the western European social democracies, unlike their homicide rates, are on average about the same as ours, though they are higher in some countries and lower in others, just as in this country they are higher in some states and lower in others. What is clear is that they have been much more successful than we have in preventing homicide, but not in preventing suicide. Thus, their total lethal violence rates are lower than ours, but that is entirely due to their much lower homicide rates.

There are several facts about the causes and prevention of the different forms of lethal violence that are true cross-culturally, however, and that are important for us to recognize if we are going to be able to expand our knowledge of these problems as issues in public health and preventive medicine. The first is that in both the US and Western Europe – and indeed, in all developed countries – people are more likely to commit suicide than homicide. Second, that there is a universal tendency for the rates of both forms of violence to increase or decrease together, which can be coupled with evidence that the same preconditions that cause increases or decreases in either form of violence tend to have the same effect on the other. For example, in both the USA and Western Europe, increases in unemployment rates are regularly followed by increases in suicide rates, and increases in other measures of economic inequality, by increases in homicide rates (Wilkinson, 1994, 1996, & 1998). Third, there is also evidence that there are statistically significant correlations between the nature of the political party in power – liberal (meaning left-wing) or conservative (right-wing) – and in the same behavioral and economic outcomes just referred to. For example, not only in the USA, but also in the UK and Australia, the election of conservative political parties has been followed, throughout the entire twentieth century, by increases in unemployment rates and economic inequality, and also by increases in the rates of both suicide and homicide (and other violent crimes; Page, Morrell, & Taylor, 2002; Shaw, Dorling, & Smith, 2002). Thus, there appear to be certain laws concerning the epidemiology of these important constituents of public health and preventive medicine that are truly universal.

When we compare our children with those of 16 other economically developed nations, we find that the USA has by far the highest poverty rate among its children (defined as less than 50% of the country's median income), as of 1994 – a rate of 25%. Our rate was 2.5 times as high as the average rate in sixteen Western European countries, where the average childhood poverty rate was 10% (Harris, 1996). Not only do we have the highest absolute childhood poverty rate, we also have the highest rate of relative poverty in the developed world. What I mean by that is that the gap in income and wealth between the richest and the poorest children in our country is far greater than it is in any other developed nation for which we have comparable data. For example, if we compare children whose family income is at the 90th percentile of income with those at the 10th percentile, we find that the gap between the richest and the poorest in the USA as of 1991 was $54,600, whereas the gap in 16 countries in Western Europe was $29,600, or only slightly more than half the level of inequality that we have in our society (Harris, 1996).

That is an important fact to notice, since many of the studies referenced above have shown that it is relative rather than absolute poverty that predicts homicide rates. That is true because relative economic inferiority to others in one's reference group is precisely what provokes the feelings of shame, inferiority, failure, envy, being a victim of injustice, and other feelings that tend to precipitate violent behavior. Whereas when everyone is poor (assuming the poverty is above the subsistence or survival level, i.e.

people are not actually starving to death), if they are all equally poor, and there is no richer comparison group, there is no shame in being poor. And where feelings of shame and inferiority are less frequent and intense, there is less violence.

But it is not only with respect to economic affairs that we discriminate against our young people. We not only fail to give the young an equitable share of our economic resources (a kind of passive aggressiveness, though the results can be literally deadly), we are also far more punitive toward them than we are toward adults (in a number of specific respects), more punitive in some ways than we were even in the recent past, and far more punitive toward them than the adults of any other developed country are toward their children all of which amounts to a very active form of aggressiveness. In saying that I do not mean to deny that we have, fortunately but also belatedly, begun to undo some of the worst and most cruel forms of our mistreatment of our children. For example, until 2005 the USA was one of only six nations on earth (including Iran and Saudi Arabia) that still executed its own children. As late as 2002, 22 U.S. states still authorized the execution of juvenile offenders. In 2005, our Supreme Court, in an unusual alliance between its conservative and its liberal members, finally declared that executing children (17 or younger) for whatever "crimes" they had committed (as if the concept of a "child" committing a "crime" even made any sense) was no longer in conformity with our evolving understanding of the limitations in children's capacities for judgment and impulse control (Lane, 2005).

As mentioned above, we have more and more frequently resorted to transferring children charged with a crime even at very young ages to adult courts and prisons. We have also invented more punitive programs custom-designed for children, such as so-called boot camps and scared straight programs – despite the fact that both of these approaches, like adult prisons for children, have been shown to increase rather than reduce rates of recidivism and future violence.

The USA is still one of only two nations on earth (the other being Somalia) that has refused to ratify the United Nations Convention on the Rights of the Child (CRC), which the General Assembly adopted 20 years ago, in 1989. Although President Bush Sr. did not sign this convention, President Clinton did do so, in 1995. However, he did not submit it to the Senate, where ratification of it was clearly impossible since it was actively opposed by politically and religiously conservative Republican leaders who commanded a majority in that body, from the Senate Majority Leader, Bob Dole, to the Chairman of the Foreign Relations Committee, Jesse Helms. The debate over ratification of the CRC has effectively been split along partisan lines ever since, with President Bush Jr. also opposing it and Democratic leaders such as former President Carter and President Obama supporting ratification. The main conservative objections to the CRC since 1995 have been that it would prevent US parents and other adults from continuing to engage in the following forms of violence against children:

1. To execute our own children (a policy that became moot when the US Supreme Court agreed with the CRC in 2005 that this practice violated children's legitimate rights);

2. To sentence them to life imprisonment with no possibility of parole (as the laws in 20 states currently permit);
3. To engage in their corporal punishment both at home, where it is legal in all but one state, and in schools, where it remains legal in 23 states but could be in all, given a 1977 Supreme Court decision that declared it not to be cruel and unusual punishment – except, of course, when applied to adults. This is in contrast to most other democracies, in which the striking of a child by an adult is regarded as assault and battery both in school and at home, just as it would be if inflicted on an adult. As one commentator has pointed out, this dispute has divided popular practice from expert opinion: "...while the American Academy of Pediatrics shares the [CRC] Committee's negative view of corporal punishment, 'as of 1985 90% of parents used corporal punishment on toddlers, and more than 50% continue such punishment up through early teen years, sometimes several times a week'" (Smolin, 2006). To be fair, 27 states have banned corporal punishment in schools, and the number of physical assaults on school children by hands or weapons that are known to the US Department of Education has been dropping, from 1.4 million in the 1979–1980 school year to 365,000 by 1997–1998 (the latter years of the Clinton administration). Almost all of those assaults occurred in Southern states, which a *New York Times* article referred to as the "Belt Belt" (Wilgoren, 2001). This makes it less surprising that that is the *region* with the highest homicide rates in the country, just as the USA is the *country* with the highest homicide rates of any economically developed democracy.
4. To deprive them of health care by failing to guarantee or provide affordable health care for all children, at least 10% of whom currently have no health insurance, in contrast to every other affluent democracy on earth, where such care is universal, one result of which, not surprisingly, is the fact that our infant and child mortality rates are the highest of any developed nation.
5. To avoid reducing the level of poverty among our children as effectively as we have among the elderly, and as effectively as all other developed nations have, since the Convention requires all states to ensure that every child in the USA has "a standard of living adequate for the child's physical, mental, spiritual, moral, and social development." Many conservatives are horrified by this requirement, as they feel that it would cost the taxpayers too much money if we stopped providing an inadequate standard of living for many of our children. They are equally horrified by the requirement that "The USA Congress and the President must in this decade attack the problem of child poverty with the same vigor as their predecessors attacked the problem of elderly poverty," as they fear that paying this much attention to children's rights would "undermine parents' rights as we know it [sic] in the USA" (Klicka & William, 2007) – meaning, apparently, the right of adults to continue making our country unique among the democratic nations of the world in the degree to which we kill, assault, neglect, impoverish, and otherwise abuse our children in the ways just enumerated.

I end this essay with a question. We all know how strongly Republicans claim to be in favor of "family values," and how vociferously they claim that Democratic policies destroy families. And yet families, by definition, include children. How can you be in favor of family values and yet be in favor of policies that do not merely hurt children, they actually kill them, as the Republican party has been for most of the past century? Capital punishment of children kills children. Adult prisons kill children (and provoke them to kill themselves). Poverty kills children. Lack of access to health care kills children. Access to guns kills children (children are at far greater risk of dying from gunfire, whether from suicide, homicide, or so-called accident, when there is a gun in their house than when there is not). Corporal punishment kills children (because it so often escalates to lethal child abuse). Having an unemployed parent has been shown to increase the likelihood that a child will die from so-called accidental death. I could go on. But the point, I think, is clear: is it possible that Americans, at least when they decide to vote Republicans into power, do not love children after all, since the Republican party has either supported or brought about, and the Democratic party has opposed or eliminated, all of the policies just mentioned? We know that in ancient Rome's highly patriarchal society, children were regarded as the property of their fathers so that the law gave them the power of life and death over their children. That is, fathers who did not approve of their children could literally execute them, and it was not considered to be murder. Is not something like that going on when we elect Republicans? Is the very loud lip-service that Republicans give to "family values" an example of their being, like Hamlet's mother, a lady who doth protest too much?

One characteristic that may help to explain why the USA is unique among the affluent countries of the world in its violence toward its own children, and in their resulting violence toward themselves and each other, is a cultural and historical factor that I had not noticed the extent and influence of until I spent some time away from this country. During the 1990s, I had the opportunity to spend 2 years in England as a Visiting Fellow at the Institute of Criminology of Cambridge University, and I noticed for the first time that England was the country that the Puritans had left, and America was the country they came to. The degree to which Puritanism has dominated American culture and values only became obvious to me, and I could see how ubiquitous its influence was, when I had been away from the USA for awhile. For example, we are the nation that has carried what can be called "pharmacological puritanism" to greater extremes than any other country on earth. You will remember H. L. Mencken's definition of puritanism as the sneaking suspicion that somebody, somewhere, is having a good time (La Monte & Mencken, 1910). So, of course, we have been the only Western nation to prohibit alcohol, and we have also been the most rabid supporters of the "war on drugs" (which was declared in 1969 at the beginning of the next period of Republican hegemony, by Nixon). Both of those policies of criminalizing drugs and imprisoning people for using them, rather than merely educating people as to their potential health hazards and offering them help in overcoming their inability to use them safely, have been among the most powerful stimulants of violence in our history. That is, both of those wars on drugs have been followed by the largest epidemics of violence in our history.

To the extent that we have voted conservative Republicans into power, we have also lagged behind every other developed nation in outgrowing our opposition to homosexuality and contraception, and our attachment to the corporal punishment of our children. For there is an even more direct way in which Puritanism stimulates punitiveness and violence by adults toward children and thus of violence by children toward themselves and each other. I am speaking of the motto "Spare the rod and spoil the child," the ultimate defense of a pattern of violence toward children that would be a crime if committed on adults.

In Piaget's (1966) research on moral development in children, he found that the most primitive form of moral reasoning, which is engaged in by the youngest and most immature children, is what he called "gerontocratic," which is based on the assumption that the ultimate moral authority, indeed the ultimate source of morality, is the older generation (i.e. the parents); that moral authority resides not in one's own conscience but in these more powerful external authorities so that whatever they say is right is right because they say it is: in other words, that might is right, those who are more powerful have the right to enforce their moral authority (i.e. their power) by means of violence, and since parents, who are older, have the power, they have moral authority, including the right to enforce that authority by means of corporal punishment, and even capital punishment. One example of the essence of this moral value system is the commandment to children to "honor" their father and mother – with no reciprocal obligation of parents to honor their children.

It is understandable why this would be the first understanding very young children would have of what morality consists of. But as Piaget (1966) noticed, many adults never outgrow this type of moral value system. This is an authoritarian, gerontocratic, patriarchal, hierarchical, despotic, antidemocratic moral value structure, which is endorsed, consciously or unconsciously, by those whose social, political, and economic preferences are to give the highest priority to the needs of adults and the elderly, and to regard children as the least important members of the human family. I want to ask whether the policies of the Republican party are guided by this kind of gerontocratic value system, since it would seem that it would perfectly describe the policies toward children that they have supported over the past century or more – a set of policies that benefit adults at the expense of children, the strong at the expense of the weak, and the rich at the expense of the poor.

Fortunately, Piaget noticed that there is a more mature moral value system, a democratic, antiauthoritarian one that is based on one's own internalized conscience so that one is capable of treating both those who are younger, weaker, or poorer than oneself with respect as people who are as capable of learning and growing as anyone else is, and of treating those who are older, stronger, or wealthier as not necessarily being infallible so that one can question, criticize and, when necessary, repudiate the orders given by external authorities. This is the kind of moral value system that the Convention on the Rights of the Child (1989) is attempting to foster and encourage, which is exactly why the principles it endorses are so threatening to those who are wedded to authoritarian, patriarchal styles of moral reasoning, and violent, punitive methods of child-rearing.

References

Albelda, R., & Folbre, N. (1996). *The war on the poor: A defense manual.* New York: The New Press.

Bartels, L. M. (2008). *Unequal democracy: The political economy of the new gilded age.* New York: Princeton University Press.

Bartlett, J. (1992). *Familiar quotations.* Boston: Little Brown.

Black, C. (1991, February 10). Robbing baby Peter to pay aging Paul. *Boston Globe,* A32

Bridge, J. A., Greenhouse, J. B., Weldon, A. H., Campo, J. V., Kelleher, K. J., et al. (2008). Suicide trends among youths aged 10 to 19 years in the USA. *JAMA, 300,* 1025–1026.

Carter, D. (2005). *Stonewall: The riots that sparked a gay revolution.* New York: St. Martins Griffin.

CDC. (2007). Suicide Trends Among Youths and Young Adults Aged 10-24 Years – USA, 1990-2004. *Morbidity and Mortality Weekly Report, 56,* 905–908.

Center for Disease Control (1987). *Vital statistics of the USA.* National Center for Health Statistics

Eckholm, E. (2009, September 11). *Last Year's Poverty Rate Was Highest in 12 Years.* New York Times. Retrieved from http://www.nytimes.com/2009/09/11/us/11poverty.html?fta=y

Fingerhut, L. A., & Kleinman, J. C. (1990). International and interstate comparisons of homicide among young males. *JAMA, 263,* 3292–3295.

Fox, J. A. (December 13-14, 1998/2000). *Demographics and USA homicide: Trends by age, sex, and race for 1976-1998 and beyond.* Paper prepared for the Harry Frank Guggenheim Violent Crime Drop Conference, New Orleans.

Fox, J. A. (1996). *Trends in juvenile violence: A report to the USA attorney general on current and future rates of juvenile offending.* Washington, DC: US Department of Justice, Retrieved from http://bjs.ojp.usdoj.gov/content/pub/pdf/tjvfox.pdf

Friedan, B. (1963). *The feminine mystique.* New York: W.W. Norton and Company Inc.

Gilligan, J. (2003). Shame, guilt & violence. *Social Research, 70,* 1149–1180.

Gilligan, J. (1999). Structural violence. In R. Gottesman (Ed.), *Violence in America: An encyclopedia.* New York: Charles Scribners Sons.

Harrington, M. (1962). *The other America.* New York: Macmillan.

Harris, I. B. (1996). *Children in jeopardy: can we break the cycle of poverty?* New Haven, CT: Yale University Press.

Henry, A., & Short, J. (1954). *Suicide and homicide: Some economic, sociological and psychological aspects of aggression.* New York: The Free Press.

Holinger, P. C. (1987). *Violent deaths in the USA: An epidemiologic study of suicide, homicide, and accidents.* New York: Guilford Press.

Holinger, P. C., et al. (1994). *Suicide and homicide among adolescents.* New York: Guilford Press.

Hsieh, C., & Pugh, M. D. (1999). Poverty, income inequality, and violent crime: A meta-analysis of recent aggregate data studies. In I. Kawachi, P. B. Kennedy, & R. G. Wilkinson (Eds.), *The society and population health reader: Volume I, income inequality and health* (pp. 278–296). New York: The New Press.

James, O. (1995). *Juvenile violence in a winner-loser culture: Socio-economic and familial origins of the rise of violence against the person.* New York: Free Association Books.

Kempe, C. H., Silverman, F. N., Steele, B. F., Droegemueller, W., & Silver, H. K. (1962). The battered-child syndrome. *JAMA, 181,* 17–24.

Klicka, C. J., & William, A. E. (2007). *The UN Convention on the Rights of the Child. The most dangerous attack on parents' rights in the history of the USA.* Purcellville, VA: Home School Legal Defense Association.

La Monte, R., & Mencken, H. L. (1910). *Men versus the man.* New York: Holt.

Lane, Charles (2005, March 2). *5-4 Supreme Court Abolishes Juvenile Executions.* The Washington Post, p. A01

Page, A., Morrell, S., & Taylor, R. (2002). Suicide and political regime in New South Wales and Australia during the 20th century. *Journal of Epidemiology and Community Health, 56*, 766–772.
Piaget, J. (1966). *The moral judgment of the child*. New York: The Free Press.
Rampell, C. (2009, September 4). *Teenage Jobless Rate Reaches Record High*. New York Times. Retrieved from http://www.nytimes.com/2009/09/05/business/economy/05teen.html?scp=1&sq=Recessions%20disproportionately%20hurt%20America%92s%20youngest%20and%20most%20inexperienced%20&st=cse
Reagan, R. (1982, May 4). *Remarks at Republican congressional dinner*. Washington, DC (quoted in Bartlett, John, *Familiar Quotations,* Justin Kaplan, General Editor, Boston: Little, Brown, 1992)
Richter, J. E. (1993). Community violence and children's development: Toward a research agenda for the 1990s. In D. Riess, J. E. Richter, M. Radke-Yarrow, & D. Scharff (Eds.), *Children and violence* (pp. 3–6). New York: Guilford Press.
Roosevelt, F.D. (1937, January 20). *Second inaugural address*. (Quoted in Bartlett, John, *Familiar Quotations,* Justin Kaplan, General Editor, Boston: Little, Brown, 1992)
Shaw, M. D. Dorling, D., & Smith, G. D. (2002). Mortality and political climate: how suicide rates have risen during periods of Conservative government, 1901–2000. *Journal of Epidemiology and Community Health, 56*, 723–725
Smolin, D. M. (2006). Overcoming religious objections to the Convention on the Rights of the Child. *Emory International Law Review, 20*, 110.
Stahl, Anne L., (April 1999). "Delinquency Cases Waived to Criminal Court, 1987-1996," USA Dept. of Justice: Office of Juvenile Justice and Delinquency Prevention, OJDP Fact Sheet, p. 1.
United Nations Convention on the Rights of the Child (1989). United Nations General Assembly Document A/RES/44/25. Retrieved from http://www.cirp.org
West, D. J. (1967). *Murder followed by suicide*. Cambridge, MA: Harvard University Press.
Wilgoren, J. (2001, May 3). Lawsuits touch off debate over paddling in the schools. *New York Times*
Wilkinson, R. G. (1996). *Unhealthy societies: The afflictions of inequality*. London: Routledge.
Wilkinson, R. G. (1994). *Unfair shares: The effects of widening income differences on the welfare of the young*. Ilford, Essex: Barnardos.
Wilkinson, R. (2004). Why is violence more common where inequality is greater? In J. Devine, J. Gilligan, K. A. Miczek, R. Shaikh, & D. Pfaff (Eds.), *Youth violence: Scientific approaches to prevention* (pp. 1–12). New York: The New York Academy of Sciences.
Wilkinson, R. G., Lchiro, K., & Kennedy, B. P. (1998). Mortality, the social environment, crime and violence. *Sociology of Health and Illness, 20*, 598–597.
Wolfgang, M. (1958). *Patterns in criminal homicide*. Philadelphia: University of Pennsylvania Press.

Chapter 5
Promoting a Protective Environment for Children Affected by Disaster and War

Neil Boothby and Alastair Ager

Introduction

Creating a protective environment is the basis of the United Nations' strategy for protecting the human rights of children faced with the extreme environmental threats posed by disasters and war. The "Protective Environment Framework" was developed as a basis to identify the key areas, where actions can be taken to increase the protection available to children (Landgren, 2005). It is a basis for thinking with appropriate breadth of potential influences on children's well-being, but with sufficient focus to frame clear actions that will promote protection. There are eight identified features of the "protective environment" which together can be seen to form a potential protective "shield" around children – not eliminating risks and vulnerabilities, but creating protection from their full impact. These include: government commitment and capacity; legislation and enforcement; culture and customs; open discussion; children's life skills, knowledge, and participation; capacity of families and communities; essential services; and monitoring, reporting, and oversight. We believe that all these features can be strengthened, and changes measured, through targeted support of international and national actors.

The Protective Environment Framework has seen limited application in situations of armed conflict, refugee migrations, and natural disasters. There is a prevailing assumption that it would be futile to try to strengthen protective "systems" in the midst of full-blown crises – and counterproductive in conflict settings, where the government is a major human rights violator. Some humanitarian organizations also question whether different types of child protection concerns that emerge in different types of emergencies – conflict, famine, natural disaster, and others – can be adequately conceptualized by a single emergency framework. As a result, agency preparedness and child protection work in emergencies has largely focused on the assistance to vulnerable groups, such as separated children, children associated with fighting

N. Boothby (✉)
Mailman School of Public Health, Program on Forced Migration and Health,
Colombia University, 60 Haven Avenue, New York, NY 10032, USA
e-mail: nb2101@columbia.edu

J. Garbarino and G. Sigman (eds.), *A Child's Right to a Healthy Environment*,
The Loyola University Symposium on the Human Rights of Children 1,
DOI 10.1007/978-1-4419-6791-6_5,

forces, and victims of gender-based sexual violence, for example. A vulnerable child focus is reflected in non-governmental organization (NGO) protection frameworks and recovery and reintegration services, such as tracing and reunification and creating safe spaces, is promoted as the main child protection activities in emergencies (Rakotomalala, 2003; Save the Children USA, 2005; Tearfund & National Society for Prevention of Cruelty to Children, 2003).

The lack of a systemic child protection framework has hampered efforts to plan and implement comprehensive protection responses for children in emergencies. It has resulted in ad hoc and (sometimes) anecdotal assessments that cannot be compared across communities, regions, or countries. A focus on discrete groups of vulnerable children may have a high value for immediate protection programming in emergencies, but it also leads to palliative approaches and small-scale projects that fall short of a systematic protection response and have little sustaining impact on protective enhancement in the long term. Indeed, a human rights approach to programming suggests that a wider range of interventions and systems development must be considered.

This paper addresses the following paradox: how can humanitarian actors ensure rapid responses to discrete groups of vulnerable children in emergencies – and at the same time – leverage commitments, capacities, and actions required to strengthen a protective environment for all children in the long run? It argues that it is not only possible to do so, but embracing this paradox is also what distinguishes stellar child protection responses from merely adequate ones.

The Protective Environment Framework is presented as a platform capable of bringing greater coherence to activities that strengthen child protection in wars, natural disasters, and refugee movements. Areas of the framework that need to be adapted – or, at least, flexibly applied – to systemically address child protection concerns in different types of emergencies are discussed. Key areas of focus for each of the eight framework elements are identified, and checklists of indicators to be considered in emergency assessment and planning efforts are provided.

The Protection Environment and Emergencies

The Protective Environment Framework specifies a range of factors that serve to protect children from risks and vulnerabilities in any given environment. It acknowledges the importance of actions targeted directly at minimizing such risks, such as peace dialogs aimed at ending conflict, for example. However, while such actions are taken forward, humanitarian agencies must seek to protect children in crisis settings through actions that "shield" children from ongoing risks. Accordingly, it is on such actions that the framework focuses. Although there is this principle focus on protection, clearly mitigation of the impact of risks will often serve, long term, to reduce overall sources of risk and vulnerability. There are eight key elements identified in this framework of the "protective environment for children" (Landgren, 2005) (Table 5.1).

Table 5.1 Elements of the protective environment for children

• Monitoring and reporting
• Governmental commitment to fulfilling protection rights
• Protective legislation and enforcement
• Attitudes, traditions, customs, behavior and practices
• Open discussion and engagement with child protection issues
• Children's life skills, knowledge and participation
• The capacity to protect among those around children
• Services for recovery and reintegration

Application of the "protective environment" in settings of humanitarian action may require generic adaptations. First, the tendency among humanitarian actors to only assess the impact of a given crisis on children and their immediate environment must be overcome. Assessment of potential protective mechanisms should not only focus on risks and vulnerabilities that result from the given crisis, but also take into account wider concerns that interact with crisis-related risks. Primary among these are social and economic conditions that:

- Risk the commoditization of children as economic units at a young age
- Lead to extreme gender division and inequity
- Shape childhood and adolescence in other harsh and exploitative ways

Second, a humanitarian crisis may provide unique opportunities to introduce significant positive change within one or more of the protective environment's eight elements. Recent examples of how crises provided unique opportunities to improve protective environments include the Asian tsunami and end of political conflict in Aceh; and, "Form 8" reporting requirement reform on rape and gender-based violence in Darfur.

Third, the *intent* of the government and other parties to a conflict will be a key consideration in developing protection responses for refugee and internally displaced populations (Inter-Agency Standing Committee, 2002; Slim & Eguren, 2004). If authorities are committed to the protection rights of refugees or displaced persons, collaboration and capacity building is a realistic protection strategy option, even if official systems are weak and technical competence low. In contrast, if one or both parties are resistant, abusive or directly involved in human rights violations, coercive denunciation may serve as a core advocacy strategy and substitution of assistance and services may be required.

Fourth, it is important to consider personal and political intent as multiple levels: community, district, provincial, and national levels. Even in Darfur – where the national government promotes wide-scale violence and human rights abuse – opportunities to promote a protective environment for children were identified at the state level (Ager, Boothby, & Bremer, 2009).

And fifth, it is important to focus on how a range of groups may be benefiting from a conflict. These may include:

- Governments
- Militia fighters

- Economic elites
- Members of the Diaspora outside conflict zones

Attention to hard-to-reach – and sometimes forgotten groups – may be a key to securing protective responses for children.

Areas of Emergency Focus

This section outlines key considerations and areas of focus for each of the framework's eight elements. It provides a preliminary set of assessment indicators and highlights key planning concerns.

Monitoring and Reporting

Monitoring and reporting are keys to the development of critical areas of humanitarian action, including effective targeting of humanitarian resources; keeping abreast of child rights trends; promoting informed advocacy regarding key risks and vulnerabilities; and establishing evidence regarding successful interventions. Strengthening the quality and coordination of data collection and dissemination is an important means of bolstering a protective environment for children in emergencies.

A minimal standard should be the establishment of a child protection monitoring and reporting system capable of capturing short-term changes and long-term trends. Assessment and program planning need to address key operational challenges for developing such a system, which may include:

- How to capture the breath of information required?
- How to ensure proper trend analyses?
- How to give feedback effectively on what has been captured for both program and policy action purposes?
- How to ensure coverage within and beyond established displaced persons camps?
- How to appropriately train personnel in monitoring, deploy them, and cope with security issues?
- How to address problems of retribution to reporting agencies?
- How to ensure confidentiality and reduce potential risks to victims?
- What is the role of government or other duty bearers in data collection?

There is a current "divide" between protection and human rights information collection in the UN field operations that reflects the global debate regarding the definition of these two interconnected fields as separate entities. This divide appears to have brought few benefits to reporting and monitoring of child protection issues which so clearly straddle the two (United Nations Office of Internal Oversight Services (OIOS), 2006). The former focuses on documentation of individual cases for legal follow-up and redress and requires a monitoring and reporting system based on narrative reporting on individual incidents. It is staff and time intensive – and not designed to achieve comprehensive coverage or to yield aggregate data on child rights violations. The latter seeks information for strategic planning, protection programming, and political advocacy; these needs are better met through surveys designed to establish incidence (number of child rights violations taking place at a given time) or prevalence (percentage of child population whose rights are violated) rates. To date, child protection surveys of these kinds are not standard practice. There is considerable opportunity to learn from good practice in sectors such as nutrition, where effective and efficient systems of reporting – using survey and surveillance approaches to data collection monitoring – have been developed in partnership with relevant government.

Inclusion of "child soldiering" in Security Council Resolutions (1539 and 1612) on monitoring and reporting on "grave violations" is but one of several impressive accomplishments. Recently, for example, several field operations have undertaken significant efforts to document the presence of girls and boys with fighting forces (OIOS, 2006), and data collected through these programs have been used to inform global policy (Williamson, 2007). At the same time, there is no basis in international humanitarian or human rights law for giving preeminent attention to one human rights violation over all others. The current Security Council proviso that grave violation monitoring and reporting be implemented within existing resources has clearly posed limits to the scope and depth of such efforts. The narrower war crimes focus poses particular dilemmas for UNICEF because its broader child protection mandate calls for the development of a strategy for additional focused data collection – relating to issues of child labor, juvenile justice, access to education, traditional harmful practices, etc., – in partnerships with government ministries whenever possible.

Commitment of Authorities to Fulfilling Protection Rights

Government commitment to respecting, protecting, and fulfilling child protection is an essential element of a protective environment. Very often governments deny that there is a problem in their own country, when in reality exploitation of children is found all around the world. Instead, governments need to show commitment to creating strong legal frameworks that comply with international legal standards, policies and programs, and to enforcing and implementing them to protect children.

In emergency situations, efforts to obtain commitments from authorities to fulfilling child protection rights often must be extended to the government and other duty bearers. In situations of armed conflict, these will include other parties to the conflict and armed groups that influence or control populations in remote areas of the country, for example, or in refugee or displaced persons camps. Even if acknowledgment and negotiations with other political–military actors is difficult or forbidden, obtaining the commitment of all "duty bearers" to adhering to child rights standards is an important objective.

Mandated and nonmandated international agencies may assume roles in emergencies that place them in positions of serving as "de facto" or "on-the-ground" authorities. This takes place, for example, when peacekeeping missions are undertaken and when UN or NGOs assume lead management roles or engage in direct service delivery in refugee or displaced persons camps. Their commitment and capacity to child protection must be assessed and developed as well.

The ALNAP Guidance Book on Humanitarian Protection outlines how the nature of protection problems is determined to a large extent by intent (Slim & Eguren, 2004). There are enormous protection challenges when government authorities or another party to a conflict is willfully instigating or refusing to prevent human rights violations. Intentional human rights abuse requires protective activities that are aimed at authorities and/or other duty bearers. Key modes of protection action may include denunciation (pressing authorities through public discourse into meeting their obligations) to accomplish policy change objectives, for example, and substitution (directly providing services to victims of violations) to accomplish assistance and support needs. In contrast, if authorities are not directly engaged in rights violations, protection actions may include persuasion (convincing authorities through private dialog) or mobilization (engaging leaders, political bodies or states that have the capacity to influence authorities to satisfy their obligations), and empowering national/local structures to carry out their functions to protect and assist affected populations.

As noted earlier, in addition to crisis-related events, harsh economic conditions and longstanding social and cultural factors play significant roles in promoting – or undermining – protective environments for children. The commitment of governments and other duty bearers to actively address the economic and social dimensions of a crisis is essential. Within governments, ministries of labor and social (and cultural) welfare may be well positioned to address social and economic phenomenon and practices related to child protection, including street children, abandoned babies, female circumcision, domestic violence, and sexual exploitation, among other issue. Often these ministries are among the marginalized within a government and lack financing, infrastructure, and training. They often are not operational and their presence will be limited to national and state capitals. If the goal is the development of institutions to establish mechanisms for the long term, clearly these and other key ministries will need to play significant roles.

Protective Legislation and Enforcement

An adequate legislative framework designed to protect children from abuse, and its implementation and enforcement are essential elements of a protective environment. The absence of these safeguards in emergencies may be symptomatic of a general lack of procedural protections, absence of multisectoral support services, and laws that already negatively impact women and vulnerable children. They may be highlighted even more during an emergency, along with other protection concerns, such as a lack of redress for human rights crimes.

Many countries and communities around the globe have formal and informal systems of justice, and the adequacy of protective legislation and enforcement needs to be examined across these interrelated systems. Traditional justice systems, for example, may operate at the community level, and deal with civil disputes and personal affairs, including domestic violence. Judgments are often decided by a council of elders or other local leaders, and cases are sometimes brought to them without contact with the police or any formal justice structures. Many crimes committed by children or against them may be frequently handled by such a system. Community courts often focus on restorative justice, compensation to victims and community service – rather than imprisonment or other formal punishments. Conflict and forced migration may disrupt these informal justice systems; however, the individuals who served on them remain important potential protection resources within refugee and internally displaced person camps.

Other types of informal courts include those sanctioned by government authorities. They, too, may operate at town, district or regional levels, and deal directly with minor criminal, civil, and personal cases through the application of both customary law and general principles of formal justice. Sanctioned informal courts are used to ease the caseload of the formal justice system and are thus often the first entry point into the formal justice system. Many offenses involving children will fall under the jurisdiction of these types of informal courts. It is important to assess whether or not such courts are readily trusted by the community. In politically or ethnically divided settings, they may be perceived to be highly biased because individuals serving on them are often appointed by or affiliated with government authorities.

Attitudes, Traditions, Customs, Behavior, and Practices

Family, kinship, tribal and, at times, feudal relationships are part of complex socioeconomic systems that maintain order and assign roles and responsibilities to all members of society. Of particular interest to a protective environment perspective are the expectations made of children and the features of community life that may be considered protective (or harmful) of them.

A strong commitment to family is an important feature of potential security and stability for children, for instance. The widespread practice of informal "adoption" of orphaned or separated children is usually a key indication of the strength of kinship obligation to protect and care for children, and should be part of an early situational assessment. Family stability is also linked with a strong sense of the need for moral education and a clear concern for children to be provided with clear moral precepts and example. There is also a range of social and religious customs – from alms giving, to youth groups, to traditional conflict resolution procedures – that are potentially protective as well. Expectations and obligations of protecting one's kin – widely cited as a frequent occurrence in context of emergencies – also point to social bonds that serve protective functions.

Protection assessments need to ascertain the extent to which a given emergency has disrupted the capacity of populations to fully utilize a wide range of intricate social mechanisms that have previously been used to maintain social cohesion within and between communities. Accordingly, it usually will make sense to consider means of supporting or, where they have completely failed, reestablishing traditional mechanisms that have a protective value.

There are likely to be other features of community life which – shaped by the harsh physical and economic conditions and deeply engrained cultural attitudes and practices – appear profoundly hostile to the welfare of children. Two major concerns that require careful assessment and response in emergencies are the commoditization of children as a source of labor, and the control of girls (and their sexuality) through marked gender disparity.

The commoditization of children as economic units may be exacerbated by war, famine, and confinement in displaced and refugee camps. Children – especially girls – may be required to remain home for longer period of time to care for younger siblings. Females may also be expected to assume dangerous roles, such as firewood collection in hostile environments outside of subsidized camps, for instance, because such duties would be even more threatening to males. Although emergencies may severely challenge household livelihoods, longstanding cultural norms and values regarding childhood – and especially children's roles in the household economy and gender expectations – will need to be strategically addressed in emergency settings as well.

A similar analysis is required on gender disparity and the subjugation of women. The role of girls in the household economy is a special concern, as is their engagement in the broader labor market. Access to education, informal education opportunities, and other potentially protective activities should be routinely assessed. Female circumcision, early marriage, toleration of domestic abuse, and marginalization of women from decision-making all point to the engrained nature of attitudes maintaining the vulnerability of women and girls. When these and other harmful practices are widespread, strategies more sophisticated than "awareness raising" are necessary to address such longstanding socially sanctioned patterns.

Open Discussion and Engagement with Protection Issues

At the most individual level, children need to be free to speak up about child protection concerns affecting them or other children. At the community level, parents, teachers, religious leaders and other immediate child care actors must be willing to openly acknowledge (and address) critical child protection concerns. At the national level, media attention and civil society engagement with child protection issues can strengthen a protective environment. NGOs need to take up protection as a priority. The silence must be broken.

In emergencies, particular attention must be paid to develop procedures and systems to ensure the security of children and adults who do report protection concerns. Confidentiality and attribution are but two concerns that must consistently be addressed. NGO and other civil society informants may also be vulnerable to attack, arrest, and expulsion.

Community dialog is an essential component of humanitarian response assessments, and is especially important in situations of armed conflict. There are many concerns that members of the affected population are likely to know more about a crisis than outside agencies, including, for instance:

- Nature and timing of the threats they confront
- Mindset and habits of those who threaten them
- Resources within the community
- History of previous threats and coping mechanisms
- Practical possibilities for resisting threats
- Optimal linkage between community and agency responses

Attention must also be paid to the differences that exist between international definitions and community definitions of key protection concerns. For example, there may be significant differences between global and local definitions of a separated child, domestic violence, child labor, and harmful practices, just to mention a few. Definitional misunderstandings that occur during assessment and planning phases are especially difficult to overcome.

Assessments need to take into account that some protection issues will be more openly discussed by community members than others and will not assume the problem that does not exist because people say that it does not. Communities may show a willingness to discuss conflict-related rape or child soldiers, for instance, while domestic violence and child labor remain taboo. At the same time, a natural disaster or armed conflict often prompt people to look critically at their previous attitudes and practices. In Pakistan, for example, open dialog with traditional Afghan leaders about their desire to continue to have women and girls treated by female doctors led to the establishment of home-based schools for refugee girls – institutions which were subsequently evaluated to be superior learning environments compared to "formal" schools established in camps (Rugh, 2000). Much of what was learned about supporting girls education in Pakistan continues to be applied in return communities in Afghanistan. Participatory assessment methods in northern Uganda enabled displaced women to discuss domestic violence and rape in a manner that resulted in the establishment of prevalence rates and women's ranking of these concerns as their top protection-assistance priorities (Boothby, Ager, Wessells, & Stark, 2007; Stark et al. 2009). Good practice is also emerging on how to engage children in the analyses of their own protection and well-being concerns (Boothby, Ager, & Ager, 2007). Protection mapping, free-listing, and other participatory exercises provide opportunities for children to identify and rank the risks they face; identify and rank the actions they and others may take to protect them from these risks; define what "doing well" means to them; and outline a concrete plan to achieve "well-being."

Authorities' willingness to engage in earnest dialog on key child protection should be taken into account when determining what routes will be pursued to secure commitments to child protection from them. Some milestones to consider include:

- Have authorities begun to discuss and analyze social phenomenon, such as street children, from a protection perspective? Or do they limit discussion to economics and security?
- Are they open to the issue of rape and children associated with fighting groups? Or are they silent because of the implications of acknowledging such concerns?
- Have authorities signaled a willingness to hold their own police or soldiers accountable for child rights violations? Or do they deny their involvement in such incidents?

Finally, national and international media attention to child protection concerns can help to promote a protective environment for children; however, it may also misinform public perceptions and donor response to child protection realities. Careful attention to developing media strategies that address key child protection concerns across the board is an assessment and planning concern. Agencies must be careful to distinguish their own needs to raise funds for their services or activities from the broad range of program and policy concerns in need of national and international attention.

Children's Life Skills, Knowledge, and Participation

Children are less vulnerable to abuse when they are aware of their right not to be exploited, or of services available to protect them. With the right information, children can draw upon their knowledge, skills, and resilience to reduce their risk of exploitation.

Access to education provides protection. Or does it? This advocacy refrain is only true when schools are physically safe and emotionally healing environments. During emergencies, adverse teacher–student ratios often soar to even higher levels; already harsh disciplinary practices deteriorate into public humiliation and corporal punishment; peer teasing may worsen into overt bullying; and boys and girls may be at greater risk for sexual exploitation than ever before. How to ensure these core protective ingredients are in place is a key assessment concern.

Core protective factors in schools include:

- Adequate teacher–student ratios
- Elimination of humiliation, bullying, and corporal punishment
- Safeguards against sexual abuse and exploitation

A review of education in emergencies suggests that school enrollment rates do not always drop in an emergency; sometimes, they actually increase (Ager et al. 2009; International Rescue Committee (IRC), 2006). Key factors include:

- History of enrollment previous to emergency
- Short-term economic survival needs
- Safety and distance to schools
- Presence or absence of funding for emergency education
- Fees levied by teachers and/or school committees

Particular attention needs to be paid to the educational needs of vulnerable groups, including, for example: children in female headed households; households where grandparents or older siblings are the primary caregivers; and teenage females with babies of their own. Emotional, social, and material supports are often required to enable these groups of children to realize their right to education in emergency settings.

In addition to schools, child-friendly spaces, children's clubs and youth committees have the potential not only to provide protective environments for children, but also to expose them to activities that promote choice and autonomy. In this way, programs on children's life skills should be expanded to include activities around juvenile justice and welfare decisions so that children learn to voice their opinions in a proceeding regarding placement due to abuse or subsequent care due to separation. A key factor in determining whether or not such community mechanisms are capable of fostering self-confidence and children's engagement in community affairs will be the attitudes and behaviors of the people who run them. Several evaluations have noted that an authoritarian, teacher-oriented approach to decision-making is not conducive to child participation in important community affairs (IRC, 2006; Lewis & Lockheed, 2007).

Finally, youth often actively engage in the political discourse regarding the current crisis and have strong feelings about what has happened to their communities and what lies ahead. While such participation may be valuable and broadly welcomed, particular attention during an emergency needs to be paid to political manipulation of children in schools, religious institutions, youth groups, and other social networks.

The Capacity to Protect Among Those Around Children

Health workers, teachers, police, social workers, and many others who interact with children need to be equipped with the motivation, skills, and authority to identify and respond to child protection abuses. The capacity of families and communities to protect their children is an essential element of a protective environment.

Historically, parent capacities to protect their children have been seriously compromised by conflicts, famines, and natural disasters. Crisis-affected families are often in a weaker position to provide material support for their children and may be too overburden with survival concerns to provide adequate emotional support as well.

Forced migration and economic pressures often require women to assume work roles that involve longer separations as caregivers from their children than is normal. The stress on families is exacerbated by the collapse of traditional livelihood strategies, which may involve food collection, seasonal migration, and raising livestock, for example.

The protective capacities of other important people are also likely to have been undermined. Traditional leaders may no longer be able or willing to negotiate cessations of military action; religious leaders may encourage violence rather than tolerance; health care facilities may not consistently represent a protective space for children; and schools may become indoctrination vehicles for political factions, or even recruitment grounds.

An assessment of the protective capacities of important people and institutions around children is thus essential. Assessments may need to focus on how the emergency has affected:

- Family livelihoods
- Gender, labor, and child care roles
- Teachers' roles, corporal punishment, indoctrination, and recruitment in schools
- Roles of traditional and religious leaders and their commitments to child protection (see Wessells & Strang, 2006)

As noted above, mandated and nonmandated humanitarian agencies often assume roles in humanitarian crisis that require them to serve as frontline protection providers. This takes place when international agencies administer camps for displaced persons, for example, or engage in direct assistance provision and service delivery. The presence of the international community "on the ground" as well as the services they provide is clearly a protective factor.

However, UN "protection by presence" strategies are usually extremely limited with very few agencies maintaining an active presence beyond state capitals or subsidized camps (Paul, 1999). Monitoring and reporting is therefore limited. NGOs may work in rural areas; however, they are often isolated and have no partners to whom they can refer child protection cases. Many humanitarian organizations have been unwilling to engage in child protection concerns because they do not have the capacity to respond to serious problems.

Services for Recovery and Reintegration

The eighth – and final – element of the "protective environment" involves direct services for children who have experienced protection violations or concerns. While other elements of the protective environment are focused on prevention, this element considers the resources that are available to support children when prevention activities have failed. Government services are in principle key in this area; however, the often limited capacity and reach of governments – coupled with the comparatively ample financial resources afforded to international actors – usually results in NGO delivery of the majority of recovery and reintegration services.

These types of services and activities are often the main – or exclusive – child protection focus in emergencies. Good practice now exists on separated children, and promising practice is emerging on children associated with fighting forces, psychosocial programming, gender-based violence, and holistic approaches to community reintegration (Ager, Boothby & Wessells, 2007; Ager, Stark, Akesson & Boothby, 2010). A major challenge exists, however, in dissemination of proven and promising practices between and beyond international agencies, and in collectively achieving full implementation and geographical coverage of such programs.

As discussed above, there are occasions when the development of recovery and reintegration services separate from government involvement is warranted. The provision of separate services is also easier. To be sure, working with governments and other authorities that are willing to fulfill child protection commitments, but lack the capacity in doing so, is more difficult, time consuming, and expensive (at least in the short run) than doing it alone. Some NGOs also view working with women and children as nonpolitical and thus preferable than engaging with government or other hard-to-reach duty bearers. Yet, research in emergency settings has consistently found that services and projects that exclusively focus on the individual child – and never link to broader government systems – have little to no impact on long term protective environments (Chae, Taylor, & Douglas, 2007; Paul, 1999; UNICEF Adolescent Development and Participation program, 2006).

Resolving the Good Practice Paradox

There is an old Scottish farmer's adage: if you try to catch two rabbits at the same time you are likely to lose both. Applied to an emergency response scenario – if one agency tries to provide urgent services to vulnerable groups – and at the same time tries to promote systemic solutions to child protection needs – the agency is likely to fail at both, and children are likely to suffer as a result.

A better way to resolve the good practice paradox is to promote a protection strategy that supports multiple actors' engagement in different and complementary actions within the eight elements of the protective environment framework. Simply put, the good practice paradox may be resolved through:

- Understanding the mandates, programming capacities, priorities, expertise of the agencies, and organizations on the ground
- Determining how agencies can best combine actions to meet critical needs rapidly and promote long-term solutions
- Actively coordinating these varied and complementary actions

Mandated organizations, such as UNICEF and UNHCR, will most likely be required to play both leadership roles in planning and promoting systemic responses to child protection concerns, and also supportive roles for NGO engagement in recovery and reintegration services. Taking the lead, strategic role will require emergency protection staff capable of undertaking situational analyses, making strategic links with authorities, ensuring monitoring and reporting systems evolve, and using child protection data to influence policies and programs. Expertise on vulnerable groups of children will be required as well; however, this technical expertise should be used to inform (and coordinate) NGO actions, rather than to engage in direct service delivery.

Moving Forward

Operational agencies that serve as members of the United Nations Protection Cluster Working Group on Children in Emergencies are in agreement that a move toward more systemic responses to child protection in emergencies is needed. It is our hope that the above discussion and tools such as the indicator checklist appended will be helpful in structuring this group's and others' thinking about strategy and the potential areas of intervention. However, it is clear that there are different views about the need to continue to focus on vulnerable groups of children as a priority – at least in the early phase of an emergency – as well as on the provision of "indicators" constituting general prompt questions regarding the needs relating to specific framework elements. Indeed, evolving to a more "objective" approach to indicators and "harder" targets that can be independently verified would be required if the Protective Environment Framework analysis is to have traction with government partners.

Appendix: Protective Environment Indicator Checklist

The above discussion suggests that the structure of the Protective Environment can be useful for the assessment and planning purposes in emergency settings. This section suggests a Protective Environment Indicator Checklist as a practical tool to track progress within and across emergency settings. For each element of the Protective Environment Framework, this checklist suggests key indicators, for each of which appropriate prompt questions are provided.

PROTECTIVE ENVIRONMENT INDICATOR CHECKLIST (Draft)

1. *Monitoring and Reporting*
   - GOVERNMENT CAPACITY: What is the capacity of government or other duty bearers in data collection?
   - AGENCY COORDINATION: What coordination mechanisms exist for interagency data collection on key child protection concerns?
   - CHANGES AND TRENDS: Is the child protection monitoring and reporting system capable of capturing short-term changes and long-term trends?
   - BREADTH AND SCOPE: Does the existing data collection system extend beyond monitoring child soldiers and other war crimes?

2. *Governmental Commitment to fulfilling protection rights*
   - CONVENTION COMMITMENTS: What key governmental commitments are reflected through being signatory of conventions?
   - CRC IMPLEMENTATION: What steps has government taken to implement actions consistent with the CRC?
3. *Protective legislation and enforcement*
   - NORMS: Do formal and informal justice systems abide by key international and national child protection norms?
   - SYSTEM CAPACITY: Do they have sufficient capacity to implement child protection safeguards and procedures?
   - DETENTION: Are children being detained in prisons with adults? Are they being detained by the military? Do lawyers and ombudsmen have regular access to both?
   - WELFARE: Are welfare mechanisms extended to a wider group of children who live on the margins of society, including juvenile delinquents, street children, and abandoned babies? Or is the focus only on police force, institutional care, and confinement?
   - LEGAL DEFINITIONS: Is the definition of a child in all legal (formal and informal) instances defined as any individual under age eighteen? If not, how is it defined, and how does this definition impact boys and girls differently?
   - DOCUMENTATION: Are key age and rights safeguards – birth registration and documentation – in place? Has this essential documentation been lost or stolen from refugees or internationally displaced? If so, how might it be replaced or substituted?
4. *Attitudes, traditions, customs, behavior, and practices*
   - EXPECTATIONS: What are the expectations made of children, and the features of community life that may be considered protective (or harmful) of them?
   - DISRUPTION: How has the emergency disrupted the capacity of families and communities to fully utilize the full range of intricate social mechanisms that have previously been used to maintain cohesion within and between villages?
   - HOSTILE FEATURES: What are the features of community life that appear profoundly hostile to the welfare of children, including the commoditization of children as a source of labor, and the control of girls (and their sexuality) through marked gender disparity?
   - TRADITIONAL HARMS: What traditional practices (e.g., FGM) exist that represent a significant protection risk?
5. *Open discussion and engagement with child protection issues*
   - SAFE REPORTING: What procedures and systems are required to ensure the security of children and adults who report protection concerns?
   - ANALYSIS OF THREATS: Have communities been consulted regarding the nature and timing of the threats they confront; the mindset and habits of those who threaten them; resources within the community; history of previous threats and coping mechanisms; practical possibilities for resisting threats; and optimal linkage between community and agency responses?
   - LOCAL DEFINITIONS: Do we understand local definitions of child protection and well-being?
   - WELFARE APPROACH: Have authorities begun to discuss and analyze social phenomenon, such as street children, from a protection perspective? Or do they limit discussion to economics and security?
   - OPEN TO SENSITIVE ISSUES: Are they open to the issue of rape and children associated with fighting groups? Or are they silent because of the implications of acknowledging such concerns?
   - IMPUNITY: Have authorities signaled a willingness to hold their own police or soldiers accountable for child rights violations? Or do they deny their involvement in such incidents?
   - MEDIA COVERAGE: Is media coverage reflective of key child protection concerns? Or is it overly focused on fundraising concerns?

(continued)

(continued)

6. *Children's life skills, knowledge, and participation*
   - SCHOOL ENVIRONMENT: Are core protective factors – adequate teacher–student ratios; absence of humiliation, bullying, and corporal punishment; and safeguards against sexual abuse and exploitation – in place or achievable?
   - SCHOOL ENROLLMENT: Have key obstacles to children accessing schools – history of enrollment previous to emergency, short-term economic survival needs; safety and distance to schools; presence or absence of funding for emergency education; and fees levied by teachers and/or school committees – been assessed?
   - VULNERABLE ACCESS: Are plans in place to ensure vulnerable children – female-headed households; households where grandparents or older siblings are the primary caregivers; and teenage females with babies of their own – are able to attend school?
   - PARTICIPATION PROMOTED: Has staff capable of promoting the self confidence and active participation of children been identified to organize safe space programs, youth groups, and other informal education activities?
   - POLITICAL MANIPULATION: Is youth vulnerability to political manipulation being monitored?
7. *The capacity to protect among those around children*
   - EMOTIONAL SUPPORT: Are parents and families too overburdened with survival concerns to provide adequate emotional support?
   - STRAIN ON CAREGIVERS: Are mothers and other primary caretakers assuming work roles that involve longer separations as caregivers from their children than is normal?
   - LIVELIHOOD IMPACTS: How has the crisis affected traditional household livelihood strategies, including food collection, seasonal migration, and raising livestock?
   - TEACHER SUPPORT: Have teachers or their roles changed? Does corporal punishment, indoctrination, or recruitment in schools exist?
   - RELIGIOUS SUPPORT: How have the roles of traditional and religious leaders and their commitments to child protection changed?
   - HUMANITARIAN ACCESS: How can international actors' commitment to child protection enhanced? How can humanitarian protection be extended to remote and marginalized populations?
8. *Services for recovery and reintegration*
   - KNOWLEDGE AND PRACTICE: Are knowledgeable child protection people in place and is good practice widely disseminated?
   - COVERAGE: Are recovery and reintegration services coordinated and extended to remote geographical areas and neglected groups of vulnerable children?
   - LINKAGE: Is there linkage of emergency response services to community and national child welfare and protection systems?

References

Ager, A., Boothby, N., & Wessells, M. (2007). The use of consensus methodology in determining key research and practice development questions in the field of intervention with children associated with fighting forces. *Intervention, 5*(2), 124–129.

Ager, A., Boothby, N., & Bremer, M. (2009). Using the 'protective environment' framework to analyse children's protection needs in Darfur. *Disasters, 33*(4), 548–573.

Ager, A., Stark, L., Akesson, B., & Boothby, N. (2010). Defining best practice in care and protection of children in crisis-affected settings: a Delphi Study. *Child Development, 81*(4), 1271–1286.

Boothby, N., Ager, A., & Ager, W. (2007). *A guide to the evaluation of psychosocial programming in emergencies*. New York: United Nations Children's Fund (UNICEF).

Boothby, N., Ager, A., Wessells, M., & Stark, L. (2007, May). *How do we know what works in protection? Building the evidence base*. Presentation on the Care and Protection of Children in Crisis-Affected Countries Project at the meeting of the Washington Network on Children and Armed Conflict, Washington, DC.

Chae, S., Taylor, R., & Douglas, A. (2007). *Youth engaged in service: A visionary strategy for post-conflict recovery (Innovations in Civic Partnership (ICP) Service as a Strategy Series)*. Washington, DC: Innovations in Civic Partnership.

Inter-Agency Standing Committee (IASC). (2002). *Growing the sheltering tree: Protecting rights through humanitarian action, programs and practices gathered from the field*. Geneva: IASC.

International Rescue Committee (IRC), Child and Youth Protection and Development Unit. (2006, June). *Creating healing classrooms: Guide for teachers and teacher educators: For field testing*. New York: IRC.

Landgren, K. (2005). The protective environment: Development support for child protection. *Human Rights Quarterly, 27*, 214–248.

Lewis, M., & Lockheed, M. (2007). Getting all girls into school. *Finance and Development: A Quarterly Magazine of the IMF, 44*(2) 63–68.

Paul, D. (1999). *Protection in practice: Field-level strategies for protecting civilians from deliberate harm (Relief & Rehabilitation Network Paper No. 30)*. London: Overseas Development Institute.

Rakotomalala, S. (Ed.). (2003). *Child protection: Manual for intervention in humanitarian crisis*. Terre des Hommes, Geneva, Switzerland.

Rugh, A. (2000). *Home-based girls' schools in Balochistan refugee villages: A strategy study*. Save the Children USA Pakistan/Afghanistan Field Office: Save the Children USA.

Save the Children USA. (2005, Spring). *Protecting children in emergencies: Escalating threats to children must be addressed (Policy Brief No. 1(1))*. Save the Children USA.

Slim, H., & Eguren, L. E. (2004). *Humanitarian protection: A guidance booklet (Pilot version)*. Active Learning Network for Accountability and Performance (ALNAP).

Slim, H., & Bonwick, A. (2005), Protection: An ALNAP Guide for Humanitarian Workers, London, Overseas Development Institute.

Stark, L., Roberts, L., Wheaton, W., Acham, A., Boothby, N., & Ager, A. (2009) Measuring violence against women amidst war and displacement in Northern Uganda using the 'Neighborhood Method'. *Journal of Epidemiology & Community Health*, Nov. 2009, doc 10.1136

Tearfund & National Society for Prevention of Cruelty to Children (NSPCC). (2003). *Setting the standard: A common approach to child protection for international NGOs*. Middlesex, UK: Tearfund & NSPCC.

United Nations Children's Fund, Adolescent Development and Participation program (UNICEF/ADAP). (2006, February). Global strategic planning consultation on adolescent programming in emergency and transition. *Report on Meeting November 28–30, 2005*. Geneva, Switzerland.

United Nations Office of Internal Oversight Services (OIOS). (2006). Independent review of monitoring and reporting (MRM) for children and armed conflict (CAAC). *Executive Summary, submitted to the United Nations Security Council on November 8, 2006*.

Wessells, M., & Strang, A. (2006). Religion: a two-edged sword. In Boothby, N., M. Wessells & A. Strang (eds) *A World Turned Upside Down: The Social Ecology of Children & War*. Kumarian Press.

Williamson, R. (2007). Children and armed conflict: Towards a policy consensus and future agenda – ten years after the Machel study. *Report based on Wilton Park Conference 840: March 19–23, 2007*. West Sussex, UK.

Chapter 6
When Rights and Needs Collide

Shweta Singh

Introduction

"The protection of children's rights, to help meet their basic needs and to expand their opportunities to reach their full potential" (UNICEF Convention of the rights of the child) – This simple mission statement from UNICEF in support of *The Rights of Children* is a crucial and important outcome of global advocacy (Smolin, 2000). The improved outreach and effectiveness of global communication, which has highlighted the differences in the way the world treats its children. The inadequacies of the developing world's ability to take care of its children appear severe even without taking into consideration the underlying differences between developed and developing societies with respect to political freedoms and equity in access to resources and opportunities.

The presumption that child rights and children's basic needs are in agreement and not mutually exclusive is implicit in the UNICEF mission statement. This paper seeks to examine the above contention in reference to the issues of child labor and child sex abuse in India. The factors that justify the examination of this contention include: (a) the developing world is undergoing a complex transformation, partly due to economic transformations and partly due to the influence of an emerging global culture, (b) children born in economically weaker families are at the lowest end of the continuum of choices due to their conditions of overwhelming poverty, inadequate state support, and poor quality of social support, (c) policies and social paradigms of child welfare (in a large section of the population) in developing countries resemble that of the developed world 100 years ago, which continues to embrace children as an economic asset, particularly when the socioeconomic position of the family is weak and marginalized, and (d) finally, *global child rights* policy does not adequately reflect the entire gamut of social realities and interpersonal and social relationships that children whose rights and needs collide are forced to negotiate every day.

S. Singh (✉)
Department of Social Work, School of Social Work, Loyola University Chicago,
820 N Michigan Avenue, Lewis Tower 1237, Chicago, IL 60611, USA
e-mail: ssingh9@luc.edu

J. Garbarino and G. Sigman (eds.), *A Child's Right to a Healthy Environment*,
The Loyola University Symposium on the Human Rights of Children 1,
DOI 10.1007/978-1-4419-6791-6_6, © Springer Science+Business Media, LLC 2010

My reflections from working as a consultant with UNICEF in Northern India on projects of child labor and child sex abuse inform this paper. I attempt to highlight the conflict in the realities and rights continuum among children in less developed countries. During the course of these projects, I was able to identify the underlying social text in phenomenon of child labor in the carpet industry and child abuse in Indian society. I examine the sociocultural conditions of India that sustain the need for child labor and limit the effectiveness of law and policy in countering child abuse.

Child Rights and India

The picture of child rights violation in India is stark (Segal, 1999). Carrying the responsibility for 19% of the world's children, the Indian State with a per capita income of 700$ (http://202.54.124.133/money/2005/oct/13income.htm) has approximately 46.6% children under 5 enrolled in schools, 47% children under 5 are malnourished. Furthermore, officially only 11 million children work in India, and 12.6% of total children work in hazardous occupations. More than 11,000 children are missing and remain untraced. The data on child abuse is even more daunting as there are more than 300,000 child prostitutes in India. "India has the world's largest number of sexually abused children, with a child below 16 years raped every 155th minute, a child below 10 every 13th hour and 1 in every 10 children sexually abused at any point of time" (Kacker, Varadan, & Kumar, 2007). Even the official count of total crimes against children has increased (from 2004 to 2005) by nearly 4%.

These numbers do not portray the disparity in the Indian society that stems from regional, religious, caste, and class difference as much for children as for adults. Further, since my work was limited to the northern state of Uttar Pradesh, it is important to get statistics relevant to Uttar Pradesh alone.

Why are Children's Rights and Needs in Collision?

Transformation of Society: On the Way to Development

According to Reddock (2002), the classification of countries into developed, developing, and underdeveloped was coined after the Second World War in recognition of the economic progress made by the Western and industrialized countries and the lack of progress in all the others. An alternative classification for societies – traditional, transitional, and modern – was coined by social scientists from political science and sociology. Reddock argues that although this alternative classification was based on culture, it did not relationally oppose the developmental classification but was a corollary of development. Both classifications assessed societies on the level of industrialization and urbanization and both presume the supremacy of Western culture (Evans & Stephans, 1988; Reddock, 2002; Robinson, 1998, 2001). Thus, modern and developed societies occupied the upper end, developing and transitional societies the middle, and traditional and underdeveloped societies were at the bottom of the social hierarchy.

One way to conceptualize this world is as Kinesodic[1] – a society whose social, political, and economic structures are in a state of flux. This movement encompasses: (a) the process of planned changes in the aspects of production and distribution in the economy, (b) the planned and unplanned political and sociological restructuring of institutions and the resultant change in inter- and intrainstitutional relationships, and (c) the overt and subtle resistance to change from micro and macroconstituents of tradition (Kapadia, 2002; Kinnaird & Momsen, 1993). Furthermore, due to their dynamic nature, it is difficult to assess the source, location, and impact of change. Therefore, it is a challenge to examine social issues, policy, and practice in these societies.

This process of transformation in society is a confounding factor in the phenomenon of child sex abuse and child labor (Kambhampati & Rajan, 2006). For instance, the North Indian state of Uttar Pradesh is experiencing migration from rural areas to urban, thus eroding social structures; changing social role expectations; and yet is able to maintain the continued dominance of certain social values, such as the sacrosanct nature of family unit. Similarly, the increasing pace of development has increased the export potential of smaller units and their products, resulting in an increasing number of manufacturing units that are sustained by low cost labor (Swaminathan, 1998). Carpet manufacturing units in North India are one of the most profitable export-oriented industries that make a significant contribution to the Indian economy. From a family owned, small, traditional enterprise, the industry has transformed into a tradesman-owned medium-scale business that thrives on child labor.

Role of Family and Family Values

The quality of children's lives is a function of their micro-level realities as much as the broader sociopolitical environment. However, in planning for children, the focus becomes the larger social systems and policies. At the microlevel, values of the family, community, and society direct and delimit the negotiations for living and surviving undertaken by each child. For instance, in India, in poverty-ridden marginalized households, the entire family, including young children share the responsibility of providing resources for the upkeep of the family. In marginal and low-income groups, children continue to be an economic asset and are not perceived as a source of emotional fulfillment or an economic liability (Basu, 1999). When we factor in the below poverty and on the poverty line living of the marginal groups, which provides the primary child labor, their investment in children is minimal while returns are considerable. Additionally, the state is not a guarantor of fundamental rights to children – of safety, food, shelter, and education. Thus, family is the primary provider and thus a primary unit of social affiliation for a child.

[1]Kinesodic in the primary dictionaries means - "Conveying motion; as; kinesodic substance; – applied esp. to the spinal cord, because it is capable of conveying both voluntary and reflex motor impulses, without itself being affected by motor impulses applied to it directly" (Retrieved February 20, 2004, available from http://dictionary.reference.com/).

The families of low-income marginalized groups are not likely to be patriarchal and patrilineal in their conception of roles and responsibilities. Marriage for women in these families is a common law practice rather than a legal one i.e., they are therefore easily reconfigured. Women in many instances are the primary providers of the family and even support mean financial. A large family is desirable as the child has a large share of responsibilities in the household, care giving, housekeeping, and economic support. In rural areas, children help on family farms and raise in-kind or cash income. Families require children to work as laborers in informal manufacturing units and households in urban and semiurban areas. For instance, a number of children who work in the carpet industry are from migrant and local impoverished families. Complexity of family relations and roles determines children well-being outcomes in poor households.

Role of State Policy and Programs

Government initiatives, comprising laws, policy, and programs range from the Central Children's Act passed in 1960 to the constituting of the National Commission for Protection of Children's Rights – acknowledges children's particular vulnerabilities, but does not have sufficient provision to prevent families and other external agents from exploiting these vulnerabilities. For instance, hazardous labor, unsafe and immoral labor, and bonded labor are offenses under the Indian constitution (Chowdhry & Beeman, 2001). However, this has not prevented children from working in industry, in prostitution, and in households. The state's limited accountability for the rights of the child; little actual mechanisms to monitor and hold violators of child rights accountable for their action; and the inability to provide alternative systems for nurture and care of children contribute to the ineffectiveness of these laws (Makman, 2002). Prevalence of child labor and child sex abuse represent the inability of the society and state to provide for the child's needs of safety, shelter, nutrition, and emotional love and support.

Transnational Activism and Formulating Charters of Rights

Child labor and child sex abuse have been at the center of transnational activist efforts. International laws have provided the impetus and push for legislation and enactment of laws that protect the right of children in a framework of rights (Chowdhry & Beeman, 2001). However, these laws also carry a generalized interpretation of rights that does not address contextual factors that hinder respect of those rights. In other words, the interpretation of rights for children is not framed in the context of local realities and needs. It is not able to articulate and take into consideration the negotiation process undertaken by children to survive within family itself.

Child Labor

I started the consultancy in 1998 February for a 4-month period. I was approached because of my background in social marketing with corporate sector (CII). My brief was simple – network and identify interested members of small industries on board with UNICEF agenda. I drafted the proposal and the plan and proceeded to modify in keeping with the communication officer's requirements from the project. One of the objectives of my consultancy work on child labor with UNICEF was primarily an effort to assess and advocate for child rights with small-scale carpet industries in the Badhoi carpet belt. My study was conducted around the same time as when the sanctions were very much in place and starting to show their mark on industry profits. The project fell within a broader framework of assessment of locally based small-scale industries willingness and likelihood of participation in UNICEF initiated projects on children's welfare. I think my identification with the entity of UNICEF itself made the carpet belt more amenable to the idea of child welfare. The power of rug mark was just then starting to hurt the business of these industries.

The participants in the study were largely not familiar with the concept of child rights. The pervasive use of child labor in rural farm work, rural and urban households, and in work situations, including – manufacturing units, shops, and retail – this is hardly surprising. Furthermore, as I found out during the second and third stage interview that most employers felt that the use of child labor was a family's only option and was a predominant household strategy to meet the economic needs of the family. "They need the money so the rest of the family can survive" or "All of them (the entire family) work in the unit and where will they (children) stay when the parents are working?" were the candid responses of the employers in the Bhadoi belt. The family's right to the child (labor) was unquestioned. This gives support to my earlier contention that family continues to be sacrosanct at all levels of Indian society. Therefore, the concept of child rights was not palatable outside the framework of family needs.

The small traders and industry people's enthusiasm for working with UNICEF was largely due to the export sanctions that were already in place to prevent the export of uncertified carpets that were suspected of using child labor. The participation of the manufacturing industries located in the carpet belt was perceived as an acknowledgment of child labor and willingness to work for child rights issues with UNICEF. In retrospect, though I am not sure if the workshop was a statement on the successful impact of the *rugmark*[1] advocacy in international markets or of my novice advocacy and social marketing skills. An activist organization initiated the Free Bonded laborers movement within the North Indian Carpet Belt from 1980s. The children were working for minimal or no money. Through intensive networking with international advocates and agencies, the political global will manifest itself in boycott of carpets produced with child labor.

The needs assessment of the industries role in child rights depicted a broad array of objectives and motivation. This was due to the differing levels of exposure the respondents had to the concept of child right and its general relevance to their own work. In my orientation meetings with the industry representative, I defined child-oriented work to mean advocacy and action on the child's behalf to give the child a better life. However, the respondents themselves were at varying levels of decision-making power within the hierarchy of organizations – CEOs, middle-level management, to the heads of HR and executive assistants. The only instances where the CEOs were willing to talk and participate in the information gathering exercise as far as I can remember was when the industry was really small, was located in the carpet belt, or when the organization was a representative of industries in some official capacity. The extent, to which organizations are willing to be involved, makes a difference to the organization's commitment to the issue of child rights.

The ongoing contribution of those already active in social welfare activities in child rights was framed in holistic terms – the building of a labor community and provision of health, education, and housing facilities. As part of the community level initiatives, children from lower socioeconomic strata benefited when the basic services were provided to all in the community and not just the workforce. The areas where I interacted with perceived scope for intervention were with the employed labor or industrial/manufacturing work force; family of worker, community surrounding the industry, and general activities or contribution toward promotion of child rights. Additionally, the industries in the study made financial contributions to social development work through welfare agencies working for the children's issues. For instance, an organization like TELCO provides community level interventions that target the entire community. While small industries were willing to work for child rights in the area of health and education.

Child Sex Abuse

Child sex abuse study was my second assignment with UNICEF. The objective was to conduct a field study to examine the situation of child sex abuse in primarily two districts in Uttar Pradesh – Lucknow and Gorakhpur. I collected the information from my discussions with communities, agencies working with children, families of victims, and in a few instances the victims themselves.

The isolation, stigma and taboo surrounding sex, self-permeating importance of family, and the insistent effort to maintain the family, absence of actual and practical help for the victim, and the only enforced punishment for abuser being social ostracism – these are the attributes of child sex abuse in this area (Lal, 2007). In the report, I describe the first reactions of the people that I met during the initial phase of the study – doctors and nursing staff from government hospitals and private nursing homes, psychiatrists in private practice, NGO staff members, lawyers, police staff, government run institutions for children, including juvenile homes, runaway homes, government offices, media representatives – as trepidation and curiosity. I identified my interaction with some of the agency personnel as comprising of "insinuating" and "sullen looks" in my report.

I found that in all the agencies (without exception) that I contacted, underlying the discomfort of open conversation on the issue was the recognition of child sex abuse. Thus, child sex abuse was prevalent in situations of working children, children from different social classes, in rural and urban areas, and in family and institutional settings. In addition, in community settings, the sexual abuse was largely associated with just girls. The only institution that felt comfortable talking about the issue was medical settings and its professionals. The identified cases were from regular checkups of children, legal abortions by young girls, during the treatment of injuries and diseases, and during postmortems on children. However, even here, when the doctors are in private practice and working with middle or upper middle class, there is less readiness to reporting the abuse, as compared to preserving family honor and family relations. There was also a bias across institutions in perceiving child sex abuse as a phenomenon of the slums. In addition, the agency contacts reported differing levels of incidence during the course of their professional life.

The specific strategies for intervention postincidence of child abuse are casework with children, rebuilding and reorienting the support system of both family and community, to provide practical help for the victims of child abuse. The strategies to identify and prevent child sex abuse include, educating children and primary caregivers about the high incidence rate and removing the stigma surrounding child sex abuse. To provide community level education on identification and intervention in perceived cases of abuse, i.e., change the role of community as a spectator to that of intervener. Additional interventions were the identification of institutions such as the school that could support the outreach to children outside of family for raising awareness of abuse.

I found out that the family along with community and kin undertook varying roles in child sex abuse – the prime one was that of an observer – a silent spectator who is aware of what is going on but is not willing or able to intervene. The reputation of child and family both seem to be factors in the decision to control the incidence of abuse but do not extend to the abuser being taken to law or the child to counseling, etc. The only agency with an active role of investigation is the police. They are invested with the responsibility to identify the nature of abuse, the abuser, family, and community information. The responsibility for assessment of abuse rests with legal and medical practitioners. However, intervention appeared to be a wholly individual level of motivation by a constable, a community member, or by a doctor. For instance, a doctor noted his pointed directive to uninvolved family members about the sex abuse of the child. A police constable reported his intervention to prevent a working child's sexual abuse at a roadside food-vending stall.

Juvenile homes for delinquents and for runaways and abandoned children comprised inmates with number of reported sexual crimes in intake interviews and medical examinations. The sad part was that during my visit to a couple of these institutions, I found girls were roaming around in semiclothed status and men, who were legally prohibited from entering the premises, were freely entering and leaving it. The warden's assurance of girls' safety from sex abuse within the premise sounded as false as her disbelief of the stories of rape and abuse of its residents. A report that I examined of two of the exresidents is an illustration. These two girls of 13 and 16 years ran away from home because of the threat of sex abuse (which they do not express in those very words) by the older married brother. "… from the past 5 to 6 years he tries to use us in a bad way and looks at us in front of my father, mother, and *bhabi*." According to the report filed by the girls, the parents encouraged the two girls to run away. There inability to prevent abuse might have been the motivating factor. The girls thought, "... life would be safer on the streets than at home." The girls stated their desire to be married off, but finally gave up on their parents being able to do so. The girls were picked up from their run away spot, as they were not able to find a place to sleep in and eventually stayed in the lock up for 2 days before being turned over to government girls' institution. However, the girls were returned to their homes within a month under advice from the superintendent of the institution. The superintendent in her conversation told me her disbelief about the girls' story and expressed her sorrow at the parents' bad luck in having such children.

The government agencies responsible for policy formulation, on the other hand, were not willing to share any perspective on child sex abuse. Their work was focused on vocational training and education and child sex abuse was apparently beyond the parameters of their job. A decade ago, very few lawyers, or legal practice firms were involved in the issue. Before the advent of Child line[1] in North India, even the voluntary sector stayed away from challenging and controversial issues. While the generalized understanding of the issue was apparent, there was no operational level specialized knowledge in the few NGOs that were part of the study, i.e., there was definitely no activist role perceived by the NGOs. Media coverage continues to comprise of frequent stories of minor rapes and accused being a family member. There are very few follow-up stories and hardly any social commentary in these stories. The media reports seem to lack the child rights perspective because of the coverage of stories of child sex abuse are limited to crime snippets. Mainstream English language newspapers and magazines very sporadically present the story from human rights perspectives. On a day-to-day basis, these stories were avoided "so as not to offend middle class morality over a cup of early morning tea."

The sexual abuse occurred both in the house and outside it, even though the incidence of abuse outside the house was easier to identify. In addition, the perpetrators were immediate family members, acquaintances, and strangers. There were a couple of instances of a male child being sexually abused. Sex abuse inside the family occurred over a period and was reported by the child to the mother. The child being victimized was alone over extended period with abuser, is quiet, and in some cases with a mental disability and too young to recognize sexual abuse.

In quite a few instances, the mothers were aware of the abuse but were not able to stop it. The extent of abuse perpetrated was the perpetrators perception of how much he could get away with. The potential of revictimization was present in the case of most victims. The abused child was from different family structures, including joint, single parent (mother or father), street child, child worker, and an abandoned child. The child is taught to ignore, avoid, and hide the abuse by family members, community norms, and social organizations. Family response in a number of cases is evident in the instructions to the child on coping. However, the response varies from shock, and protest to silent spectator roles. The family's long-term needs, safety, shelter, and food for everyone (including siblings) in some instances, appeared to overtake the need to protect the child.

Family and community seemed to be aware of the abuse from the start to the end. The most apparent thing in child sex abuse is that none of the involved parties wants to stand up and be seen as activists protesting against it (see Fig. 6.1).

Mother's responses to reports of abuse depict the limitations brought about by a lack of control over basic resources and the traditionalism that is in fear of men and society. Action by mothers was limited to a few cases, where the parent had lodged formal complaint of the sexual abuse or when the child was missing (see Fig. 6.2).

The reasons for the abuse ranged from easy access to a child, ineffective role of mother and family in prevention, social disorganization due to migration, disrupted sexual relations between mother and father, alcohol abuse by perpetrator, isolation in the child's company, poor family, child working, community tolerance, and passivity toward the issue. The immediate circumstances of the abuse varied. One factor was perpetrator being in the child's company alone for an extended period. Physical isolation of child in case of stranger abuse was another factor. The abuser may be a member of the immediate family such as father, uncles brother, relatives, or a servant, *rickshaw wallahs*[1], teacher, neighbor, or acquaintance. A third category was

Matrix of Involvement		
Agency	**Entry ⇨**	**Exit ⇦**
Family	*Actual abuse*	*Virtually from the beginning*
Community, Neighborhood	*Repeat incidence*	*Present as observers all the while*
Police	*Escape, complaint, on the street*	*When the legal procedure is initiated*
Homes	*Police intervention, hospitals, courts*	*With court rulings for release/til reaching an adult age*
NGO	*Community based intervention, in the field*	*Virtually from the beginning*
Doctors	*Medico-legal case, physical, psychological treatment*	*With discharge of patient*
Lawyer/court	*Cases dealing with abandoned, abused, runaway children*	*Legal settlement of child at a home/family/others*
Media	*Case worth coverage*	*Diminishing news value*

Fig. 6.1 Matrix of involvement

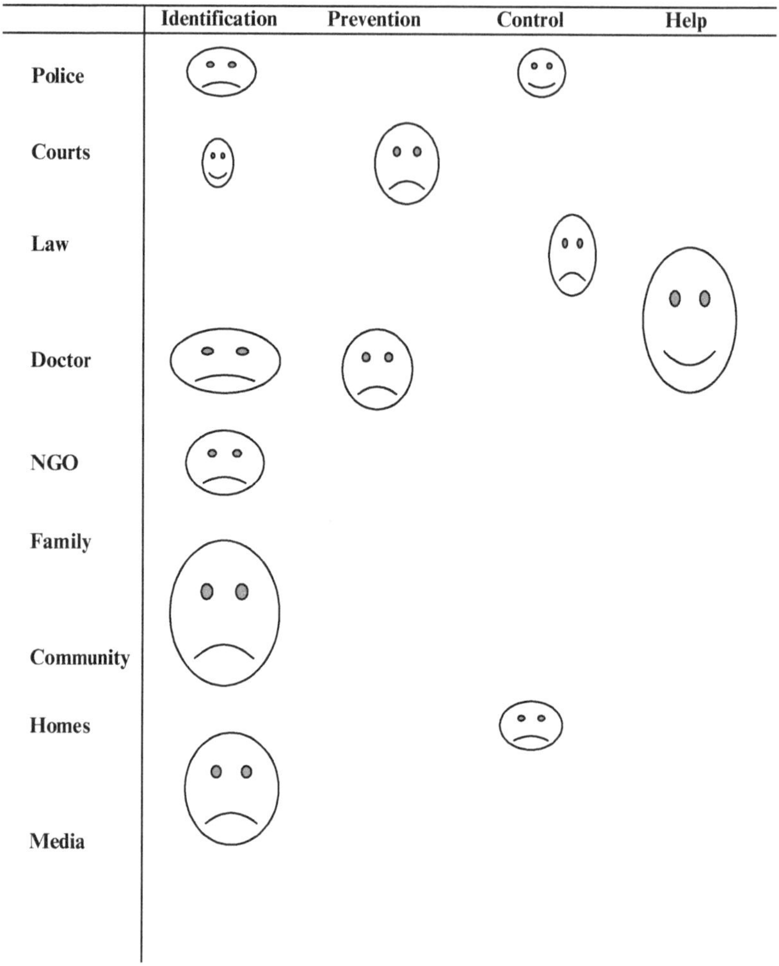

Fig. 6.2 Exit and entry into child abuse

abusers including strangers and employers. Abusers' age ranged from 15 to 50 years. Within family, the abuser has a powerful position as a provider or senior.

My recommendations for working with victims of child sex abuse focused on the prevention of revictimization and support for coping. A key aspect in this is working with the community or groups not limited to immediate family. Even the second aspect of my recommendations focused on the family – to create awareness of the crime of child sex abuse within family situations and an acceptance within families to discuss the rights of the child. My recommendations also included formulating strategies keeping the client group in mind, i.e., communities living in low-income slums vs. communities within rural areas. As these groups of people had varying community level interests and conflicts and social environments (norms). My recommendations to work with the local organizations included realization of the role played by doctors and police in identification and prevention of child sex abuse.

Family as the Center of Conflict Between Rights and Needs

While the state refuses to be an active substitute parent, the abusive and neglectful family continues to be a powerful part of the child's life. The abuse victims report the abuse or the threat of abuse to parents, primarily mothers. These reports were disregarded or no active confrontation followed in most instances. In many instances, the interaction between the abuser and the victim continues even after the abuse has been stopped or found. A child running away from home to avoid the sex abuse is a common threat in many cases in my study. In another instance, the brother repeatedly tries to abuse the sister, as he feels entitled to her in the same way his father treats his step wife. The victims of abuse are married right after the experience of abuse at ages varying from 8 to 15 years. In most instances, the husband's family abandons or harasses the girl upon finding out about the abuse.

This role of family as a site of abuse and source of support is important for conceptualizing children's lives within families, community, society, and state. The family as a unit varies in different milieus, and it is necessary to identify the structural handicaps that children face at institutional and individual levels. The structure and function of families exemplifies the need for reframing child rights to fit in the localized contexts of needs. Furthermore, there is a need to prioritize rights by specific population of children, even though – safety – shelter – and nutrition must take precedence. This will require the identification of the most marginalized and affected population groups and the proportion of children within them. In addition, the stakeholders within the localized systems must be identified – such as the AICMA, and their activities for child welfare monitored. This might be even more effective in bringing about a fulfillment of child needs than sanctions for violating them.

The route to advocacy for child rights needs to grasp the situations in which survival of the child depends upon the continuance of the same structures of exploitation that are targeted by advocacy, such as employment in carpet industry. The first stop and the primary advocacy must target the family both in context of child sex abuse and child labor. Family is the primary unit not only of nurture that a child enjoys, but is also a center for exploitation for the child. The second level of advocacy must be with the state and its negligence of its role of being a substitute for family. The child in most of the developing world does not have any form of reliable state support that will be able to meet the bare minimum of caring and nurture requirements for a child. This is apparent from the Nithari killings of children over a period of 5 years (Krishnan, Skandan, & Kochher, 2007). The presence of street children who are struggling to survive on their own also underlines this fact (Riggio, 2002). Children being conscience of their own rights is desirable, particularly in countries like the USA; a state steered system that holds violators of children's rights largely accountable. On the contrary, awareness of child rights by children in India can yield very little unless there is a system that can hold violators of those rights accountable. As a reflection, when women's rights have taken so long and are far from being universally realized, how much power can a child carry to bring about the realization of her rights?

Finally, it has to be the collective social conscience that must push for the rights of the child. The burgeoning middle class continues to employ children as household help and caregivers of other children. This is possible because the employer is able to dissociate childhood as a factor in the child whose family is marginalized. Current legislation has made minimum wages, health insurance, and contract-like situations viable for children in this kind of employment. However, a simple drafting of legislation will not result in recognition and enforcement of social will to recognize the presence and vulnerability of childhood both within one's own family and in those of poor and marginalized others.

References

Basu, K. (1999). Child labor: Cause, consequence, and cure, with remarks on international labor standards. *Journal of Economic Literature, 37*, 1083–1119.

Chowdhry, G., & Beeman, M. (2001). Challenging child labor: Transnational activism and India's carpet industry. *Annals of the American Academy of Political and Social Science, 575*, 158–175.

Evans, P., & Stephans, J. D. (1988). Studying development since the sixties – the emergence of a new comparative political-economy. *Theory and Society, 17*, 713–745.

Kacker, L., Varadan, S., & Kumar, P. (2007). *Study on child abuse: India 2007*. Ministry of Women and Child Development, Government of India. Retrieved from http://www.violencestudy.org/IMG/pdf/childabuseIndia2007.pdf

Kambhampati, U. S., & Rajan, R. (2006). Economic growth: A panacea for child labor? *World Development, 34*, 426–445.

Kapadia, K. (2002). Translocal modernities and transformations. In K. Kapadia (Ed.), *The violence of development: The politics of identity, gender, and social inequality in India* (pp. 142–179). New Delhi: Kali for women.

Kinnaird, V., & Momsen, J. (1993). *Different places, different voices: Gender and development in Africa, Asia, and Latin America*. New York: Routledge.

Krishnan, M., Skandan, K., & Kochher, J. S. (2007). *Report of the committee investigating into allegations of large scale sexual abuse, rape and murder of children in Nithari village of NOIDA (UP)*. Ministry of Women and Child Development, Government of India. Retrieved from http://wcd.nic.in/nitharireport.pdf

Lal, N. (2007). *Hidden darkness: Child sexual abuse in India*. Retrieved from http://www.asiasentinel.com/index.php?option=com_content&task=view&id=476&Itemid=34

Makman, L. H. (2002). Child crusaders: The literature of global childhood. *The Lion and the Unicorn, 26*, 287–304.

Reddock, R. (2002). Why gender? Why development? In P. C. J. Parpart & V. U. Barritreau (Eds.), *Theoretical perspectives on gender and development* (pp. 23–50). Ottawa, ON: International Development Research Center.

Riggio, E. (2002). Child friendly cities: Good governance in the best interests of the child. *Environment and Urbanization, 14*, 45–58.

Robinson, W. I. (1998). Beyond nation-state paradigms: Globalization, sociology, and the challenge of transnational studies. *Sociological Forum, 13*, 561–594.

Robinson, W. I. (2001). Transnational processes, development studies and changing social hierarchies in the world system: A Central American case study. *Third World Quarterly, 22*, 529–563.

Segal, U. A. (1999). Children are abused in Eastern countries: A look at India. *International Social Work, 42*, 39–52.

Smolin, D. M. (2000). Strategic choices in the international campaign against child labor. *Human Rights Quarterly, 22*, 942–987.
Swaminathan, M. (1998). Economic growth and the persistence of child labor: Evidence from an Indian city. *World Development, 26*, 1513–1528.
UNICEF. *Convention on the rights of the child*. Retrieved from http://www.unicef.org/crc/

Part III
Human Rights as a Tool for Social Change

Chapter 7
The UN Convention on the Rights of the Child: An Instrument for Creating a Healthy Environment for the Child

Jaap E. Doek

Introduction

The United Nations (UN) Convention on the Rights of the Child (CRC) was drafted between 1980 and 1989 in a rather political and complicated process with an open-ended working group of the then UN Commission on Human Rights (Doek, Cantwell, & Detrick, 1992; LeBlanc 1995; Legislative History 2007). The text of the CRC as proposed was unanimously adopted by the General Assembly of the UN on 20 November 1989 (United Nations Convention on the Rights of the Child, 1989). It is the most universally ratified human rights treaty in the history of the UN. By their ratification, 193 states have committed themselves to respect for and a progressive full realization and implementation of the rights of the child as enshrined in the CRC.

Only two states have not ratified the CRC: Somalia, due to the fact that it does not have an internationally recognized government and USA for lack of political will. But USA did ratify the two Optional Protocols to the CRC on the Involvement of Children in Armed Conflict and on the Sale of Children, Child Prostitution, and Child Pornography.[1] There is reason to believe that the new administration will work toward ratification since there are no obstacles that cannot be addressed in reservations if they pose serious legal problems (Todres, Wojcik, & Revaz, 2006).

---

[1] It goes beyond the scope of this article to present the arguments, pros and cons about the ratification of the CRC by USA; see in this regard, e.g., Emory International Law Review, Volume 20, Spring 2006, Number 1 with various contributions to Special Spring 2006 Symposium on; What's wrong with rights for children. But USA did submit its initial reports on the implementation of the Optional Protocols to the CRC (UN Doc. CRC/C.OPAC/USA/1, 22 June 2007 and CRC/C/OPSC/USA/1, 16 July 2007). They were discussed with the UN Committee on the Rights of the Child on May 22, 2008, in Geneva, resulting in Concluding Observations with recommendations for further actions (UN Doc. CRC/OPAC/USA/CO/1, 25 June 2008 and UN Doc. CRC/C/OPSC/USA/CO/1, 25 June 2008).

J.E. Doek (✉)
UN Committee on the Rights of the Child, Amsterdam, The Netherlands
e-mail: JaapEDoek@cs.com

J. Garbarino and G. Sigman (eds.), *A Child's Right to a Healthy Environment*,
The Loyola University Symposium on the Human Rights of Children 1,
DOI 10.1007/978-1-4419-6791-6_7, © Springer Science+Business Media, LLC 2010

A Committee on the Rights of the Child (hereafter: the CRC Committee) has been established in accordance with art. 43 of the CRC. This committee is a body of 18 experts elected by representatives of the States Parties to the CRC in charge of monitoring the implementation of the CRC by the States Parties (Gras, 2001). This is done on the basis of reports regularly submitted by States to the CRC Committee and of reports submitted by UN agencies and NGOs. In addition, the CRC Committee issues so-called General Comments, documents in which the Committee provides States Parties and all others interested in the CRC with guidance on the interpretation and implementation of the CRC (Belser, Hanson, & Hert, 2009). I will come back to the work of the CRC Committee in the second part of this chapter. But first I shall discuss the importance of the CRC for the creation of a healthy environment for the child.

The CRC and the Right of the Child to a Healthy Environment

The CRC is not only the most ratified but also the most comprehensive human rights treaty. It covers and elaborates not only the civil and political rights of the child, but also her/his economic, social, and cultural rights. The CRC is often and in the first place associated with the protection of the child. And indeed, the CRC contains quite a number of provisions requiring States Parties to take effective legislative, social, and other measures to protect the child against all forms of physical and mental violence while in the care of parents or other caregivers (art. 19); against all forms of commercial and/or sexual abuse and exploitation, trafficking, sale, and other forms of exploitation (art. 32–36); against torture, and inhuman and degrading treatment (art. 37); and the recruitment and use in armed conflict (art. 38 and the Optional Protocol on the involvement of children in armed conflict).

These provisions are important for the creation of a healthy environment, given the fact that they also call for prevention. But the CRC presents the child not only as an object of protection, a traditional approach in other human rights treaties; see for instance art. 24 ICCPR: "Every child shall have .... the right to such protection measures as are required by his status as a minor, on the part of his family, society, and the State," and a similar provision in art. 10(3) ICECSR.[2]

The key importance of the CRC is the recognition of the child as a subject of rights, rights holder with evolving capacities to exercise her/his rights. A recognition reflected, e.g., art. 12 requires States Parties to assure to the child the right to express her/his views in all matters affecting the child, and that these views are given due weight in accordance with her/his age and maturity (see for detailed interpretation of this key provision United Nations General Comment No. 12 (2009)).

[2] I will limit myself to the role of parents, but it should be noted that art. 5 also mentions "the members of the extended family or community as provided for by local customs, legal guardians or other persons legally responsible for the child"; in other words, guidance and directions to the child in her/his exercise of rights could and should also be provided by others

The CRC does not only see the child as recipient of protection, but also as an active participant not only in judicial and administrative proceedings (see art. 12(2) and art. 9(2) CRC), but also in all matters affecting the child. Another and equally important characteristic of the CRC is that the child is not left to his evolving capacities as a rights holder. The child is seen as member of her/his family and it is fundamental for the full harmonious development of her or his personality that the child grows up in a family environment (Preamble, par. 6 CRC). In this regard, it should be noted that the school also plays an important role because art. 29 CRC requires that the education of the child shall be directed to, among others, the development of the child's personality, talents, and mental and physical abilities to their full potential; see for more information United Nations General Comment No. 1 (2001). Within this family environment, the parents have the primary and common responsibility for the upbringing and development of the child as explicitly recognized in art. 18 CRC. The best interests of the child shall be the basic concern of parents. This responsibility encompasses, according to the CRC, the rights and duties of parents to provide, in a manner consistent with the evolving capacities of the child, appropriate direction and guidance in the exercise by the child of the rights recognized in the CRC (art. 5); and the responsibility to secure, within their abilities and financial capacities, the conditions of living necessary for the development of the child (art. 27(2)CRC).

But this recognition of the rights and duties of parents does not mean that they are the only ones responsible for the creation of a healthy environment for their child.

Both articles 18 and 27 of CRC explicitly provide for responsibilities of the State in general and in rather specific terms. Art. 18(2) contains a provision that can be considered as a key element of the State's responsibility, and is often not given the attention it deserves:

> States Parties shall render appropriate assistance to the parents in the performance of their child-rearing responsibility and not only for e.g. parents who are in need of assistance because of their shortcomings or difficulties but for all parents and with a very specific and important goal: to promote and guarantee (the implementation of) the rights enshrined in the CRC.

In addition to this support and in order to actually provide it, the State shall ensure the development of institutions, facilities, and services for the care of children. Article 27 containing the right of the child to an adequate standard of living expects States Parties to take appropriate measures (in accordance with national conditions and within their means) to assist parents to implement this right which shall include to provide, in case of need, material assistance and support programs particularly with regard to nutrition, clothing, and housing.

Of course, States Parties do have many more obligations under the CRC. For instance, the obligation to ensure – when appropriate in a progressive manner – the respect for and implementation of the child's right to, e.g., freedom of expression and freedom of association, the right to the highest attainable standard of health and to education. These and other obligations of the State have to be translated into measures that should contribute to the creation of a healthy environment for the child, while the State should fully respect and take into account the responsibilities of the parent(s) and the child as a rights holder with evolving capacities to exercise her/his right. One could say that the implementation of children's rights takes place in a triangle of the child, the parent, and the State.

> What do all these rather abstract provisions mean in more concrete terms? The CRC Committee has elaborated these (and other) provisions of the CRC in very concrete recommendations in its General Comments. By way of example I will focus on Early Childhood and on Adolescents, topics which also have been addressed in United Nations General Comment No. 7 (2006) and United Nations General Comment No. 4 (2003) respectively.

Early Childhood

The CRC Committee emphasizes that article 12 applies also to the (very) young children. Research and observations show that these children are acutely sensitive to their surroundings, acquire understanding of the people, places, and routines in their lives very rapidly, make choices and communicate their feelings and ideas and wishes long before they are able to communicate through the conventions of spoken and written language. Therefore, States Parties should take all appropriate measures to ensure that the concept of the child as a rights holder with freedom to express views and the right to be consulted is implemented from the earliest stage in ways appropriate to the child's capacities, best interests, and rights to protection from harmful experiences. In this regard, the State should promote active involvement of parents in the creation of opportunities for young children to exercise their rights progressively within their every day activity in all relevant settings (United Nations General Comment No. 7, 2006, par. 14).

Assistance to Parents

The CRC Committee acknowledges that the realization of children's rights during early childhood (a period of most extensive and intensive parental responsibility related to all children's rights covered by the CRC) to a large degree depends on the well-being and resources available to parents. Therefore, the Committee recommends States Parties to develop an integrated policy that would include assistance and, where necessary, interventions that impact indirectly on parent's ability to promote the best interests of the child (e.g., taxation and benefits, adequate housing, and working hours) as well as those that have more immediate consequences (e.g., prenatal health services, home visitors, and parent education and counseling; United Nations General Comment No. 7 (2006), par. 20). In that regard, special attention must be paid to the most vulnerable groups of young children, e.g., girls, children living in poverty, children with disabilities, orphans, children infected with/affected by HIV/AIDS, and children belonging to minorities.

Parent–Child-State

The CRC Committee has repeatedly underscored the importance of early childhood education (an importance confirmed by research). In the light of responsibility of the parent, the right of the child to a full and harmonious development, and the obligation of the State, the Committee makes, e.g., the following recommendations (United Nations General Comment No. 7 (2006), par. 29):

> States Parties in providing the assistance to parents as required in art. 18(2) should take all appropriate measures to enhance parent's understanding of their role in their children's early education, encourage child-rearing practices which are child-centred, encourage respect for the child's dignity and provide opportunities for developing understanding, self-esteem and self-confidence;
>
> States Parties should at all time aim to provide programmes (for early childhood development) that complement the parents' role and are developed as much as possible in partnership with parents (….) in developing the child's personality, talents and mental and physical abilities to their fullest potential.

Adolescents

After a brief description of adolescence as a period characterized among others by rapid physical, cognitive, and social changes, including sexual and reproductive maturation with various challenges in the transition to adulthood, the CRC Committee expresses (United Nations General Comment No. 4, 2003) its concern that States in implementing their obligations under the CRC have not given sufficient attention to the specific concerns and needs of adolescents as rights holders.

In United Nations General Comment No. 4 (2003), the Committee pays particular attention to the creation of a safe and supportive environment for adolescents. It emphasizes the role of parents, public authorities, and others working with or for children to create, with a view to provide adolescents with a meaningful opportunity to express their views freely in all matters affecting them (art. 12 CRC), an environment based on trust, information-sharing, the capacity to listen, and sound guidance that is conducive for the equal participation of adolescents including in decision-making processes (United Nations General Comment No. 4 (2003), par. 4).

In terms of parental assistance, the CRC Committee provides States Parties with various recommendations, e.g., to provide adequate information and support to parents to facilitate the development of a relationship of trust and confidence, in which issues regarding, for example, sexuality and sexual behavior, and risky life-styles can be openly discussed, and acceptable solutions can be found that respect the adolescent's rights and their evolving capacities to exercise them (United Nations General Comment No. 4 (2003), par. 12); and to give special attention, guidance, and support to adolescents and parents whose traditions and norms may differ from those in the society where they live.

The creation of a safe and healthy environment requires that States Parties do take effective measures, including the establishment of counseling and support services (United Nations General Comment No. 4 (2003), par. 18):

> To prevent and address problems relatively common among adolescents such as mental disorders, psychosocial illness (e.g. eating disorders, self-destructive behaviour, depression) and suicide, but also various forms of violence in and outside schools and in institutions;
>
> To prevent and eliminate harmful traditional practices that threaten the healthy development and life of adolescents such as early marriage, female genital mutilation and honour killings.

With a view to the adolescents' evolving capacities to exercise their rights, the Committee is of the opinion that States should ensure that all adolescents are provided with and have access to adequate information essential for their health and development and for their ability to participate meaningfully in society. In that regard (and with reference to art. 3, 17 and 24 CRC), adolescents should be provided with access to sexual and reproductive health information, including on family planning and contraceptives, the dangers of early pregnancies, the prevention of HIV/AIDS, and the prevention and treatment of sexually transmitted infections (STI; United Nations General Comment No. 4 (2003), par. 28).

Finally, States Parties should in this regard

> Enact laws or regulations to ensure that confidential advice concerning treatment is provided to adolescents so that they can give their informed consent. Such laws or regulations should stipulate an age for this process, or refer to the evolving capacities of the child;
>
> To provide training for health personnel on the rights of adolescents to privacy and confidentiality, to be informed about planned treatment (United Nations General Comment No. 4 (2003), par. 33).

After this (incomplete) picture of the interpretation of provisions of the CRC, which can provide the child with a healthy environment, the key question remains: Are they implemented and how?

The Implementation of the CRC

In a report of the UN Secretary General presented to the General Assembly of the UN in 2007 (UN Doc. A/62/259, 15 August 2007), one can find a global picture of progress made in the realization of the rights of the child and more specifically in the light of the International Plan of Action "A World Fit for Children" adopted at a Special Session of the General Assembly of the UN in May 2002 (UN Doc. A/S-27/19 Rev. 1.). This report focuses almost exclusively on developments in the areas of health, education, violence, and HIV/AIDS.

Progress has been, e.g., in reduction of infant mortality and increase of immunization (measles death reduced with 60%), but routine immunization still fails to reach 27 million children. Substantial progress has been made in providing iodized salt to households but each year, 38 million newborns in the developing world are unprotected from lifelong consequences of brain damage associated with iodine deficiency. But adolescent health remains a challenge in several respects and the report does not provide any information on progress made in this regard. More and other information are provided with the same mixed picture of (some) progress and remaining challenges (Doek, 2007b) in education, in the prevention of violence against children, and exploitation of children (Pinheiro, 2006). But I like to focus on the instruments and processes for an effective implementation of the CRC at the national level, with attention for the monitoring role of the CRC Committee.

Implementation of the CRC at the National Level

By ratifying the CRC, the State – that is, its government – assumed (voluntarily) the legal obligation to undertake all appropriate legislative, administrative, and other measures for the implementation of the rights enshrined in the CRC (art. 4). Given the rich content of the CRC meeting that obligation requires a lot of different actions to be carried out under the responsibility of different ministries or departments.

Given the complexity of the CRC including, e.g., the interdependence of many of the rights it contains, the implementation can easily become fragmented and inconsistent.

With a view to establish a comprehensive policy at the national level, the CRC Committee has recommended the State Parties to undertake General Measures of implementation (see United Nations General Comment No. 5, 2003). This set of General Measures is meant to create an infrastructure for the implementation of the CRC. These measures are legislation, coordination, budget allocation, data collection, ongoing awareness raising actions and training of professionals, active involvement of NGOs, and an independent monitoring body such as a children's ombudsperson. The development and implementation of these measures must be guided by the so-called General Principles of the CRC: non-discrimination (art. 2); best interest of the child (art. 3); the right to life, survival, and development (art. 6); and the right of the child to express views and to participate (art. 12; Doek, 2007a).

To make this rather general approach more concrete and by means of an example: in order to create a healthy environment for the (very) young child, the government has to enact adequate legal provisions and regulation not only for the protection, but also for the healthy development of this child. In addition, various social measures must be taken, e.g., to provide parents with support and counseling where necessary. As I said, the Committee has given detailed recommendations in this regard (GC. No 7, 2005). All these measures do require effective coordination and cooperation between various ministries (Justice, Health, Education, and Social Affairs) and the allocation of sufficient budgets. In order to assess the impact of these measures, collection of relevant data is necessary.

Although it is fair to say that most States Parties to the CRC have taken a variety of measures for its implementation, particularly in the area of legislation, and also in terms of developing specific programs, e.g., on (prevention of) violence against children, sexual exploitation, trafficking, child labor, and juvenile justice, the reality on the ground shows that the implementation of all these measures is often either insufficient or even completely lacking (African Report, 2008).

So the key question is, what can/should be done to actually implement the CRC provisions and create a healthy environment for the child? First, and to avoid misunderstandings, the State is the primarily responsible for taking all necessary actions for the realization of the child's right to a healthy environment. The CRC committee has – as said and illustrated before – provided the States Parties with rather specific guidance and recommendations on the measures they should take. At the same time, it is the role of the parliament to control the government in its performances in the field of children's rights and to put pressure on the government if it fails to meet its obligations under the CRC. But keep in mind that States cannot meet these obligations overnight, and that the role of parliament can be among others to urge the government to develop and implement a national comprehensive plan for a progressive implementation of the CRC (there is a manual for parliamentarians with guidance for their role in implementing the CRC). But experiences have shown that it is not enough to rely on the (political) willingness of a government and/or members of parliament to actually provide/allocate the necessary financial and other resources for the implementation of the CRC.

It is crucial that the civil society is as much as possible involved in the (promotion of the) implementation of the CRC, in particular via NGOs, advocacy groups, and professional organizations. The history so far has shown that there are in almost all States, parties to the CRC NGOs active in the field of children's rights. It can be said that the CRC, compared to other human rights treaties, has – from a global perspective – the largest active constituency. These NGOs have proven that they can, through all kinds of actions, campaigns, and targeted lobbying, contribute in a significant manner to respect for and implementation of the rights of the child at the national level.

The other very important factor in the promotion of children's rights is UNICEF, particularly in over 150 developing countries in which it has country offices. They integrate as much as possible the implementation of the CRC into their country programs and use the specific provisions to support, e.g., programs to prevent and eliminate violence in schools and to provide primary health care with special attention for marginalized and vulnerable groups of children (art. 2 CRC, non-discrimination).

Finally, it is important that every country establishes an independent body for monitoring the implementation of the CRC, such as a children's ombudsperson or commissioner, or a section in an existing National Human Rights Institution. Because such a body can, as experiences have shown, in quite a number of countries, play the role of advocate for and voice of children, and can as a watchdog keep the government on its toes. In some countries, these bodies also have the power to receive and investigate individual complaints of children, a power which can not only provide the individual child with remedies, but can also contribute to a better understanding of the meaning of the rights of the child in the daily reality (United Nations General Comment No. 2, 2002).

In short, there are different mechanisms available to contribute to the de facto ensuring of respect for and implementation of the rights of the child at the national level. Maximum energy and money should be invested in an effective functioning of these mechanisms.

Monitoring of the Implementation of the CRC at the International Level

The CRC does, like the other human treaties, provide for a mechanism for international monitoring of the States Parties performance in meeting the obligations under the CRC. This international accountability is important not only as an addition to national accountability, but also as a motor for national efforts to improve implementation of the CRC.

The CRC Committee (see intro) has been established for the purpose of examining the progress made by States Parties in achieving the realization of their obligations under the CRC. States are obliged to regularly submit periodic reports to this committee, and other information which form the basis for an examination of the progress made and the remaining challenges in a dialog between the Committee and a delegation of the State Party (art. 42 & 44). The results of this dialog/examination are presented in the so-called Concluding Observations containing concerns and specific recommendations of the CRC Committee to the government of the State concerned. These recommendations should be and in fact are used in many countries as ammunition for NGOs, UN agencies, and others for furthering the implementation of the CRC.

At the international level, the CRC committee does not have the power to investigate individual complaints, a power all other human rights treaty bodies have. Efforts are underway to establish this power, but it may take many years to have concrete results.

But in some regions, there are more (Inter American and European Courts) or less (African Court for Human Rights) effective courts where individual complaints can be filed. They are not especially meant for children, but they pay increasing attention to the rights of children as enshrined in the CRC. Their role in guaranteeing the implementation of children's rights may become more and more important in the years to come.

In conclusion, the CRC contains quite a number of substantive provisions meant to create and support a healthy environment for children, and there is a variety of instruments available at the national and the international level to make sure that these provisions are more than promises on paper.

References

African Report. (2008). *The African report on child wellbeing 2008: How child-friendly are African Governments?* Addis Ababa: The African Child Policy Forum.

Belser, E. M., Hanson, K., & Hirt, A. (2009). *Sourcebook on International children's rights.* Berne/Brussels: Stampfli/Bruylant.

Doek, J. (2007a). The CRC general principles. In J. Zermatten (Ed.), *18 Candles, the convention on the rights of the child reaches majority* (pp. 31–42). Sion, Switzerland: Swiss Agency for Development and Cooperation.

Doek, J. E. (2007b). The eighteenth birthday of the convention on the rights of the child: Achievements and challenges. *Journal of Law Reform, 41*, 61–75.

Doek, J., Cantwell, N., & Detrick, S. (1992). *The United Nations convention on the rights of the child. A guide to the travaux preparatoires.* Dordrecht: Martinus Nijhoff.

Gras, J. (2001). *Monitoring the convention on the rights of the child.* Helsinki: The Erik Castren Institute of International Law and Human Rights. Research Reports 8/2001.

LeBlanc, L. J. (1995). *The convention on the rights of the child: United Nations lawmaking on human rights.* Lincoln and London: University of Nebraska Press.

Legislative History. (2007). *Legislative history of the convention on the rights of the child: Volume I and II.* New York: United Nations Office of the High Commissioner on Human Rights.

Pinheiro, P. S. (2006). *World report on violence against children.* Geneva: United Nations. Retrieved from http://www.unicef.org/violencestudy/Cover%20World%20Report%20on%20Violence%20against%20Children.pdf

Todres, J., Wojcik, M. E., & Revaz, C. R. (2006). *The UN convention on the rights of the child. An analysis of treaty provisions and implications of U.S. ratification.* Ardsley, NY: Transnational Publishers.

United Nations Convention on the Rights of the Child (1989). *United Nations General Assembly Document A/RES/44/25.* Retrieved from http://www.cirp.org

United Nations General Comment No. 1 (2001). *The aims of education* (UN Doc. CRC/GC/2001/1. 17 April 2001).

United Nations General Comment No. 12 (2009). *The right of the child to be heard* (UN Doc. CRC/C/GC/12, 1 July 2009, Advance unedited version).

United Nations General Comment No. 2 (2002). *The role of independent national human rights institutions in the promotion and protection of the rights of the child* (UN Doc. CRC/GC/2002/2, 15 November 2002).

United Nations General Comment No. 4 (2003). *Adolescent health and development in the context of the Convention on the Rights of the Child* (UN Doc. CRC/GC/2003/4, 1 July 2003).

United Nations General Comment No. 5 (2003). *General measures of implementation of the convention on the rights of the child* (UN Doc. CRC/GC/2003/5, 27 November 2003).

United Nations General Comment No. 7 (2006). *Implementing child rights in early childhood* (UN Doc. CRC/C/GC/7/Rev.1, 20 September 2006).

Chapter 8
The Right to a Family Environment for Children of Prisoners

Robin Kimbrough-Melton

As the "natural environment for the growth and well-being" of children (Convention on the Rights of the Child, 1989, preamble), the family has long enjoyed special protection within international human rights law (e.g. International Covenant on Civil and Political Rights, 1976, art. 23 & 24; International Covenant on Economic, Social, and Cultural Rights, 1976, art. 10; Universal Declaration of Human Rights, 1948). However, the concept of the *family environment* as the optimal setting for the development of children first appears in the Convention on the Rights of the Child (1989). The Convention recognizes that the "child ....should grow up in a family environment, in an atmosphere of happiness, love and understanding" (preamble). To achieve this objective, the Convention directs governments to provide "necessary protection and assistance" to families so that they can fully assume their responsibilities within the community (preamble). These responsibilities include preparing children to be full participants in society.

The use of the phrase *family environment* is particularly important to children who are separated from their parents often for reasons beyond their control. In too many situations, children are separated from their parents, either temporarily or permanently, with little, if any, input about where they live and whether they will have contact with their parents (Bernstein, 2005; Braman, 2004; Seymour, 1998). They may be placed in settings away from their siblings and other relatives. If they remain with relatives, it may be with little ongoing emotional and financial support.

This chapter examines the application of the right to a family environment to a rapidly growing population of children who face such circumstances: the children of incarcerated parents. Although the chapter focuses on children with parents in jail or prison, many other children face similar challenges because their parents are detained for violations of immigration law. In addition, many children have parents who are in the criminal justice system but who are living in the community (e.g. probation, parole, community supervision). Depending on the circumstances, these

R. Kimbrough-Melton (✉)
Institute on Family and Neighborhood Life, Clemson University,
225 South Pleasantburg Drive, Suite B 11, 29607 Greenville, SC, USA
e-mail: rkimbro@clemson.edu

J. Garbarino and G. Sigman (eds.), *A Child's Right to a Healthy Environment*,
The Loyola University Symposium on the Human Rights of Children 1,
DOI 10.1007/978-1-4419-6791-6_8,

children may face challenges similar to children of prisoners, including periods of involuntary separation.

The War on Drugs: Casting a Wide Net

Nearly 40 years ago, the USA declared a war on drugs and adopted a policy of imprisonment as a means of protecting the public safety. In 1970, 196,429 persons were in state and federal prisons. By February 2008, however, one in 100 American adults (Pew Center on the States, 2008) – more than *2.3 million* people – were behind bars. More than five million others are on probation or parole. Hence, more than seven million adults are under some form of correctional control in the USA (Pew Center on the States, 2009). This gives the USA the dubious distinction of being the global leader in the rate of incarceration, far outpacing nations like China, Russia, and Iran. China, which has a much larger population than the USA, still incarcerates only 1.5 million. Russia has the next highest rate of incarceration in the world at 890,000 inmates (Pew Center on the States, 2008).

The policy to incarcerate was premised on the assumption that crime would be reduced if dangerous and violent criminals were taken off the streets. By the mid-to-late 1980s, however, the jails and prisons were full of people who had committed nonviolent drug and drug-related offenses. Commentators disagree about the impact of incarceration on lowering crime rates. If there has been a positive impact, however, it has been small (JFA Institute, 2007). In some communities, crime has decreased, in others it has remained stagnant, and in still others, crime has increased.

The use of incarceration as a means of controlling crime and enhancing public safety has become a massive public health problem. Aside from capturing low-level offenders who might more productively serve their time in the community, mass incarceration has had significant adverse outcomes for the families of offenders. Quite simply, the use of incarceration has restructured family relationships across generations, reshaped communities, destroyed friendships, and reduced material and emotional resources to masses of children whose relationships with their parents have become the *collateral damage* of this policy.

In the USA, criminal justice policies are individually-focused, thus any adverse impacts on the loved ones of offenders, including their children, have generally not been considered relevant. As a result, the growing imprisonment of parents has created a level of vulnerability and deprivation for their children by effectively excluding them from material and social resources. The loss of a parent to incarceration and the associated stigma often diminishes social capital for children of prisoners (Hagan & Dinovitzer, 1999).

Both men and women have been adversely affected by the policy to incarcerate. In some neighborhoods, men simply are gone. Washington, DC, is a case in point. A 3-year ethnographic of male incarceration in the District of Columbia at the turn of the century revealed that the use of incarceration had been as harmful, and sometimes more harmful, to families of the incarcerated as to the prisoners themselves

(Braman, 2002). If then-prevailing policies were continued, 75% of African American men living in Washington at the time could expect to be incarcerated at some point in their lives (Braman, 2002).

The impact of corrections policies on women was also not fully considered (Chesney-Lind, 2002). In the 30-year period beginning in 1977, the number of female prisoners in state or federal prisons increased 816% from 12,279 to 112,498. By December 2008, more than 214,000 women were held in jails and prisons in the USA (Sabol, West, & Cooper, 2009; Minton & Sabol, 2009). Many others were on probation or parole. Although women are still a much smaller segment of the overall criminal justice population than are men, the rate of incarceration is growing faster among women.

This unprecedented increase in the confinement of women can be tied directly to the War on Drugs and related sentencing reforms. Drug and drug-related offenses (e.g. forgery, prostitution, fraud, shoplifting, and stealing) comprise the vast majority of crimes for which women have been incarcerated. Unlike their male counterparts, women are more likely to be minimally involved in the drug trade, if at all (Frost, Greene, & Pranis, 2006). More often, they are supporting their own drug habit or living with partners engaged in the drug trade. Their peripheral role often has meant that they have had less leverage in plea bargaining than their male counterparts (Kimbrough-Melton & Koons-Witt, in press).

The majority of incarcerated men and women are parents. Approximately 75% of women and 65% of men in state prisons nationwide report being parents (Schirmer, Nellis, & Mauer, 2009) and their numbers have been increasing. Using data collected from inmates, Mumola (2000) reported that the number of children with a mother in prison nearly doubled from 1991 to 1999, while the number of children with a father in prison increased by 58% during the same period.

The incarceration of parents – both mothers and fathers – often is detrimental to children. Because mothers are more likely than fathers to be caring for children at the time of their arrest and incarceration, children are more likely to be directly affected by maternal incarceration in their daily life. Therefore, the dramatic increase in maternal incarceration in the twenty-first century (122% from 1991 to 2007) and the possibility of adverse outcomes for their children have generated increased attention by state and federal policymakers alike.

Children with Incarcerated Parents: A Large and Diverse Population

Prevalence

Because no single agency documents the number of children affected by parental incarceration, the best estimates of the impact of incarceration on American children comes from inmates' self-report during their orientation to prison. On average, mothers in state prison report that they have 2.4 children and fathers report that they have 2 children. Accordingly, more than two million children were estimated to have a parent in prison in 2008 (LaVigne, Davies, & Brazzel, 2008). When probation and parole are also considered, the figure jumps to as many as ten million – one in seven American children (Glaze & Bonczar, 2009). To put this statistic into context, in 2007, England and Wales identified 140,000 children of prisoners, and Scotland reported 13,500 (Marshall, 2008).

Children affected by parental incarceration tend to be young, poor, and black or Hispanic (Mumola, 2000). The average age of children in Mumola's study was 8, with 58% under age 10 and 22% under age 5. As of July 2007, African American and Hispanic children were, respectively, 7.5 and 2.5 times more likely than White children to have a parent in prison (Glaze & Maruschak, 2008).

The Impact of Incarceration on the Well-Being of Children

Children of prisoners may be one of the most at-risk populations of children in the USA today. The scarcity of research about the impact of parental incarceration on them has prompted concern among service providers, government officials, and academics alike. Moreover, little is known about the interaction of parent incarceration with a host of other factors (e.g. poverty, academic problems, parent mental health and substance abuse problems, chaotic lifestyles, and ongoing involvement in criminal activity) that often are present in the lives of these children. Very few studies – most using small samples – document the experiences of children from their own point of view. Research has primarily focused on the problems of children of prisoners without considering their entire lives (Johnston, 1995). Nonetheless, the evidence is sufficient to conclude that most children experience parental incarceration as a challenging and potentially traumatic event (Hairston, 2007). The majority of children of incarcerated parents display problems related to parent–child separation, long-term traumatic stress, and inadequate quality of care (Johnston, 1995).

Parent–Child Separation

The degree to which separation as a result of parental incarceration is significantly different from other forms of parent–child separation is not yet well understood. As in cases of divorce, parental separation because of incarceration may initiate a series of dramatic changes in the lives of children: moving to a new neighborhood, changing schools, substantially lowered standard of living, loss of contact with the absent parent, and decline in parental well-being and mental health (Dunn, 2004; Hetherington & Clingempeel, 1992). Maternal incarceration has been shown to be especially disruptive of the everyday lives of children (LaVigne et al., 2008). Children experiencing maternal incarceration are more likely than those with a father incarcerated to be removed from their home and placed with relatives, usually grandparents, or with foster parents (Hagan & Dinovitzer, 1999; LaVigne et al.). In her study of the relationships of children of incarcerated mothers, Poehlmann (2005) found that the majority of the children (60%) had lived with one caregiver since the incarceration of their mother but 40% had lived with at least two caregivers. Of the 40%, 30% had changed caregivers four or more times since the incarceration of their mother.

Children of prisoners are more likely than other children in general to experience accumulated risk, including poverty, single-parent home, low maternal education, parental mental illness, substance abuse, and large family size (Dallaire, 2007; James & Glaze, 2006; Murray & Farrington, 2005). Although parent incarceration per se does not necessarily contribute to adverse outcomes for children of prisoners (DeHart & Altshuler, 2009), the continuing severe stress that many families experience increases the likelihood of problems.

Other factors that may be unique to children of prisoners can also exacerbate the negative impact of separation. For example, because children of prisoners often live with relatives, especially if their mother is incarcerated, siblings sometimes have to be separated among relatives (Hagan & Dinovitzer, 1999; Johnston, 1995). Moreover, children with mothers incarcerated are more likely to experience permanent separation because of the time limits that were established by the Adoption and Safe Families Act of (1997) for the initiation of termination of parental rights. From 1997 to 2002, terminations of parental rights involving parental incarceration increased by approximately 250% (Genty, 2003). Finally, the separation of children from their parents because of parental incarceration is often exacerbated by the "social, community and institutional stigma" (Hairston, 2007, p. 2) associated with incarceration.

Long-Term Traumatic Stress

Aside from the day-to-day life challenges facing many children of prisoners, the initial experience of losing a parent or parents often is traumatic. In general, children with incarcerated parents react to separation from their parent in much the same way as any other child. Most often, they experience crying, sadness, and/or repeatedly calling for and looking for mothers (Poehlmann, 2005). They may also experience confusion (52%), anger (40%), sleep problems (32%), and developmental regression (22%) (Poehlmann, 2005). Younger children often do not have the developmental skills to cope with the loss of a parent, and older children may feel the need to hide the incarceration because of stigma. Other studies have relied on parental reports of children's behavior and direct contact with children of prisoners to document a variety of negative outcomes, including behavioral problems, school-related difficulties, depression, low self-esteem, aggressive behavior, and general emotional dysfunction (Hagan & Dinovitzer, 1999). Some children who visited their mothers in prison showed signs of posttraumatic stress disorder, including depression, feelings of anger and guilt, flashbacks about their mothers' crimes or arrests, and experiences with hearing their mother's voices (Kampfner, 1995).

The criminal justice system itself is a source of traumatic events for children. Witnessing the arrest of a parent or returning home from school to an empty house when a parent is arrested during school hours can exacerbate emotional and behavioral problems. The arrest of a parent is one of the only situations in which parent–child separation occurs without regard given to the circumstances of the child, or for that matter, the existence of a child. Stories abound of children who come home from school to find their parents absent and who fend for themselves until discovered by a neighbor or other adult and reported. Kampfner (1995) found that children of incarcerated mothers were more likely to report long-term recall of the trauma of separation from their mothers than were children from similar high risk backgrounds but without maternal incarceration.

Although many children with parents incarcerated experience adverse outcomes, not all do. Some appear to be resilient in the face of terribly difficult experiences. The degree to which children experience difficulties is related to their age at the time of the incarceration, the gender of the parent removed from the home, and the level of ongoing support the children receive after the parent's incarceration. In her research on attachment relationships in children with incarcerated mothers, Poehlmann (2005) found that children were more likely to have secure relationships when the children lived in stable caregiving arrangements, when they reacted to the incarceration of their mother with sadness rather than anger, and when they were older.

Inadequate Quality of Care

Children separated from their parents because of incarceration are more likely than children separated from their parents for other reasons to experience diminished quality of care in their care giving arrangements. In a study of youth from 11 rural counties in North Carolina, Phillips, Erkanli, Keeler, Costello, and Angold (2006) determined that children who had parents incarcerated were 130% more likely than children in the general population to experience family instability. Similarly, children who had parents involved with the criminal justice system but not incarcerated were 80% more likely than children in the general population to experience family instability (Phillips et al., 2006).

Moreover, Phillips et al. (2006) found that children who had incarcerated parents or parent figures were 80% more likely to live in households characterized by economic strain. If fathers were living with their minor children at the time of their imprisonment, the financial well-being of the family may decline significantly if the father was the primary breadwinner.

Regardless of which parent is incarcerated, a child's quality of care may not improve significantly on release of the parent. Aside from the usual challenges (e.g. accessing employment, housing, treatment) facing inmates on reentry, restrictions on the provision of services to drug offenders make it even more difficult for reentering offenders to find the support necessary to do well. Effects on children may last far beyond their parent's imprisonment (Hagan & Donovitzer, 1999).

A Children's Bill of Rights

Growing concern over the potential vulnerability of children with incarcerated parents and the lack of attention to them led a coalition of advocates, social service providers, governmental representatives, and others who work with these children to develop a set of "rights" to protect them when their parents are arrested or incarcerated (San Francisco Children of Incarcerated Parents Partnership, 2005). Time and time again, the coalition witnessed the devastation to children of prisoners when their very existence, much less their needs or interests, was not acknowledged by law enforcement, the courts, and correctional agencies.

As the Coalition noted,

> They have...committed no crime, but the penalty they are required to pay is steep. They forfeit, in too many cases, virtually everything that matters to them: their home, their safety, their public status and private self-image, their source of comfort and affection. Their lives and prospects are profoundly affected by the numerous institutions that lay claim to their parents – police, courts, jails and prisons, probation and parole – but they have no rights, explicit or implicit, within any of these jurisdictions (San Francisco Children of Incarcerated Parents Partnership, 2005, p. 5).

In the words of children of prisoners, they should have the right to:

1. Be kept safe and informed at the time of my parent's arrest.
2. Be heard when decisions are made about me.
3. Be considered when decisions are made about my parent.
4. Be well cared for in my parent's absence.
5. Speak with, see, and touch my parent.
6. Support as I struggle with my parent's incarceration.
7. Not be judged, blamed, or labeled because of my parent's incarceration.
8. A lifelong relationship with my parent.

Although the statement does not rise to the level of a legally recognized and enforceable claim or entitlement, recent action by the California Assembly (SCR 20, 2009) to adopt a resolution encompassing the bill of rights will ensure that the statement is distributed to children of incarcerated parents. The resolution also invites discussion by the relevant state agencies of ways to use the bill of rights as a framework for analysis and decision making about services to children.

The rights encompassed in the bill of rights are as much psychological as they are policy-and program-oriented. At the core, they require someone to do something to *acknowledge* children, to *engage* them, and to *support* them even when their interests collide with the interests of those in authority or with their incarcerated parents or caregivers. As the Coalition has noted, even if the statement of rights is recognized by the various institutions involved with their parents and taken seriously, "children of prisoners would still face a daunting array of obstacles and traumas" (San Francisco Children of Incarcerated Parents Partnership, 2005, p. 5).

The CRC's Right to a Family Environment

The concept of a *family environment* first appears in the preamble of the Convention on the Rights of the Child (1989), where it is described as the optimal setting for the "full and harmonious development" of the child's personality. Living in a *family environment* is equated with living in "an atmosphere of happiness, love and understanding" (preamble).

Melton (1996) has argued that the choice of the words *family environment* was inspired in part because it suggests a set of relationships that are more encompassing than the biological parents of a child. It does not diminish the fundamental role of parents in raising their children (see Convention, 1989, arts. 3, 5, 7, 9, & 10). Rather, it emphasizes "function" over "form." Because the language starts from the child's perspective about the relationships that are most important to him or her, family structure becomes unimportant. Thus, in situations where a child cannot live with his or her biological parents, the child still can live in a *family environment*.

Melton (1996) has argued further that the phrase *family environment* rather than *family* creates a legally enforceable right. Although it is not possible for the state to ensure that every child has a family, it is possible for governments to facilitate environments that nurture and support the child's relationships both in the community and in the institutions. In the community, steps can be taken to engage caregivers, extended family, friends, and neighbors in the care of children. In correctional institutions, connections between parents and children are being encouraged by organizing family centers and special visiting days where parents and their children can interact in a family-like setting.

The strong preference in the Convention for family-like environments is consistent with the general approach of international human rights law that rights derive from the inherent dignity of the child or person. Like the Children's Bill of Rights, the Convention establishes a framework for policy and programmatic change that starts from the perspective of the child. The primary difference between the Bill of Rights and the Convention's right to a family environment is the emphasis of the former on the parent relationship and the importance of the relationship to the child even when they are separated. The Convention's right to a family environment similarly protects the parent–child relationship by requiring governments to preserve family relationships (arts. 5 &7). A child has the right to know and be cared for by his or her parents (art. 7) and "to maintain personal relations and direct contact with both parents" (art. 9). However, the language of the Convention is also more expansive in encompassing the extended family, community and legal guardians (see arts. 3 & 5), and recognizing their role in providing direction and guidance to the child.

Because the various articles of the Convention (1989) are read together, the Convention also is much more expansive in the obligations of governments. The duty of the government to protect the child's right to a family environment goes beyond formal preservation of relationships to substantive entitlements that support an environment conducive to family life (Melton, 1996). Concretely, the Convention recognizes the right to "standard of living adequate for the child's physical, mental, spiritual, moral and social development (art. 27)." This includes nutrition, clothing, housing, and general material needs (art. 27, §3), social insurance (art. 26), maternal and child health care (art. 24), access to health services (art. 24), and support needed for the prevention of child abuse and neglect (art. 19).

The obligation of governments to provide assistance within their means to parents and caregivers (art. 27, §3) is especially important to children of prisoners. Many are living with relatives, usually grandparents, who generally receive little if any financial support for their grandchildren. Because many relatives are themselves living on limited incomes, their inability to access financial assistance increases the likelihood that children will be shuttled between caregivers or separated from siblings as a way of sharing the financial load. If relatives do access medicaid or other income support services, the incarcerated parent may have an obligation to pay back the support on their release from prison. For most parents who struggle to find employment on release from prison, paying back support is very difficult to do.

Even if children continue to live with one biological parent, the family may face significant financial challenges if the incarcerated parent was working and supporting the family at the time of arrest. The incarceration of fathers often plunges families into economic distress.

The need for support, both financial and emotional, does not cease with the release of the parent from prison. Many parents, especially mothers, resume parenting on their release from prison. Barriers in accessing public housing and income support for some prisoners, and employment for most prisoners, makes it difficult for parents to pick up where they left off.

Strengthening Family Environments for Children of Prisoners

Our experience in serving children of prisoners and their families through our Building Dreams program has reinforced for us the importance of paying attention to the relationships most important to the child. Interventions for children of prisoners should strengthen the ability of their caregivers to parent while simultaneously engaging others in the community to lend support. Children of prisoners can manage trauma and stress much more effectively when they are surrounded by adults – caregivers and neighbors – who can help them cope with the crisis (Hairston, 2007). More often than not, caregivers are isolated in their parenting because of their reluctance to seek help and support. They isolate themselves for a variety of reasons. Some fear that the children will be removed from the home if they bring attention to themselves. Many find the legal process confusing and frustrating and so they are reluctant to ask basic questions about the status of their loved one. Others do not understand how the formal service system works and so they are not effective in securing services. Still others are engaged in antisocial behaviors that would place them at risk if they reached out. Finally, many do not access help because of the stigma associated with having a family member incarcerated. Our experience with Building Dreams, a program that provides support (e.g. mentoring, connections to informal networks and formal social services) to children of incarcerated parents and their caregivers, affirms that, for many families, the harsh impacts of parental incarceration on children can be ameliorated when comprehensive, community-based support is easily accessible, provided early, and in nonjudgmental ways.

In serving children of prisoners and their families, we have embedded our work in the context of our broader community initiative – *Strong Communities for Children* – aimed at building the capacity of communities to keep kids safe (Melton, this volume; see also Melton & Holaday, 2008; Melton, 2009). The fact that Strong Communities were available to families in only a portion of the counties served by Building Dreams gave us a foundation for understanding the importance of broad-based community support. We simply have not been able to provide the level of service and support to families of the incarcerated living in counties not served by Strong Communities.

The essence of Strong Communities is the mobilization of community members to enhance the likelihood that families will have access to needed services and supports as well as to strengthen informal social support. Based on principles of respect and dignity, Strong Communities was premised on the idea that children and families should not have to become clients to access help. They should be able to get help where they are, when they need it, in a form that they can use it, with ease, and without stigma.

Strong Communities started from the premise that if residents understand the challenges facing families, they will become engaged in creating opportunities for children and their families to access the "conditions necessary for the child's development" (Convention, 1989, art. 27, §2). Volunteers worked with us to develop an array of supportive services (e.g. family activity centers, parent–child activities, financial counseling, general family advocacy), some of which were universally available to families and others that were targeted to families with high needs. The supportive services that were developed as a part of Strong Communities – even the more intensive services – were available to families free of charge in a variety of community settings (e.g. schools, fire departments, parks, churches, family resource centers, and recreation centers).

Strong Communities was distinctive in two other ways that made it much easier for families of the incarcerated to feel comfortable about receiving help. First, the message of the Strong Communities was that every parent needs help at some time or another. Efforts to normalize the receipt of help and to create opportunities for reciprocity fostered an environment, where families in Building Dreams could open up about their circumstances without feeling stigmatized or ashamed. When families opened up, community members began to understand the challenges faced by children impacted by incarceration, and they responded compassionately to integrate these families into community life.

Second, in an effort to strengthen social connectedness within the service area, Strong Communities emphasized the development of informal networks of support. Considerable research exists to demonstrate the importance of social capital to the well-being of children (Coulton, Crampton, Irwin, Spilsbury, & Korbin, 2007; Coulton & Korbin, 2007; Freisthler & Campton, 2009). Building Dreams families benefited from informal networks in several ways. Families were the recipients of services that ranged from a new house for a family whose mobile home was condemned, to help with mental health counseling, to respite for grandparent caregivers, and to access to health services. Other families benefited from the advocacy of community members. When a family of seven siblings, most of whom had been severely abused, were at risk of separation because the Department of Social Services did not have a home that could take all of the children, a church network stepped in to offer support so that the Department was comfortable placing the children with a relative caregiver. Still other families in Building Dreams received assistance from professionals (e.g. lawyers, financial counselors, medical personnel) who volunteered their expertise to help others.

Conclusion

Children with parents in prison have been an under recognized and underserved population until recently. Although research on the life trajectories of these children is only beginning to emerge, concern over their well-being has led organizations throughout the USA to begin identifying strategies for providing treatment for children of prisoners with humanity. The "right to a family environment" in the Convention onthe Rights of the Child provides a platform from which to begin constructing useful and appropriate support for children of prisoners. Embedding such support within the community is an effective strategy not only for the concrete support that can be generated, but also for the increased understanding and compassion that occurs when community members have an opportunity to help their neighbors. Governments can be instrumental in facilitating the development of such support.

References

Adoption and Safe Families Act, 42 U.S.C. section 629 (1997).

Bernstein, N. (2005). *All alone in the world: Children of the incarcerated.* New York: New Press.

Braman, D. (2002). Families and incarceration. In M. Mauer & M. Chesney-Lind (Eds.), *Invisible punishment: The collateral consequences of mass imprisonment* (pp. 117–135). New York: New Press.

Braman, D. (2004). *Doing time on the outside: Incarceration and family life in urban America.* Ann Arbor, MI: University of Michigan Press.

California Senate Concurrent Resolution 20 (2009).

Chesney-Lind, M. (2002). Imprisoning women: The unintended victims of mass imprisonment. In M. Mauer & M. Chesney-Lind (Eds.), *Invisible punishment: The collateral consequences of mass imprisonment* (pp. 79–94). New York: New Press.

Convention on the Rights of the Child, U.N. Doc. A/Res/44/25 (1989).

Coulton, C. J., & Korbin, J. E. (2007). Indicators of child well-being through a neighborhood lens. *Social Indicators Research, 84*, 349–361.

Coulton, C. J., Crampton, D., Irwin, M., Spilsbury, J., & Korbin, J. E. (2007). How neighborhoods influence child maltreatment: A review of the literature and alternative pathways. *Child Abuse and Neglect, 31*, 1117–1142.

Dallaire, D. H. (2007). Incarcerated mothers and fathers: A comparison of risks for children and families. *Family Relations, 56*, 440–453.

DeHart, D. D., & Altshuler, S. J. (2009). Violence exposure among children of incarcerated mothers. *Child and Adolescent Social Work Journal, 26*, 467–479.

Dunn, J. (2004). Understanding children's family worlds: Family transitions and children's outcomes. *Merrill-Palmer Quarterly, 50*, 224–235.

Freisthler, B., & Campton, D. (2009). Environment and child well-being. *Children and Youth Services Review, 31*, 346–348.

Frost, N., Greene, J., & Pranis, K. (2006). *Hard hit: The growth in the imprisonment of women, 1977–2004*. New York: Women's Prison Association.

Genty, P. M. (2003). Twelfth annual symposium on contemporary urban challenges: Damage to family relationships as a collateral consequence of parental incarceration. *Fordham Urban Law Journal, 30*, 1671–1684.

Glaze, L. E., & Bonczar, T. P. (2009). *Probation and parole in the United States, 2008 (NCJ 228230)*. Washington, DC: Bureau of Justice Statistics.

Glaze, L. E., & Maruschak, L. M. (2008). *Parents in prison and their minor children, (NCJ 222984)*. Washington, DC: Bureau of Justice Statistics.

Hagan, J., & Dinovitzer, R. (1999). Collateral consequences of imprisonment of children, communities, and prisoners. *Crime and Justice, 26*, 121–162.

Hairston, C. F. (2007). *Focus on children with incarcerated parents: An overview of the research literature*. Baltimore, MD: Annie E. Casey Foundation.

Hetherington, E. M., & Clingempeel, W. G. (1992). Coping with marital transitions: A family systems approach. *Monographs of the Society for Research in Child Development, 57*, 2–3.

International Covenant on Civil and Political Rights, U.N. Doc. A/6316 (1966), *entered into force* March 23, 1976.

International Covenant on Economic, Social, and Cultural Rights, U.N. Doc. A/6316 (1966), *entered into force* January 3, 1976.

James, D. J., & Glaze, L. E. (2006). *Mental health problems and prison and jail inmates*. Washington, DC: Bureau of Justice Statistics.

JFA Institute. (2007). *Unlocking America. Why and how to reduce America's prison population?* Washington, DC: Author.

Johnston, D. (1995). The care and placement of prisoners' children. In K. Gabel & D. Johnston (Eds.), *Children of incarcerated parents* (pp. 103–123). New York: Lexington Books.

Kampfner, C. J. (1995). Post-traumatic stress reactions of children of imprisoned mothers. In K. Gabel & D. Johnston (Eds.), *Children of incarcerated parents* (pp. 89–102). New York: Lexington Books.

Kimbrough-Melton, R. J. & Koons-Witt, B. J. (in press). *Will they be back: Reentry of adult female offenders in South Carolina*. Columbia, SC: South Carolina Correctional Association

LaVigne, N. G., Davies, E., & Brazzell, D. (2008). *Broken bonds: Understanding and addressing the needs of children with incarcerated parents*. Washington, DC: Urban Institute.

Marshall, K. (2008). *Not seen. Not heard. Not guilty. The rights and status of the children of prisoners in Scotland*. Edinburgh, UK: Scotland's Commissioner for Children and Young People.

Melton, G. B. (1996). The child's right to a family environment. Why children's rights and family values are compatible. *American Psychologist, 51*, 1234–1238.

Melton, G. B. (2009). How strong communities restored my faith in humanity: Children can live in safety. In K. A. Dodge & D. L. Coleman (Eds.), *Preventing child maltreatment: Community approaches* (pp. 82–101). New York: Guilford.

Melton, G. B. & Holaday, B.J., (Eds.). (2008). Strong communities as safe havens for children [Special Issue]. *Family and Community Health 31*(2).

Minton, T. D., & Sabol, W. J. (2009). *Jail inmates at midyear 2008: Statistical tables (Report No. NCJ 225709)*. Washington, DC: Bureau of Justice Statistics.

Mumola, C. J. (2000). *Incarcerated parents and their children*. Washington, DC: Bureau of Justice Statistics.

Murray, J., & Farrington, D. P. (2005). Parental imprisonment: Effects on boys' antisocial behavior and delinquency through the life-course. *Journal of Child Psychology and Psychiatry, 46*, 1269–1278.

Pew Center on the States. (2008). *One in 100: Behind bars in America in 2008*. Washington, DC: Pew Charitable Trusts.

Pew Center on the States. (2009). *One in 31: The long reach of American corrections*. Washington, DC: Pew Charitable Trusts.

Phillips, S. D., Erkanli, A., Keeler, G. P., Costello, E. J., & Angold, A. (2006). Disentangling the risks: Parent criminal justice involvement and children's exposure to family risks. *Criminology and Public Policy, 5*, 677–702.

Poehlmann, J. (2005). Representations of attachment relationships in children of incarcerated mothers. *Child Development, 76*, 679–696.

Sabol, W. J., West, H. C., & Cooper, M. (2009). *Prisoners in 2008 (Report No. NCJ 228417)*. Washington, DC: Bureau of Justice Statistics.

San Francisco Children of Incarcerated Parents Partnership. (2005) Children of Incarcerated Parents: A Bill of Rights, San Francisco: Author. (www.sfcipp.org)

Schirmer, S., Nellis, A., & Mauer, M. (2009). *Incarcerated parents and their children: Trends 1991–2007*. Washington, DC: Sentencing Project.

Seymour, C. B. (1998). Children with parents in prison: Child welfare policy, program, and practice issues. *Child Welfare, 77*, 469–493.

Universal Declaration of Human Rights, U.N. Doc. A/810 at 71 (1948).

Chapter 9
A Child's Right to an Environment That Prevents Obesity: Ethical Considerations

Garry Sigman

Introduction

The addition of children's rights to the human rights agenda was articulated and organized into specific areas by the Geneva Declaration of the Rights of the Child in 1924 at the League of Nations. It is stated that "mankind owes to the child the best that it has to give" (Parsi, 2002, p. 495). More specific principles were laid out in the Declaration of the Rights of the Child, proclaimed by the United Nations (UN) General Assembly (1959). For example, article 2 states

> The child shall enjoy *special protection*, and shall be given opportunities and facilities, by law and by other means, to enable him to develop physically, mentally, morally, spiritually and socially in a healthy and normal manner and in conditions of freedom and dignity.

The UN Convention on the Rights of the Child (1989) was put forward as the most comprehensive document to date, and helps to address children's circumstances in the modern world. It is this "special protection" that enable a child to develop physically and mentally in a healthy manner, and this paper addresses, and wishes to apply to an area not yet anticipated in 1924, 1959, or 1989.

Child and adolescent obesity has become a serious and worldwide problem that effects physical and mental development, and risks reduction of expected life expectancy (Engeland, Bjorge, Tverdal, & Sogaard, 2004). The rising prevalence of obesity in children and adults around the globe is largely (although not exclusively) thought to reflect adverse environmental circumstances, and is thus worthy of examination in a volume that addresses the rights of children to a healthy environment. A direct derivation of the rights of children regarding obesity is a relatively newer area in the child rights' discourse, and requires investigating the nature of the obesity phenomenon and the ethical issues underlying proposed preventive and therapeutic actions.

G. Sigman (✉)
Loyola University Medical Center, 2160 S First Ave, Maywood, IL 60153, USA
e-mail: gsigman@lumc.edu

J. Garbarino and G. Sigman (eds.), *A Child's Right to a Healthy Environment*, The Loyola University Symposium on the Human Rights of Children 1,
DOI 10.1007/978-1-4419-6791-6_9, © Springer Science+Business Media, LLC 2010

Obesity is a primary risk condition for the *non-communicable diseases*, along with cancer, cardiovascular disease, diabetes, and hypertension, which have increased in prevalence in the developed and non-developed world (Amuna & Zotor, 2008). Just as children who face risk of the most common *communicable diseases* that have plagued children, such as pneumonia, diarrhea malaria, HIV, and neonatal infections have required, protection so too does becoming obese by reduction of risk in the areas of education, relief of the conditions of poverty, and programs to target the disease. However, non-communicable diseases differ though, in ways that engender ethical considerations.

First, non-communicable diseases are "diseases of lifestyle," so that any attempts by clinicians or policy planners require involving the "choices" of individuals as to how they live. In our case, it invokes the lifestyle of parents and caregivers in the interest of their children. Second, the morbidity and mortality of these conditions, while present in children, are mostly diseases of adulthood, while the risk is developed during the childhood years. This "silent" risk places a special burden on health promotion and prevention. How this is done and "to whom" bring up very important ethical questions, such as who is responsible for taking on this burden? Who are the appropriate shareholders? What public policies should endeavor to involve them? Finally, unlike communicable diseases, where the organization and provision of medical care (supplying immunization, medical examinations, prescription, and distribution of drugs) are necessary interventions to help reduce childhood mortality, the child obesity problem seems to require more non-medical solutions. The necessary focus on the community, groups, economic, and governmental entities requires mobilization. Children with severe health risk are appearing at health care providers' clinics in unprecedented numbers. Most available medical treatments are limited, often ineffective, unstudied, and possibly risky. Thus, Ethical challenges also arise within the confines of the examining office as to what should be done for these patients.

This article will briefly review the epidemiology of childhood obesity, thereby exploring the burden of the problem and discuss the mandate to act. The various influences upon childhood obesity will be discussed, utilizing an ecological model in which biology, and environment effect behaviors that are either "obesogenic," favoring obesity, or "leptogenic" (from the hormone leptin, which is made in adipose cells), favoring slimness. These factors that influence obesity invoke ethical challenges that include the public health agenda and the clinical care of obese child and adolescent patients. We will then apply the ethical considerations derived from the unique challenge of child obesity to the issue of child rights and discuss the "special protections" needed to combat this modern epidemic.

Epidemiology and Implications

Whether we act or not depends upon evidence of child obesity prevalence, recent trends and documentation of adverse health effects (Lobstein, Baur, & Uauy, 2004). Here I will review these areas. The biomedical definition of obesity in childhood and adolescence is excessive fatness or adiposity to a total body weight. Body mass index (BMI; weight in kilograms divided by the height in meters squared) is generally used in children and adults to characterize body weight levels. Children's BMIs, unlike adults, are compared to a reference population of children of the same sex and age, in order to derive a percentage. Overweight is defined as above the 85th percentile and obesity is defined as over the 95th percentile.

Currently, one in three children in the United States are overweight or obese. This approaches one in two in African-American and Hispanic children. For children aged 6–19 years, the prevalence of children with a BMI > 95% has risen by a factor greater than fourfold. The rise is not a recent trend, but has occurred over the past 30 years. It appears that the greatest rise in the population was between the survey periods from the 1970s to the 1990s. Not only had the rate of childhood obesity risen, but also children at the highest percentiles had higher BMIs than that observed in past years (Ogden et al., 2006). So, the amount of children who became obese rose, and the (fattest) of the children got (fatter).

Increase in the prevalence of childhood overweight and obesity is not limited to USA. The highest prevalence is in North America, Australia, and Europe (Janssen et al., 2005). Childhood obesity had also increased in some economic developing countries and urban populations (Wang & Lobstein, 2006). A more recent increase in obesity rates have occurred in the near and Middle East as well as in countries in the Asia-Pacific, Sub-Saharan region of Africa, and Central and South America. In some developing countries, overweight exceeds underweight among women (Mendez, Monteiro, & Popkin, 2005) and children (Wang, Monteiro, & Popkin, 2002).

Data suggest that childhood obesity predicts adult obesity. This prediction is the greatest for higher BMI levels and older ages. More overweight children are likely to track to adulthood than normal weight children, and more overweight adolescents than overweight children are likely too as well (Deshmukh-Taskar et al., 2006).

The health implications of this higher rate of obesity are dramatic for children and for the adults that they will become. Obesity in adults is known to be a risk factor for atherosclerosis, heart disease, stroke, non-insulin dependent diabetes, hypertension, cancer, gall bladder disease, and renal failure. Obesity in childhood and adolescence dramatically increases the risk of coronary heart diseases in adulthood. By 2035, at this rate of prevalence, it is estimated that there will be at least 100,000 excess cases of heart disease in USA (Ebbeling & Ludwig, 2008).

As the prevalence of obesity rose in children, and the severity of obesity increased, children began presenting to health care facilities with some of these adult-type diseases. The prevalence of what was formally called "adult-onset" diabetes (now type II diabetes) has increased by a factor of tenfold for children and teens (Ludwig, 2007). Obese children manifest other health problems as well, including dermatologic, orthopedic, pulmonary, and other endocrine and metabolic disease processes.

The rate of adolescent obesity, in 2002, is projected to increase the prevalence of obese 35-year-olds in 2020 to a range of 30–37% in men, and 34–44% in women (Bibbins-Domingo, Coxson, Pletcher, Lightwood, & Goldman, 2007). There are now some studies that demonstrate these projections. A group of Norwegian adolescents were followed into adulthood (an average of 32 years) and manifested a mortality rate for those whose BMIs were above the 90% between ages 14 and 19 years, to 80% higher than those whose adolescent BMI was 25–75%. Overweight teens had an intermediate mortality rate (Engeland et al., 2004).

The ethical implications relating to the change in epidemiology arise both from doubt and a sense of urgency. Research relating to prediction of later morbidity and mortality from childhood obese states is limited. Although BMI is considered the best available screening tool for clinical practice, it is not without problems in its predictive value. It only provides an approximate correlation to the biomedical definition of obesity; it provides no specific information about cardiovascular risk, for example ratio of adipose to lean body tissue, or waist to hip ratio (Ebbeling & Ludwig, 2008). Its predictability as a risk factor is limited, as many children and adolescents might be obese, but lack other risk factors for cardiovascular disease, and are not demonstrably at risk. Should obesity be considered a risk factor, or a disease? This leads to questions such as how should the prevention and care of obesity be prioritized and funded. Issues arise regarding the analysis of the epidemiological facts, and the sense of urgency that might arise. Controversy exists as to whether the urgency that is being described is "political" in the sense that it benefits the pharmacology, health care, and weight loss industry (Campos, Saguy, Ernsberger, Oliver, & Gaesser, 2006). The mandate to "do something" can lead to either appropriate, empirically sound, and efficacious interventions or (1) diversion of scarce resources away from more pressing needs; (2) a tendency to blame, to find single parties culpable in the problem, and to attack their practices – demonizing some parties, e.g., food industry, or parents or schools; and (3) a call for the use of newer technological approaches, e.g., drugs, surgery before consideration, and development of effective prevention and less dangerous treatments that are sound and efficacious.

The terms "epidemic" and "crises" are often used in relationship to the increase in child obesity. Use of these terms reinforce and invoke urgency. Obesity rates over the last 50 years have risen significantly, and are associated the current rates of childhood diabetes and pre-diabetic states. The data suggest that the call for prompt action now is a reasonable conclusion, but it called for prompt action before now; the trend is not new. The dramatic increases in adult and childhood obesity had begun in the 1970s and 1980s. In fact, the most recent data from the NHANES surveys from 2003 to 2006 suggest that prevalence of high BMI has not significantly changed between 1999 and 2006. Perhaps the threshold of medical complications (the rise in childhood diabetes, metabolic syndrome, and liver disease) has helped the health care sector to mobilize, but along with the public health sector, it appears to be late action.

Now or before, problem or "epidemic," action is required. But, do we have the data to support prompt effective action? Or, do we act because we know we should without waiting for good data? Can we act upon the best data that we have? The complexity of the disorder, the need for preventive action above all, and the disparate populations that effect obese children lead to careful ethical evaluation of what to do, how to do it, and to whom.

The Complex Etiology of Childhood Obesity: Implications

The nature of obesity is complex, a process that includes bio-genetic, socio-cultural, and psychological aspects. The influences ultimately determine whether energy intake is greater than energy use, over the long term, which results in obesity. It is best understood as an ecological phenomenon, where many influences are bi-directional. Figure 9.1 is a summary of those factors. No single influence predominates for this multi-factorial problem. Preventive and corrective action will require multidimensional change. The environmental changes that are associated with the increase in rates of child obesity cannot solely be changed by the parties, who at this time are widely thought to be "responsible" for dealing with the problem, namely parents/caretakers and health care providers. The implication of this for public health and medical care will be further developed as we survey the domains that influence the problem.

Biological Influences on Childhood Obesity

Biological and physiological causes of obesity in children are a starting point in order to clarify what can be prevented and treated. Three primary characteristics obesity will be discussed:

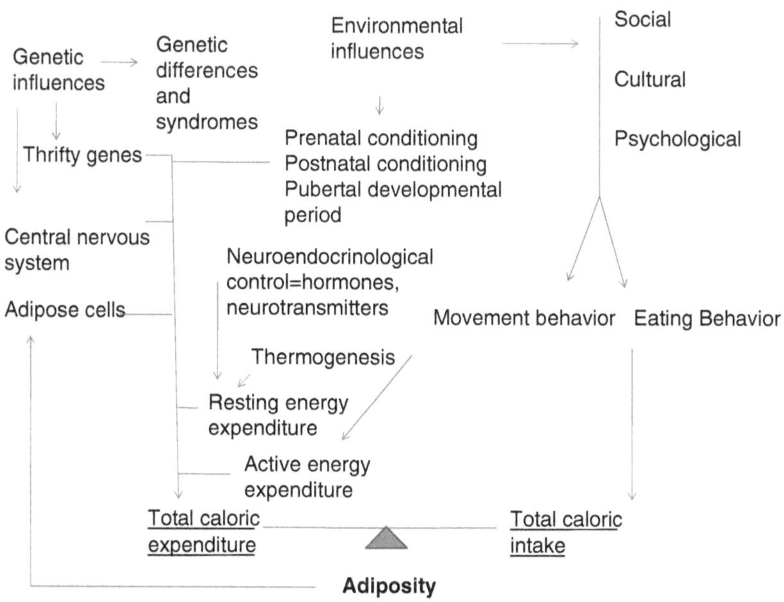

Fig. 9.1 Obesity etiology

- Etiology is multi-factorial; not correlated with single influences.
- *Thrifty genes* make obesity a common phenomenon and genetic factors affect individual levels of adiposity.
- *Body weight homeostasis* is a biological phenomenon that prevents effective treatment of obesity.

How much adipose tissue is stored in the body depends upon the dynamic balance between energy expenditure and energy intake. Expenditure and intake, both sides of the energy equation, are influenced by biogenetic phenomena, environmental and psychological factors. For infants and young children, most important influences are related to genetically determined and developmentally conditioned neuro-endocrine control of body weight regulation, as well as parent/caretaker feeding practices and expectations of the caretaker regarding physical activity needs. For older children, adolescents, and adults, all the factors affecting younger children are operative, and in addition, the elements of social effects, knowledge, and self-awareness, choice of food and activity, and psychological characteristics come into play.

Genetics plays a significant role in causing obesity in individuals. The overriding genetic influence refers to the "thrifty gene" hypothesis. Humans, having evolved from periods of their past environments where food was necessary for survival but was not always readily available, developed mechanisms where energy when available, would be more readily stored (Prentice, Rayco-Solon, & Moore, 2005). Thus, it appears that man has been selected to survive episodic famine and seasonal hungry periods, and is rather unsuited to the present period of a plethora of calories available in many areas of the world. This is termed thrifty genotype and is considered a genetic endowment of Homo-sapiens. It has also been discovered that there are individuals who have tendency to store adipose tissue above and beyond that conferred by genotype, and that the tendency has origin in the fetal period and/or the immediate post-natal period. Data support the tendency for fetuses that are growth deprived and have early catch-up growth in the first post-fetal months to develop increased adiposity and be at risk for diabetes in the child and adult years (Adair, 2008). This seems to be an acquired tendency to hold energy in response to the fetal environment, and it is through a mechanism of neuro-endocrine conditioning. Early under nutrition or over nutrition in effect "rewires" the brain, making the body tolerant of excess fat.

Genetics also plays a role in conferring unique susceptibility to obesity in individuals and their family pedigrees. Evidence of heritability is high. It is estimated that up to 40% of the variability in childhood BMI is attributable to genetic influences (Wardle, Carnell, Haworth, & Plomin, 2008). Animal models for single-gene disorders causing obesity have led to exploration of specific genes that may affect humans (Casper, Sullivan, & Tecott, 2008). Research has identified various specific genetic mechanisms for human obesity.

The rapid rise in obesity in the past decades cannot be explained by a change in the genotype of individuals beyond our tendency to store fat, and any unique genotypes in families. It does indicate an interaction between genes and environment.

Changes in availability and palatability of foods and reduction in amounts of physical exertion have resulted in an overall shift up of obesity in populations. Environmental influences override any obesity resistant genotypes at a population level.

Body weight homeostasis is an important physiological factor in the obesity problem. Multiple studies of mammals, including humans, indicate that body weight is regulated and that physiological mechanisms help to resist large changes in weight, especially downward changes (Coll, Farooqi, & O'Rahilly, 2007). Genes encode for molecular components of this regulatory system (Rosenbaum & Leibel, 1998). There are "catabolic" neuronal pathways in the brain's hypothalamus that respond to circulating signals that are secreted in response to feeding, and result in reduced food intake (through the sensation of satiety) and increased energy expenditure. The most important signals are from leptin, which is secreted in the adipose tissue; insulin from the pancreas, and cholecystokinin and peptide YY from the gastrointestinal tract. In response to dieting and weight loss, a corresponding and opposite mechanism occurs, which is "anabolic," increases appetite and lowers energy expenditure. Those signals include the hormone ghrelin and growth hormone (Popovic & Duntas, 2005). This system is inhibited in response to a plethora of available calories. It appears, from clinical, physiological, and molecular studies, that the anabolic system is far more efficient than the catabolic, and this explains the relatively easier mechanism of weight gain compared to that of weight loss. The environmental and behavioral obesogenic factors seem to create a dysregulation, or insensitivity of the catabolic side of this regulatory system. This provides the biological basis for the obesity epidemic (Schwartz et al., 2003).

It also explains the relatively poor success that most obese children and adults have with dieting to lose weight. Many can lose weight in the short term but have difficulties with sustaining the weight loss (Mann et al., 2007). Low energy intake results in the anabolic regulatory, physiologic, increased hunger, food-seeking behavior, and lower basal metabolic rate. Short-term weight loss attempts often fail – both independent and physician-guided attempts (Rossner, Hammarstrand, Hemmingsson, Neovius, & Johansson, 2008); successes depend upon long-term changes (Shick et al., 1998). Because of these physiologic effects on the human organism, prevention is more readily attainable than weight loss once obese.

The biogenetic contributions to obesity give rise to these implications: Individuals with obesity producing genotypes or regulatory adjustments due to an adverse fetal period are affected in ways that transcend what their own attitudes and actions might be able to do for obesity. Their biology is working against them and they are more likely fated to be obese compared to others. The larger cultural attitude that "it's their own fault" if they are obese is a falsehood. This is especially troublesome for children who suffer from stigma and who are bound to be obese by biological and environmental factors, both of which are not within their control, because dieting and weight loss efforts work against "thrifty genes" and neuro-endocrine regulation of body weight; therefore, prevention is better than treatment. Approaches that deal with the problem after it happens are prone to difficulty and would tend to blame the victim (and their families), if treatment is not successful. Since the older the child, the more likely that obesity will persist, we can consider childhood a critical period; failure to prevent obesity in children seals their biological fate. Therefore, they might require prevention interventions that are morally justifiable.

Environmental Contributions to Childhood Obesity

Environmental factors have resulted in high levels of obesity in genetically susceptible children. Many factors that have changed in areas where obesity rates have risen influence the ultimate balance between energy intake and expenditure. Many cross-sectional studies and longitudinal studies have explored these influences, but the ecological nature of the problem prevents knowledge of the relative influence of each. Most theorists have suggested that these primary factors have resulted in more childhood obesity (1) food, (2) physical activity, (3) transportation patterns, (4) a change in use of time, and (5) increased media consumption. The environment dramatically influences these critical lifestyle factors.

A useful paradigm that we will utilize is described in Swinburn, Egger, and Raza (1999), where they divide important influences into the *macro-environment*, including transportation infrastructure, government policy and law, the economy (including the food economy), the media, social determinants, cultural mores, and health systems, as well as the *micro-environment*, including communities, neighborhoods, schools, peer groups, and families. Our discussion will proceed from the macro to the micro. Physical, economic, political, and socio-cultural aspects of environment are pertinent to providing an obesogenic milieu. Thus, many parties or sponsors are identifiable as contributing to the epidemic and for potential, interventions: government (federal, state, and local), industry and media, community organizations, health care organizations, charitable groups, schools, legal community, individuals, parents and families, and youth themselves.

The Obesogenic Macro-Environment and Ethical Issues

The major importance of environmental factors has been demonstrated by analyzing the changes that have occurred in areas of the world where obesity is a more recent and more rapidly developing problem. These changes have occurred: Increased availability of foods high in fat, sugar, and salt; changes in production of food and marketing in developing countries; growth of fast food outlets of large trans-national corporations; and changes in patterns of work and leisure that occur because of economic changes in the region and are sustained by media's influences on consumer choice and lifestyle. The increase in prevalence of child obesity in USA and European countries has preceded other developing countries in the world because these obesogenic macro-environmental phenomena had been in place. Specific changes in environments supporting greater intake of sweetened food and drink, high fat food and all in larger portion sizes, more snacks, more ready-to-eat foods, and more restaurant eating provide more storable energy to the population (Anderson & Butcher, 2006). Availability of lower fat and nutritious foods has decreased in many areas. Energy expenditure has been affected by environments, which have resulted in less walking to school and elsewhere, fewer physical education classes, less play outside the home, and more use of cars, escalators, elevators, and automatic doors.

Governmental Policy

Governmental policy, whether national and local, has been recognized to influence obesity-related factors. The influences that have been discussed are (1) food production farm subsidies that favor production of corn syrup and, therefore, low cost and high sugar and high fat food availability (Schwartz & Brownell, 2007); (2) food programs under government supervision, such as the food stamp program, and school lunch programs which might influence food availability to underserved groups and children in school settings; (3) policies and standards regarding food quality and labeling; (4) educational policy (e.g., the food pyramid); (5) government and industry relationships, such as those affecting food manufacturers and advertisers, the political aspects of these relationships; and (6) state and community sponsoring awareness and preventive efforts. An issue of concern for children is the abundance of food advertising seen by children, especially on television. A 2005 review by the Institute of Medicine of the National Academies concluded that food marketing influences children's food preferences, consumption, and health (McGinnis, Gootman, & Kraak, 2006).

Various applications of law have been attempted or are being considered (Alderman, Smith, Fried, & Daynard, 2007). Evaluation of extant and proposed government policy has resulted in a vigorous dialog. Calls for public policy changes in order to remedy the problem, e.g., government regulation of food choices by taxes, regulation of food industry, and prohibiting direct advertising to children have engendered concerns about government's over-involvement in areas of personal choice and personal responsibility. "My eating habits or yours don't justify the government's involvement in the kitchen" (Kersh & Morone, 2002, p. 145). Food is linked to individual satisfaction and lifestyle, so strategies that strive to change personal food behavior often are viewed as intrusive.

Is there a government level justification to interfere with industry and personal choice in relation to child obesity? This is not a new precedent, governmental-level regulations have been applied to other areas of personal freedom, e.g., seat belts, car seats, traffic laws, and drug laws sentence checked by author and is correct. Acceptance at a societal level of such policy interventions, especially those aimed at advertising to children and regulation of school foods, depends upon whether there is real concern about obesity and whether children are considered the helpless "victims" of the obesogenic environment.

The Economy

The economy has influenced rates of childhood obesity. Personal income affects food choices and physical activity. Costs of food production, manufacturing, distribution, and retailing determine types of foods that are made available to the population. The marketing and production of food and beverages, which are preferentially desired by children and adolescents for their availability, price, and palatability, have coincided with rising obesity rates (Hawkes, 2007).

Social Determinants

The socioeconomic and demographic makeup of various sub-populations has an effect on child obesity rates. The rates of childhood obesity are higher in areas of greater poverty in developed countries and in developing countries that have a rising GNP (Monteiro, Conde, Lu, & Popkin, 2004; Ogden et al., 2006). Many mechanisms for this relationship include single parent or dual working parent families, lack of affordable healthy food, less supermarkets, more fast food restaurants, ethnically targeted food marketing, less opportunity to organize and provide healthy home environments for children, less opportunity to supervise children's activities, less neighborhood safety, and less affordable and available places for exercise (Kumanyika, 2008).

Obesity rates significantly differ by race/ethnicity. The prevalence of overweight Mexican-American male children and adolescents is significantly higher than that of overweight white children. For females, overweight rates for Mexican-American and black children and adolescents are significantly higher than white children (Ogden et al., 2006). Part of these differences relates to the effects of relative poverty as discussed above. Other parts relate to socio-cultural environmental influences in underserved communities. Traditional obesogenic cuisines, prevalent obesity norms, and body image ideals (above-average prevalence of obesity in adult female), female roles, maternal diabetes during pregnancy, parental attitudes and practices that may lead to overfeeding children, above-average levels of consumption of certain high calorie foods and beverages, under-funded schools (less fitness resources, soft-drink availability, and lower quality foods), food insecurity, higher stress levels, and increased TV time have all been hypothesized as contributing to obesity in ethnic groups in which obesity is most prevalent.

Beyond ethnic-specific cultural issues, there is an influential cultural attitude toward thinness and "fatness" that affects all groups in society. As evidenced from the advertising of the multi-billion dollar weight loss industry as well as the restaurant and food industry, we live in a "bulimic" society, where the message is eat all you want, but lose weight whenever you want, or you will not be respected. Thinness signifies control, beauty, success, attractiveness and cleanliness. In contrast, the lack of thinness represents laziness, ugliness, and is non-hygienic and not desirable. Our children and teens are continuously exposed to this "adult" cultural attitude, and this exposure is similar to ways that we expose children to the excesses of the adult world. Children's unique physical and psychological characteristics put them in danger with are not with this overeat and diet attitude. Indeed, teens without guidance assume that the best way to lose weight is to "diet," an entity that can be defined by a myriad number of unhealthy and "quick fix" approaches, for instance self starvation and taking diet pills.

This cultural milieu creates a pervasive stigma for overweight children, who are effected from young ages of childhood. There is a relationship between a child's obesity and likelihood of being bullied (Janssen, Craig, Boyce, & Pickett, 2004). The effects of weight bias on children include effects on self-esteem, depression, body dissatisfaction, problematic peer relations, suicidal ideation and ultimately lower SES, eating disturbances, and decreased physical activity. Body dissatisfaction, lower self-esteem, embarrassment, a reluctance to engage in physical activities, and unhealthy weight loss practices (self-starving) can contribute to the overweight condition by causing mood-related eating and binging (Puhl & Latner, 2007; Puhl, Moss-Racusin, & Schwartz, 2007; Puhl, Moss-Racusin, Schwartz, & Brownell, 2008). Awareness of stigma should guide interventions. There have been mandates for mandatory BMI screening, for instance (Justus, Ryan, Rockenbach, Katterapalli, & Card-Higginson, 2007), but this would likely add to stigmatic effects upon children in a public environment (CNMC, 2008).

The ethical implications of the prevalent inequities in childhood obesity as well as cultural influences are considerable. Dietary and lifestyle characteristics are imbedded in an ecology that is influenced by macro-environmental forces of economic factors, ethnic/group membership, and cultural attitudes. Many of the changes an individual parent or care-taker might consider are beyond individual choice. Public health and clinical interventions seek to alter individual behaviors of parents and children by giving advice about eating and exercise. While it seems necessary and indeed seems the only thing that can be done, it is inequitable, because it puts the burden on individuals despite other realities. In addition, within the perception of those from minority groups, the health message might be obscured by the cultural mandate for a socially acceptable appearance. The majority culture is characterized by an undue emphasis on thinness and creates a normative discontent about body in females (Baskin, Ahluwalia, & Resnicow, 2001). Are obesity-related interventions perceived as paternalistic demands for conformity to dominant culture, or appropriate health messages? Health advice from the majority culture can be met with distrust. The overemphasis upon weight control might not be an ideally psychologically healthy aspect of majority culture. Do our methods of intervention (telling people to eat healthier foods and exercise more) feel stigmatizing for minority parents and kids?

Health Care Systems

Health care systems, including standards of health care of medical care givers are part of the macro-environment that might affect obesity. Medical systems are focused, via training, culture, and economics, upon diagnosis and treatment and are less proficient at preventive interventions (Perrin et al., 2008). In addition, primary care physicians' practices are not optimized for chronic care and behavioral change counseling, which is not reimbursed, as well as for acute care and medical procedures. There are many underinsured segments of society, and those segments often include children who are obese or at risk. Indeed, health care reimbursement favors procedures and short-term interventions rather than the type of preventive and long-term interventions that might help prevent child obesity (Homer & Simpson, 2007; Tsai, Asch, & Wadden, 2006).

Can obesity be remedied utilizing the traditional medical interventions of short term health counseling promotion, medications and surgery? For child obesity, treatment is fraught with great difficulty. Because child obesity is associated with significant morbidities, health care professionals attempt to intervene without strong tools. The evidence base of interventions is fragmented and small scale, and there are significant questions of efficacy and sustainability in most health care settings. Indeed, the most effective interventions that have been researched have occurred in multi-disciplinary settings, largely unavailable to most children and parents (Hughes et al., 2008; Spear et al., 2007). Recent expert recommendation for treatment calls for types of interventions unavailable to most practitioners (Spear et al.). Care that is necessary for the rising numbers of obese children must be sustained and multi-disciplined. Prevention and treatment need reimbursement on par with other health care services. Our health care system currently does not make this available to providers and families.

The clinician when caring for an obese child, aware of the health risks, is compelled to intervene utilizing the resources available. Since obesity is a very difficult problem to treat and success rates are low, the age old medical ethics principle of *first, no harm* becomes prominent. Obese children and adolescent care requires frequent monitoring, adherence to medical "prescriptions" for food and exercise, ones that are difficult for care givers and patients to follow. This results in concerns among pediatricians of non-adherence, and sets up a potentially contentious relationship, especially for the most severely obese children. Indeed, investigations of child abuse and neglect have been called for in cases of extreme obesity (BBC News, 2007). Those children are also at higher risk in the medical system to be exposed to drugs and surgery, both methods lacking a well established record of effectiveness and safety (Inge et al., 2004).

The Community Environment

The community environment includes the local area infrastructure, the commercial environment, and the school environment. Analysis of studies attempting to clarify the relative contributions of these factors has been equivocal, perhaps due to methodological problems (Holsten, 2008). Availability of fast foods effects overweight in adolescents' more than younger children (Rosenheck, 2008). The school environment has been questioned as an obesogenic influence because of decreasing time for physical education, unhealthy foods available in vending machines, and school-supported marketing of foods with low nutritional value (Molnar, Garcia, Boninger, & Merrill, 2008; Story, Kaphingst, & French, 2006). There are a lack of interventions reported, targeting specific childhood racial and ethnic subgroups. Researches on community interventions that are ethnically and racially specific and that have been efficacious are needed for community public health planners to utilize evidence-based approaches (Economos & Irish-Hauser, 2007).

Macro-environmental changes, due to the ecological complexity, require critical appraisal of preventive interventions as well as contribution of sponsor's involvement at many levels of society. The public has demonstrated concern over the problem of child obesity (Evans, Finkelstein, Kamerow, & Renaud, 2005). However, the multi-factorial contributions to the problem would require concern at many levels of private and public sponsorship in order to create favorable change or the macro-environment. A useful demonstration paradigm has occurred in Western Europe, in which sponsors were contacted to determine changes that would be acceptable and useful (Millstone & Lobstein, 2007). The needs of children might challenge philosophical and legal concepts of commercial freedom and government support of free commerce. For example, the Sydney Principles' for reducing the commercial promotion of foods and beverages to children, adopted by the International Obesity Task Force (Swinburn et al., 2008), suggest that children's rights call for marketing restrictions. Advocacy for projects that deal with multiple sponsors is needed to support upstream change (Dietz, Bland, Gortmaker, Molloy, & Schmid, 2002).

The Obesogenic Micro-Environment and Ethical Issues

The micro-environment includes where adults and children live their lives within their homes and in their schools and communities. The overriding influences on child obesity in this sector, the structure and needs of the family, as well as parenting attitudes and practices, attitudes and behaviors of other influential adults (extended family, school, and community), and peer attitudes and behaviors.

Research has supported the effect of parenting on childhood obesity. Breast feeding has shown to be protective (Arenz, Ruckerl, Koletzko, & von Kries, 2004; von Kries, Koletzko, Sauerwald, & von Mutius, 2000). Parenting practices, such as exerting pressure and restriction of foods has contributed to subsequent obesogenic eating styles in children (Faith & Kerns, 2005). Overly permissive styles can also contribute to unhealthy eating, lack of exercise, and television watching, and lack of sleep (Knutson & Van Cauter, 2008). In addition, the risk of obesity is increased by physical abuse, verbal abuse, humiliation, neglect, strict upbringing, physical punishment, and conflict or tension (Ventura & Birch, 2008).

Parental knowledge and attitudes also are pertinent (Crawford, Timperio, Telford, & Salmon, 2006). In many minority parents, attitudes and behaviors may be supportive of higher level of obesity compared to than in non-minority parents. Many parents underestimate their child's level of overweight. Studies have shown that shown that Latina mothers, and those with low income and lower levels of education do not view their preschool children as overweight (Hackie & Bowles, 2007; He & Evans, 2007; Jain et al., 2001). Some positive attitudes about overweight might persist in those who come from backgrounds where thinness is related to illness, poverty or drug addiction (Kumanyika & Grier, 2006).

Gender considerations affect child obesity as well. Women are mostly responsible for organizing, preparing and providing food to children (Warin, Turner, Moore, & Davies, 2008). Gender and class-based aspects of mothering are not often explored or understood in the area of health promotion. Experiences of women from different social classes, and their understanding of their role as mothers might differ from counseling requests for individual behavioral change.

Family environmental issues provide complex fields of influence embedded in a multi-layered environment, which include tastes, traditions, convenience requirements/choices, foods available at home, food/meal routines, feeding styles, family members' weight status and diet, attitudes toward overweight individuals' weight status, encouragement of physical activity, and rules regarding TV use.

Culpability and responsibility are primary ethical issues in child obesity. Dietary and lifestyle occur within an ecological context including macro and micro-environmental factors. The act of directing behavior (giving advice) either in clinical settings or via public forum that is incongruous with forces beyond individual choice is ethically troublesome. There is a presumption of parental liberty in our attitudes and law, resulting in relative freedom from intrusions of state, and yet many children are becoming obese. Is "letting" a child become obese a dereliction of parental responsibility? Should there be individualized interventions based upon BMI screening in order to protect certain children? Are the risks to children less important than the rights to privacy or commercial freedom?

Environments, Ethics and Children's Rights

We have derived these ethical questions from our discussion of the nature of child obesity. They are summarized as follows:

- Does protection of children require coerced action and a paternalistic approach at a public health and clinical level, or can efficacious educational and preventive interventions be developed?
- Whose culpability/responsibility is childhood obesity in view of complex, multi-level influences? Does culpability mandate responsibility for ameliorating interventions?
- What action is mandated when results of action are not clear? What are the priorities for action?
- Uneven social determinants exist in childhood; can interventions be socially, ethnically, and racially appropriate (efficacious and respectful)?

- There are definite stigmatic aspects of being an obese child; can we steer clear of inadvertent harm to children and families in our interventions by providing developmentally appropriate interventions; identification of child/teen patients that does not add to stigma and, prevention of eating disordered behavior?

The ecological influences on child obesity that have been discussed create a challenge to help children prevent and reduce obesity. Analyzing the problem of child obesity as a "rights" issue, in addition to a public health challenge may add moral authority to public consideration of changes that are needed (Greenway, 2008). Supporting and promoting their rights require considerations that are child specific and can help guide preventive and therapeutic interventions, both at a public health, and a clinical level:

1. Children need special protection in this obesogenic world environment. They are an at-risk population whose "biological fate" is dependent on macro- and micro-environmental influences. Children's health has been harmed by changes in the environment. Therefore, child and adolescent health must become a more active consideration in factors such as building communities for healthier movement, altering community food environments; regulating food advertising; and developing government sponsored nutrition, educational, and health programs. Precedent for regulations and policies that protect the public health already exists for other health risks, e.g., motor vehicle injury, alcohol, and tobacco, and are justifiable to protect children.
2. Public health interventions will be most effective if they address *upstream* effects on children's health, looking at the macro-environmental level and the community level, rather than focusing upon individual family behavior.
3. Public health and *prevention* model *is better than treatment* model. This derives from the nature of the obese state.
4. *Despite the need for action, interventions should be evidenced-based and strive to do no harm.* Some approaches and treatments do have the potential to harm, rather than help, especially if fragmented from socio-cultural considerations or derived from untested methods.
5. *Interventions need to be developmentally appropriate.* Psychosocial and developmental uniqueness of children and adolescents, requires a measured approach different than the approaches utilized for adult weight loss. Health, rather than weight, should the be goal of prevention and treatment. A weight focus, by itself, is likely to result in child, parent, and health provider frustration and despair, contributing to stigma, and blaming children and parents.
6. *Intensive medical interventions should only involve severe obesity with severe obesity-related complications.* In view of our knowledge of health risk and treatment risk, we are not justified in providing treatments that might harm rather than help.
7. All interventions must *address stigma and social attitudes.*
8. Socio-cultural mediators require research and analysis of subcultures and sub-populations so that interventions are grounded in cultural traditions and norms unique to groups at risk.
9. Environmental change that helps prevent and reduce child obesity requires *sponsors working together* to ensure effective change and to avoid unintended consequences.

References

Adair, L. S. (2008). Child and adolescent obesity: Epidemiology and developmental perspectives. *Physiology & Behavior, 94*, 8–16.

Alderman, J., Smith, J. A., Fried, E. J., & Daynard, R. A. (2007). Application of law to the childhood obesity epidemic. *Journal of Law, Medicine & Ethics, 35*, 90–112.

Amuna, P., & Zotor, F. B. (2008). Epidemiological and nutrition transition in developing countries: Impact on human health and development. *Proceedings of the Nutrition Society, 67*, 82–90.

Anderson, P. M., & Butcher, K. E. (2006). Childhood obesity: Trends and potential causes. *Future of Children, 16*, 19–45.

Arenz, S., Ruckerl, R., Koletzko, B., & von Kries, R. (2004). Breast-feeding and childhood obesity – A systematic review. *International Journal of Obesity and Related Metabolic Disorders, 28*, 1247–1256.

Baskin, M. L., Ahluwalia, H. K., & Resnicow, K. (2001). Obesity intervention among African-American children and adolescents. *Pediatric Clinics of North America, 48*, 1027–1039.

BBC News (2007, February 27). *Obese boy to remain with mother*. Retrieved from www.news.bbc.co.uk/1/hi/health/6402113.stm.

Bibbins-Domingo, K., Coxson, P., Pletcher, M. J., Lightwood, J., & Goldman, L. (2007). Adolescent overweight and future adult coronary heart disease. *New England Journal of Medicine, 357*, 2371–2379.

Campos, P., Saguy, A., Ernsberger, P., Oliver, E., & Gaesser, G. (2006). The epidemiology of overweight and obesity: Public health crisis or moral panic? *International Journal of Epidemiology, 35*, 55–60.

Casper, R. C., Sullivan, E. L., & Tecott, L. (2008). Relevance of animal models to human eating disorders and obesity. *Psychopharmacology, 199*, 313–329.

Children's National Medical Center (CNMC) (2008). *Children's national medical center policy statement: Childhood obesity*. Retrieved from www.childrensnational.org/files/PDF/advocacy/OnCapitolHill/Obesity_Statement.pdf.

Coll, A. P., Farooqi, I. S., & O'Rahilly, S. (2007). The hormonal control of food intake. *Cell, 129*, 251–262.

Crawford, D., Timperio, A., Telford, A., & Salmon, J. (2006). Parental concerns about childhood obesity and the strategies employed to prevent unhealthy weight gain in children. *Public Health Nutrition, 9*, 889–895.

Deshmukh-Taskar, P., Nicklas, T. A., Morales, M., Yang, S. J., Zakeri, I., & Berenson, G. S. (2006). Tracking of overweight status from childhood to young adulthood: The Bogalusa Heart Study. *European Journal of Clinical Nutrition, 60*, 48–57.

Dietz, W. H., Bland, M. G., Gortmaker, S. L., Molloy, M., & Schmid, T. L. (2002). Policy tools for the childhood obesity epidemic. *Journal of Law, Medicine & Ethics, 30*, 83–87.

Ebbeling, C. B., & Ludwig, D. S. (2008). Tracking pediatric obesity: An index of uncertainty? *JAMA, 299*, 2442–2443.

Economos, C. D., & Irish-Hauser, S. (2007). Community interventions: A brief overview and their application to the obesity epidemic. *Journal of Law, Medicine & Ethics, 35*, 131–137.

Engeland, A., Bjorge, T., Tverdal, A., & Sogaard, A. J. (2004). Obesity in adolescence and adulthood and the risk of adult mortality. *Epidemiology, 15*, 79–85.

Evans, W. D., Finkelstein, E. A., Kamerow, D. B., & Renaud, J. M. (2005). Public perceptions of childhood obesity. *American Journal of Preventive Medicine, 28*, 26–32.

Faith, M. S., & Kerns, J. (2005). Infant and child feeding practices and childhood overweight: The role of restriction. *Maternal & Child Nutrition, 1*, 164–168.

Greenway, J. (2008). Childhood obesity: Bringing children's rights discourse to public health policy. *Community Practitioner, 81*, 17–21.

Hackie, M., & Bowles, C. L. (2007). Maternal perception of their overweight children. *Public Health Nursing, 24*, 538–546.

Hawkes, C. (2007). Regulating and litigating in the public interest: Regulating food marketing to young people worldwide: Trends and policy drivers. *American Journal of Public Health, 7*, 1962–1973.

He, M., & Evans, A. (2007). Are parents aware that their children are overweight or obese? Do they care? *Canadian Family Physician, 53*, 1493–1499.

Holsten, J. E. (2008). Obesity and the community food environment: A systematic review. *Public Health Nutrition, 14*, 1–9.

Homer, C., & Simpson, L. A. (2007). Childhood obesity: What's health care policy got to do with it? *Health Affairs (Millwood), 26*, 441–444.

Hughes, A. R., Stewart, L., Chapple, J., McColl, J. H., Donaldson, M. D., Kelnar, C. J., et al. (2008). Randomized, controlled trial of a best-practice individualized behavioral program for treatment of childhood overweight: Scottish childhood overweight treatment trial (SCOTT). *Pediatrics, 121*, e539–e546.

Inge, T. H., Krebs, N. F., Garcia, V. F., Skelton, J. A., Guice, K. S., Strauss, R. S., et al. (2004). Bariatric surgery for severely overweight adolescents: Concerns and recommendations. *Pediatrics, 114*, 217–223.

Jain, A., Sherman, S. N., Chamberlin, L. A., Carter, Y., Powers, S. W., & Whitaker, R. C. (2001). Why don't low-income mothers worry about their preschoolers being overweight? *Pediatrics, 107*, 1138–1146.

Janssen, I., Craig, W. M., Boyce, W. F., & Pickett, W. (2004). Associations between overweight and obesity with bullying behaviors in school-aged children. *Pediatrics, 113*, 1187–1194.

Janssen, I., Katzmarzyk, P. T., Boyce, W. F., Vereecken, C., Mulvihill, C., Roberts, C., et al. (2005). Comparison of overweight and obesity prevalence in school-aged youth from 34 countries and their relationships with physical activity and dietary patterns. *Obesity Reviews, 6*, 123–132.

Justus, M. B., Ryan, K. W., Rockenbach, J., Katterapalli, C., & Card-Higginson, P. (2007). Lessons learned while implementing a legislated school policy: Body mass index assessments among Arkansas's public school students. *Journal of School Health, 77*, 706–713.

Kersh, R., & Morone, J. (2002). The politics of obesity: Seven steps to government action. *Health Affairs (Millwood), 21*, 142–153.

Knutson, K. L., & Van Cauter, E. (2008). Associations between sleep loss and increased risk of obesity and diabetes. *Annals of the New York Academy of Sciences, 1129*, 287–304.

Kumanyika, S. K. (2008). Environmental influences on childhood obesity: Ethnic and cultural influences in context. *Physiology & Behavior, 94*, 61–70.

Kumanyika, S. K., & Grier, S. (2006). Targeting interventions for ethnic minority and low-income populations. *Future of Children, 16*, 187–207.

Lobstein, T., Baur, L., & Uauy, R. (2004). Obesity in children and young people: A crisis in public health. *Obesity Reviews, 5*, 4–104.

Ludwig, D. S. (2007). Childhood obesity – The shape of things to come. *New England Journal of Medicine, 357*, 2325–2327.

Mann, T., Tomiyama, A. J., Westling, E., Lew, A. M., Samuels, B., & Chatman, J. (2007). Medicare's search for effective obesity treatments: Diets are not the answer. *American Psychologist, 62*, 220–233.

McGinnis, J. M., Gootman, J. A., & Kraak, V. I. (2006). *Food marketing to children and youth: Threat or opportunity*. Washington, DC: National Academies Press.

Mendez, M. A., Monteiro, C. A., & Popkin, B. M. (2005). Overweight exceeds underweight among women in most developing countries. *American Journal of Clinical Nutrition, 81*, 714–721.

Millstone, E., & Lobstein, T. (2007). The PorGrow project: Overall cross-national results, comparisons and implications. *Obesity Reviews, 2*, 29–36.

Molnar, A., Garcia, D. R., Boninger, F., & Merrill, B. (2008). Marketing of foods of minimal nutritional value to children in schools. *Preventive Medicine, 47*, 504–507.

Monteiro, C. A., Conde, W. L., Lu, B., & Popkin, B. M. (2004). Obesity and inequities in health in the developing world. *International Journal of Obesity and Related Metabolic Disorders, 28*, 1181–1186.

Ogden, C. L., Carroll, M. D., Curtin, L. R., McDowell, M. A., Tabak, C. J., & Flegal, K. M. (2006). Prevalence of overweight and obesity in the United States, 1999–2004. *Journal of the American Medical Association, 295*, 1549–1555.

Parsi, M. R. (2002). A world tailored for children and the young: The children and the young around us and the child and the adolescent within each of us. *Minerva Pediatrica, 54*, 489–506.

Perrin, E. M., Vann, J. C., Lazorick, S., Ammerman, A., Teplin, S., Flower, K., et al. (2008). Bolstering confidence in obesity prevention and treatment counseling for resident and community pediatricians. *Patient Education and Counseling, 73*, 179–185.

Popovic, V., & Duntas, L. H. (2005). Brain somatic cross-talk: Ghrelin, leptin and ultimate challengers of obesity. *Nutritional Neuroscience, 8*, 1–5.

Prentice, A. M., Rayco-Solon, P., & Moore, S. E. (2005). Insights from the developing world: Thrifty genotypes and thrifty phenotypes. *Proceedings of the Nutrition Society, 64*, 153–161.

Puhl, R. M., & Latner, J. D. (2007). Stigma, obesity, and the health of the nation's children. *Psychological Bulletin, 133*, 557–580.

Puhl, R. M., Moss-Racusin, C. A., & Schwartz, M. B. (2007). Internalization of weight bias: Implications for binge eating and emotional well-being. *Obesity (Silver Spring), 15*, 19–23.

Puhl, R. M., Moss-Racusin, C. A., Schwartz, M. B., & Brownell, K. D. (2008). Weight stigmatization and bias reduction: Perspectives of overweight and obese adults. *Health Education Research, 23*, 347–358.

Rosenbaum, M., & Leibel, R. L. (1998). The physiology of body weight regulation: Relevance to the etiology of obesity in children. *Pediatrics, 101*, 525–539.

Rosenheck, R. (2008). Fast food consumption and increased caloric intake: A systematic review of a trajectory towards weight gain and obesity risk. *Obesity Reviews, 9*, 535–547.

Rossner, S., Hammarstrand, M., Hemmingsson, E., Neovius, M., & Johansson, K. (2008). Long-term weight loss and weight-loss maintenance strategies. *Obesity Reviews, 9*, 624–630.

Schwartz, M. B., & Brownell, K. D. (2007). Actions necessary to prevent childhood obesity: Creating the climate for change. *Journal of Law, Medicine & Ethics, 35*, 78–89.

Schwartz, M. W., Woods, S. C., Seeley, R. J., Barsh, G. S., Baskin, D. G., & Leibel, R. L. (2003). Is the energy homeostasis system inherently biased toward weight gain? *Diabetes, 52*, 232–238.

Shick, S. M., Wing, R. R., Klem, M. L., McGuire, M. T., Hill, J. O., & Seagle, H. (1998). Persons successful at long-term weight loss and maintenance continue to consume a low-energy, low-fat diet. *Journal of the American Dietetic Association, 98*, 408–413.

Spear, B. A., Barlow, S. E., Ervin, C., Ludwig, D. S., Saelens, B. E., Schetzina, K. E., et al. (2007). Recommendations for treatment of child and adolescent overweight and obesity. *Pediatrics, 120*(Suppl. 4), S254–S288.

Story, M., Kaphingst, K. M., & French, S. (2006). The role of schools in obesity prevention. *Future of Children, 16*, 109–142.

Swinburn, B., Egger, G., & Raza, F. (1999). Dissecting obesogenic environments: The development and application of a framework for identifying and prioritizing environmental interventions for obesity. *Preventive Medicine, 29*, 563–570.

Swinburn, B., Sacks, G., Lobstein, T., Rigby, N., Baur, L. A., Brownell, K. D., et al. (2008). Sydney principles' for reducing the commercial promotion of foods and beverages to children. *Public Health Nutrition, 29*, 1–6.

Tsai, A. G., Asch, D. A., & Wadden, T. A. (2006). Insurance coverage for obesity treatment. *Journal of the American Dietetic Association, 106*, 1651–1655.

United Nations Convention on the Rights of the Child (1989). United Nations General Assembly Document A/RES/44/25. Retrieved from http://www.cirp.org.

Ventura, A. K., & Birch, L. L. (2008). Does parenting affect children's eating and weight status? *International Journal of Behavioral Nutrition and Physical Activity, 5*, 15.

von Kries, R., Koletzko, B., Sauerwald, T., & von Mutius, E. (2000). Does breast-feeding protect against childhood obesity? *Advances in Experimental Medicine and Biology, 478*, 29–39.

Wang, Y., & Lobstein, T. (2006). Worldwide trends in childhood overweight and obesity. *International Journal of Pediatric Obesity, 1*, 11–25.

Wang, Y., Monteiro, C., & Popkin, B. M. (2002). Trends of obesity and underweight in older children and adolescents in the United States, Brazil, China, and Russia. *American Journal of Clinical Nutrition, 75*, 971–977.

Wardle, J., Carnell, S., Haworth, C. M., & Plomin, R. (2008). Evidence for a strong genetic influence on childhood adiposity despite the force of the obesogenic environment. *American Journal of Clinical Nutrition, 87*, 398–404.

Warin, M., Turner, K., Moore, V., & Davies, M. (2008). Bodies, mothers and identities: Rethinking obesity and the BMI. *Sociology of Health & Illness, 30*, 97–111.

Chapter 10
Anchoring and Empowering Children: A Child's Right to Participation Within a Healthy Environment

Edmund B. Bruyere

"We are not the sources of problems;
we are the resources that are needed to solve them".

Voices from the World's Children
Children's Forum 2002

Introduction

I begin this chapter with the question, has the USA done enough to anchor all children living in the USA to the relationships, experiences, and opportunities vital to empowering them with the capacities necessary to exert their right to participation? With an estimated 13 million children living in poverty (Faas & Cauthen, 2008), 1.3 million living in homelessness (National Law Center on Homelessness and Poverty (NLCHP), 2007), 8.5 million without health insurance (National Center on Health Care (NCHC), 2009), 92,854 incarcerated males (OJJDP, 2008), and 25% not graduating from high school, (President Obama, 2009) the answer to this question appears to be a resounding no.

With the plight of so many children, we have an obligation to act and move toward permanent change. To date, 193 of our global counterparts have chosen to do this exactly by ratifying the UN Convention on the Rights of the Child (CRC, 1989), which contains 39 substantive and interconnected articles meant to anchor and empower all children to exert their right to participation (Hart, Price-Cohen, Farrell-Erickson, & Flekkoy, 2001; UN General Comment no. 12, 2009 (GC-12, 2009c)). It is important to note that the USA (Somalia also has not ratified the CRC but intends to do so in the near future) remains the only industrialized country to stand in contempt of this international social and moral consensus (Bedard, 2007).

E.B. Bruyere (✉)
Department of Psychology, Loyola University,
6525 N Sheridan Road, 669 Damen Hall, Chicago, IL 60626, USA
e-mail: ebruyere@luc.edu

J. Garbarino and G. Sigman (eds.), *A Child's Right to a Healthy Environment*,
The Loyola University Symposium on the Human Rights of Children 1,
DOI 10.1007/978-1-4419-6791-6_10,

Thus, this chapter explains the benefits associated with socially, spiritually, and psychologically anchoring children living in the USA to the relationships, experiences, and opportunities vital to promoting their right to participation. I do this by indentifying the substantive articles related to a child's right to participation, explaining the concepts of social, spiritual, and psychological anchoring, highlighting research conducted by the Search Institute which demonstrates the significant benefits of anchoring children, and conclude by calling for ratification of the UN Convention on the Rights of the Child by the USA.

Participation and the Evolving Capacities of a Child

While the UN Convention of the Rights of the Child's (CRC) principle of "participation" is best understood through an evaluation of the relation of the 39 substantive articles within the CRC as a whole, Article 12 is recognized as specifically addressing a child's right to participation (UN Committee on the Rights of the Child General Comment no. 12 (GC-12), 2009). Article 12 asserts that children be afforded opportunities to express themselves, verbally as well as nonverbally, and to voice opinions in matters relevant to them (Lansdown, 2005). However, while it is acknowledged that adults respect and consider the expressions and opinions of children, this does not equate to granting them every wish or request. Rather, parents as well as other adults are encouraged to consider the relevance of the topic, maturity level, and if the matter under consideration is in the "best interest of the child" (Hart, 2002; Articles 3 and 18). Similarly, Articles 13–15 and 31 grant *all* children the right to expression, thought and religion, association and assembly, and play.

Because a child's right to participation depends on social environments providing equal opportunities for participation (GC-12, 2009c), it is relevant to briefly highlight the CRC's principle of nondiscrimination. Article 2(1) asserts:

> States Parties shall respect and ensure the rights set forth in the present Convention to each child within their jurisdiction without discrimination of any kind, irrespective of the child's, or his/her parent's, or legal guardian's race, color, sex, language, religion, political or other opinion, national, ethnic or social origin, property, disability, birth or other status.

Each of the aforementioned rights is vital to promoting a child's *evolving capacities* (Article 5; Lansdown, 2005). Evolving capacities refer to the "processes of maturation and learning whereby children progressively acquire knowledge, competencies and understanding, including acquiring understanding about their rights and about how they can best be realized" (p. 8, UN Committee on the Rights of the Child General Comment no. 7 (GC-7), 2005). The evolving capacities of a child are influenced by the extent to which they are socially, spiritually, and psychologically anchored to healthy relationships, experiences, and opportunities (Lansdown, 2005). As we see later in this chapter, the more children are anchored to the relationships, experiences, and opportunities vital to exerting their right to participation, the more likely they are to thrive and be protected from risk. Thus, in accord with the theme of this text, child participation depends in large part on being raised in a socially healthy environment.

Social Anchoring

We turn now to an explanation of *social anchoring*. Social anchoring refers to grounding children in healthy families, other adult relationships, and communities (Garbarino, 1999). According to Melton (2005a), a leading child rights scholar in the USA, these social anchors are at the heart of the CRC (see preamble, articles 4, 18, 26, 28–29, 30, 31). As he explains, "individual rights (i.e., participation) lack meaning without social relatedness and social cohesion" (Melton, 2009). The family stands at the forefront of this assertion (GC-7, 2005; Melton, 1996).

Participation begins at birth when newborns and infants participate in reciprocal interactions in which their behavior appears to be indiscriminate but meaningful (Flekkoy & Kaufman, 1997; GC-7, 2005). For example, although they lack verbal ability, all infants, regardless of culture, communicate by engaging in survival behaviors meant to obtain responses from caregivers. The function of these interactions generally will lead to an attachment relationship which will predict healthy (or unhealthy) human development (Ainsworth, 1978; Sroufe, Egeland, Carlson, & Collins, 2005), consequently empowering them with the evolving capacities necessary for exerting their right to participation (GC-7, 2005).

Researchers have identified four attachment relationships influenced by the type of caregiving infants and children receive (*securely-attached, anxious-resistant, anxious-avoidant,* and *disorganized-disoriented*; Ainsworth, 1978; Main & Solomon, 1990). The most developmentally facilitative relationship is *securely-attached* – achieved through accepting sensitive and responsive caregiving. "Normal" infants who develop a securely-attached relationship will likely show considerably better psychological and behavioral outcomes, and therefore, will be better prepared to exert their right to participation. Securely-attached children are more likely to cope with stress effectively and less likely to develop depression, conduct problems, and to engage in alcohol and drug use, than children who are not securely-attached (Sroufe et al., 2005).

Beyond infancy, the influence of family remains stable. Children continue to need the protection, support, love, and guidance (preferably through an authoritative style of parenting) of parents as well as others. The Committee on the rights of the Child (GC-12, 2009c) recommends ratifying nations develop and promote parent education programs directed at teaching parents an authoritative style of parenting which has been found to be more respectful of child participation and the human rights of children in general. These programs should address:

- "The relationship of mutual respect between parents and children
- The involvement of children in decision making

- The implication of giving due weight to the views of every family member
- The understanding, promotion and respect for children's evolving capacities" (p. 20, GC-12, 2009c)

Other Adult Relationships

Vygotsky (1986) proposed that child development is influenced through social and cultural interactions with parents, family, as well as others like nonrelated adults (Benson, 2007; Grossman & Bulle, 2006). Nonrelated adults (e.g., mentors, coaches, teachers, clergy, and family) influence a child's "zone of proximal development" – the point between what can be learned on one's own and what can be learned with the intervention of a teacher. This is significant because it is a mechanism for learning how to function both psychologically and behaviorally within society and to become empowered to exert the right to participation.

To illustrate the power of nonrelated adult role models, I offer a personal anecdote. My son, Eddie III, who lives with his mother in Nebraska, spent the summer with me last year. Shortly after arriving, I noticed behaviors indicating that he was suffering deficits in intrapersonal competence (e.g., poor self-esteem, low self-confidence, and depression). As a father who loves his son deeply, I contacted his mother to discuss my concerns. We agreed upon a strategic intervention to boost his self-esteem, confidence, and affect. Having read about the positive influence of *martial arts,* the first part of our plan included enrolling Eddie in karate classes with one of the sports most successful athletes – Jon Fonto. I should specify that I was not encouraging my son to gain skills to become violent with others but rather the skills necessary to boost his intrapersonal competence.

The second part of our plan included encouraging Eddie to apply for a part-time job through our community youth job center. Our intentions in doing this were to strengthen his job skills and financial competence. What I did not expect from his employment was the positive influence of an intergenerational relationship he developed with a well-respected community member and a long time resident of our community – an 80-year-old Syd Zinney.

Eddie's enthusiasm for learning karate was exciting to observe. Equally impressive was the dedication and effort he put forth working for Mr. Zinney. As the next few months passed, I developed a deep level of respect and admiration for both of the men in my son's life. Jon and Mr. Zinney made an incredible impression on Eddie. Jon challenged him physically and mentally, and with the effort he put forth in the dojo, resulted in earning a yellow belt. With Mr. Zinney, he learned valuable life lessons, to take pride in his work, and gained a deeper respect for me. Over the course of the summer, Eddie went from being depressed, and having relatively low levels of self-esteem and confidence, to a young man filled with pride and confidence, as well as joy. When he left to attend college, it was obvious he was taking an important "can do" attitude with him.

The influence of these experiences with nonrelated adults and the corresponding psychological and behavioral outcomes are not unique to those displayed by my son. A large body of research supports the psychological value of participation with nonrelated adults (Benson, 2007; Cochran & Bo, 1989; Pretty, Andrewes, & Collett, 1994; Svedhem, 1994; Talmi & Harter, 1998; Werner, 1993). To illustrate, research has show that relationships with nonrelated adults are significantly related to greater levels of self-worth and hope for the future (Talmi & Harter, 1998). Likewise, relationships with nonrelated adults have also been found to decrease feelings of loneliness, depression, aggression, and delinquency. Finally, research has also found that youth who develop meaningful relationships with three or more nonrelated adults for at least 3 years, are less likely to use alcohol and drugs, smoke cigarettes, and engage in juvenile crime (Benson, 2007).

Healthy Communities

Child participation depends on the social and economic health of communities (Barnes, Katz, Korbin, & O'Brien, 2006). For example, investigating the influence of social and economic stress on rates of child maltreatment, Garbarino (1976) found child maltreatment to be significantly related to inadequate neighborhood social support and economic stress. Another study reported that 97% of youth living in Chicago do not feel that the adults in their communities value or like them (Scales & Leffert, 2004). Research suggests that children who do not feel safe are less likely to participate when living in unsafe conditions (UNICEF, 2003), to view adults as dependable, to play, and/or to engage in cultural activities. In addition, children who feel unsafe are more likely to do poorly in school, isolate themselves from others, have less hope for the future, and engage in risk behavior, than peers who feel safe (Schwab-Stone et al., 1995).

What are the outcomes associated with living in a healthy community? A study evaluating the strength of 112 communities across the USA, found the number of community strengths (strong families, schools, community involvement, and positive peer influence) to promote child participation and positive psychological and behavioral outcomes (Blyth & Leffert, 1995). These findings are in line with research conducted by Theokas et al. (2005). Conducting exploratory factor analysis, they found ecological assets (e.g., family, community, and school) to predict individual asset accumulation (evolving capacities), which in turn was found to influence positive outcomes (school success, display of leadership, helping others, maintaining good health, delay of gratification, valuing diversity, and overcoming adversity; outcomes include youth who develop into citizens who contribute to self, family, community, and society). It was concluded that healthy communities provide youth with caring, safe and supportive environments, relationships that value youth, opportunities for participation, and set clear expectations for behavior.

Spiritual Anchoring

To fully understand the construct of *spiritual anchoring*, it is necessary to provide a basic definition of spiritual development. Spiritual development is defined as, the process through which human beings develop an inner self which transcends the concrete superficial nature of the world in which they live to connect with a personal identity and divine spirit marked with purpose, meaning, love, compassion, and moral integrity (Benson, Roehlkepartain, & Rude, 2003; Garbarino & Bedard, 1996). The outcome of spiritual development, of course, is spirituality.

Spiritual anchoring is addressed under Article 27 of the CRC which asserts, "States Parties recognize the right of every child to a standard of living adequate for the child's physical, mental, *spiritual*, moral and social development." It is one component associated with promoting a child's full personhood (GC-1, 2001), a personhood which is the goal of the CRC (Melton, 2005b).

Spiritual development is nurtured from birth and is first influenced by relationships with parents and other family members. Healthy spiritual development depends upon positive human experiences, meaning that threats to well-being such as poverty (Article 4), maltreatment (Article 19) and other forms of trauma can, and often do, severely affect one's connection with the spiritual self (Garbarino, 1999). To illustrate, Reinert and Edwards (2009), found the experience of child sexual abuse to predict feeling less attached to God, as well as viewing God as unloving, controlling and distant. Of course, children are malleable, so when they are anchored in specific relationships, experiences, and opportunities the more likely they are to overcome adversity.

It is widely recognized by many cultures living within our nation that as children mature, one of the most influential ways of spiritually anchoring children is through participation in faith-based organizations (Lerner & Dowling, 2002; e.g., churches, synagogues, mosques). The value of participation within faith based organizations has been substantiated by Dowling, her colleagues (2004) who conducted structural equation modeling to account for the mediating effect of religiosity and spirituality in predicting thriving behavior among a sample of 1,000 youth (age 12). They found spirituality to be a predictor of thriving behavior; this relation was found to be significantly stronger when youth were participating in faith based activities.

One of the benefits of faith-based organizations is that they connect youth to older adults. The significance of intergenerational relationships to child development lies in the power of one generation passing to another: Knowledge and wisdom, skills, rules for behavior, and a value system; if we look at the influence of peers, these places allow children of the same value system to participate together in environments which are safe, conducive to developing faith in God, encourage and support play, and influence civic responsibility.

Schools (private and public) also play a powerful role in spiritual anchoring. Considering the extensive amount of time children spend in school, it is vital that we recognize these as places meant to influence the development of the "whole child" – including spiritual development (Articles 27 and 29; Hart et al., 2001). In regards to the aims of education, General Comment No. 1 from the UN Committee on the Rights of the Child (2001, para 12) states,

> Article 29(1) insists upon a holistic approach to education which ensures that the educational opportunities made available reflect an appropriate balance between promoting the physical, mental, spiritual and emotional aspects of education, the intellectual, social and practical

> dimensions, and the childhood and lifelong aspects. The overall objective of education is to maximize the child's ability and opportunity to participate fully and responsibly in a free society. It should be emphasized that the type of teaching that is focused primarily on accumulation of knowledge, prompting competition and leading to an excessive burden of work on children, may seriously hamper the harmonious development of the child to the fullest potential of his or her abilities and talents.

The last sentence of the previous quote implies that teachers, administrators, and policy makers should leave competitive activities on the field, and look to the wide body of pedagogical literature illustrating the value of cooperative learning and self-competition in promoting spiritual as well as cognitive and socioemotional development (GC-12, 2009c; Johnson, Johnson, & Holubec, 1998; Scales & Taccogna, 2000). Cooperative learning is a method of teaching which brings students together as teams to work toward achieving a common goal. One of the main benefits of cooperative learning is that it encourages social interactions between students, who due to personal differences (e.g., cultural, race, ability level, and age), may have never participated with each other. In terms of outcomes, which are healthy for the spirit, cooperative learning fosters relationship building, problem solving, and conflict resolution skills, enhances self-esteem, instills an appreciation for diversity, and promotes prosocial behavior. Basically, it takes the focus away from "me," to a focus on "we." But there is a place for "me" in the classroom.

Although I was well known among my family and friends as a fierce competitive athlete, I was never more competitive than I was with myself in the classroom. This self-competitiveness began in the fifth grade when my class had the unique opportunity to be visited by the Minneapolis Fire Chief who came to speak with us about fire safety. Like many of my classmates, I had boyhood dreams of becoming a firefighter, so I was awestruck by his presence. Before he left that day, he challenged us to complete a fire safety activity which required developing a fire safety and evacuation plan for our homes. The extra credit assignment was divided into two different levels of accomplishment. Those who accomplished the first level earned a silver captain's badge, whereas those willing to do the extra activities required of the second level, earned a gold fire chief badge. I put all of my effort into successfully earning the gold badge.

I am convinced that the fire safety activity and corresponding external reward served as the impetus for my goal setting personality. However, this was not about the external reward, but rather the spiritually significant intrapersonal feelings I gained from challenging myself and becoming successful. You see, despite the physical and psychological abuse I was suffering at home at the hands of my parents, my accomplishments in school helped me feel good about myself. This internal drive motivated me to work harder, and to eventually reach a point where I could help others. In addition, these feelings helped me to realize that my life had meaning and purpose.

My purpose for telling this story is to illustrate the power that teachers and community members hold within the context of our classrooms. These honorable people have the power to influence spiritual development through interaction and instruction focused on nurturing the souls of our children. Thus, the classroom should not only focus on the core academic areas of reading, writing, science and math, but also should stimulate the whole child through activities which promote spiritual development; spiritual development which when combined with a socially healthy environment is likely to psychologically anchor children (GC-1, 2001).

Psychological Anchoring

The culmination of social and spiritual anchoring is referred to as *psychological anchoring*. When children are socially and spiritually anchored, they develop the psychological resources necessary to actively cope with risk factors which may compromise becoming empowered to exert their right to participation (Garbarino, 1999). To illustrate, analyzing data from a sample of at-risk youth (N=2,226), Molnar, and his colleagues (2008) found greater social support to be negatively related to aggression and juvenile delinquency, suggesting that social support from nonrelated adults influences empowers children with the evolving capacities necessary to avoid participating in aggressive and delinquent crime. Similarly, conducting structural equation modeling to test social control theory (which suggests that juvenile crime is associated to a lack of social connection and deficiencies in intrapersonal competence) researchers found high self-esteem, positive school attitudes, prosocial behavior, purpose in life, and prosocial bonds to protect youth from juvenile delinquency; fear of harm, victimization, and abuse in the home were found to predict juvenile delinquency (Dukes & Stein, 2001). These studies illustrate that the more youth are socially and spiritually anchored, the greater likelihood they will be psychologically anchored, and consequently protected from developing mental illness and engaging in behavior which may compromise their right to participation. To illustrate the true power of psychological anchoring, we turn now to the Search Institute's 40 Developmental Assets.

The 40 Developmental Assets: The Manifestation of the Human Rights of Children

For over five decades, the Search Institute – a nonprofit organization – located in Minneapolis, Minnesota has been conducting research evaluating child and adolescent development. Consequently, surveys of approximately 3 million students across the USA in grades K-12 reveal that there are 40 developmental assets vital to promoting child well-being and preventing risk behaviors (Benson, 2007). These assets are the nutrients of a socially healthy environment, and therefore, are vital to promoting the participation rights of children.

The 40 developmental assets are both external and internal (Benson, 2007). External assets include the anchors of *support*, *empowerment*, *boundaries and expectations*, and *constructive use of time*. These external assets account for the extent to which youth are anchored in healthy relationships, experiences, and opportunities. The remaining 20 internal assets are categorized under a *commitment to learning*, *positive values*, *social competencies*, and *positive identity* (see search-institute.org for a full list of the assets). These internal assets reflect the CRC's emphasis on a child's evolving capacities. Research strongly suggests that the more youth are socially, spiritually, and psychologically anchored, the greater likelihood they will thrive, and be protected from risk.

Thriving is a process of "adaptive developmental regulation which results in young people who move beyond their own self-interest and place value on, and commit to, action supportive of a social system promoting equity, democracy, social justice, and personal freedom – leads to prospering" (p. 22, Lerner & Dowling, 2002). Thriving involves a healthy change process resulting in developmental regulation which serves to counter many of the at-risk behaviors and negative outcomes (e.g., violating the rights of others, incarceration, drug and alcohol use) experienced by many youth today, moving them closer to reaching their true personhood. Again, a personhood is espoused by the UN Convention on the Rights of the Child (Melton, 2005b).

The Search Institute has indentified eight indicators of thriving: School success, display of leadership, helping others, maintaining good health, delay of gratification, valuing diversity, and overcoming adversity (Lerner & Dowling, 2002). Moreover, they have found a positive relation between level of assets and thriving indicators. That is, as asset levels increase, so does thriving. Conversely, the fewer levels of assets present in the lives of youth, the more they tend to do poorly. Scales and his colleagues (2000) found the asset framework to explain as much as 43% of the variance in thriving indicators, even after controlling for demographic variables. In addition, the asset framework has been found to account for as much as 66% of the variance in explaining overall risk behavior (e.g., alcohol, tobacco, illegal drugs, sexual intercourse, depression-suicide, antisocial behavior, violence, school problems, driving and alcohol, and gambling; Leffert, Benson, Scales, Sharma, Drake, & Blyth, 1998).

It is worth mentioning that the vision of the Search Institute is similar to that of the CRC. Specifically, it envisions: "A world where all young people are valued and thrive." In addition, it recognizes the following as "rights" of kids:

1. The "best interest of the child" should be strongly considered when making decisions and drafting policy (Article 3)
2. Poverty is acknowledged as the greatest threat to child well-being and should be subsequently eradicated (preamble and Article 4)
3. End all forms of discrimination (Article 2)
4. Promote the rights essential to human development – survival, protection, growth, and development. Children need to grow up in healthy families and communities (Articles 5–6, & 27)
5. Ensure access to a quality education (Articles 23, & 28–29)

6. Promote policies which protect children from the danger of violence, abuse, exploitation and discrimination (Article 2 & 19)
7. In accordance with the evolving capacities of the child, every child has the right to participation (Search Institute, 2008; Articles 12–15, & 31)

While the Search Institute and the CRC share common visions, they do differ in one fundamentally important way. The CRC is a legally binding international treaty meant to guide ratifying governments in legislating policy and programming (Melton, 2005b). In doing so, governments are required to place the "best interest" of children and families at the forefront of policy decisions (Melton, 1996). On the other hand, the Search Institute's asset framework and research supporting it are the manifestation of the human rights of children. Meaning, in addition to being a tool for indicating the needs of children, the research is indicative of whether a society is respecting the human rights of children, particularly at the community level. Thus, it is logical to argue that if the human rights of children are being met within the USA, research should indicate that every child is being socially, spiritually, and psychologically anchored, and consequently thriving and not being exposed to risk (Melton, 2009).

Asset Research

Where do youth living in the USA stand in regards to average levels of developmental assets? A study, which includes 6th–12th grade students ($N=148{,}189$), found 17% of youth experiencing 0–10 assets placing them *at risk* for negative outcomes, 42% experiencing 11–20 assets making them *vulnerable* to negative outcomes, 32% experiencing an *adequate* amount of assets with 21–30, and only 8% were found to be *thriving* with 31–40 assets. These findings suggest that approximately 50% of youth across all sociodemographic groups are either at-risk or vulnerable to negative outcomes and risk behavior (Benson, 2007). More profoundly, this research strongly suggests that we are failing to ground a large percentage of children in the social, spiritual, and psychological anchors vital to promoting their right to participation.

How do at-risk and thriving youth differ in terms of negative outcomes? Research has found that students experiencing 0–10 assets are thirty-eight times more likely to report using illegal drugs than peers experiencing 31–40 assets; in terms of cigarette use, these same students are approximately ten times more likely to report using cigarettes than thriving peers. Similarly, 34% of at-risk students compared to 3% of thriving students were found to be engaging in sexual intercourse three or more times in their lifetime, and 62% of at-risk students reported engaging in three or more violent acts in the past year compared to only 6% of thriving peers. Finally, at-risk students were fifteen times more likely to report using alcohol than thriving peers (Benson, 2007; Benson, Roehlkepartain, & Sesma, 2004). I should state that these findings are almost identical to findings from previous studies conducted by the Search Institute (Benson, 2007). What these studies clearly demonstrate is that asset accumulation has the power to promote thriving behavior and prevent risk.

Power of the Assets to Promote

The assets have been shown to predict thriving behavior. In a study following the academic progress of middle school students (*N*=370) across time, researchers found a significant relation between the level of assets and GPA (Roehlkepartain, Benson, & Sesma, 2003). That is, students reporting 0–10 assets were found to have a GPA of 2.1, those experiencing 11–20 a GPA of 2.8, 21–30 a GPA of 3.1, and finally 31–40 assets a GPA of 3.3. Another study of inner city youth (*N*=462) found that youth experiencing 20–40 assets (placing them in the adequate to thriving range) were also participating and succeeding in school, valuing diversity, maintaining good health, delaying gratification, and participating in activities helping others (Scales et al., 2000). These findings mirror a Search Institute (2003) survey (*N*=148,189) which found only 4% of thriving students to be experiencing school problems compared to 44% of at-risk peers, and 88% of thriving students compared to 27% of at-risk students to be maintaining good health. On a similar note, 96% of thriving students compared to 62% of at-risk students reported helping others one or more hours per week (Benson, 2007). Other studies have found asset accumulation to predict better standardized test scores and school attendance (Benson; Connell, Halpem-Felsher, Clifford, Crichlow, & Usinger, 1995).

Power of the Assets to Prevent

Asset accumulation has also been found to prevent risk behavior. Using structural equation modeling to conduct a secondary analysis of Search Institute data (*N*=200), De Carvalho (2007) found thriving behavior and asset levels to be negatively related to juvenile delinquency. In other words, as the number of assets accumulated, thriving behavior increased and juvenile delinquency decreased.

Studies have found several specific assets to be negatively related to delinquency. In a study using the asset framework to test social control theory, which suggests that delinquency is related to a lack of social connection and deficiencies in internal assets, Dukes and Stein (2001) found high self-esteem, positive school attitudes, prosocial activity, purpose in life, and prosocial bonds to protect youth from engaging in deviant behavior; fear of harm, victimization, and abuse in the home predicted juvenile delinquency. Finally, after controlling for demographic variables, Leffert and her colleagues (1998) found positive peer influence, personal restraint, school engagement, time at home, resistance skills, and peaceful conflict resolution to account for 39% of the variance in explaining protection from antisocial behavior.

Several of the assets categories have been found to be important protective factors across ethnic groups (Native American, White, African American, Hispanic, Asian). In an aggregate sample of approximately 218,000 students in grades 6–12, the Search Institute (2003) found boundaries and expectations, commitment to learning, positive values, and social competencies significantly related to antisocial behavior, a predictor of juvenile delinquency. As implied, not all assets are relevant to each ethnically diverse group, nonetheless, the asset research consistently shows that it is the accumulation of assets that promotes thriving and prevents risk behavior (Benson, 2002).

Assets and Economic Equality

This chapter would be incomplete without discussing the relation between economic equality, and thriving and risk behavior. While income level has been found to account for a small amount of the variance in explaining the interplay between asset accumulation, and thriving and risk behavior (Benson, 2007; Leffert et al., 1998; Scales et al., 2000), economic equality does matter. Research has consistently found that on average, youth living in poverty experience three fewer assets that their more affluent peers (Benson, 2007). This discrepancy stands counter to the CRC's emphasis on nondiscrimination (Article 2).

One way poverty (in particular, chronic, pervasive, and intergenerational poverty) may influence asset accumulation through its effects on a child's sense of safety (Asset 10) within the home. Poverty, parental stress, and a lack of parental social support have been found to predict child maltreatment and neglect (Brooks-Gunn & Duncan, 1997; Brown, Cohen, Johnson, & Salzinger, 1998; Sroufe et al., 2005). A study of maltreated children found effects on social competence (an internal asset category) and self-esteem (positive identity) to predict internalizing and externalizing behavior at age 12 (Kim & Cicchetti, 2004). Another found fear of harm, victimization, and abuse in the home to predict juvenile delinquency (Dukes & Stein, 2001). These studies suggest that poverty is indirectly yet negatively related to thriving behavior, and a predictor of risk behavior.

Poverty also sends a socially toxic message that is counter to empowering children to exert their right to participation. That is, "within this land of wealth and social opportunity you are excluded." Garbarino (1999) highlights the psychological and spiritual toll of poverty during an interview with a young man serving life behind bars for murder. Garbarino is asked by Warren, "When you were growing up, were you poor or regular?" (p. 174)? Warren's question suggests the feelings of shame and inadequacy – feelings counter to the internal assets related to positive identity (Assets 37–40). Thus, poverty contributes to undermining the social, spiritual, and psychological anchoring of children (Garbarino, 1999), consequently preventing many children from being empowered to exert their right to participation.

> "For evil to triumph it is enough only that good men do nothing"
>
> Edmund Burke

We have been informed of the significance of the social, spiritual, and psychological anchors vital to empowering children to exert their right to participation. Thus, we have an obligation to act. For many years, we have seen study after study strongly suggesting that the well-being of many children is getting worse rather than better. Much of this research illustrated the plight of the mix of kids who represent the 13 million living in poverty (Faas & Cauthen, 2008), 1.3 million living in homelessness (NLCHP, 2008), 8.5 million without health insurance (NCHC, 2008), 92,854 incarcerated males (OJJDP, 2008), and 25% not graduating from high school (President Obama, 2009). The major difference between previous research and more recent findings is in the strong evidence highlighting that youth from *all* walks of life are not only at risk for negative developmental outcomes, but they are also not being empowered to exert their right to participation.

For years now, child and family advocates have been calling for a permanent national family agenda (Benson, 2002; Bronfenbrenner, 1979; Garbarino, 1992; Kamerman, 1996; Zigler & Muenchow, 1984). Because our current political system has the ability to undermine child and family-friendly policies which promote child and family well-being, we can bring about permanency in child and family protection through ratification of the United Nations Convention on the Rights of the Child (Bruyere & Garbarino, 2009). With a permanent blueprint for structural change in place, a child and family-centered national policy would no doubt require youth, parents, policy makers, and scholars to come together for one single purpose – to assure that our next generation of citizens, participate in the democratic process which assures the continuation of our society.

We have an obligation to act and move toward permanent change – to not do so would be reprehensibly irresponsible. Make no mistake about it; change will be slow. But for moral change to occur, it always takes people moving one step in a direction which is morally right. To date, 193 of our global counterparts have made this commitment to their children and families. Will we?

References

Ainsworth, M. D. S., Blehar, M. C., Waters, E., & Wall, S. (1978). *Patterns of attachment: A psychological study of the strange situation*. Hillsdale, NJ: Erlbaum.

Barnes, J., Katz, I., Korbin, J. E., & O'Brien, M. (2006). *Children and families in communities: Theory, research, policy and practice*. West Sussex, UK: John Wiley & Sons.

Bedard, C. (2007). *Children's rights are human rights*. Chicago, Loyola University Press.

Benson, P. L. (2002). Adolescent development in social and community context: A program of research. *New Directions for Youth Development, 95*, 123–147.

Benson, P. L. (2007). *All kids are our kids: What communities must do to raise caring and responsible children and adolescents* (2nd ed.). NY: Jossey Bass.

Benson, P. L., Roehlkepartain, E. C., & Rude, S. P. (2003). Spiritual development in childhood and adolescence: Toward a field of inquiry. *Applied Developmental Science, 7*, 205–213.

Benson, P. L., Roehlkepartian, E. C., & Sesma, A. (2004). Tapping the power of community: The potential of asset building to strengthen substance abuse prevention efforts [Electronic version]. *Search Institute Insights & Evidence, 2*, 1–14.

Blyth, D. A., & Leffert, N. (1995). Communities as contexts for adolescent development: An empirical analysis. *Journal of Adolescent Research, 10*, 64–87.

Bronfenbrenner, U. (1979). *The ecology of human development: Experiments by nature and design*. Cambridge, MA: Harvard.

Brooks-Gunn, J., & Duncan, G. (1997). The effects of poverty on children and youth. *The Future of Children, 7*, 55–71.

Brown, J., Cohen, P., Johnson, J. G., & Salzinger, S. (1998). A longitudinal analysis of risk factors for child maltreatment: Findings of a 17-year prospective study of officially recorded and self-reported child abuse and neglect. *Child Abuse and Neglect, 22*, 1065–1078.

Bruyere, E. B., & Garbarino, J. (2009). The ecological perspective on the human rights of children. In S. B. Kamerman, S. Phipps, & A. Ben-Arieh (Eds.), *From child welfare to child well-being: An international perspective on knowledge in the service of making policy: A special volume in honor of Alfred J. Kahn*. New York: Springer.

Cochran, J. K., & Bo, I. (1989). The social networks, family involvement, and pro- and anti-social behavior of adolescent males in Norway. *Journal of Youth and Adolescence,* 18, 377–398.

Connell, J. P., Halpem-Felsher, B. L., Clifford, E., Crichlow, W., & Usinger, P. (1995). Hanging in there: Behavioral psychological, and contextual factors affecting whether African American students stay in high school. *Journal of Adolescent Research,* 10, 41–63.

De Carvalho, J. (2007). *A causal analysis of developmental assets, behaviors, and delinquency among Hispanic youth in Texas* (Doctoral dissertation, University of Texas). Retrieved from http://dspace.uta.edu/bitstream/handle/10106/316/uta-etd-1440.pdf;jsessionid=58C846F4971281FE6B42E920EFAC1666?sequence=1

Dodge, K. A. (1993). Social-cognitive mechanisms in the development of conduct disorder and depression. *Annual Review of Psychology, 44*, 559–584.

Dowling, E. M., Gestsdottier, S., Anderson, P. M., von Eye, A., & Lerner, R. M. (2003). Spirituality, religiosity, and thriving among adolescents: Identification and confirmation of factor structures. *Applied Developmental Science, 7*, 253–260.

Dukes, R. L., & Stein, J. A. (2001). Effects of assets and deficits on the social control of at-risk behavior among youth: A structural equations approach. *Youth & Society, 32*, 337–359.

Faas, S., & Cauthen, N. K. (2008). Who are America's poor children: The real story. *National Center for Children in Poverty*. Retrieved from http://www.nccp.org

Flekkoy, M. G., & Kaufman, N. H. (1997). *The participation rights of the child: Rights and responsibilities in family and society*. Bristol, PA: Jessica Kingsley Publishers.

Garbarino, J. (1976). A preliminary study of some ecological correlates of child abuse: The impact of socioeconomic stress on mothers. *Child Development,* 47, 178–185.

Garbarino, J. (1992). *Children and families in the social environment* (2nd ed.). New York: Aldine de Gruyter.

Garbarino, J. (1999). *Lost boys: Why our sons turn violent and how we can save them*. New York: The Free Press.

Garbarino, J., & Bedard, C. (1996). Spiritual challenges to children facing violent trauma. *Childhood, 3*, 467–478.

Grossman, J. B., & Bulle, M. J. (2006). Review of what youth programs do to increase the connectedness of youth with adults. *Journal of Adolescent Health, 39*, 788–799.

Hart, S. N. (2002). Making sure the child's voice is heard. *International Review of Education,* 48, 251–258.

Hart, S., Price-Cohen, C., Farrell-Erickson, M., & Flekkoy, M. (2001). *Children's rights in education*. Philadelphia: Jessica Kingsley Publishers.

Johnson, D. W., Johnson, R., & Holubec, E. (1998). *Cooperation in the classroom*. Edina, MN: Interaction Book Company.

Kamerman, S. (1996). Child and family policies: An international overview. In E. F. Zigler, S. L. Kagan, & N. W. Hall (Eds.), *Children, families and government*. New York: Cambridge University Press.

Kim, J., & Cicchetti, D. (2004). A longitudinal study of child maltreatment, mother-child relationship quality and maladjustment: The role of self-esteem and social competence. *Journal of Abnormal Child Psychology, 32*, 341–354.

Lansdown, G. (2005). *The evolving capacities of the child*. Florence, Italy: UNICEF.

Leffert, N., Benson, P. L., Scales, P. C., Sharma, A. R., Drake, D. R., & Blyth, D. A. (1998). Developmental assets: Measurement and prediction of risk behaviors among adolescents. *Applied Developmental Science,* 2, 209–230.

Lerner, R. M., & Dowling, E. M. (2002). Positive youth development: Thriving as the basis of personhood and civic society. *New Directions for Youth Development,* 95, 11–33.
Main, M., & Solomon, J. (1990). Procedures for identifying infants as disorganized/disoriented during the Ainsworth Strange Situation. In M. T. Greenberg, D. Cicchetti, & E. M. Cummings (Eds.), *Attachment in the preschool years* (pp. 121–160). Chicago, University of Chicago Press.
Melton, G. (1996). The child's right to a family environment. *American Psychologist,* 51, 1234–1238.
Melton, G. (2005a). Building humane communities respectful of children: The significance of the Convention on the Rights of the Child. *American Psychologist, 60*, 918–926.
Melton, G. (2005b). Treating children like people: A framework for research and advocacy. *Journal of Clinical Child and Adolescent Psychology,* 34, 646–657.
Melton, G. (2009, November). *Twentieth anniversary of the United Nations Convention on the Rights of the Children.* Paper presented at the Symposium on Counting Children in Sydney, Australia.
Molnar, B. E., Cerda, M., Roberts, A. L., & Buka, S. L. (2008). Effects of neighborhood resources on aggressive and delinquent behaviors among urban youths. *American Journal of Public Health, 98*, 1086–1093.
National Center on Health Care (2009). *Health insurance coverage.* Retrieved from http://www.nchc.org/facts/coverage.shtml
National Law Center on Homelessness and Poverty (2007). *2007 annual report.* Retrieved from http://www.nlchp.org
President Obama, B. (2009). *Remarks by the President to the Hispanic Chamber of Commerce on a complete and competitive American education.* Washington, DC. Retrieved from http://www.whitehouse.gov
OJJDP. (2008). *Statistical briefing book.* Retrieved from http://ojjdp.ncjrs.gov
Pretty, G. M., Andrewes, L., & Collett, C. (1994). Exploring adolescents' sense of community and its relationship to loneliness. *Journal of Community Psychology, 22*, 346–358.
Reinert, D. F., & Edwards, C. E. (2009). Attachment theory, childhood mistreatment, and religiosity. *Psychology of Religion and Spirituality, 1*, 25–34.
Roehlkepartain, E. C., Benson, P. L., & Sesma, A. (2003). *Signs of progress in putting children first: Developmental assets among youth in St. Louis Park, 1997–2001.* Available at http://www.childrenfirst.org
Scales, P. C., Benson, P. L., Leffert, N., & Blyth, D. A. (2000). Contribution of developmental assets to the prediction of thriving among adolescents. *Applied Developmental Science,* 4, 27–46.
Scales, P. C., & Leffert, N. (2004). *Developmental assets: A synthesis of the scientific research on adolescent development.* Minneapolis, MN: Search Institute.
Scales, P. C., & Taccogna, J. (2000). Caring to try: How building students' developmental assets can promote school engagement and success. *NASSP Bulletin,* 84, 69–78.
Schwab-Stone, M. E., Ayers, T. S., Kasprow, W., Voyce, C., Barone, C., Shriver, T., et al. (1995). No safe haven: A study of violence exposure in an urban community. *Journal of American Academy of Child and Adolescent Psychiatry,* 34, 1343–1352.
Search Institute. (2008). *Child rights and assets.* Retrieved from http://www.search-institute.org
Sroufe, L. A., Egeland, B., Carlson, E. A., & Collins, W. A. (2005). *The development of the person: The Minnesota study of risk and adaptation from birth to adulthood.* New York: Guilford Press.
Svedhem, L. (1994). Social network and behavior problems among 11-13 year old school children: A theoretical and empirical basis for network therapy. *Acta Psychiatrica Scandinavica,* 89, 4–84.
Talmi, A., & Harter, S. (1998). *Pathways to better outcomes: Special adults as sources of support for young adolescents.* Paper presented at the biennial meetings of the Society for Research on Adolescence, San Diego, CA.
Theokas, C., Almerigi, J. B., Lerner, R. M., Dowling, E. M., Benson, P. L., Scales, P. C., et al. (2005). Conceptualizing and modeling individual and ecological asset components of thriving in early adolescence. *Journal of Early Adolescence, 25*, 113–143.

UNICEF. (2003). *The state of the world's children 2003*. Retrieved from http://www.unicef-irc.org

UNICEF. (2007). *Child poverty perspective: An overview of child well-being in rich countries*. Retrieved from http://www.unicef-irc.org

United Nations Committee on the Rights of the Child. (2009a). *General comment no. 1: The aims of education*. Retrieved from http://www2.ohchr.org/english/bodies/crc/comments.htm

United Nations Committee on the Rights of the Child. (2009b). *General comment no. 7: Implementing child rights in early childhood*. Retrieved from http://www2.ohchr.org/english/bodies/crc/comments.htm

United Nations Committee on the Rights of the Child. (2009c). *General comment no. 12: The right of the child to be heard*. Retrieved from http://www2.ohchr.org/english/bodies/crc/comments.htm

United Nations Convention on the Rights of the Child. (1989). United Nations General Assembly Document A/RES/44/25. Retrieved from http://www.cirp.org

Vygotsky, L. (1986). *Thought and language*. Cambridge, MA: MIT Press.

Werner, E. E. (1993). *A longitudinal perspective on risk for learning disabilities*. Paper presented at the annual conference of the Learning Disabilities Association of America, San Francisco, CA.

Zigler, E., & Muenchow, S. (1984). How to influence social policy affecting children and families. *American Psychologist, 39*, 415–420.

Part IV
Cultural and Social Impediments to a Healthy Environment for Children

Chapter 11
Child Slavery and the Global Economy: Historical Perspectives on a Contemporary Problem

John Donoghue

Introduction

In the fall of 1649 on the docks of a large slave trading port, sailors strained, sweated, and swore through their work, hauling cargo, hoisting sails, and mending rigging, making ready for a voyage to the colonies. As the sailors prepared to weigh anchor, a crowd of parents gathered along the shoreline, grieving for their children who had been kidnapped and brought aboard the ship. As their children struggled for breath in the suffocating stench and stifling heat of the ship's hold, the parents grew despondent, desperate to redeem their children from a future of death-dealing labor in the scorching fields of the English Chesapeake or Caribbean. A sympathetic witness noted that when the slave ship began to sail into the distance, the parents followed along the water's edge, "crying and mourning for their children's redemption from slavery" (Bullock, 1649, pp. 13–14; Harlow, 1923, p. 300; Linebaugh & Rediker, 2000, p. 110).

When I describe this scene to an audience, I invite them to guess where it took place. Invariably, the response is "the west coast of Africa." It is a good answer. Most people, scholars included, rightfully associate trans-Atlantic slave trading with the horrors endured by millions of Africans and their descendants. Statistics, of course, support this assumption. Between 1500 and 1800, of the fifteen million migrants who came to the Americas, twelve million arrived from Africa in chains. Another two million Africans died during the middle passage, while an additional two million perished within their first two years of enslavement (Davis, 2006, pp. 93–95, 116–117, 235–236; Rediker, 2007, pp. 5, 347). But while these statistics are horrifying, they are still abstractions; standing alone, they cannot convey slavery's catastrophic human cost or the magnitude of its historical significance. The profitability of African slave labor and African slave trading fueled global capitalism's first wave of expansion and financed the West's eventual rise to global hegemony.

J. Donoghue (✉)
Department of History, Loyola University, 6525 N Sheridan Rd, Chicago, IL 60626, USA
e-mail: jdonoghue@luc.edu

J. Garbarino and G. Sigman (eds.), *A Child's Right to a Healthy Environment*, The Loyola University Symposium on the Human Rights of Children 1,
DOI 10.1007/978-1-4419-6791-6_11,

In the mid-nineteenth century, sectional disputes over slavery's expansion exploded into civil war in the United States, where over 600,000 died in the carnage; measured in proportion to the current American population, this figure stands at an astonishing six million (Gilpin, 2008; Stout, 2006). But the federal government's abandonment of reconstruction decimated what Lincoln called the "new birth of freedom" won by black soldiers and their white comrades. Consequently, the late nineteenth and early twentieth centuries brought African–Americans Jim Crow, disenfranchisement, waves of pogrom-like lynching, and systemic poverty stemming from job discrimination and segregation (Hahn, 2003). While many European, Asian, and Hispanic immigrant groups faced hard times during this period in the way of labor exploitation and cultural prejudice, none endured anything approximating the suffering of African–Americans. As Hurricane Katrina revealed in our own time, slavery's legacies of racism and racial inequality have metastasized in the soul of American life, and continue to define, for the worse, American citizenship, social privilege, and economic opportunity. Taking this malignant legacy into view, the slavery scholar David Brion Davis concluded that slavery in the United States, within the wider sweep of slavery's global history, amounted to "the ultimate form of inhuman bondage" (Davis, p. 3).

Although correct, Davis' conclusion, as well as his entire analysis of the "rise of slavery" must be joined by a more profound understanding of how American life in general, and class exploitation in particular, became racialized. In short, the racial boundaries defining slavery and freedom did not arrive intact with waves of European and African migrants. Since race is a product of history rather than biology, it had to be made, even invented, to draw the line between who would experience the worst forms of oppression in America and who could seize upon its manifold opportunities. In ways surprising to us in the present, for much of the seventeenth century, whites and blacks in the British Empire endured the common experience of slavery – a hidden history that can help explain the persistence of slavery in today's global economy (Allen, 1997; Amussen, 2007; Beckles, 1989; Morgan, 1975; Roediger, 2000).

Revisiting the historical account of the kidnapped children described in the introduction can help us understand how slavery still persists in a world which largely regards slavery as a thing of the past. Far from an entrepôt on the coast of West Africa, the slave trading port mentioned above was London, where for close to a century, slave ships embarked illegally for British colonies with tens of thousands of stolen "white" people. Most of these unfortunates, as I will discuss later, were children and teenagers, whom colonial planters purchased and put to work against their will, to plant, tend, and harvest two of the global economy's most lucrative commodities, tobacco and sugar. Tragically, since they made up the majority of those enslaved in Britain's colonies, young people came to embody one of the most valuable "commodities" of the day. Of course, nobody, today or yesterday, is born into the world as a commodity; consequently, European children, like European, African, and Indian people of all ages, had to be transformed, in economic terms, into commodities. In pursuing this course, the predators who brought slavery into the British Atlantic showed an extraordinary capacity for grounding profitable economic innovation in exploitation, violence, and terror. Unfortunately, the same case can be made in today's global economy; for despite its de jure abolition, slavery does not merely persist, it thrives, mostly through the deception and coercion of millions of children into unpaid work, a proof positive of slavery's resilient ability to adapt to changing political and economic contexts. In retrospect, it seems that the relentless quest to expand profits by exploiting labor has brought us back to the future, to a savage state of epidemic, child slavery. The aim of this chapter is to explain how this happened.

Our study begins with an elusive question: why did a system that enslaved mostly young people from the British Isles develop in the seventeenth-century British Empire? To answer this question, we must recognize that like today, the seventeenth century was a time of rapid political and economic change that took place on a global scale, connecting the lives of Europeans, Africans, and Native Americans in unprecedented form and intensity. This new phase of global interconnectedness owed to two world-transforming events. The first of these events involved the rise of the modern nation through empire building, a process that began in Europe early in the fifteenth century. By the middle of the sixteenth century, Europe's first superpower, Spain, had expanded its imperial reach beyond the Iberian Peninsula and across the Atlantic and into the Pacific, conquering much of the Caribbean and present-day Central and South America as well as parts of southeast Asia. Over the course of the next two centuries, Portugal, France, the Netherlands, and Great Britain would compete with Spain and each other to acquire and develop wealth-producing colonies (Elliot, 2006; Greene, 2007; Pestana, 2004).

As European empires expanded, so did global networks of finance, production, and commerce, part of a larger transformation from traditional forms of economic organization to increasingly capitalistic ones. Before the age of empire and capital, a moral consensus existed in the western world that economies should work to produce an abundance of wealth so that everybody, across a divinely ordained, rigidly stratified social hierarchy could avail themselves, in very unequal proportions, to the basic necessities of life, particularly to the material benefits derived from access to the "commons," or the lands, food, fuel, and building material held in trust by the local community. Access to the commons, reflected in the structural organization of European economies, evolved into a sacred right. The new logic of capitalism challenged all this by striving to define the ends of economic organization as the private accumulation of exponentially multiplying wealth (Kennedy, 2008; Linebaugh, 2008, pp. 46–68; Thirsk, 1985; Tilly, 1981, Chap. 7; Wood & Wood, 1997).

In parts of seventeenth-century Europe, but especially on the British mainland, the drive toward private accumulation stripped millions of their common rights. This occurred most clearly through the enclosure, or privatization, of the commons, which deprived the rural masses of life's basic, material necessities. Enclosure also eroded older conceptions of economic justice, when the pursuit of wealth at the expense of another's welfare was widely regarded as sinful. Consequently, the capitalist-styled changes sweeping the British mainland during the early modern period uprooted millions, creating a massive population of desperately poor people, many of whom flocked to port cities, especially London, whose population more than quadrupled during the early modern period. As a result, English port cities swelled with human beings on the margins of survival, leaving tens of thousands of children vulnerable in increasingly dysfunctional environments (Beier, 1985, 1989; Blomely, 2007, pp. 1–21; Griffiths, 2008; Patriquin, 2004, pp. 196–216; Winthrop, 1630).

Across the Atlantic, as colonial settlement stripped Native Americans of their own common rights by enclosing land into private property, planters cleared another route to profit maximization by driving down labor costs in ways more ruthless than those that their counterparts in Britain had employed. In particular, colonial legislatures, consisting almost exclusively of planters and merchants tied to the production and commerce of cash crops, passed laws that abolished the protection servants and wage workers enjoyed in England under the common law. Over the course of the seventeenth century, these colonial labor statutes transformed workers from Europe into the temporary, chattel property of their owners. "Whites" served terms from four to ten years. Some Africans were enslaved for life while others served temporary terms. Like the relatively few whites who survived temporary slavery, Africans could and did become freemen of the colony. Consequently in the seventeenth century, in contrast to most periods in American history, the institution of slavery drove white and black workers together, not apart. An event known as Bacon's Rebellion clearly illustrates this exceptional situation. In 1676, free and enslaved whites and blacks under the nominal leadership of Nathaniel Bacon combined in an armed attempt to overthrow the plantocracy regime ensconced at Jamestown. By the end of the rebellion, Jamestown lay in ashes, burned to the ground by the insurgents, who based their claim to freedom and access to material necessities as a "common right." In response, colonial legislatures passed increasingly violent and terroristic labor codes to more effectively discipline and racially divide plantation workers whose interracial solidarity threatened the plantocracy's domination of colonial society (Allen, 1997; Beckles, 1995, pp. 572–583; Blackburn, 1997, pp. 217–261; Dunn, 1984, pp. 157–194; Galenson, 1981; Menard, 2001; Morgan, 1976, pp. 250–337; Palmer, 1998; Pestana, 2004, pp. 183–212; Salinger, 1997, pp. 311–338; Steinfeld, 1991; Tomlins, 2001, pp. 5–43). Although both temporary and permanent forms of slavery in Britain's colonies clearly violated the English common law, both made cash crop production, not to mention the traffic of human beings, immensely profitable ventures. Indeed, slave trading, even more than voluntary European migration, brought Britain's far-flung Atlantic colonies together into a unified, political and commercial empire (Beckles, 2001, pp. 218–240; Bliss, 1994). British traders did venture to Africa for slave cargos at this time, but for most of the seventeenth century, Dutch and Spanish dominance kept Britain's share of the trade small (Hair & Law, 2001, pp. 264–285; Paige, 1984). This consequently made black slaves scarce and prohibitively expensive in the Chesapeake. On the contrary, in the British West Indies, geographic proximity to Dutch, Portuguese, and Spanish slave-trading routes made access to African slaves easier, which in part explains why Barbados and Jamaica transitioned to racialized slavery earlier than Britain's North American colonies. Colonists also enslaved Native Americans, mostly women and children, whom they took captive after killing most of their male relations in what the settlers called "just wars." Indians were enslaved temporarily and permanently. They were also traded from British North America to the West Indies in return for enslaved Africans (Guasco, 2007, pp. 389–411; Jordan, 1961, pp. 243–250). "Natives" captured in other "just" colonial wars fought closer to Britain formed another critical part of the empire's early enslaved population. During the middle of the seventeenth century, Britain traded Catholics who were taken captive in the conquest of Ireland into colonial slavery, sometimes transporting the Irish in ships engaged in the African slave trade (Beckles, 1990, pp. 503–522; O'Callaghan, 2000; Rodgers, 2007, pp. 145–156). Although estimates of the number of Irish sold into temporary slavery range from 30,000 to over 100,000, it is clear that children were specifically targeted by the British government. For instance, in September 1655, Henry Cromwell, Lord Lieutenant of Ireland and son of Lord Protector Oliver Cromwell, planned to enslave thousands of Irish boys and girls. He hoped that enslaved Irish girls could help multiply the number of "English" colonists (Birch, 1742, pp. 15–30).

The empire, however, hardly limited itself to enslaving Irish children. In 1651, the Guinea Company, equipped with a parliamentary charter to trade for slaves in Africa, instructed its agents to purchase boys around fifteen years of age. But most often, the government tapped its own rich reserve of what political economists call "surplus labor," which encompassed tens of thousands of children as well as adults. In 1618, the Privy Council ordered orphans to be taken up and shipped to Virginia. By the mid-seventeenth century, this process expanded, with soldiers rounding up thousands of convicts, vagabonds, and girls and women of "loose character." Through government contracts, these "rogues" were put aboard ships and transported into temporary slavery in the colonies. Again, as with the enslavement of the Irish, the enslavement of the desperate English poor intensified during the mid-seventeenth century, when for a brief period, revolutionaries led by Oliver Cromwell abolished the monarchy, centralized state power, and engaged in the first systematic attempt to organize Britain's Atlantic colonies into a coherent, profit-generating empire. Mobilizing the most vulnerable sections of the British population to meet the rising demand for cheap colonial labor thus became a state imperative. As the most vulnerable among the desperately poor throughout history have always been children, it should not be surprising that many among the thousands swept off of English streets and scoured from its jails were children (Allen, 1997, p. 64; Amussen, 2007, p. 224; Johnson, 1970, pp. 17–51).

Even taken together, however, the amount of children and teenagers enslaved by these legal means did not exceed those whom "kidnappers" and "spirits," contrary to the laws of both empire and colony, delivered into bondage. During the seventeenth century, the terms "kidnappers" and "spirits" entered the lexicon, as innovative forms of child exploitation made new language necessary to articulate old crimes in their new capitalist context. "Kidnapping" (a corruption of "kid nabbing"), or "spiriting away" a person, involved deceptively luring, or in the term of the day, "inveigling" a person into forced labor, usually young people as the prefix of "kid" makes clear. Sometimes kidnappers resorted to force and coercion when false promises involving sex, alcohol, light work, and high pay failed. Parliament first noted this practice in 1618, sixteen years after the founding of Jamestown. William Bullock, a Virginia tobacco planter, wrote that the "the usual way for getting servants is by a sort of men nicknamed spirits…[whose victims are] persuaded…that they shall go into a place where food will drop into their mouths: and being thus deluded, they take courage and are transported." Lured by spirits in this way, the children we encountered at the outset of this article most likely spent several weeks languishing in "cooks shops," or provisioning warehouses on the Thames docks, concentrated for the most part in the St. Katherine's neighborhood. Spirits delivered their victims to these "cook shops," where they were kept "prisoner" for sometimes as long as six weeks "until some master [meaning a ship captain] fetches them off." Here, indentures could be forged or coerced to circumvent curious customs officials, but the corruption of this realm of the imperial bureaucracy was so endemic that spirits sometimes dispensed with indentures altogether. With or without a bogus indenture in hand, the captain would pay the owner of the shop around three pounds for the spirits' fee and the cost of feeding the captive children. The captain would then add this fee to the five pound cost of transporting the children to the colonies, where he would sell the children to planters, increasing the price for profit or negotiating the equivalent in land, tobacco, or sugar (Bullock, 1649, pp. 13–14).

Remember that William Bullock wrote that kidnapping provided the "usual way" to mobilize the plantation labor supply destined for the Chesapeake. It should also be noted that Bullock found fault with this system, as the shocked and traumatized children taken captive by spirits made for poor workers once they arrived in the new world. Other planters remarked that workers being delivered to Virginia were so young that they should have come equipped with "cradles" (Pestana, 2004, p. 189). The Virginia Assembly took note that many children showed up without indentures; this posed a problem, since Parliament, in a half-hearted attempt to thwart illegal trafficking, required all transported workers to leave England with indentures. The Assembly responded to the problem by creating a uniform term of service for children who arrived without indentures, stating that they would serve until the age of twenty-one. Evidently, returning the victims of spirits to their homes in England remained beyond the realm of possibility in a colony perennially in need of fresh, exploitable labor. That Bullock called for the elimination of the spirit trade to reform the labor supply system reveals the massive scope and scale of this sordid commerce. One ring alone, working in the London neighborhood of St Katherine's, delivered approximately 6,000 souls into colonial bondage between 1658 and 1670. One witness reckoned that the ring reached the height of its capacity when it lured 840 Londoners into slavery in one year (Allen, 1997, pp. 76, 92, 143, 178; Beckles, 1989, pp. 50–51; Henning, 1823, pp. 99–100, 181, 184, 224, 229–233, 239, 253–256, 259–263, 266, 269, 271, 273, 278–279, 283).

This evidence prompts important questions: if spiriting and other means of slave trading along with voluntary migration had brought tens of thousands of workers to the colonies, why did the demand for more rise so rapidly? Shouldn't natural population reproduction have modified the overseas demand for workers? Unfortunately, a combination of endemic disease and overwork killed off several generations of seventeenth-century colonial workers, although overwork killed more since it could destroy outright or leave a person in a state too weak to successfully battle disease (Allen, 1997, pp. 76, 92, 143, 178, 323 FN 180; Morgan, 1976, pp. 175–177). Young people suffered most from these conditions because their weaker constitutions made them more vulnerable to disease and death from overwork. But they also died in greater numbers because they outnumbered other groups within the enslaved population. Stepping back from the details, a bigger picture emerges, where children and teenagers, rendered vulnerable through rapid, market-driven change in Britain, were reconfigured by slave traders and slave owners into labor commodities; their work, in turn, enriched a growing empire, one whose commercial consolidation through slave trading did much to advance capitalism's global reach.

Although nobody can legitimately dispute the fact that these young people were horribly exploited, the question remains of whether or not they and others in temporary bondage actually endured "slavery." Using the term "slavery" here might strike many readers as odd, since their history text books used the phrase "indentured servitude" to characterize what I have called "temporary slavery." Despite "indentured servitude's" seeming entrenched position in the lexicon of early American studies, my own research has rendered this term so unsatisfactory, so misleading, and so biased that I have dispensed with it altogether in my scholarship.

"Indentured servant" is misleading first because tens of thousands were deceived into working against their will; they did not give the kind of free and clear consent that English indentures required. Secondly, the term confuses because it conjures up images of English servants, who could expect their masters, under the force of law, to fulfill contractual obligations that prohibited physical abuse and guaranteed proper food, clothing, and shelter as well as training in a trade. Additionally, unlike in England, colonial law made it possible to discipline "servants" through a form of terror that gave master's extended control of their labor time; in this way, courts hearing masters' complaints about their workers' drunkenness, theft, fornication, bastardy, and running away, among other infractions, sentenced the accused to extended terms of service, in some cases, doubling the time "contracted." English courts punished servants through fines and jail time as proscribed by common law precedents, not through rewards to masters measured in elongated control of unfree labor. Furthermore, no servant in England ever became the chattel property of a master; in the colonies, masters owned both the labor and person of their "indentured servants," a new order of labor relations that masters painfully reinforced by branding their servants with white hot irons, a practice unimaginable in Old England. These unfortunates could be bought and sold according to the whim of their masters, and many changed hands several times before they died or their terms expired. During their bondage, the temporarily enslaved endured the same brutal violence and material deprivation as lifelong slaves; sometimes, due to their cheap purchase price and terminal service, they were treated even worse than lifelong slaves by planters who wanted to exploit as much labor as possible from slaves they could not control forever.

Ultimately, using the term "indentured servitude" adopts the rhetorical cloak planters employed to conceal, under the guise of normal master–servant relations, the new system of slavery they invented in the colonies. Planters knew well that rendering their countrymen into chattel property, even temporarily, ran counter to English law as well as the tradition that Christians should not enslave other Christians. Indentured servitude therefore became the plantocracy's euphemism for slavery, a term their partisans deployed to dissuade an increasingly alarmed English public that Englishmen were enslaving other Englishmen "beyond the seas" (Allen, 1997, pp. 124–147; Amussen, 2007, pp. 13, 17, 108, 121–129, 143, 155, 227; Beckles, 1995, pp. 572–584; Morgan, 1976, pp. 126–129, 216–218, 281–282). Leading partisans of this stripe included William Bullock, whom we've met before, and Martin Noell, a London trader in Atlantic commodities who served both Oliver Cromwell and Charles II as an advisor on colonial trade. Both Bullock and Noell bought, owned, and sold people from around the British Isles, a fact that renders farcical their denials, made in print and in the halls of Parliament, that colonial planters "made merchandise" of Christians (Bullock, 1649, pp. 13–14; Rutt, 1828, pp. 258–259). Finally, the conditions endured by "indentured servants" also meet widely accepted sociological criteria that scholars use to define slavery, past and present; for our purposes here, this makes "bond-slave" a more conceptually precise and historically accurate term than "indentured servant" (Davis, 2006, pp. 30–32; Patterson, 1982, pp. 21–27).

The testimony of Charles Bailey, sold into bond-slavery as a teenager in the 1640s, reveals the conditions he and tens of thousands of others endured. Recalling his own experience in Virginia, Baily wrote:

> {I endured}hunger, cold, nakedness, beatings, whippings, and the like...for many times was I stripped naked, and tied up by the hand, and whipped, and made to go barefoot and bare-legged in cold and frosty weather, and hardly cloaths to cover my nakedness, besides the sore and grievous labor which I was continually kept at during which time my poor soul would be often bemoaning itself concerning my soar captivity and misery...I had hard labor, and my daily exercise was beyond the common manner of slaves, for mine was often night and day...my very outward man would have been laid in the dust as several of my then fellow labourers were...Lord forgive them for what they did to them and me, for I am sure the poor creatures had better have been hanged, then to suffer the death and misery they did. (Baily, 1663, pp. 8–9)

Bailey suffered this slavery at precisely the same time that Bullock denied that it existed in Virginia. Noting, as Bailey did, the high mortality among "bond-slaves," historians themselves should be wary of drawing rigid lines between "bond-slavery" and lifelong slavery in the seventeenth century; being kidnapped into bond-slavery often involved a de facto life sentence, where victims would be systematically worked to death by their masters. For instance, on a Maryland plantation:

> a master having a sick servant...and observing...that there was no probability of his enjoying any more service from him, made him, sick and languishing as he was, dig his own grave... the others being to busy to dig it, having their hands full attending to the tobacco. (Dankers & Sluyter, 1680, p. 217)

Instead of the fixed asset, high stakes investment lifelong slaves represented to planters, Bailey's account illustrates how bond-slavery rendered children and others the "disposable people" of the seventeenth century, a phrase used by modern slavery scholar and abolitionist Kevin Bales to describe those held in bondage in today's global economy (Bales, 1999).

Bailey's account also reveals how young bond-slaves often came into that awful condition, as he, like thousands of others, had been kidnapped into forced labor as a teenager. While in Gravesend, a port town on the Thames between London and the English Channel, Bailey

> met with one Bradstreet, who was commonly called a "spirit," for he was one of those who did entice children and people away for Virginia; he fell into discourse with me, and I being in tender years, he did cunningly get me on board a ship, which was then there riding ready for to go to those parts, and I being once on board, could never get on shore, until I came to America, where I was sold as a bond-slave for 7 years. (Baily, 1663, pp. 8–9)

Despite its unlawfulness, corruption and a lack of political will allowed kidnapping to flourish as the first dominant form of human trafficking in the colonial Chesapeake for most of the seventeenth century. It should be noted, however, that even had Parliament and local government displayed more initiative in cracking-down on spirits, the British state made more work for them by cultivating an acute demand for colonial labor. The state did this by creating a colonial bureaucracy to oversee and tax a burgeoning empire of colonies that produced cash crops through slave labor. Even though bond-slavery contradicted English law, the state did nothing to abolish or even modify its practice in the colonies; this despite the Act of 1650 and the first set of Navigation Acts (1651), which asserted Parliament's sovereignty over the colonies. Clearly, the state prioritized its share of colonial profits over the freedom of its own subjects. And so, by directly encouraging the expansion of profitable yet exploitative capitalist enterprises around its Atlantic empire, the state ensured that spirits would continue to ply their sordid trade, thus rendering its own laws against spiriting exercises in disingenuous futility.

Space does not permit a thorough account of how and why the African slave trade replaced spiriting as the dominant form of human trafficking first in the West Indies and then in the Chesapeake. Nor can we spend much time discussing how and why racialized, chattel slavery replaced non-racialized bond-slavery as the most pervasive form of labor exploitation. It should be noted, however, that popular resistance to spiriting certainly drew negative attention to the practice, making the continuation of bond-slavery increasingly problematic.

Like most progressive reforms, the fight against spiriting and bond-slavery began in the streets, undertaken by people directly affected by injustice. Although we noted earlier that parents mourned their kidnapped children as they sailed away into slavery, parents, relations, friends, and neighbors did more than cry; they fought, desperately and effectively, when they caught a spirit in the act. Dozens of cases appear in London's seventeenth-century archives of riots that broke out when crowds confronted spirits. The tumults themselves, with the property destruction that accompanied them, drew Parliament's attention to the spiriting trade, resulting in the anti-kidnapping laws discussed above (CSPD, 1661–1666, pp. 220, 254–259, 278).

Additionally, during the English Revolution, puritan republicans pitted the freedom of political and religious liberty against the "slavery" of absolute monarchy and religious intolerance. Radicals within the revolutionary cadre, many of whom had spent time in the colonies, also issued manifestos decrying spiriting and bond-slavery as the clearest kinds of "slavery" that the revolution should sweep away in the name of godly justice. One radical faction led by an ex-New Englander named Thomas Venner even launched two ill-fated rebellions to restore the Republic and redeem the "enslaved consciences and bodies" of those who had been spirited away to the colonies. In New England itself, the Rhode Island assembly passed a law abolishing both bond-slavery and permanent slavery in 1652. This effort was led by Samuel Gorton, a man with Quaker-like beliefs who had also spent time in London during the English Revolution, where he supported the democratic republicanism of the Leveller movement, preaching to members in the same churches from which Thomas Venner would later gather his rebels (Donoghue, 2004, pp. 47–68; Linebaugh & Rediker, 2000, pp. 104–112).

A century later, Britons would sing a national anthem with the refrain, "Britons never, never, never would be slaves," a phrase that contradicted past realities while glorifying England's imperial power and cherished tradition of liberty. Britons never sang, of course, about their enslavement of millions of Africans, who by the early eighteenth century, dominated the empire's labor force.

The wealth and power that the transition to racialized, permanent slavery brought the British Empire make it difficult to understand how and why the imperial government voluntarily abolished the slave trade in 1807 and slavery itself in 1832. In one of the most famous studies of British abolition, Eric Williams argued that while Britain experienced its industrial take-off at home during the late eighteenth century, slavery's profitability declined to the point that made it too costly to pursue in light of money to be made by exploiting nominally "free labor" in a new age of industrial capitalism. Over the past 20 years, scholars such as Seymour Drescher, David Eltis, Roger Anstey, Stanley Engerman, and Barbara Solow challenged Williams' thesis, showing how slavery's profitability actually reached its zenith at the point where Williams traced its decline. In view of the changing scholarly consensus, David Brion Davis concluded that British abolition marked a rare moment in history when moral principles trumped profits in the construction of state policy (Anstey, 1975; Bender, 1992; Davis, 2006, pp. 231–249; Drescher, 1977, 1987; Eltis, 1987; Engerman & Solow, 2004).

Davis goes too far, however, in attributing abolition to the morals of the state itself. In contrast, the historians Peter Linebaugh and Marcus Rediker focus more appropriately on the lived morality of the democratic, international, human rights movement that eventually made slave trading and holding unacceptable to the British public. Through relentless, decades-long campaigning, the activists who made this movement represented a social cross-section from around the empire, ranging from slaves and escaped slaves, to sailors and soldiers, textile workers, rural laborers, miners, middle-class manufacturers, and Methodist ministers. Their activities included helping slaves escape slavery, investigating slave ship and plantation conditions, gathering testimonies from former slaves and sailors engaged in the slave trade; publishing slave memoirs, and graphic accounts and visual depictions of slavery and slave trading; staging of public protests and boycotts; and the submission of petitions containing hundreds of thousands of signatures to Parliament (Davis, 2006, Chap. 10; Linebaugh & Rediker, 2000, Chaps. 8–9). To co-ordinate these and other efforts, white and black activists in Britain formed organizations such as the Society for the Abolition of the Slave Trade (1787) and the Anti-Slavery Society (1823). Inspired by prophetic figures such as John Woolman and Anthony Benezet, American Quakers began organizing against slavery in 1763. Their work spawned successor groups during the late eighteenth century, who united moral outrage with republican principles to refute pro-slavery arguments. A generation later, radical New England reformers, free blacks, and escaped slaves, supported by British sympathizers, founded the American Anti-Slavery Society, a group which framed its opposition to slavery on the higher law of moral justice to override constitutional defenses of slavery. At about the same time, the most immediately successful anti-slavery organization, the Underground Railroad, conducted mainly by free blacks, helped hundreds of thousands of slaves from the south escape to freedom. The most direct response to slavery, the rebellions of the enslaved themselves, were integral to the history of abolition. The Haitian Revolution, which resulted in slaves overthrowing their masters to establish an independent republic, inspired successor rebellions around the West Indies, South America, and the American south. Collectively, these rebellions put the lie to arguments advanced by pro-slavery forces that the slaves' lack of self respect kept them content in their state of bondage. Interestingly, as Davis himself has shown, the Jamaican and Demaran rebellions of the early nineteenth century proceeded through designs that slaves hatched in league with white abolitionists. The point here is that a century-long tradition of radical thinking and mass-organization eventually pushed the British Empire and the United States into abolishing the slave trade and slavery; in each case, human rights movements, inspired by the actions of slaves themselves, pushed powerful governments to act in morally powerful ways. Abolitionism was far from a white-dominated, middle class reform movement. Without such pressure from below, it is hard to imagine how, where, and when abolition would have occurred when it did (Aptheker, 1989; Bredlinger, 2007; Brown, 2006; Dubois, 2004; Jackson, 2009; Slaughter, 2008; Snodgrass, 2007).

Thanks in part to the leadership of black and white British and American abolitionists, freedom from slavery became the first internationally recognized human right, as ratified by the League of Nations in 1926. This ideal transferred readily into practice, as far as ending legal slavery and slave trading, two institutions deeply embedded in the rise of global capitalism. But in terms of ending illegal slave trading and slavery itself in all their myriad forms, abolition, in light of global capitalism's prioritization of maximized profits, remained an elusive aspiration rather than a concrete reality.

Tragically, the roots of this dilemma may be traced back to the way in which states implemented the abolition of slavery in the nineteenth century. While ending the forms of slave trading and slavery publicized by grass-roots abolitionists,

European powers and the United States pursued policies that allowed and even directly encouraged other forms of unfree labor to flourish. As a case in point, once the British abolished slavery in the West Indies, they supervised the shipment of indentured Indian and Chinese workers onto sugar plantations, where they labored in conditions at least comparable to slavery. Why? The imperial state placed more of a premium on maximizing sugar profits to maintain a competitive edge over European rivals than in stamping out the bloody and exploitative labor practices involved in sugar production. In India itself, the imperial state presided over cotton, tea, coffee, and spice production, as well as railroad-building and other construction projects, all of which directly or indirectly made use of unfree labor. Within the United States, the Republican Party traded an end to federally governed reconstruction in return for southern support in the 1876 presidential election. Even before this bargain for partisan power, but particularly so in its wake, southern states passed draconian penal codes aimed at black men. Incarcerating blacks for even the most minor crimes under these laws, southern states gained revenue by hiring-out black prisoners to private corporations, who maximized their own profits by violently coercing convict labor in industries that ranged from road building to mining to brick making. Millions were exposed to these forms of bondage. Thus, even in the midst of the era of state-sponsored abolition, the pecuniary and political priorities of governments in the United States and the United Kingdom trumped their pretenses toward protecting human rights through the abolition of slavery (Blackmon, D. 2008; Chatterjee, 2005; Fierce, 1996; Lai, 1993; Mancini, 1996; Oshinsky, 1996).

The state priorities which prolonged the existence of slavery in the nineteenth and twentieth centuries have unwittingly helped to spark the resurgence of slave trading and slavery, especially child slavery, in our own time. While it would take volumes to comprehensively demonstrate and document how this has happened, the history may be clearly if incompletely summarized. After World War II, multinational corporations, their benefactors in western governments, and the global economic institutions they organized such as the IMF, World Bank, and later the WTO, gained increasing control over the global economy. Working in concert, these institutions set a premium on increasing the volume and value of trade between former imperial powers and the post-colonial societies of the "global south" in Latin America, Asia, and Africa. During the Cold War, at the height of the era of colonial liberation movements, corporations, western governments, and international economic institutions mustered their collective power to consolidate the strength of global capitalism by effectively re-colonizing the global south. World Bank and IMF loans, along with global free trade agreements such as GATT opened up post-colonial societies for "integration into the free market." But these programs advanced in ways that undercut the democratic freedoms that were, at least as western powers and global economic groups argued, part and parcel of capitalism's world-wide expansion (Goldman, 2005; Meier, 2005; Woods, 2006). Although it died from a thousand wounds in the global south, democracy in the region received its death blow from the violent and illegal campaigns western nations waged to eliminate socialist political competition. A list includes but is not limited to the sabotage of democratic elections in Vietnam (1954) and Guatemala

(1954); the assassination of elected leaders in Congo (1964) and Chile (1972); coups in Syria (1948), Iran (1956), Iraq (1958), Indonesia (1965), Uganda (1971), and Thailand (1976); terrorist campaigns throughout the 1980s in Central and South America; hot wars in Vietnam from 1948 to 1975; and proxy wars in Angola, South Africa, Congo, and the Sudan (ca. 1950–1991). The statistics bear mute witness to the human carnage: thousands "disappeared" in Chile, tens of thousands killed and tortured by CIA-trained and US-funded terrorists in Central America and Iran, millions of Vietnamese killed during wars with France and USA, three million dead during Suharto's US sanctioned atrocities in Indonesia, tens of millions killed by regimes brought into power and/or supported by the West throughout the entirety of the African continent (Blum, 1995; Grandin, 2006; Johnson, 2004; Kinser, 2007; Kornbluth, 2004; Nzongola-Ntalaja, 2002; Turner, 2007; Weiner, 2007).

Unfettered, post-cold war free market expansion has only exacerbated the catastrophic impact of these atrocities, committed as they were to expand the global, economic, and political hegemony of western nation-states and their multinational, corporate clients. While the void of post-cold war socialist competition made the blunt force of violence and terror less necessary, the cumulative effect of cold war carnage worked to undermine the rule of law in the world's post-colonial societies, leaving a legacy of corruption and political instability in its wake. With corrupt dictators competing for power with each other and with domestic rivals, cycles of civil and regional wars have continued to wash the global south in blood, and in the cases of central and western Africa, have culminated in genocides whose collective scale exceeds that of the Holocaust. Meanwhile, despite the revolutions of the mid-twentieth century that freed colonies from the direct control of imperial powers, the wealth of the global south continues to flow into the coffers of their past imperial masters.

Why has this happened? First, taken together, the political elite of the global south, who owe their power to foreign nations and multi-national corporations, have proven all too eager to waste the wealth and souls of their citizens at the behest of neo-imperial patrons. Furthermore, with the rise of the United States as the world's dominant power in the 1990s, the US-dominated IMF and World Bank pressured nations in the global south to make "structural adjustments" that would curtail labor and environmental regulations to create a more "business friendly" environment in order to attract foreign investment. Structural adjustments also meant cutting public spending on health care, education, and other social services in order to free up state revenue to pay off the debts nations incurred from IMF and World Bank loans. This has effectively rendered nations of the global south into the bond-slaves of the world's most ruthless capitalist powers. Particularly in Africa and the Caribbean, "free market" integration through WTO and World Bank-mandated tariff reductions brought in a flood of cheap imports from developed nations that ruined many domestic industries. This in turn prompted more IMF and World Bank loans, thus deepening the problem of national debt bondage in the global south. The WTO also supported economic reforms calculated to take advantage of each post-colonial society's "competitive advantage" in cash-crop, energy, or extraction industries. This transition in turn used up land formerly devoted to food production. Collectively, structural adjustments have left the people of the global south hungry despite their former self-sufficiency in food production, poor despite the wealth of their natural resources, and economically enslaved to their task-masters in the global north. Ultimately, structural adjustments kill people in the global south; the AIDS epidemic swept through these regions as the IMF and World Bank pillaged the treasuries of civil societies there. As a result, with less and less to spend on health care, life spans plunged in Africa and South Asia from their apex in the mid-1980s (Blackmon, P. 2008, pp. 179–202; Harvey, 2005, 2007; Nanwani, 2008, pp. 199–226; Peet, 2003; Perkins, 2008; Stiglitz, 2003; Teunissen & Akkerman, 2005).

In short, political and economic foreign intervention, combined with corruption and violence from within, have returned the global south to a state of nature, where life, to quote Thomas Hobbes, has again become nasty, brutish, and short. Unsurprisingly, and according to plan, the volume of global trade continues to reach historical heights as profits for multi-national corporations expand apace. Making matters worse, an explosion of population growth has accompanied the decline of civil society in the global south. Within the last fifty years, the world's population has soared from two to six billion, with the greatest increases realized in the regions with already failing public infrastructures. This situation has left millions in the global south vulnerable for economic exploitation, leading directly to the resurgence of slavery in our own time.

Predictably, women and children, the most vulnerable segments of post-colonial populations, have suffered the most from this process; like the children of the seventeenth century, they are the disposable people of today's global economy.

Kevin Bales, the leading scholar on modern slavery, has reckoned there are approximately twenty-seven million people in bondage today. This figure represents the highest number of people ever enslaved at one time in history. The International Labor Organization (ILO), an agency funded by the United Nations, has arrived at a lower figure of twelve million. The ILO estimates that close to 80% of those enslaved today are women and children; Bales' own figures correspond proportionately (Bales, 2004, p. 4; Bales, 2005, pp. 87–11; ILO).

Much like the seventeenth-century British Empire, in today's global economy, race does not determine who remains free and who will be enslaved; instead, as Professor Bales argues, sheer vulnerability based upon age, gender, and class within a wider context of political corruption, and capitalist exploitation have again become the predictors of who will be enslaved. Additionally, slavery today, like in the seventeenth-century British Empire, can only be properly described as a long spectrum of various kinds of bondage, ranging from bond-slavery to life-long slavery. In another chilling parallel between this past and our own present, due to an ever-expanding population of vulnerable young people, slaves can be purchased for exceptionally low prices, making the value of their labor high while simultaneously reducing the value of their lives in the eyes of their masters. In a startling, inflation-adjusted contrast with racialized slavery in the Antebellum south, Kevin Bales has estimated that a slave in 1850 Mississippi cost $1,400, while a person may be purchased in Ghana today for as little as $30. Although there is no legal footing to assert temporary or lifetime ownership over these slaves, there is no compelling need to (Bales, 2004, pp. 9–11; Bales, 2007, pp. 9–20). Slavery flourishes illegally where the rule of law has succumbed to widespread corruption. Here, as with seventeenth-century Britain, governments act in profitable though illegal concert with global entrepreneurs. In Myanmar, for example, Halliburton contracted in 1998 to build an oil pipeline. The Myanmar government, in turn, forced its ethnic minorities into slavery to build the pipeline, much like the seventeenth-century British Empire delivered Irish children into the hands of slave-owning tobacco and sugar planters. Neither Halliburton nor the Myanmar government, like the seventeenth-century colonial legislatures, acknowledges that their labor systems rely at least in part upon slave labor (Waldman, 2000).

Within this context, in ways reminiscent again of the seventeenth century, drawing rigid lines between those temporarily or permanently enslaved makes little sense, since slave owners today exploit their slaves as long as local conditions allow them to and as long as the work of their slaves remains profitable. For example, the completion of the Halliburton pipeline made the Myanmar slaves expendable; the job was over so feeding and clothing idle slaves just meant an added cost to Halliburton and the Myanmar government. In another example, brothel owners in South Asia regularly enslave children for prostitution. These children work as sex slaves as long as they remain desirable to pedophiles and free of sexually transmitted diseases. When the children age or fall ill, they are put out on the street. The large supply of vulnerable people, especially children, their low cost, and the illegality of slavery make modern slaves disposable, rending their lifetime control unnecessary and sometimes less profitable, since it costs more to keep and feed a slave, and less to work them to death or abandon them when their profitability diminishes (Bales, 2005, pp. 35, 65–68; ILO-IPEC, 1998; Sage & Kasten, 2006, p. 4).

Rapid population growth and the horrific socio-economic conditions extant in the global south have made the work of today's "spirits" much easier. Chillingly, like the seventeenth century, most children are enslaved today by kidnappers who lure their victims into bondage through deception. Traffickers of this variety endeavor to convince poor children or their families to sign contracts for attractive though fictional jobs abroad, offers that are sometimes accompanied by promises of employer-subsidized, higher education. These contracts seemingly help children escape their immediate, miserable circumstance and bleak future prospects. But instead of good jobs and higher education, these children are enslaved and sold abroad, usually as prostitutes, textile operatives, and domestic and agricultural workers. This international, slave-trading network keeps brothels and textile mills in the global south in business. It also helps explain how slave labor persists in the "massage parlors," sweat shops, citrus groves, and sugar fields of the United States and other powerful, developed nations (Aronowitz & Peruffo, 2001; Bales, 2005, pp. 154–171).

While they account for over half of those trafficked across borders, millions of child slaves work against their will within their own nations. Unlike the early British Empire, where child slaves worked mainly on colonial plantations, today's child slaves labor in domestic industries that range beyond agriculture to include the sex trade, military service, mining, textiles, and light and heavy manufacturing. Too often, they are trapped in a world of bond-slavery occasioned by the desperate financial straits suffered by their families. Bond-slavery occurs with disturbing regularity in India, often cited as an economic miracle of the post-Cold War global economy. The textiles (especially rugs), cigarettes (known as beedis) and cash crops made and grown there are often the product of bond-slave labor. Government corruption ensures that many will never escape this fate, as a slave-owning farmer who also holds a position in the Indian Department of Labor recently told an abolitionist doing field research (Bales, 2005, pp. 1–4, 16–17, 20, 32–34, 88; Basu, 2002). Other children are kidnapped and forced into military service. There they are given drugs to anesthetize them to the atrocities they are forced to commit on behalf of official or para-military forces locked in political struggles to control their nations' corrupt political institutions. This practice prevails in Africa and South Asia, and often bleeds into other forms of child slavery used for public works projects, diamond mining, prostitution, and drug trafficking (CSUCS, 2006; Francis, 2007, pp. 207–231; UNICEF, 2002). Meanwhile, as the governments of world powers devote money to stop human trafficking, their foreign policies as nations and within global economic institutions continue to produce and further aggravate the conditions which make people, especially children, vulnerable to enslavement.

While it may be true that the number of people enslaved today represents the lowest proportion in world history, modern slavery still represents a grave, global crisis. First, slavery's survival amounts to a gross violation of human rights that jeopardizes the lives and well-being of millions of children. Secondly, slavery remains a drag on economic growth in the global south. First, the persistence of slavery keeps the wages of free workers low; low disposable income in turn drives down per capita consumption; this results in dwindling revenues for local businesses and limits the prospects for likely entrepreneurs. Consequently, the millions of people living on less than two dollars a day continues to grow, as does the amount of children, who if not enslaved, work long hours for little pay. This ghastly fact helps explain the pervasive market share and profitability of multi-national corporations like Nike, who relocate production sites to the global south to take advantage of cheap child labor. This notwithstanding the fact that Nike, like most multi-nationals, originated in nations like the United States, which have banned child labor as an institution repulsive to the standards of modern civilization. Meanwhile, local economies in the global south invariably suffer because corporations like Nike employ children for wages too low to sustain regional growth. If Nike paid higher wages in the global south, the parents who now find it necessary to send their children off to work could earn wages high enough to send their children to school. But as the situation stands now, poorly educated children, upon reaching adulthood, do not possess the skills to compete for good jobs in the global economy. They will most likely send their own children to work, deepening a cycle of unnecessary poverty and exploitation. These circumstances also sustain the growth of modern slavery, making it easier for modern-day spirits to seduce children or their families eager to find a better life for them; other families turn reluctantly to bond-slavery in order to survive. Despite the large expansion of the middle class in regions like India in recent years, the long-term economic outlook remains grim for the vast majority of people in India itself and the global south as a whole. This can be largely but not exclusively attributed to the exploitative character of multi-national corporate capitalism, which continuously pulls millions into an expanding vortex of deception, poverty, bondage, and the hell of hopelessness.

And so despite the de jure abolition slavery, slavery exists today at the extreme end of a long spectrum of economic and political injustice rooted in the world's most powerful public and private institutions. Taking heed from Britain's example, we should realize that forbidding slavery and child labor at home while helping it flourish abroad enslaves us all to a morally abhorrent, economic regime, one that depends upon murderous political tyranny and rapacious corruption, thrives through the exploitation of children, and generates inequalities offensive to our professed notions of justice. Moreover, this global economic regime, which exercises power in its own name at the expense of the global public good, justifies itself by making soul-less materialism and crass consumerism the object of all work; in the end, this demeans the dignity of all labor. To conflate any of this with the onward march of democracy requires us to embrace Orwellian double-speak, that "freedom is slavery."

To conclude, the more familiar system of racialized, chattel slavery, which crystallized in the British Empire by the early eighteenth century, grew out of an earlier, seventeenth-century system, where multiple forms of slavery existed side by side. Although race always defined the line between temporary and lifelong bondage in the colonial period, race did not always define the line between slavery and freedom. In fact, for the better part of the seventeenth century, most slaves in the empire, especially in the Chesapeake region, became so due to their sheer vulnerability to enslavement, not by virtue of their race, which in the modern meaning of the term did not yet exist. As poor children made up the majority within the enslaved population, age and class became the key criterion for determining vulnerability to enslavement. This cannot be explained outside the context of Europe's transition to capitalism and the rise of the western nation-state through empire building, interdependent processes that created the supply and demand for child slaves.

Gazing through this historical perspective involves a long look in the mirror, where the image of the twenty-first-century global economy casts back a reflection of its blood-soaked seventeenth-century predecessor. Modern slavery more resembles that which existed in the seventeenth-century empire, rather than that of the eighteenth- or nineteenth-century slave societies of colonial Britain and the American south. In the seventeenth century, the empire's long spectrum of unfree labor was dominated by disposable bond-slaves, most of whom were children. The parallel continues through the fact that today, vulnerability shaped by age, class, and gender rather than race determines who will be enslaved. Strikingly, vulnerability to enslavement, in both the seventeenth and twenty-first centuries, stems largely from global upheavals occasioned by complementary developments in imperial power struggles and capitalist economic expansion. The traffic in modern slaves also resembles that which occurred between the British Isles and the colonies during the seventeenth century, when spirits illegally deceived young people into bondage. Additionally, like the former British Empire, today's world powers pass laws against trafficking, while their foreign policies create the conditions in which slavery flourishes.

Drawing again from history, we realize that in the nineteenth century, Britain and the United States, followed later by the world's other empires, summoned the requisite political will to abolish lifelong slavery and slave trading in all of its forms. But this occurred only after a half century of relentless political pressure from self-organized groups of citizens (today we would call them NGOs). This perspective reveals that ending slavery today can only be achieved by marshalling the political will of the world's dominant states, the only organizations with the most power to affect slavery's complete abolition.

On the contrary, governments can pass all the anti-trafficking laws they wish to, and devote as much money as their legislatures see fit to effect their enforcement. But as long as their own foreign policies, and those they pursue through the governing bodies of the global economy continue to breed the conditions in which slavery flourishes, children and adults will continue to suffer, in Prof. Jim Garbarino's words, the worst of "the dark side of the human experience."

It would serve us all well to remember that power never voluntarily extends itself in self-less directions; in the end, the state must be pushed into a new age of abolition. A democratically organized, international peoples' movement, more than any member of Parliament or Congress, brought the African slave trade and racialized slavery to an end in the nineteenth century. We hold the power now to complete the work begun by the abolitionists of the past. The work has already begun. Groups with thousands of members around the world like Anti-Slavery International and its US affiliate Free the Slaves emancipate slaves and lobby national governments to pass and enforce anti-trafficking laws. Like the hundreds and thousands of ordinary people in the late eighteenth and nineteenth centuries, the ordinary people in today's abolitionist movements are capable of extraordinary things. But based upon historical perspective, I contend that today's abolitionists cannot limit themselves to emancipation campaigns and re-adjustment programs. Instead, we must broaden our efforts through direct confrontations with the national and global institutions whose policies have created the conditions in which resurgent child slavery has taken root. Ultimately, this more systematic approach will move us closer to providing children everywhere with a healthy environment, a goal inextricably linked to the future success of the abolitionist movement.

References

Allen, T. (1997). *The invention of the White race* (Vol. 2). New York: Verso.

Amussen, S. (2007). *Caribbean exchanges: Slavery and the transformation of English society*. Chapel Hill, NC: University of North Carolina Press.

Anstey, R. (1975). *The Atlantic slave trade and British abolition*. Atlantic Highlands, NJ: Humanities Press.

Aptheker, H. (1989). *Abolitionism: A revolutionary movement*. Boston, MA: Twayne Publishers.

Aronowitz, A. A., & Peruffo, M. (2001). *Smuggling and trafficking in human bondage: The phenomenon, the markets that drive it, and the organizations that promote it*. Turin: United Nations Interregional Crime and Justice Research Institute.

Baily, C. (1663). *A true and faithful warning unto the people and inhabitants of Bristol*. London.
Bales, K. (1999). *Disposable people: New slavery in the global economy*. Berkeley, CA: University of California Press.
Bales, K. (2004). *New slavery: A reference handbook*. Denver, CO: ABC-CLIO.
Bales, K. (2005). *Understanding global slavery*. Berkeley, CA: University of California Press.
Bales, K. (2007). *Ending slavery: How we free today's slaves*. Berkeley, CA: University of California Press.
Basu, A. K. (2002). *Targeting child labor in debt bondage: Evidence, theory and policy implications*. Florence: UNICEF.
Beckles, H. M. (1989). *White servitude and black slavery in Barbados, 1627–1715*. Knoxville, TN: University of Tennessee Press.
Beckles, H. M. (1990). A "riotous and unruly lot": Irish indentured servants and freemen in the English West Indies, 1644–1713. *William and Mary Quarterly, 47*, 503–522.
Beckles, H. M. (1995). The concept of 'White Slavery' in the English Caribbean during the early seventeenth century. In J. Brewer & S. Staves (Eds.), *Early modern conceptions of property*. London: Routledge.
Beckles, H. M. (2001). The hub of empire: The Caribbean and Britain in the seventeenth century. In N. Canny (Ed.), *The origins of empire: The Oxford history of the British Empire*. New York: Oxford University Press.
Bender, T. (1992). *The anti-slavery debate: Capitalism and abolitionism as a problem in historical interpretation*. Berkeley, CA: University of California Press.
Birch, T. (1742). *The state papers of John Thurloe* (Vol. 4). London: Woodward.
Blackburn, R. (1997). *The making of new world slavery: From the baroque to the modern, 1492–1800*. New York: Verso.
Blackmon, D. (2008a). *Slavery by another name: The re-enslavement of Black people in America from the Civil War to World War II*. New York: Doubleday.
Blackmon, P. (2008b). Rethinking poverty through the eyes of the International Monetary Fund and the World Bank. *International Studies Review, 10*, 179–202.
Bliss, R. M. (1994). *Revolution and empire: English politics and the American colonies in the seventeenth century*. New York: Manchester University Press.
Blomely, N. (2007). Making private property: Enclosure, common right and the work of hedges. *Rural History, 18*, 1–21.
Blum, W. (1995). *Killing hope: US military and CIA interventions since World War II*. Monroe, ME: Common Courage Press.
Bredlinger, I. A. (2007). *To be silent would be criminal: The antislavery influence and writings of Anthony Benezet*. Lanham, MD: Scarecrow Press.
Brown, C. L. (2006). *Moral capital: Foundations of British abolitionism*. Chapel Hill, NC: University of North Carolina Press.
Bullock, W. (1649). *Virginia impartially examined and left to public view*. London.
Chatterjee, I. (2005). Abolition by denial: The South Asian example. In G. Campbell (Ed.), *Abolition and its aftermath in Indian Ocean Asia and Africa: Studies in slave and post-slave societies and cultures*. New York: Routledge.
CSUCS. (2006). *Child soldiers and disarmament, demobilization, rehabilitation and reintegration in West Africa: A survey of programmatic work on child soldiers in Côte d'Ivoire, Guinea, Liberia and Sierra Leone*. London: Coalition to Stop the Use of Child Soldiers.
Dankers, J., & Sluyter, P. (1680). *Journal of a voyage to New York*. New York: Long Island Historical Society (Ann Arbor, MI: University Microfilms, 1966).
Davis, D. B. (2006). *Inhuman bondage: The rise and fall of slavery in the New World*. New York: Oxford University Press.
Donoghue, J. (2004). Unfree labor, imperialism, and radical republicanism in the Atlantic world, 1630–1661. *Labor: Studies in Working-Class History of the Americas, 1*, 47–68.
Donoghue, J. (2010). 'Out of the Land of Bondage': The English revolution and the Atlantic origins of abolition. *American Historical Review, 115* (October 2010).

Drescher, S. (1977). *Econocide: British slavery in the era of abolition*. Pittsburg, PA: University of Pittsburgh Press.

Drescher, S. (1987). *Capitalism and anti-slavery: British mobilization in comparative perspective*. New York: Oxford University Press.

Dubois, L. (2004). *A colony of citizens: Revolution and slave emancipation in the French Caribbean*. Chapel Hill, NC: University of North Carolina Press.

Dunn, R. (1984). Servants and slaves: The recruitment and employment of labor. In J. Greene, P. Jack, & J. R. Pole (Eds.), *Colonial British America: Essays in the new history of the early modern era*. Baltimore, MD: Johns Hopkins University Press.

Elliot, J. H. (2006). *Empires of the Atlantic world: Britain and Spain in America, 1492–1830*. New Haven, CT: Yale University Press.

Eltis, D. (1987). *Economic growth and the ending of the Trans-Atlantic slave trade*. New York: Oxford University Press.

Eltis, D., Behrendt, S. D., Richardson, D., & Klein, H. S. (1999). *The Trans-Atlantic slave trade: A database on CD-ROM*. Cambridge: Cambridge University Press.

Engerman, S., & Solow, B. (2004). *British capitalism and Caribbean slavery: The legacy of Eric Williams*. New York: Cambridge University Press.

Faust, D. G. (2008). *This republic of suffering: Death and the American Civil War*. New York: Knopf.

Fierce, M. C. (1996). *Slavery revisited: Blacks and the southern convict lease system, 1865–1933*. Brooklyn, NY: Africana Studies Research Center.

Francis, D. J. (2007). 'Paper protection' mechanisms: Child soldiers and the International protection of children in Africa's conflict zones. *Journal of Modern African Studies, 45*, 207–231.

Galenson, D. (1981). *White servitude in colonial America: An economic analysis*. New York: Cambridge University Press.

Goldman, M. (2005). *Imperial nature: The World Bank and struggles for social justice in the age of globalization*. New Haven, CT: Yale University Press.

Grandin, G. (2006). *Empire's workshop: Latin America, the United States, and the rise of the new imperialism*. New York: Metropolitan Books.

Greene, J. P. (2007). Colonial history and national history: Reflections on a continuing problem. *William and Mary Quarterly, 64*, 235–250.

Griffiths, P. (2008). *Lost Londons: Change, crime, and control in the capital city, 1550–1660*. New York: Cambridge University Press.

Guasco, M. (2007). To 'doe some good upon their countrymen': The paradox of Indian slavery in early Anglo-America. *Journal of Social History, 41*, 389–411.

Hahn, S. (2003). *A nation under our feet: Black political struggles in the rural south from slavery to the great migration*. Cambridge, MA: Harvard University Press.

Hair, P., & Law, R. (2001). The English in Western Africa to 1700. In N. Canny (Ed.), *The origins of empire: British overseas enterprise to the close of the seventeenth century*. New York: Oxford University Press.

Harlow, V. (1923). *A history of Barbados 1625–1685*. Oxford: Clarendon Press.

Harvey, D. (2005). *The new imperialism*. New York: Oxford University Press.

Harvey, D. (2007). *A brief history of neoliberalism*. New York: Oxford University Press.

Henning, W. W. (1823). March 1642–1643, Act XXVI. Being a collection of all the laws of Virginia from the first session of the legislature, in the year 1619: Vol. I, 1619–1620. New York: R. & W. & G. Bartow.

Hill, C. (1972). *The world turned upside down: Radical ideas during the English revolution*. New York: Viking.

ILO. Retrieved from http://www.ilo.org/global/Themes/Forced_Labour/lang--en/index.htm.

ILO-IPEC (1998). Trafficking in children for labour exploitation including child prostitution in the Mekong Sub-region: A research report. In: *International Programme on the Elimination of Child Labour*. Bangkok: International Labor Organization.

Jackson, M. (2009). *Let this voice be heard: Anthony Benezet, Father of Atlantic abolitionism*. Philadelphia, PA: University of Pennsylvania Press.

Jefferson, J. C. (1888). *Middlesex county records* (Vol. 3). London: Middlesex County Record Society.
Johnson, C. (2004). *The sorrows of empire: Militarism, secrecy, and the end of the republic*. New York: Metropolitan Books.
Johnson, R. C. (1970). The transportation of vagrant children from London to Virginia, 1618–1622. In H. S. Reinmuth (Ed.), *Early Stuart studies: Essays in honor of David Harris Willson*. Minneapolis, MN: University of Minnesota Press.
Jordan, W. (1961). The influence of the West Indies on the origins of New England slavery. *William and Mary Quarterly, 18*, 243–250.
Kennedy, G. (2008). *Diggers, levellers, and agrarian capitalism: Radical political thought in seventeenth century England*. Plymouth, MA: Lexington Books.
Kinser, S. (2007). *Overthrow: America's century of regime change from Hawaii to Iraq*. London: Times Books.
Klein, N. (2007). *The shock doctrine: The rise of disaster capitalism*. New York: Metropolitan Books.
Kornbluth, P. (2004). *The Pinochet File: A declassified dossier on atrocity and accountability*. New York: New Press.
Lai, W. L. (1993). *Indentured labor, Caribbean sugar: Chinese and Indian migrants to the British West Indies, 1838–1918*. Baltimore, MD: Johns Hopkins University Press.
Linebaugh, P. (2008). *The Magna Carta Manifesto: Liberties and commons for all*. Berkeley, CA: University of California Press.
Linebaugh, P. L., & Rediker, M. (2000). *The many-headed hydra: Sailors, slaves, commoners, and the hidden history of the revolutionary Atlantic*. Boston, MA: Beacon.
Mancini, M. G. (1996). *One dies, get another: Convict leasing in the American South, 1866–1928*. Columbia, SC: University of South Carolina Press.
Mapping of Corruption and Governance Measurement Tools in Sub-Saharan Africa (2008). *Report of Transparency International: The global coalition against corruption*.
Meier, G. M. (2005). *Biography of a subject: An evolution of development economics*. New York: Oxford University Press.
Menard, R. R. (2001). *Migrants, servants, and slaves: Unfree labor in colonial British America*. Aldershot, England: Ashgate.
Morgan, E. (1975). *American slavery – American freedom: The ordeal of colonial Virginia*. New York: Norton.
Morgan, K. (2007). *Slavery and the British Empire: From Africa to America*. New York: Oxford University Press.
Nanwani, S. (2008). Holding multilateral development banks to account: Gateways and barriers. *International Community Law Review, 10*, 199–226.
Nzongola-Ntalaja, G. (2002). *The Congo: From Leopold to Kabila: A people's history*. New York: Zed Books.
O'Callaghan, S. (2000). *To hell or Barbados: The ethnic cleansing of Ireland*. Channel Islands: Brandon.
Oshinsky, D. (1996). *"Worse than Slavery": Parchman farm and the ordeal of Jim Crow Justice*. New York: New Press.
Paige, J. (1984). *The letters of John Paige, London merchant, 1648–58*. London: London Record Society.
Palmer, C. A. (1998). *The worlds of unfree labour: From indentured servitude to slavery*. Aldershot, England: Variorum.
Patriquin, L. (2004). The agrarian origins of the Industrial Revolution in England. *Review of Radical Political Economics, 36*, 196–216.
Patterson, O. (1982). *Slavery and social death: A comparative study*. Cambridge, MA: Harvard University Press.
Peet, R. (2003). *Unholy trinity: The IMF, World Bank, and WTO*. New York: Zed Books.
Perkins, J. (2005). *Fair trade for all: How trade can promote development*. New York: Oxford University Press.

Perkins, J. (2008). *The secret history of the American empire*. New York: Plume.
Pestana, C. G. (2004). *The English Atlantic in an age of revolution*. Cambridge, MA: Harvard University Press.
Rediker, M. (2007). *The slave ship: A human history*. New York: Viking.
Reynolds, D. (2005). *John Brown, abolitionist: The man who killed slavery, sparked the Civil War, and seeded civil rights*. New York: Knopf.
Rodgers, N. (2007). The Irish in the Caribbean, 1641–1837: An overview. *Irish Migration Studies in Latin America, 5*, 145–156.
Roediger, D. (2000). *The wages of Whiteness: Race and the making of the American working-class*. New York: Verso.
Sage, J., & Kasten, L. (2006). *Enslaved: True stories of modern day slavery*. New York: Palgrave Macmillan.
Salinger, S. V. (1997). Labor, markets, and opportunity: Indentured servitude in early America. *Labor History, 38*, 311–338.
Slaughter, T. P. (2008). *The beautiful soul of John Woolman, apostle of abolition*. New York: Hill & Wang.
Smith, A. E. (1947). *Colonists in bondage: White servitude and convict labor in America, 1607–1776*. New York: Norton.
Snodgrass, M. E. (2007). *The underground railroad: An encyclopedia of people, places, and operations*. New York: Sharpe.
Steinfeld, R. (1991). *The invention of free labor: The employment relationship in English and American law and culture, 1350–1870*. Chapel Hill, NC: University of North Carolina Press.
Stiglitz, J. (2003). *Globalization and its discontents*. New York: Norton.
Stout, H. S. (2006). *Upon the altar of freedom: A moral history of the Civil War*. New York: Viking.
Teunissen, J. J., & Akkerman, A. (2005). *Helping the poor? The IMF and low-income countries*. Leiden: FONDAD.
Thirsk, J. (1985). *The agrarian history of England and Wales, Vol. 5, 1640–1750: Agrarian Change*. Cambridge: Cambridge University Press.
Thompson, E. P. (1991). *Customs in common: Studies in traditional popular culture*. New York: New Press.
Tilly, C. (1981). *As sociology meets history*. New York: Academic Press.
Tomlins, C. (2001). Reconsidering indentured servitude: European migration and the early American labor force, 1600–1775. *Labor History, 42*, 5–43.
Turner, T. (2007). *The Congo wars: Conflict, myth and reality*. New York: Zed Books.
UNICEF. (2002). *East Asia and the Pacific regional office, adult wars, child soldiers: Voices of children involved in armed conflict in the East Asia and Pacific region*. Bangkok: UNICEF.
Virginia Magazine of History and Biography (1898–1899).
Waldman, P. (2000, October 27). Pipeline project in Myanmar puts Cheney in spotlight. *Wall Street Journal*.
Weiner, T. (2007). *Legacy of ashes: The history of the CIA*. New York: Doubleday.
Williams, E. (1994). *Capitalism and slavery*. Chapel Hill, NC: University of North Carolina Press (originally published in 1944).
Winthrop, J. (1630). A model of Christian charity. *Collections of the Massachusetts Historical Society, 7*, 31–48 (Boston, MA: Massachusetts Historical Society, 1838).
Wood, A. (2006). Fear, hatred and the hidden injuries of class in early modern England. *Journal of Social History, 39*, 803–826.
Wood, E. M., & Wood, N. (1997). *A trumpet of sedition: Political theory and the rise of capitalism, 1509–1688*. New York: New York University Press.
Woods, N. (2006). *The globalizers: The IMF, the World Bank, and their borrowers*. Ithaca, NY: Cornell University Press.

Chapter 12
In Harm's Way in America: The Burden of Gun Violence

William French

Introduction

Gun violence in the USA annually accounts for vast suffering and death, yet many of us have become so habituated to it that we fail to grasp its scale or impact. It takes a heavy toll on American children, especially children in America's inner cities. While its direct carnage is quite massive, its indirect impacts are quite pervasive as well. We, as a society, suffer decade after decade by failing to understand the range of impacts of our national policies of open firearm access that allow a spread of handguns and other firearms to proliferate across homes and communities throughout our country (Garbarino, 1999; Kopel, 1995; Prothrow-Smith, 1991). We lead the developed nations of the world in firearm homicides, and our children, families, and society at large pays a heavy price (Cook & Ludwig, 2000). In 1998, the City of Chicago, for example, in a lawsuit against some gun manufacturers and gun store operators sought to recover monies that the city incurred in 4 years of police, medical, and other municipal expenses required for addressing firearm violence. The costs borne by the city and its taxpayers were estimated at $433 million (Butterfield, 1998, 2002).

We are presented by the gun lobby with a seemingly coherent but deeply distorting picture of the role of guns in our communities and our homes, and because of the immense political power of the National Rifle Association and the rest of the gun lobby, decade after decade, we fail to have a sustained national engagement with the true costs and scale of the carnage wrought by our present gun access policies. We thus fail, decade after decade, to implement gun control policies and other measures that might reduce the annual suffering of children, families, and communities caused by firearm violence.

W. French (✉)
Department of Theology, Center for Christian Ethics, Loyola University,
6525 N Sheridan Rd, 443 Crown Center, Chicago, IL 60626, USA
e-mail: wfrench@luc.edu

J. Garbarino and G. Sigman (eds.), *A Child's Right to a Healthy Environment*,
The Loyola University Symposium on the Human Rights of Children 1,
DOI 10.1007/978-1-4419-6791-6_12,

Guns are symbolically and culturally freighted with meaning and laden with fundamental notions about our identity as individuals, communities, and about our nation as a whole. Obviously, gun violence discussions in the last 40 years have become deeply politicized. Gun control has been a central point of contestation in the so-called *culture wars* (Frank, 2004). These "wars" have obviously been pushed for political gain in both local and national elections. The Democratic Party has tended to be for more stringent gun control, especially handgun control measures while the Republican Party has tended to align itself with the National Rifle Association's condemnation of gun control.

The Democratic Party under President Clinton made gun control a priority, but since then the Democratic Party has reduced its prioritization of focus on gun violence and the need for more robust gun control and violence prevention measures. There may be two major reasons for this. First, the good news is that homicide numbers in general, and firearm homicide numbers in particular, rose across the late 1980s and early 1990s to an alarming peak in 1993. Since then the USA has seen a significant dropping off of homicide and firearm homicide numbers. The bad news is that while we have dropped from the peak in 1993 of 17,048 firearm homicides, our 2006 level of 11,566 remains a lot of human carnage: Traumatized families, ripped communities, lost dreams, and fear (USDOJ, 2009). Second, it seems that the Democrats have calculated that Al Gore may well have lost the Presidency to George Bush over gun rights concerns in West Virginia and Tennessee that pushed enough voters to flip those states to the Republican candidate. Democrats have clearly backed away from making gun violence a top priority since then, and it is likely that they have calculated that it is simply too costly politically. Accordingly, the national discussion about gun violence has diminished as both the Republican and the Democratic Parties have decided to turn attention to other issues. But significant carnage, family suffering, and societal impact continues even if the national political discussion has by and large moved on.

In what follows, I suggest that we can begin to grasp the diffuse trauma and tragedy of America's annual pageantry of gun violence when we compare its scale with that of the casualties of the 9/11 terrorist attacks. This process of comparison allows us to open our eyes to the scale of damage and begin to test out the possibility that our domestic gun violence deserves to be recognized as a genuine national security priority. Discussions of WMD – weapons of mass destruction – are housed typically in International Studies, Strategic Theory, and War and Peace discussions. I want to appropriate this term and suggest that it is an apt description for our national scale of firearms violence wrought by the proliferation of small arms across our society. If it is wise to worry about nuclear proliferation, it is similarly wise to worry about small arms proliferation. Both can kill – and in great numbers. Similarly, I aim to use distinctive categories from Just War Theory – namely, collateral damage – to illuminate how both intentional gun violence and indeed mere gun ownership take one into the terrain of explicit moral responsibility. Simple gun ownership requires a high level of vigilance to prevent alternative uses for a gun initially purchased with the intention of its use in target practice or hunting.

I will examine the societal debates about gun violence and gun control. Specifically, I will show how the general descriptions of the main dynamics shaping America's gun violence that are repeated, decade after decade, by the National Rifle Association, and the rest of America's gun lobby are deeply flawed. And because these descriptions misdiagnose the problems so markedly, they are used to justify deeply inadequate public policies meant to preserve easy public access to guns. I will conclude by examining how debates about gun violence and gun control are so heated in part because they sit squarely on the key ideological divide between the affirmation of the value of individual rights and the affirmation of the priority of the common good. Our "culture wars" are mobilized often for political purposes, and the center of these "wars" often is the charged debate between individualist and communitarian philosophical emphases. Where many worry intensely about infringing on "gun rights," I note that the English medieval right to bear arms develops out of a core affirmation of the need to defend the common good and well-being of the community. If *rights* are an important moral lens, so too is an affirmation of the centrality of the common good. And surely, discussions of *gun rights* cannot be allowed to blind us, decade after decade, to the rights of children and families to have a healthy environment. Defense of the well-being of the community in the late middle ages may well have justified the requirement that able-bodied people bear arms so as to be able to help protect the community. But today, the need for community protection may well require not so much the bearing of arms as the restraining of the proliferation of arms.

Gun Violence as Mere Local News

Different frameworks for understanding concentrate our attention on various features of reality and block attention to other features. They shape the world that we attend to and extend concern about. It has long been difficult for our society to grasp the scale of our national gun violence because of the way it tends to present itself in discrete episodes of carnage with one, two, or three dead spread in seemingly disconnected events of tragedy flung across time and the expanse of our country. Such events are typically ugly – 7/11 Store holdups gone awry; crazed lover kills beloved; drunken shoot out at local bar; back alley assaults, and, of course, gang shootings. These stories have repeated themselves across the decades and across our land and regularly receive short-lived media notice as tragic but local news items. Such episodes numb us with their frequency and mechanical repetition. Not surprisingly, this repetitiveness of the local news stories of gun violence leads over time to a sense that gun violence is simply a sad but fixed part of the fabric of American life. In this way, huge scales of violence become "normalized," and we as a society become accustomed to these sad stories as simply given features of life and not patterns that can and should be engaged and changed.

Episodic Attention then Business as Usual

But over the years, the country has witnessed shocking cases where the gun casualties are so numerous that national media attention is drawn and sustained. Gun fire that brings down ones and twos does not break into national attention. But the Columbine High School shootings in Littleton Colorado in May 1999 and other large-scale spectacular events of gun violence since then do change the equation and break into the national news cycle. At Columbine, two white suburban high school students shot and killed 12 of their school mates and a teacher before shooting themselves. Thirteen victims and two perpetrators were dead (Gibbs, 1999).

While national attention focuses on the unusual event of the largely white suburban high school mass shooting, no media outlet seemed interested in the story that Chicago, for example, was doing only slightly less than the equivalent of a Columbine High School scale massacre each week. While Columbine got the headlines, Chicago, LA, New York, Detroit, and the rest had their normal flow of gun fire and family suffering and tearful funerals go by with only local notice and little national attention. When urban center violence is "normalized" in the national mind, people tune out – it is so ugly and depressing after all. Only gun violence episodes that break the expected norm or pattern trigger national media attention and hence prompt a national focus and discussion (Trout, 2009).

After Columbine, we have seen that a regular procession of high profile cases of mass shootings have commanded – even if fleetingly – national media attention. On March 21, 2005 at the Red Lake High School Indian Reservation in Minnesota, a student went on a rampage and shot and killed ten of his classmates and grandparents. On April 16, 2007, we had the deadliest shooting rampage in American history at Virginia Tech in Blacksburg, Va. An emotionally imbalanced student shot and killed 32 people before killing himself. And again, we have the recent shooting at Northern Illinois University on February 15, 2008 where Stephen Kazmierczak shot and killed six people (Herbert, 2009).

While these larger episodes of gun violence slaughter do capture the national news stage briefly, almost no policy change has developed from these new occasions of national exposure. While the shock over the Columbine High School killings triggered a sustained national discussion about gun issues, since then each episode of mass gun violence seems to register less and less of a national impact. We, as a nation, appear to be growing accustomed now even to these episodic large events of firearms carnage.

The Asymmetry of Moral and Strategic Concern: Gun Carnage and the Drama of 9/11

A key problem with American gun violence is that it presents no immediately clear grand narrative or frame by which we can cognitively gather all of its distinct episodes of carnage into a meaningful whole that captures and holds our national attention, moves us to tears, pushes us to grasp, and engages the scale of the problem. It is instructive to compare our country's robust reaction to the 9/11 attacks to our country's easy conscience, decade after decade, regarding far greater levels of carnage wrought annually by home grown firearm violence.

The 9/11 attacks fixated the world's attention in good part because the carnage was so intensely concentrated in remarkably potent visuals of an identifiable "ground zero." The compactness of the drama of the 9/11 carnage intensified the concentration of moral attention and national feeling. In contrast, the relative diffuseness of our numerous but small scale gun violence events – scattered here and there across the land – obscures our moral attention to the scale of firearm casualties. Even casualty levels of ones and twos repeated enough can rise to massive numbers. And any weapon, like the handgun, that across a year and across our land can generate such numbers deservers to be understood as a "weapon of mass destruction." WMD needs to be recognized not just as an appropriate term used to describe the nuclear, biological or chemical weapons of foreign military or terrorist threats. WMD can, I believe, be appropriately applied to help name rightly the true scale of our domestic gun violence casualties. Weapons proliferation is dangerous whether it is in the international sphere or within our national borders. We should have dual concern about both nuclear proliferation and local handgun proliferation. In my childhood, our elementary school ran "duck and cover" drills in case of nuclear attack. We lived 20 miles northwest of Washington, DC, so we were a bit sensitized to the threats posed in the Cold War. Today, my children's elementary school runs *lock down* drills in case of crazed gun assaults. Nuclear weapons and small arms may differ markedly, but both constitute a real intrusive threat into the lives of children and into America's communities.

Indeed in the last few years, there has been growing recognition that America's policies of relatively easy gun access are allowing Mexican drug cartels to arm themselves with weapons smuggled in from our country. As the *New York Times* (2009) has recently reported, Mexico in 2008 suffered from 6,200 drug-related murders, a doubling from the previous year. A report to Congress holds that over 90% of the guns that were recovered in Mexican drug violence cases across the last 3 years were initially sold by American gun dealers, gun shops, and gun shows primarily in Texas, California, and Arizona (McKinley, 2009). Mexican leaders are now calling for our country to impose stricter gun regulation. It seems that the cost of America's gun policies is no longer just the fact that American citizens – like our soldiers in Iraq and Afghanistan – are being asked daily to walk in "harm's way." Indeed, our national policies would now seem to impose a burden on Mexican citizens asking them also to walk in "harm's way" as well (Renner, 1997). This means that to grasp the true scale of the US firearm violence, we should be incorporating the Mexican data of its dead who have died due, in significant part, to the US gun sales.

Another element of 9/11's remarkable drama lay in how the attacks came from foreign sources. This immediately cast the events as the rarest of events – an attack on America's mainland – our *homeland* – sheer *terrorism*. The 9/11 attacks were immediately grasped as of utmost importance, the true stuff of war, but by contrast, our homegrown patterns of gun violence appear as rather boring, politically meaningless and common, deeply ugly, and mere criminal justice matters: The stuff for police chiefs, social workers, and maybe mayors to worry about, but not Presidents and international leaders (Hedges, 2003).

Given the horrific drama of the terrorist threat, the scale of our national resolve to address that threat came as no surprise. We developed a Department of Homeland Security, vastly upgraded airport security, changed our foreign policy, spent untold vast sums on a war in Afghanistan to take down the Taliban government that had allowed Al-Qaeda to operate, and later on a more controversial war on Iraq, ostensibly to prevent Saddam Hussein from giving weapons of mass destruction to terrorist organizations. One may well disagree with the direction of our nation's actions in response to 9/11, but one cannot deny that the nation responded vigorously to the murder of 3,000 and the potential threat of more murder to come (Hoge & Rose, 2005).

What is so remarkable is the contrasting lack of any robust and sustained national outcry against the far greater home grown firearm carnage that killed far more Americans in 2001 than did any foreign terrorists. In 2001, 11,671 Americans were killed in firearm homicides and that prompted little sustained national discussion (USDOJ, 2009). The nation felt compelled to provide significant financial compensation to help ease the horrific suffering of the families of the victims of 9/11. But no such national financial generosity has ever been forthcoming to help ease the trauma and the loss experienced by the far greater number of families devastated each year by the loss of loved ones due to home-grown firearm violence. Why is the former class of families deemed more deserving of help than the latter? Why is the latter class of families' suffering and loss deemed less deserving somehow of national concern and national response? If we are going to have a Department of Homeland Security, then it would seem that it should extend its reach beyond protection against foreign terrorists. We get security briefings in America's airports, but many of our urban center neighborhoods need such briefings just as much. For our "homeland" communities to be genuinely secure, we need policies designed to reduce the casualty flows that occur from homegrown threats employing firearms.

A Gathering of Diffuse Ground Zeros': Chicago's Vigil Against Violence

The catastrophe of 9/11 with its delimited duration and sharply defined "ground zeros" concentrated the moral attention of the nation and people around the world intensely. By contrast, America's domestic gun violence tends to diffuse its mini-episodes of drama in far-flung tragic events seemingly unconnected one from the other and enjoying no overarching grand narrative of war or international threat to offer a frame of interpretation, focus, and meaning. It thus requires greater intentionality and imagination to intellectually gather together the annual impact of American firearm violence. To achieve this focus in the case of gun violence is a distinct moral achievement requiring a communal effort and aided on occasion by public rituals of mourning.

Years ago, I was privileged to join in one such community-based attempt to gather in the broad impact of gun violence welling up across a year in a fixed geographical zone – the Southside of Chicago. I taught for a year in Willibrord Catholic High School on Chicago's Southside at 115th Street in Roseland and lived in Chicago's Hyde Park neighborhood for a number of years as I worked on my doctorate at the University of Chicago. I heard about a group of Southside religious and civic leaders who started a memorial service held in the evening of the first Sunday of every month to remember and mourn those of the Southside murdered that year. They gathered at 35th and State in the shadows of the Stateway Gardens Public Housing Complex. Led by Rev. Susan Johnson, people gathered to hold onto the memory of loved ones, to sing and pray, to be comforted and to try to heal. Each service included a reading of the names of the South Side's murdered dead for that year. The slate was washed clean on the New Year so that January's list was short. I attended the May 31, 1995 gathering and the build-up of the list included 150 dead. The names were read as the evening darkened and our candles glowed brightly.

I returned on the New Year's Eve – December 31, 1995. America's gun violence was in the tail end of its highest carnage years. I will not forget that evening. We who gathered – black, white, Hispanic, poor, middle class, and many police officers – prayed, sang, and shivered in the gathering cold and dark. I and most others had tears in our eyes. We read the names of the Southside's murder victims for the year. I stood in line to read my list of 11 names – Gregory McWilliams, William Stewart, Norma Wade, Yvette Fleming, and the rest – may God rest their souls and heal their families. The list went on and on as we stamped freezing feet. We – a band of maybe 150 of the living – tried to hold onto the memory of the 407 who were murdered in the Southside of Chicago that year (Kalven, 2002; Terry, 2007). Statistics are one thing, but names catch in the throat (Trout, 2009). A country that too quickly forgets its episodes of violence and its dead would do well to develop more of these public rituals that gather the community and require a pause and an acknowledgment of pain and loss and connections severed. If we had more such community-wide civic rituals of remembrance and mourning, perhaps we as a national community would over years be able to grasp the price we pay for policies of easy gun access and inattention to gun violence patterns.

Guns Impact on Children: Leading Causes of Death

Gun violence has an immense impact on the lives of children in the USA in direct and indirect ways (Fingerhut & Christoffel, 2002; Friedman, 2006; Garbarino, Bradshaw, & Vorrasi, 2002). Many children each year are killed or injured by gunfire. Likewise, high rates of gun violence mean that too often the adults – the parents, uncles, aunts, and other caregivers – upon whom children depend are themselves killed or injured. The ripple effects of firearms possession and use ebb widely.

According to the Centers for Disease Control and Prevention (CDC hereafter) in 2005, homicide was the second leading cause of death of children up to and including the age of 19. It accounted for 11.1% of all deaths and of homicide deaths 70.4% were firearm homicides. The leading cause of death was unintentional injury, but this category includes 172 accidental firearm deaths. The fourth leading cause of death was suicide, and of these suicides 43% were the result of gunshots. Gun violence thus plays a major role in three of the four leading causes of death (Bergen, Chen, Warner, & Fingerhut, 2007; CDC, 2005, 2009).

For the cohort between 10 and 19, unintentional injury remained the leading cause of death, followed by homicide is second and suicide is third. 1.7% of unintentional injury deaths were due to firearm accidents. Homicides accounted for 13% of all deaths and of those remarkably 82% were firearm homicides. Suicides, the third leading cause of death, accounted for 10.8% of total deaths and of suicides 43.7% occurred through the use of a gun. If you break out the data for 10–19-year-old white females, suicide is the third leading cause of death and homicide drops to fourth. For white males, 10–19, suicide is number two and homicide is number three. For black females, homicide is number two and suicide is sixth. For black males aged 10–19, homicide is the first place leading cause of death comprising 40% of total deaths (CDC, 2009).

Gender and Racial Differentiates in Homicide Victim Rates: Our National Shame

In 2005, 798 of homicide victims were under age 14, 827 were between the ages of 14–17, 4,329 were between the ages of 18–24, 4,389 were between 25 and 34 (USDOJ, 2007b). Most very young homicide victims are killed without the use of a gun. By age 6, however, 34% are killed with the use of a gun, and by age 12, 54% of homicide victims are dying by gunfire. Between the ages of 15 and 20, roughly 75% of homicide victims are killed by gunfire (USDOJ, 2007g).

According to Centers of Disease Control figures, in 2005, 126 children, aged 12 or under, were killed in firearm homicides – 77 boys and 49 girls; 42 of these kids were white boys, 34 were black boys, 27 were white girls, and 18 were black girls. The average firearm homicide rate per 100,000 of this age group stood at 0.24 (Bergen et al., 2007).

Older children – teenagers – fared much worse. That year saw 1,846 young people, aged 13–19, killed in firearm homicides for a death rate of 6.24. Strikingly, 987 were black male teens, and 626 were white male teens. The firearm homicide death rate per 100,000 for black males in this age cohort (2,448,239 in total) stood at 40.31. The death rate for white boys in this age group (11,827,582 in total) stood at 5.29. Firearm homicides among black female teens stood at 84 (total 2,381,094) for a homicide death rate per 100,000 of 3.53. For white female teens, there were 87 firearm homicides (11,196,667 in total) for a homicide death rate of 0.78 (Bergen et al., 2007; Zimring & Hawkins, 1999).

The next age grouping – ages 20–30 – exhibits even more glaringly, the horrific carnage being borne by the African American community due to firearm violence. The total firearm homicide death rate per 100,000 for this age cohort in 2005 stood at 11.91. The homicide death rate for white females stood at 1.54, and for black females it jumps to 6.97. For white males, it was 8.77 while for black males it soars to 95.53. Black men in this age group are almost 11 times more likely to be murdered with a gun than white men and 13 times more likely to be so murdered than black women (Bergen et al., 2007).

Is not this a searing hole in America's heart? America, of course, cannot forget the carnage scale of 9/11. But we as a society need to clutch other ranges of pain and suffering close to our hearts too. Just in 2005 alone, 1,972 of American kids died in firearm homicides. That is roughly 2/3rd of the casualties of the 9/11 attacks. In 2005 alone, the firearm homicide death toll among black men aged 20–30 was slightly higher than the 9/11 loss of life (Bergen et al., 2007).

How can one not feel ashamed that these casualty flows do not seem to concentrate our nation's attention? What kind of country has our country become? Have we no compassion or moral vision or seriousness left?

Gun Violence Data: Grasping the Scale of the Problem

The good news is that the US homicides have dropped significantly from their peak in 1991 of 24,703 to 16,692 in 2005 (USDOJ, 2007c). The bad news is that this last figure is still a lot of dead people. Likewise, firearm homicides have dropped significantly from their peak of 17,048 in 1993 to 11,566 in 2006 (USDOJ, 2009). The Centers for Disease Control and Prevention gives slightly higher figures – 12,352 – for 2005 homicide firearm deaths (Kung, Hoyert, Xu, & Murphy, 2008; CDC, 2009a). The bad news is that either figure still constitutes a huge national hemorrhaging of blood with waves of suffering and trauma rippling out across too many families and communities. In 2006, sadly the total number of homicides went up slightly to stand at 17,034 with firearms serving as the lethal weapon in almost 68% of all homicides (USDOJ, 2009). In 2005, handguns were used in 8,478 homicides, with "other guns" – rifles or shotguns – being used in 2,868 homicides (USDOJ, 2007g).

The bulk of perpetrators of homicides are males and most victims of homicide are males. Across the years from 1976 to 2005, the offending rates for males were roughly eight times higher than those for females, and the victimization rates for males were roughly three times higher than those rates for females. Across those years, males were the victims of homicide in 76.5% of the cases while female victims made up 23.5% of the victim pool. 88.8% of the homicides had a male perpetrator. In 2005, the homicide victimization rate per 100,000 stood at 9 for males and 2.3 for females with 13,122 males and 3,545 females killed (USDOJ, 2007e).

For the years 1976–2005, the "victimization rates for males were three times higher than the rates for females. The offending rates for males were eight times higher that the rates for females. Approximately one-third of murder victims and almost half the offenders are under the age of 25. For both victims and offenders, the rate per 100,000 peaks in the 18–24 year-old age group" (USDOJ, 2007f).

There are huge racial disparities in homicide victimization rates. In 2005, the victimization rate per 100,000 for whites was 3.3 while for blacks it tragically stood at 20.6, and for the class dubbed "other" it stood at 2.5. In terms of numbers of homicide victims, 2005 saw 8,017 whites murdered, 7,999 blacks murdered, and 437 others murdered (USDOJ, 2007h).

It is worth noting that across the years 1976–2005 most murders were intraracial. For example, 86% of white victims were killed by whites and 94% of black victims were killed by blacks (USDOJ, 2007h). In 2005, 44.6% of homicides consisted of a white offender and a white victim, 8.8% consisted of a black offender and a white victim, 3.2% consisted of a white offender and a black victim, and 42.2% consisted of a black offender and a black victim (USDOJ).

Gun Violence as a Leading Cause of Urban Communities' Loss of Social Capital

William Julius Wilson's magisterial sociological analyses *The Truly Disadvantaged* and *When Work Disappears* were heavily informed by his studies of Chicago's Southside and Westside communities (Wilson, 1987). Wilson provides a detailed sociological understanding of the impact on many urban American areas like Chicago when heavy industry left and unemployment rates rose dramatically. Poverty increases coupled with increased availability of guns helped encourage increased crime rates, neighborhood decay, a loss of political clout, and commercial and industrial investment. In such regions, increasingly, families feel increased threat and loss of quality of life. Wilson analyzes the powerful dynamic of "out migration" from urban areas experiencing rising poverty and crime rates. It, he argues, has never been just so-called *White flight* to the safer and better off suburbs, but a generalized middle class and lower middle class flight of all racial groups – of Black families, Hispanic families, and Asian families, as well.

Such *outmigration* of the middle and working classes, Wilson argues, increases the "concentration of poverty" in various districts and cuts their political clout, civic and economic vitality, tax base, and city services. Increased crime rates render such neighborhoods unattractive to commercial or industrial reinvestment, and this sustains high patterns of unemployment and consequent poverty and hopelessness. Gun violence, I would argue, has been historically a key factor in this dynamic of outmigration – of middle-class flight – and a key obstacle in luring companies, stores, and developers to reinvest in – and middle-class families to relocate in – hard hit urban communities.

While urban gun violence patterns are but one factor among a wide number that have encouraged the growth of America's suburban areas and the depopulation of many of our urban districts, still it is a significant element in families' choices of outmigration. And once such outmigration occurs, the very geographical distancing of growing suburban populations seems to go hand in hand over the decades with an emotional distancing from the realities and scale of urban firearm violence. What impacts on 'those people' is not really my problem. Over time, too many Americans seem to have accustomed ourselves with a notion that high firearm violence and wide-spread family suffering is a sad, but normal and indeed inevitable feature of everyday life in many inner-city districts.

The Gun Lobby's Account of Our Gun Violence Problem

The National Rifle Association and the rest of the gun lobby have put forth, over the last four decades, a sustained picture of our gun problem, but it is a picture that fails to attend to a range of important data and concerns. Thus, it distorts more than it illumines. They portray our society as sharply and rather rigidly divided between two key classes of people – law abiding citizens and criminals. The core problem of firearm violence is narrowed into a tightly circumscribed issue – the intentional use of guns for criminal purposes. Guns in the hands of ordinary citizens remain valorized as a potent social good – providing opportunities for wholesome sports-like target shooting that can engage the entire family or hunting that can link people to the great outdoors in all its majesty. And in learning the skills and practices of these sports, kids can come to connect to deep elements of America's historic past. Thus, guns, hunting, and target shooting are said to support "family values" and patriotic values (Burbick, 2006; Sugarmann, 1992).

Indeed the intensity of the concentration on the criminal use of guns grounds another potent argument why ordinary citizens deserve open access to firearms. The emphasis on the criminal threat of gun violence to one's home or person grounds the argument that citizens and households need armed defense against potential armed attack. Guns are said to offer prudent parents and individual citizens some deterrent protection against home invasion and assault. This concern for personal and home defense against hostile strangers has been the gun lobby's rationale for pushing state legislatures' to pass "right to carry laws" allowing citizens to carry concealed handguns. It has also been the core appeal of many handgun companies in trying to increase sales to women – by marketing smaller handguns designed to fit into a purse (Sugarmann & Rand, 1994).

So the overall policy agenda the gun lobby advocates is one where guns are to be kept maximally accessible to "law abiding citizens" but significantly restricted against the criminal element. This simultaneous valorization of open access and strict restriction leads to the gun lobby pushing for policies that would require immediate identification and background checks so that gun sales at gun shows can be processed immediately. One would not want a stand up American citizen to have to wait 2 weeks to get their gun. Strict background checks at the point of gun sales are to be used to prevent guns from falling into the hands of "criminals," or the insane or children. The gun lobby pushes consistently for both maximally broad access to gun purchases for most citizens and for strict prosecution of criminal use of firearms. Hence, we have the logic enshrined in the NRA's famous slogans – "Guns Don't Kill People. People Kill People," "If Guns Are Outlawed, then Only Outlaws Will Have Guns," and the more edgy "An Armed Society is A Polite Society." But it is important to remember some of the rejoinders. One is: "Guns Don't Kill People, People Kill People, but They Do It with Guns."

The Gun Lobby's Blind Spots: Firearm Suicides and Data on Homicide Perpetrators

The gun lobby's interpretation is fundamentally flawed, in that it ignores two massive realities at the core of American firearm violence. The gun lobby's obsession with criminal use of guns by hostile strangers leads them to ignore the massive impact on America's families and communities of firearm suicides and the fact that in the vast majority of firearm homicides, the perpetrators are not hostile strangers but rather family members, friends, or acquaintances. It seems that the strict line so emphasized by the gun lobby between "law abiding citizens" and "criminals" understood always as "hostile strangers" is a fiction.

Because the NRA and the rest of the lobby concentrate their attention so tightly on the threat posed by violence from hostile strangers, the suffering that is borne into American homes and communities by vast numbers of firearm suicides is systematically ignored because it does not fit the category of crime. However, public health and medical professionals because of their broader concern for overall societal health, pay equal concern for both firearm homicide data, and firearm suicide trends. Both suicides and homicides kill and maim and spread widening ripples of suffering and trauma. Both threaten children and families and both bring unnecessary suffering into American's homes and communities and high costs to the treasuries of cities and states (Hemenway, 2004).

Conveniently lost in this view of the problem is any serious moral wrestling with the suffering caused by the US firearm suicides, which annually have long surpassed firearm homicide numbers. While the rates of firearm homicide are tragic enough, we get a truer picture of the scale of gun violence in America when we add the rates of firearm deaths by suicide and accidental shooting. The suicide of someone else may pose no direct threat to our security, but the pain of loss to the suicide victim's family and friends can be as devastating as if the victim had been murdered. Families, schools, and communities lose loved ones through firearm homicides, suicides, and accidents, and there are strong moral and public policy reasons to try to reduce the victim rates wherever we can.

In 2005, there were 17,002 firearm suicides cases in the USA (out of a total 32,637 suicides). So roughly 52% of suicides are with the use of a gun. It is estimated that the ingestion of drugs or poison are involved in 70% of all nonfatal suicide attempts, but less than 12% of successful suicides. By comparison, one study suggests that over 90% of suicide attempts using guns prove lethal (Kung et al., 2008).

A second major inadequacy of the gun lobby's understanding of gun violence lies in its sustained emphasis on the threat from "hostile strangers." This concern has potent emotional force. For example, in the NRA's flagship monthly magazine *The American Rifleman* readers over the years are exposed regularly to a column "The Armed Citizen." It describes in detail the cases of personal assault or threat and the cases of home invasion where an individual or homeowner uses a gun to deter the attack. But this portrayal should not blind us to the criminological data that holds that the primary threat in firearm violence is from a family member, friend, or acquaintance, who when drunk or enraged by an argument, grabs a gun. Much rides on whether we attend to this data or ignore it. The gun lobby in choosing to ignore it holds that law abiding citizens rightfully feeling threatened by potentially hostile and criminal strangers should protect themselves by getting a firearm for home or personal protection. Thus, they advocate bringing a gun into the home or onto one person as a positive safety choice, an insurance policy to help deter, or defend against hostile attack.

But the best criminological data shows that hostile strangers are not the main threat in firearm homicides. The data makes clear that by bringing firearms into the home, one is simply making these guns more available and on call possibly for that tragic day in the future when a family member, a friend, or acquaintance visiting – perhaps drinking too much or perhaps in a fit of anger – grabs what is readily present and shoots. Whereas the gun lobby views the classification of people as somehow ontologically set as "law abiding citizens" or "criminals," the real stuff of life is more messy and fluid. We need not go back to the Genesis account where Cain kills his brother Abel out of jealously to recognize that brothers kill brothers, and friendships can twist and that real people when drunk or stoned can do things that are out of character. With regularity, those with no criminal infraction record tragically cross the line. There is a first time for everything. Every criminal starts out as a "law abiding citizen." Zimring and Hawkins (1997) estimate that roughly 75% of gun homicides are committed by acquaintances, friends, or family.

It would seem that wide proliferation of guns into American homes does not promote family or community security, but distinctly enhances insecurity and mayhem and profound loss and suffering.

Guns and Consumer Product Safety

Almost all firearm suicides and accidents are by law-abiding citizens, and many firearm homicides are committed by individuals with no previous criminal record. Thus, the Violence Policy Center in Washington, DC argues that policies that allow wide availability of guns to "law-abiding" citizens while struggling to keep them out of the hands of criminals will accomplish little (Sugarmann & Rand, 1994).

While accepting the need for waiting periods for gun purchases, the Center doubts that this will reduce our domestic carnage.

Instead, along with a growing number of legislators, policy analysts, physicians' groups, and big city mayors, the Center wants to change the basic frame of interpretation about gun issues: From one centered in concern about violence by strangers to one that understands guns as "inherently dangerous consumer products," deserving strict public safety and regulatory oversight. This *consumer product safety* approach seeks to restrict the flood of firearms into homes and communities across the land.

The Consumer Product Safety Commission (CPSC), established by Congress in 1972, was granted regulatory oversight over almost all consumer products to insure their general safety, but Congress specifically exempted firearms and ammunition from regulatory coverage. Thus, no federal agency has the power to "ensure that firearms manufactured and sold are safe for their intended use" or "to prohibit the manufacture or sale of new firearms technology that poses a significant threat to public safety" (Sugarmann & Rand, 1994, p. 5). While the Bureau of Alcohol, Tobacco and Firearms (BATF) can regulate the sale and transfer of firearms and ammunition, it still suffers from significant underfunding and the hostility of the National Rifle Association (NRA) and many conservative members of Congress.

By focusing on guns as *inherently dangerous products* and threats to public safety, this movement calls for outright bans on certain weapons, greatly expanded waiting periods for gun purchases, limits on the number of gun purchases an individual may make in a month or year, requirements that guns be locked up away from children, and significantly higher registration fees for gun dealers. The Violence Policy Center, for example, would have Congress set bans on the manufacturing, sales, ownership, and transfers of assault weapons, handguns, and other especially hazardous firearms. Present handgun owners would be allowed to keep their weapons until death, when their survivors would have to turn the gun into law-enforcement officials. Shotguns and rifles for sport could still be sold and owned, but there would be greater federal regulatory powers to keep new developments in rifle and shotguns within safe limits and to extend the ban on assault-style rifles (Sugarmann & Rand, 1994).

Gun Ownership, Collateral Damage, and Hidden Externalities

The term "collateral damage" has been prominent in the recent years in American newspapers regarding stories about American bombers killing civilians while targeting military sites in our Wars in Iraq and in Afghanistan (Hedges & Al-Arian, 2008; Walzer, 1977). This terminology has deep traditional roots in the development across the centuries of the just war tradition, a tradition of moral reasoning that has strongly shaped the articulation in the last two centuries of the international rules of warfare. The core of this moral tradition holds that in war, it is morally permissible to target enemy soldiers but not permissible to target one's opponents' civilians, their noncombatants. The intentional killing of civilians, this teaching holds, is quite simply "murder" – a war crime. However, unintentional killings of civilians in war – caused by bombing or shooting intended against enemy soldiers or other legitimate military targets but which goes wide of the mark – has long been distinguished from murder and dubbed collateral damage. Where murder of civilians in war has long been held as a grievous wrong and punishable as a war crime, "collateral damage" has been understood to refer to regrettable accidents, for which there is no direct moral or legal culpability, no court martial, military punishment or international condemnation.

This ethical distinction flows in good part from a tradition of reasoning in historic Roman Catholic ethics given prominent highlighting in the writings of Thomas Aquinas, where he notes that a single decision can lead to double effects, one intended and another unintended. This tradition long held that one bears direct moral responsibility for the range of one's intended effects, but not for one's unintended effects, dubbed side-effects. Such effects, like the stray bombing killing a civilian family, are classed as tragic and regrettable events, but finally true accidents for which no moral or legal culpability flows to the agent who released the bomb.

But in recent decades, this whole notion of giving collateral damage a moral pass as a pure accident has been strongly challenged. Further distinctions seem to be warranted because we accept in many other spheres of human action how direct moral responsibility is not tightly restricted solely to the class of directly intended effects but flows more broadly to include unintended but foreseeable harms that may flow from one's action. For example, a core area in medical malpractice cases is grounded in the notion that moral agents often deserve to be held directly morally and legally responsible for our unintended but still foreseeable impacts that damage others. The whole legal theory of negligence is based on holding that the sphere of direct moral responsibility, and hence potential culpability, is not restricted to just the range of intended outcomes, but also to the broader range of destructive outcomes that an agent should have been able to foresee and take due care to avoid.

I believe that the analysis of collateral damage in the ethics of combat offers an important lens for helping to focus attention on important aspects of America's annual pageantry of gun violence. The gun lobby's reductionistic polarization of law-abiding citizens and criminals cashes out in a stress on two classes of acts gun homicides and gun accidents. This directly parallels the similar distinction of murder and pure accident that the classic just war theory enshrined in its understanding of collateral damage. The NRA and the rest of the gun lobby tend to focus so intently on intentional firearm homicide, that all other impacts of the gun use like gun suicides get treated like mere collateral damage, regrettable, but inevitable events in which the gun purchaser or owner bears no negligence or responsibility. The gun lobby assumes an ability to grasp the complexity of gun use as bifurcated between the seemingly positive uses (home defense, sports-hunting, target shooting, and the satisfactions of collecting) and other negative criminal and destructive uses of guns.

When the key moral focus is placed so intensely on intentional choice in discrete acts of firearm homicide, then the complex moral terrain of responsibility surrounding the decision to purchase a gun and bring it into a home or carry it on one person is allowed to remain in the shadows. The NRA and the gun lobby want the whole debate to be within the frame of criminal justice concerns – condemn criminal use and prosecute harshly. The public health perspective and the consumer product safety perspective, and that of big city mayors want to highlight not only the moral responsibility or irresponsibility involved in discrete decisions to pull the trigger, but also to reflect on the grave moral responsibilities involved in the decision to buy a gun and thus introduce that weapon into a home or an apartment.

We need to deconstruct the myth of control in the NRA's slogan: "Gun's don't kill people, people kill people." It distorts by suggesting that people's initial intentionality when they purchase a gun is clear and that they can sustain strict control over the built-in lethality of weapons across the decades. This view of guns suggests that the issue of moral and legal responsibility is engaged only at the intentionality of the point of actual purchase, the initially intended targeting and firing.

But important issues of moral and legal responsibility are raised for individuals when they decide to purchase guns and to bring them into a home and for cities, states, and national communities when they fail to develop adequate restrictions on gun sales. The fact that a gun can be put to multiple uses across its lifetime lies behind the growing movement to consider guns as inherently dangerous consumer products and public health threats. It suggests that we consider guns as analogous to land mines or bombs – artifacts whose lethality may slumber, but may later be triggered by persons other than the original purchaser or current owner (Winslow, 1997). Firearms, even if bought initially for the most peaceable and innocuous of reasons, e.g., target shooting – can still be used later by the owner or others to kill oneself or others.

If those who purchase lethal instruments bear a high burden of responsibility for even the collateral damage they cause, then those who use guns – to make profits, to have good salaries in Washington, DC lobby headquarters, to gain pleasure from sport, to gain feelings of security at home – bear responsibility when these lethal instruments are used later and often by others to cause destruction to self and others. Such tragic outcomes may well not have been intended, but they should have been foreseen.

The attempts a few years ago by cities to bring lawsuits against various gun manufacturers and sellers helped further an important societal conversation about the morality of guns. Many of the initial cases brought by major cities have been blocked in the courts, but at least these cases have prompted a discussion about *societal-borne*, but heretofore undiscussed costs due to gun violence (Butterfield, 1998, 2002). As with cases of environmental pollution and cigarette smoking, the sale and use of guns often imposes high social and economic costs on the general public – costs that the public – as neighbors, citizens, and taxpayers – has not volunteered to bear. Gun buyers and sellers have been allowed to pass the significant social and medical costs of gun ownership and use onto society at large, a society that has remained until quite recently generally unmindful of the massive scale of such impacts, these hidden externalities (Cook & Ludwig, 2000; Finkelstein, Corso, & Miller, 2006).

Guns as a Symbolic Center of the Culture Wars

The issues of gun control are so hotly contested because they lie near the center of America's "culture wars," straddling the philosophical fault line between strict individualism and communitarianism (Bellah et al., 1985). The National Rifle Association (NRA) draws deeply on America's historic emphasis on individual rights, especially the Second Amendment's guarantee of "the right of the people to keep and bear Arms."

The issues of firearm violence in America have been so reified across 30 years political clashes that many are extremely bored with the tired and predictable character of the arguments presented. For many people, gun rights, target practice, hunting, gun threats, and firearm homicide are felt deeply and are wrapped tightly to one's sense of identity and community. For the last 30 years, guns have served as a wedge issue between the two national parties. Democrats have been relatively more concerned to push gun control policies and Republicans more concerned to protect gun rights of individuals. Many in the gun rights camp stress that the 2nd Amendment that speaks of the right to keep and bear arms holds that this is the primary right because it is the concrete possession against a potentially tyrannical government that allows a community to actually engage in protecting all their other rights. Much of this cultural wars divide grows out of the tension between individualist models of society and more communitarian understandings (Gitlin, 1995; Wills, 1999).

Much of the volatility of the debates about guns in America arises, I believe, comes from the complex ways guns have been understood as related to the American identity. "Gun rights" are housed in the Bill of Rights in the 2nd Amendment. This, not surprisingly, has pushed for a popular framing of gun issues as an individual rights and liberty question about keeping open the access to gun purchases, gun sports, and guns for home and personal security. But while the emphasis in the USA falls on gun rights, the emphasis in the United Kingdom (from which we historically get our stress on gun rights) seems ironically to fall on our civic responsibilities.

Joyce Lee Malcolm (1994) is a historian who tracks out the development of the British right to bear arms upon which much of the American colonial thinking draws. Tellingly, she concludes that this "right" arises out of a historically deeper strand of English law and sensibility, namely, that which is concerned about civic responsibilities to protect the community of the town or village. Her research suggests that the English "right to bear arms" developed in the Middle Ages out of a communitarian emphasis on common civic responsibilities and interests in deterring criminals and in protecting one's family along with one's neighbors. Gun rights, that in contemporary America are pushed so stridently as a matter of individual liberty, it seems, developed from historic English affirmations of gun duties and responsibilities owed to the protection of one's entire community. She notes that an obligation of a *police duty* was imposed in the Middle Ages on able-bodied Englishmen and women to keep "watch and ward" duties of protecting the town or village.

This communal responsibility demanded that people be armed and ready to raise a "hue and cry" to warn the community of criminal action or attack. The key value was civic safety. The firearm was a means to affecting that goal, not a fetish and end all in itself that the contemporary American gun lobby has turned it into.

Both American gun laws and our constitutional interpretations about the meaning of the 2nd Amendment seem to be stalemated in our national conflict over individualist vs. communitarian understandings of our national project. We have a history of a defined right to bear arms articulated in the United States arising from a Medieval English communal stress on an obligation to render civic responsibility for the wellbeing of the neighborhood and town. Historically the United States Supreme Courts have focused on this 2nd Amendment "right to bear arms" and concluded that it does not affirm an individual right to own a gun, but rather a communal right that allows for greater restrictions to be imposed on individual's access to gun ownership. The full wording of the 2nd Amendment reads: "A well regulated Militia, being necessary to the security of a free State, the right of the people to keep and bear arms, shall not be infringed."

The 1939 Supreme Court held in the case of *United States v. Miller* that the 2nd Amendment did not grant any individual right to gun ownership. It interpreted the Amendment's preamble about a "well-regulated Militia" as defining the frame in which the right was to be interpreted (Henigan et al., 1995). This allowed for fairly robust state and city laws to restrict gun ownership, especially handgun ownership. But we live in interesting times. After 8 years of the Presidency of George Bush, his realigned Supreme Court overturned *US v. Miller* in its holding on June 26, 2008 in its case *District of Columbia v. Heller*. This case struck down a District of Columbia law prohibiting the ownership of guns and this likewise struck down a similar law in Chicago and other municipalities. The Court has held that American's now have an individual right to bear arms (Doherty, 2008; Tushnet, 2007). This landmark case renders many city laws that ban handguns as null and void, but it is a narrow holding and the grand debates and cases regarding gun restrictions will continue.

The *culture wars* debates between individualist and communitarian understandings of the American project now are being placed on vivid display in the holdings of the US Supreme Court. One hopes that as the Court deliberates over the constitutional interpretation issues that it will give equal attention to the real world consequences of its holdings on the well-being of children, families and communities across America. One hopes that our country can recover some of the old English stress that gun ownership must be evaluated with a keen eye toward the well-being of the community.

Conclusion

Concern about gun rights must not be allowed to override the rights of children and families to enjoy a healthy environment. Homeland security is not just about protecting the American society from the threat by foreign terrorists, but if it is to be a genuine security, it must include sustained attention and response to reduce our home grown firearm violence patterns. National media focus and political discussion concentrates sustained attention to the courage and valor of American soldiers who are asked to walk in harm's way, yet too often we as a nation turn our backs to the fact that our policies of easy gun access have helped insure that a whole generation of young people, especially those growing up in inner city core areas, are forced to walk daily in harm's way also right in our own communities. Gun violence is of a scale that it needs to be thought of as a top national security problem worthy of serious engagement and deserving serious funds and educational resources to be committed to violence reduction policies. Guns are weapons of mass destruction. Gun control measures need of course to be tied to serious efforts to promote economic reinvestment and job creation in many of our nation's urban core neighborhoods, small towns, and rural areas. Today, as in late Medieval England, the right to bear arms must serve the core value of protecting the common good of society. Tighter gun control measures by themselves will not solve all of our gun violence problems, but they do remain an important step toward insuring a healthy environment for our children and families.

References

"The Armed Citizen," in The American Rifleman 155:12 (December 2007): 8.

"The Armed Citizen," in The American Rifleman 156:3 (March 2008): 8.

Bergen, G., Chen, L. H., Warner, M., & Fingerhut, L. A. (2007). *Injury in the United States: 2007 chart book*. Hyattsville, MD: National Center for Health Statistics.

Bellah, R., Madsen, R., Sullivan, W. M., Swidler, A., & Tipton, S. M. (1985). *Habits of the heart: Individualism and commitment in American life*. New York: Harper & Row.

Burbick, J. (2006). *Gun show nation: Gun culture and American democracy*. New York: The New Press.

Butterfield, F. (1998, November 13). Chicago is suing over guns from suburbs. *New York Times*. Retrieved from http://www.nytimes.com.

Butterfield, F. (2002, January 3). Suit against gun makers gains ground in Illinois. *New York Times*. Retrieved from http://www.nytimes.com.

Center for Disease Control and Prevention. (2009a). National Center for Health Statistics fast stats A to Z. Retrieved from http://www.cdc.gov/nchs/FASTATS/homicide.htm.

Center for Disease Control and Prevention. (2009b). WISQARS. 10 leading causes of death and injury. (United States: 2005, All races, both sexes, ages 1–19). Retrieved from http://www.cdc.gov/injury/images/LC-Charts/10LC_overall_2005b-a.pdf.

Center for Disease Control and Prevention. (2009c). WISQARS. Youth violence. Retrieved from http://www.cdc.gov/ViolencePrevention/youthviolence/stats_at-a_glance/lcd_10-24.html.

Cook, P. J., & Ludwig, J. (2000). *Gun violence: The real costs*. Oxford: Oxford University Press.

Death and American guns in Mexico. (2009, June 25). *New York Times*. Retrieved from http://www.nytimes.com.

Doherty, B. (2008). *Gun control on trial: Inside the Supreme Court battle over the Second Amendment*. Washington, DC: Cato Institute.

Fingerhut, L. A., & Christoffel, K. K. (2002). Firearm-related death and injury among children and adolescents. *The Future of Children, 12*, 25–37.

Finkelstein, E. A., Corso, P. S., & Miller, T. R. (2006). *The incidence and economic burden of injuries in the United States*. Oxford: Oxford University Press.

Frank, T. (2004). *What's the matter with Kansas: How conservatives won the heart of America*. New York: Metropolitan Books.

Friedman, D. (2006). *Saving our children: An in-depth look at gun violence in our nation and ours Schools*. Bloomington, IN: Author House.

Garbarino, J. (1999). *Lost Boys: Why our sons turn violent and how we can save them*. New York: Anchor Books.

Garbarino, J., Bradshaw, C. P., & Vorrasi, J. A. (2002). Mitigating the effects of gun violence on children and youth. *The Future of Children, 12*, 73–85.

Gibbs, N. (1999, May 3). The monsters next door: A special report on the Colorado school massacre. *Time Magazine*. Retrieved from http://www.timemagazine.com.

Gitlin, T. (1995). *The twilight of common dreams: Why America is wracked by culture wars*. New York: Metropolitan Books.

Glick, S. (1994). *Female persuasion: A study on how the firearms industry markets to women and the reality of women and guns*. Washington, DC: Violence Policy Center.

Hedges, C. (2003). *War is a force that gives us meaning*. New York: Anchor Books.

Hedges, C., & Al-Arian, L. (2008). *Collateral damage: America's war against Iraqi civilians*. New York: Nation Books.

Hemenway, D. (2004). *Private guns public health*. Ann Arbor, MI: University of Michigan Press.

Henigan, D. A., Nicholson, E. B., Hemenway, D., & Helfand, I. (1995). *Guns and the Constitution: The myth of Second Amendment protection for firearms in America*. Northhampton, MA: Aletheia Press.

Herbert, B. (2009, April 14). The American way. *The New York Times*. Retrieved from http://www.nytimes.com.

Hoge, J. F., & Rose, G. (Eds.). (2005). *Understanding the war on terror*. New York: Foreign Affairs.

Kalven, J. (2002). *The vigil against violence*. View from the Ground. Retrieved from http://www.viewfromtheground.com/archive/2002/10/the-vigil-against-violence.html.

Kopel, D. B. (Ed.). (1995). *Guns: Who should have them?* Amherst, NY: Prometheus Books.

Kung, H. C., Hoyert, D. L., Xu, J., & Murphy, S. L. (2008). Death final data: 2005. *National Vital Statistics Report, 56*, 1–121. Retrieved from http://www.cdc.gov/nchs/data/nvsr/nvsr54/nvsr54_10.pdf.

Malcolm, J. L. (1994). *To keep and bear arms: The origins of an Anglo-American right*. Cambridge: Harvard University Press.

McKinley, J. C. (2009, February 29). U.S. Is arms bazaar for Mexican cartels. *New York Times*. Retrieved from http://www.nytimes.com.

Minino, A. M., Anderson, R. N., Fingerhut, L. A., Boudreault, M. A., & Warner, M. (2006). Deaths: Injuries, 2002. *National Vital Statistics Reports, 54*, 1–125. Retrieved from http://www.cdc.gov/nchs/data/nvsr/nvsr54/nvsr54_10.pdf.

Prothrow-Stith, D., & Weissman, M. (1991). *Deadly consequences: How violence is destroying our teenage population and a plan to begin solving the problem*. New York: Harper Collins.

Renner, M. (1997). *Small arms, big impact: The next challenge of disarmament*. Washington, DC: Worldwatch Institute.

Sugarmann, J. (1992). *National Rifle Association: Money, firepower, & fear*. Washington, DC: National Press Books.

Sugarmann, J., & Rand, K. (1994). *Cease fire: A comprehensive strategy to reduce firearm violence*. Washington, DC: Violence Policy Center.

Terry, D. (1995, April 4). Chicago Journal; Remembering the dead in a vigil against violence. *New York Times*. Retrieved from http://www.nytimes.com.

Trout, J. D. (2009). *The empathy gap: Building bridges to the good life and the good society*. New York: Viking Press.

Tushnet, M. V. (2007). *Out of range: Why the Constitution can't end the battle over guns*. Oxford: Oxford University Press.
U.S. Department of Justice, Bureau of Justice Statistics. (2004). Key Facts at a Glance: Firearm Deaths by Intent, 1991–2001. Retrieved from http://www.ojp.usdoj.gov/bjs/glance/tables/frmdth.htm.
U.S. Department of Justice, Bureau of Justice Statistics. (2007a). Homicides by racial composition of victims and offenders. Retrieved from http://www.ojp.gov/bjs/homicide/tables/ovracetab.htm.
U.S. Department of Justice, Bureau of Justice Statistics. (2007b). Homicide trends in the U.S.: Age trends. Retrieved from http://www.ojp.usdoj.gov/bjs/homicide/teens.htm.
U.S. Department of Justice, Bureau of Justice Statistics. (2007c). Homicide trends in the U.S.: Long term trends and patterns. Retrieved from http://www.ojp.usdoj.gov/bjs/homicide/hmrt.htm.
U.S. Department of Justice, Bureau of Justice Statistics. (2007d). Homicide trends in the U.S.: Long term trends, Homicide Victimization, 1950–2005. Retrieved from http://ojp.usdoj.gov/bjs/homicide/tables/totalstab.htm.
U.S. Department of Justice, Bureau of Justice Statistics. (2007e). Homicide trends in the U.S.: Trends by gender. Retrieved from http://www.ojp.usdoj.gov/bjs/homicide/gender.htm.
U.S. Department of Justice, Bureau of Justice Statistics. (2007f). Homicide trends in the U.S.: Trends by race. Retrieved from http://www.ojp.gov/bjs/homicide/tables/vracetab.htm.
U.S. Department of Justice, Bureau of Justice Statistics. (2007g). Homicide trends in the U.S.: Weapons used. Retrieved from http://www.ojp.usdoj.gov/bjs/homicide/tables/weaponstab.htm.
U.S. Department of Justice, Bureau of Justice Statistics. (2007h). Homicide victims by race. Retrieved from http://www.ojp.gov/bjs/homicide/tables/vracetab.htm.
U.S. Department of Justice, Bureau of Justice Statistics. (2007i). Percent of all homicides by racial composition of victims and offenders. Retrieved from http://www.ojp.gov/bjs/homicide/tables/ovracetab.htm.
U.S. Department of Justice, Bureau of Justice Statistics. (2007j). Racial differences exist, with blacks disproportionately represented among homicide victims and offenders. Retrieved from http://www.ojp.gov/bjs/homicide/race.htm.
U.S. Department of Justice, Bureau of Justice Statistics. (2009). Key facts at a glance: Crimes committed with firearms, 1973–2007. Retrieved from http://www.ojp.usdoj.gov/bjs/glance/tables/guncrimetab.htm.
Walzer, M. (1977). *Just and unjust wars: A moral argument with historical illustrations* (pp. 151–157). New York: Basic Books.
Wills, G. (1999). *A necessary evil: A history of American distrust of government*. New York: Simon & Schuster.
Wilson, W. J. (1987). *The truly disadvantaged: The inner city, the underclass, and public policy*. Chicago: University of Chicago Press.
Wilson, W. J. (1996). *When work disappears: The world of the new urban poor*. New York: Alfred A. Knopf.
Winslow, P. C. (1997). *Sowing the dragon's teeth: Land mines and the global legacy of war*. Boston: Beacon Press.
Zimring, F. E., & Hawkins, G. (1997). *Crime is not the problem: Lethal violence in America*. Oxford: Oxford University Press.

Chapter 13
The Right to a Healthy Social Environment: Protecting Children from Social Toxicity

James Garbarino

To live in fear and falsehood is worse than death.

–Boyce, M. (2001).

Introduction

Some kids are smarter than others. Some are better looking than others. Some are kinder and more sensitive than others. Some are more talented than others. Some are more confident than others. But all these differences pale in comparison with what kids share and kids do not change much at their core over the years. They want to be valued and accepted. They want to be safe. They want to learn and explore. They want to play and have fun. They need to find meaning in their lives and make a spiritual connection (Garbarino, 1995).

It is not these core themes and concerns that change. Rather, it is the cultural, psychological, and social messages and tools that are available to them as they go about the universal business of growing up (Garbarino, 1995). The nature of these messages and tools does have an effect on the process of growing up, however. Some ennoble; others degrade. Some promote social order; others promote chaos. Some are good; some are bad. Some result in young adults who want to serve humanity and carve out a spiritually meaningful life for themselves, like the kids I read about who raised money in their school to help Hurricane Katrina victims a thousand miles away. Others result in teenagers like the ones I watched on a "reality" program on television who to a person said their goal in life was "to be rich and famous."

When the social environment spreads "fear and falsehood," it becomes poisonous to the development of children and youth, much as when the physical environment is poisoned and misused it can undermine their physical well-being (Garbarino, 1995).

J. Garbarino (✉)
Center for the Human Rights of Children, Department of Psychology, Loyola University, 1032 W Sheridan Rd, 119 Coffey Hall, Chicago, IL 60660, USA
e-mail: jgarbar@luc.edu

J. Garbarino and G. Sigman (eds.), *A Child's Right to a Healthy Environment*, The Loyola University Symposium on the Human Rights of Children 1,
DOI 10.1007/978-1-4419-6791-6_13,

This is particularly true for kids who are especially vulnerable to developmental harm because of their difficult temperament or mental health problems.

Social toxicity refers to the extent to which the social environment of children and youth is poisonous, in the sense that it contains serious threats to the development of identity, competence, moral reasoning, trust, hope, and the other features of personality and ideology that make for success in school, family, work, and the community (Garbarino, 1995). Like physical toxicity, it can be fatal – in the forms of suicide, homicide, drug-related and other life style-related preventable deaths. But mostly, it results in diminished "humanity" in the lives of children and youth by virtue of leading them to live in a state of degradation, whether they know it or not.

What are the social and cultural poisons that are psychologically equivalent to lead and smoke in the air, PCBs in the water, and pesticides in the food chain? We can see social toxicity in the values, practices, and institutions that breed feelings of fear about the world, feelings of rejection by adults inside and outside the family, exposure to traumatic images and experiences, absence of adult supervision, and inadequate exposure to positive adult role models. These feelings and experiences arise from being embedded in a shallow materialist culture, being surrounded with negative and degrading media messages, and being deprived of relationships with sources of character in the school, the neighborhood, and the larger community (Eron, Gentry, & Schlegel, 1994).

For example, research on the impact of televised violence indicates that its effect on increasing aggressive behavior by child viewers is equivalent to the effect of smoking on lung cancer – namely, that it accounts for about 10–15% of the variation (Eron et al., 1994). In this sense, violent television is a social toxin. By the same token, all the various "isms" – racism and sexism, for example – that diminish the worth of targeted groups are toxins in the sense that they are linked to negative developmental outcomes.

The bias against homosexuals has a similarly negative effect. Although the term homophobia is widely accepted, it may not be the most useful way to approach this issue (allowing the offending bigots to say, "I don't fear homosexuals, I just don't like them and think they are unnatural or deviant."). There is no alternative widely accepted (with terms like "homonegativity" and "heterosexualism" being offered but not widely used in public). Although it took decades of advocacy to do so, the professional psychological community has acknowledged that whatever we may call the bias against homosexuals, there is no scientific foundation for it. For example, in 1973, the American Psychiatric Association's Board of Trustees declared that "homosexuality per se implies no impairment in judgment, stability, reliability, or general social or vocational capabilities" and came out squarely against public and private discrimination against gays and lesbians (American Psychiatric Association, 2000).

This has not ended homophobic actions, of course. A study of high school students published in 1998, found that in comparison with heterosexual kids, gay, lesbian, and bisexual youth were five times more likely to miss school because they felt unsafe, four times more likely to be threatened with a weapon at school, twice as likely to have their property damaged at school, and three times more likely to require medical treatment after a fight at school (despite the fact that they were four times *less* likely to be involved in fighting at school; Garofalo, Wolf, Kessel, Palfrey, & Durant, 1998).

As reported earlier, it was not until 1973 that the American Psychiatric Association's Board of Trustees declared that "homosexuality per se" is not pathological, and came out squarely against public and private discrimination against gays and lesbians. Things have changed for the better on this fundamental issue of human rights, the right to be who you are, albeit too late for many earlier generation. Now, many more people are comfortable with the idea of homosexuality and in relationship with real live homosexuals, and many more gay and lesbian individuals feel safe enough to come out (Garbarino, 2008). A cursory tour through prime time television and mainstream movies makes that clear.

However, rejection and hatred directed at gays and lesbians is one of the few forms of negative bias that can still be expressed openly in America by politicians, religious leaders, and other public figures. After all, even as late as 1998, the American Psychiatric Association's Board of Trustees thought it necessary to issue a statement saying that it opposes any psychiatric treatment which is based upon the assumption that homosexuality per se is a mental disorder or the a priori assumption that a patient should want to or try to change his/her sexual orientation. And, it is still true that openly homosexual individuals are barred from serving in the US military – and they continue to be discharged once their "secret" is officially acknowledged.

Homophobia, racism, sexism. All these dimensions of social toxicity are important, but superseding and infusing them all is spiritual emptiness, the loss of a sense of living in a positive meaningful universe beyond the material experience of day-to-day life. When there is no meaning beyond the material, there is no life beyond going to the shopping mall. I heard this once in its most terrible form when a 19-year-old who had just been sentenced to life in prison (for killing a police officer) said he was going to kill himself. "Why?" I asked. "Because I am never going to the mall again," he replied. Indeed, if kids live only for their commercial lives, there really is no life left when denied access to the shopping mall that gives their lives material meaning (Garbarino, 1999).

Just as some children are more vulnerable than other children to physical poisons in the ground and in the air, some children are more vulnerable to social toxicity. Emotionally troubled and temperamentally vulnerable children living in a socially toxic environment are like psychological asthmatics living in an atmospherically polluted city. It seems that young children are most vulnerable to aspects of life that threaten the availability and quality of care by parents and other caregivers while adolescents are most vulnerable to toxic influences in the broader culture and community, like pornography on the internet and violent video games in the mall.

Adolescence is mostly and usually the crystallization of childhood experience, and so the youth most at-risk are those who develop psychological vulnerabilities in childhood and then face social deprivation and trauma in adolescence (Loeber & Farrington, 1999). This is why research reveals that in some (positive) neighborhoods, only 15% of 9-year-olds who have developed a chronic pattern of aggression, bad behavior, acting out, and violating the rights of others (kids who might be diagnosed with "Conduct Disorder") become serious violent delinquents, while in other (negative) neighborhoods the figure is 60%!

At-risk and marginalized youth act as "social weathervanes," in the sense that they indicate the direction of social change in their societies. The particular cultural and social pathologies present in a society will generally be most evident in the lives of these youth. For example, when the old Soviet system in Eastern Europe collapsed, adolescent drug abuse became epidemic (Kelly & Amirkhanian, 2003). The epidemic in Thailand and the Philippines is child prostitution (Mulhall, 1996). Where the drug economy overwhelmed the justice system, murderous violence became epidemic in Colombia (Wadlow, 2002).

In each case, psychologically vulnerable youth were most affected. They are the youth who already have accumulated the most developmental risk factors – youth who enter adolescence with a history of malfunctioning families, youth with unstable and reactive temperaments, and youth with emotional disabilities.

Amidst all the confusion and the temptations and the blind alleys of modern life, we can always gain clarity by asking, "does this contribute to my character development" (Lickona, 2004)? If it does not, we must go back to the drawing board. Years ago a colleague of mine had a bumper sticker on his office door that read: "You can change the world…but unless you know what you are doing, please don't."

The nature of my work has exposed me to some of the dark side of America and to some of its moral and political limitations (Garbarino, 2008). I traveled to New Orleans in 2006, a year after the Katrina Hurricane hit New Orleans, and I saw reconstruction mired in racism, the interests of the affluent class trumping the needs of the poor, and "politics as usual." Two years later, there are still reports that emergency aid has been diverted and wasted, to the detriment of meeting the basic needs of many residents of the city (Briscoe, 2007).

I have been to Cambodia and seen how American arrogance during the Vietnam War in the 1960s and 1970s all but guaranteed the success of Pol Pot's Khmer Rouge in taking over the country and thus setting in motion the years of insane slaughter that followed (Garbarino, Kostelny, & Dubrow, 1991). I have been to Nicaragua and seen the toll taken on lives and spirits by American support for the Contras' war against the Sandinistas during the 1980s. I have repeatedly been to the Middle East and seen how American decades of pro-Israeli bias and unwillingness to recognize the legitimate national aspirations of the Palestinians allowed that conflict to fester and continue to the ugly point it has reached today.

And perhaps most to the point, among all the nearly 200 nations of the world the USA stands nearly alone (Bedard, 2007), one of only two UN members which have not ratified the UN Convention on the Rights of the Child. The other is Somalia, which can at least offer the defense that it does not have a functioning central government empowered to enact ratification. Two toxic forces have blocked ratification. The first is the fundamentalist impulse in American culture that fears and rejects human rights initiatives in general as a threat to the power of the entrenched interests of homophobic, patriarchal, punishment-oriented "traditional values." The second is the power of those who believe that we are above and beyond the rest of the world – "We're Number One!" – and therefore entitled to our exceptional status. Americans have a special difficulty in dealing with this issue. One of our problems is what historians have called our "historical exceptionalism." What they mean in using this term is that we tend to view our history as unique, and to reject the idea that we are like everyone else, as a people and as a country. It is a rare politician who can refrain from saying, "This is the greatest nation on Earth." Many would go so far as to say this is the greatest nation that has ever existed, unique among all countries. The theme of exceptionalism reverberates down through the decades of American history. I think we can start this process by looking backward to America of the 1950s (Kaplan, Pelcovitz, & Fornari, 2005).

America in the 1950s had just emerged from the Great Depression and World War II (Shales, 2007). During the Great Depression in the 1930s, large numbers of American workers were unemployed because of the economic crisis, and felt despair, fear, and anger that through no fault of their own they were being impoverished. Debate continues among historians and economists about the exact causes of the Depression and the strategies and tactics used to deal with it by the national government and other public policy entities. What does seem clear is that the actions of President Franklin Roosevelt, a Democrat elected to lead the nation in 1932, played an important role in inspiring demoralized unemployed workers, who prior to his arrival on the national scene felt betrayed and abandoned by the national political leadership and business leaders who were their allies. The renowned American writer John Updike (2007) was a child during the 1930s and recalls observing his own unemployed father's desolation, and his reaction to the policies and words of President Roosevelt:

> My father had been reared a Republican, but he switched parties to vote for Roosevelt and never switched back. His memory of being abandoned by society and big business never left him and, for all his paternal kindness and humorousness, communicated itself to me, along with his preference for the political party that offered 'the forgotten man' the better break. Roosevelt made such people feel less alone. The impression of recovery – the impression that a President was bending the old rules and, drawing upon his own courage and flamboyance in adversity and illness, stirring things up on behalf of the down-and-out – mattered more than any miscalculations in the moot mathematics of economics.

World War II built upon this sense of meaningfulness to create a powerful sense of confidence and solidarity. Brokaw (1998) captured all this in his book *The Greatest Generation,* and this was the launching pad for the 1950s. Despite the challenges parents of the 1950s faced with the rise of atomic war as a threat, I believe that they had an easier time of it when it came to protecting children than I did as a parent in the 1980s and 1990s, and than do parents in the world of the twenty-first Century. For one thing, the flow of information to children 50 years ago was under relatively tight and benign control. To be sure, this control had a downside (e.g., in its narrow portrayal of females and ethnic and racial minorities and the absence of people with other than heterosexual orientation). But on the plus side, television was effectively censored when it came to sex and vivid violence.

There was a strong sense that "children are watching" meant that adults should forego the pleasure and titillation of explicit sexuality on the screen (Luke, 1990). Of course, this censorship limited the ability of television and the movies to deal with some adult subjects, but in retrospect I do not think the cost was too great. Themes of sexuality, infidelity, debilitating illness, depression, suicide, and murder could be presented, but in a manner that seems muted, dignified, and subtle by today's "let it all hang out" standards.

There was violence, but it was highly stylized and sanitized. The "bad guys" were only moderately nasty, and the "good guys" subscribed to a strict code of honorable conduct. In the television environment of the 1950s, even the child of a negligent parent was at little risk sitting in front of the television set because the narrow range of available images and themes was tightly controlled by the adults who made and broadcast the programming. The same was true for movies (Luke, 1990).

The media technology of the 1950s also worked to the advantage of children (Hilmes, 2004; Luke, 1990). Special effects were primitive and not likely to produce the kind of visual trauma associated with contemporary images. The cumbersome quality of visual recording technology – limited for the most part to film – reduced to negligible the possibility that horrific events would be made available visually to the television and movie viewer, including the child viewer.

Today, the ubiquitous availability of video recording means that much of what is horrible to see will be made available for the seeing, and usually by children as readily as by adults (Garbarino, 2002). Consider the horror of the attack on Pearl Harbor in 1941 versus the attack on the World Trade Center 60 years later. The former was visually witnessed by a relative handful of children; the latter was seen via videotape by virtually every child in America – over and over again, in many cases. Repeat this for every violent and traumatic image over and over again, from the big events like plane crashes to the little events like ritual beatings purveyed over local television news as well as over You-Tube and other internet sites that cater to kids. This exposure to traumatic imagery is one important feature of the social toxicity which compounds the problem of parents and other caring adults in helping children deal with growing up in the age of terror. But it is not the only element.

As the atomic age began, the structure of benevolent adult authority was relatively intact, at least when compared to the world of the twenty-first century America. Adults were adults, and kids were kids. The social contract between children and adults was intact and in force: Children will live in their world (under the direct supervision of empowered adults); adults will live in theirs (mostly out of sight from the innocent eyes of children). Adults were in charge and in return took responsibility for protecting children.

This empowered adults to keep children out of the adult world and the institutions of America cooperated and conspired to maintain the useful illusion that children did not have to worry because the grownups were taking care of business on their behalf. Perhaps one notable exception to this rule was to be found in the "duck and cover" scare tactics associated with the threat of atomic war. The very exceptionality of this violation of children's sense of safety is evidence of the existence of the general rule of innocence.

But with each new year after 1950, children's visual access to scary stuff increased, whether it be horrific violence of war and crime, parental incapacitation, family break up, the clay feet of political leaders, or the sweaty details of sexuality. Today's routine exposure of children to social toxicity means that today's child is already reeling from the sense of a broken social contract with the adult world before we even begin to factor in the challenges of living in the age of terror. Thus, if ever there was a time for parents to take up the mantle of "responsibility," it is now. Mediating the child's exposure to the dark side of human experience in today's already toxic social environment will continue to be one of the principal challenges for "good" parents in the years to come.

One of the casualties of both trauma and social toxicity in general is social trust and faith in the future. Adults who grew up confined to the images and messages of a child sized world may have a solid world view to sustain their social trust and faith in the future, but children who are growing up in an age in which mass media can and do bring vivid trauma to children from an early age onward may not. A study of adults seeking psychiatric intervention found that among those who had suffered a traumatic event at a young age, nearly three quarters replied "yes," when they were asked, "Have you given up all hope of finding meaning in your life?" Among those who were adults before they experienced trauma the comparable figure was much lower – 20%. Parents must display empathic parenting grounded in the awareness of developmental processes when children are faced with trauma, lest they slip into a profound sense of meaninglessness.

For most of us, seeing life from a spiritual perspective necessitates a shift in our thinking. It requires that we see ourselves as spiritual beings, first and foremost. This means that we acknowledge our spiritual identities and existence in addition to the physical and psychological realities of living as a human organism. This recognition includes the awareness of the primacy of spiritual existence, a shift to recognizing oneself as a spiritual being first and foremost. Even for many who see themselves as religious, this recognition requires a fundamental shift: from a materialist metaphysic of body first, consciousness second, to spirit first, and body second.

What are the requisite elements of this shift? One is a transcendent organizing belief in a coherent spiritual existence (a Higher Power, a spiritual Source, a spiritual Creator, an all benevolent higher spiritual being). Another is a belief in oneself as being connected in spirit to the Higher Power and to other human beings as other spiritual peers having a physical experience and the centrality of love in this approach to the world. The third concerns the way we approach reality in our efforts to understand and improve it. Each informs our analysis of how the search for meaning in the lives of children and youth facing issues of life and death makes an enormous difference in our understanding human development. This is not just a matter of impersonal analysis. It is a matter of real lives shaped and defined by how well we do in guaranteeing each child's basic human right to a healthy social environment, how well we do it converting social toxicity to a socially healthy state in which all the "isms" and other cultural poisons that affect kids are replaced with nurturing acceptance.

References

American Psychiatric Association. (2000). *APA position statement on psychiatric treatment and sexual orientation, December 11, 1998*. Retrieved from http://www.psych.org/psych_pract/copptherapyaddendum83100.cfm

Boyce, M. (2001). Zoroastrians: Their religious beliefs and practices. London: Routledge.

Bedard, C. (2007). *Children's rights are human rights*. Chicago: Loyola University Press, Center for the Human Rights of Children.

Briscoe, D. (2007). *Katrina: A systematic failure*. Retrieved on September 07, 2007 from http://www.msnbc.msn.com/id/20546339/site/newsweek/

Brokaw, T. (1998). *The greatest generation*. New York: Random House.

Eron, L. D., Gentry, J. H., & Schlegel, P. (1994). *Reason to hope. A psychosocial perspective on violence & youth*. Washington, DC: American Psychological Association.

Garbarino, J. (1995). *Raising children in a socially toxic environment*. San Francisco: Jossey-Bass.

Garbarino, J. (1999) Lost Boys: Why Our Sons Turn Violent and How We Can Save Them. NY: Free Press.

Garbarino, J. (2002). Foreword: Pathways from childhood trauma to adolescent violence and delinquency. *Journal of Aggression, Maltreatment & Trauma, 6*(1), 22–29.

Garbarino, J. (2008). Children and the dark side of human experience: Confronting global realities and rethinking child development. NY: Springer

Garbarino, J., Kostelny, K., & Dubrow, N. (1991). *No place to be a child: Growing up in a war zone*. New York: Lexington Books.

Garofalo, R., Wolf, C., Kessel, J., Palfrey, J., & Durant, R. H. (1998). The association between health risk behaviors and sexual orientation among a school based sample of adolescents. *Pediatrics, 101*(5), 895–902.

Hilmes, M. (2004). *The television history book*. London: British Film Institute.

Kaplan, S. J., Pelcovitz, D., & Fornari, V. (2005). *The treatment of children impacted by the World Trade Center attack*. New York: Hawthorn.

Kelly, J. A., & Amirkhanian, Y. A. (2003). The newest epidemic: A review of HIV/AIDS in central and eastern Europe. *International Journal of STD & AIDS, 14*(6), 361–371.

Lickona, T. (2004). *Character matters: How to help our children develop good judgment, integrity, and other essential virtues*. New York: Touchstone.

Loeber, R., & Farrington, D. (1999). *Serious and violent juvenile offenders: Risk factors and successful interventions*. Thousand Oaks, CA: Sage.

Luke, C. (1990). *Constructing the child viewer: A history of the American discourse on television and children, 1950–1980*. New York: Praeger.

Mulhall, B. P. (1996). Sex and travel: studies of sexual behaviour, disease and health promotion in international travellers – a global review. *International Journal of STD & AIDS, 7*(7), 455–465.

Shales, A. (2007). *The forgotten man: A new history of the great depression*. New York: HarperCollins.

Updike, J. (2007). *Laissez-faire is more: A revisionist history of the depression*. The New Yorker, July 02.

Wadlow, R. (2002). *Violence in Columbia, 1990–2000: Waging war and negotiating peace*. St. Paul, MN: Professors World Peace Academy.

Index

Kolibri 360 GmbH
Ferdinand-Jühlke-Straße 7
99095 Erfurt, Deutschland
produktsicherheit@kolibri360.de